MW00773935

'Despite its inauspicious title, this much welcomed and highly readable volume offers a cogent, theoretically grounded argument about the EU's need for stabilizing hegemonic leadership to ensure continued cooperation and harmony. As an important antidote to the slew of new books which view Europe's future through a glass darkly, it provides a refreshing and compelling assessment of the EU's resilience in the face of an onslaught of four potentially crippling crises. Webber's suggestion that a "Weimar" or a "Hanseatic" hegemonic coalition could underwrite future European stability is sure to provoke much discussion and inspire subsequent research on the health of the European Union. A must-read for all students of the EU and of International Relations.' – **Professor Beverly Crawford Ames**, *University of California Berkeley, USA*

'This fascinating and well-written book couldn't be timelier. Well organized, thorough, and filled with historical facts, it explores the Eurozone, Ukraine, Refugee and Brexit Crises and their political and economic roots. It is an essential reference for everyone with an interest in the crisis politics in the European Union.' – **Professor John Ryan**, *London School of Economics, UK*

'Webber offers a fascinating account and interpretation of EU crises overtime and challenges the Monnet statement that "Europe's integration proceeds ahead through crises". Disintegration is a possible outcome if stability is not provided by an hegemonic (benevolent) state (Germany). The thesis is disputable but provides a fertile ground for debate and future research. A must-read for all scholars and students interested in European integration (and *disintegration!*).' – **Professor Yves Mény**, *European University Institute, Italy*

'Douglas Webber's insightful and comprehensive study enriches our understanding of the nature and depth of the EU's multiple crises since 2009 and the integrative and, more importantly, disintegrative dynamics they triggered. This timely book makes an important contribution to our theoretical understanding of the EU's integrative and disintegrative dynamics of the last decade and of Germany's key role therein. A must read for all those interested in the future of the EU and in European (dis)integration theory.' – **Professor Joachim Schild**, *Trier University, Germany*

'It has often been claimed that Europe rebounds more strongly from crisis, but this time may be different. In *European Disintegration?* Douglas Webber analyzes the resilience of the European project against the multidimensional crisis of the past long decade: Euro, Ukraine, Schengen, Brexit. His is an astute discussion of the impact of a long-neglected factor: the varying presence of a hegemon capable and willing to pick up the slack when the chips are down. The quadruple crisis of the EU became a litmus test of Germany's ability to provide stabilizing leadership, and the hegemon has been at best "hobbled". This is a beautifully crisp and clear book – but not one for the faint-hearted.' – **Professor Liesbet Hooghe**, *University of North Carolina at Chapel Hill, USA*

'The core conclusion of Webber's analysis of the crises roiling the EU is that it may well fail to survive them if the pan-European commitments of Germany – its "reluctant hegemon" – should falter. His is an argument that deserves our closest attention.' – **Professor Martin Rhodes**, *University of Denver, USA*

'Webber's work sets a new benchmark in comprehending the varied picture of crisis, integration and disintegration within the European Union. By imaginatively inverting existing theories of integration he boldly challenges us to consider the possibility that it is, above all, Europe's "hobbled hegemon", Germany, that poses the greatest threat of future disintegration in the EU.' – **Dr Ben Wellings**, *Monash University, Australia*

THE EUROPEAN UNION SERIES

General Editors: Neill Nugent, William E. Paterson

The European Union series provides an authoritative library on the European Union, ranging from general introductory texts to definitive assessments of key institutions and actors, issues, policies and policy processes, and the role of member states.

Books in the series are written by leading scholars in their fields and reflect the most up-to-date research and debate. Particular attention is paid to accessibility and clear presentation for a wide audience of students, practitioners and interested general readers.

The series editors are **Neill Nugent**, Emeritus Professor of Politics at Manchester Metropolitan University, UK, and **William E. Paterson**, Honorary Professor in German and European Studies, University of Aston. Their co-editor until his death in July 1999, **Vincent Wright**, was a Fellow of Nuffield College, Oxford University.

Feedback on the series and book proposals are always welcome and should be sent to Andrew Malvern, Red Globe Press, 4 Crinan Street, London N1 9XW, or by e-mail to **andrew.malvern@macmillaneducation.com**

General textbooks

Published

Laurie Buonanno and Neill Nugent **Policies and Policy Processes of the European Union**

Desmond Dinan **Encyclopedia of the European Union**
[Rights: Europe only]

Desmond Dinan **Europe Recast: A History of the European Union (2nd edn)**
[Rights: Europe only]

Desmond Dinan **Ever Closer Union: An Introduction to European Integration (4th edn)**
[Rights: Europe only]

Mette Eilstrup Sangiovanni (ed) **Debates on European Integration: A Reader**

Simon Hix and Bjørn Høyland **The Political System of the European Union (3rd edn)**

Dirk Leuffen, Berthold Rittberger and Frank Schimmelfennig **Differentiated Integration**

Paul Magnette **What is the European Union? Nature and Prospects**

John McCormick **Understanding the European Union: A Concise Introduction (7th edn)**

Brent F. Nelsen and Alexander Stubb **The European Union: Readings on the Theory and Practice of European Integration (4th edn)**
[Rights: Europe only]

Neill Nugent (ed) **European Union Enlargement**

Neill Nugent **The Government and Politics of the European Union (8th edn)**

John Peterson and Elizabeth Bomberg **Decision-Making in the European Union**

Ben Rosamond **Theories of European Integration**

Sabine Saurugger **Theoretical Approaches to European Integration**

Ingeborg Tömmel **The European Union: What it is and How it Works**

Esther Versluis, Mendeltje van Keulen and Paul Stephenson **Analyzing the European Union Policy Process**

Hubert Zimmermann and Andreas Dür (eds) **Key Controversies in European Integration (2nd edn)**

Also planned

The European Union and Global Politics

The Political Economy of European Integration

European Disintegration?

The Politics of Crisis in the European Union

Douglas Webber

BLOOMSBURY ACADEMIC
LONDON • NEW YORK • OXFORD • NEW DELHI • SYDNEY

BLOOMSBURY ACADEMIC
Bloomsbury Publishing Plc
50 Bedford Square, London, WC1B 3DP, UK
1385 Broadway, New York, NY 10018, USA
29 Earlsfort Terrace, Dublin 2, Ireland

BLOOMSBURY, BLOOMSBURY ACADEMIC and the Diana logo are trademarks of
Bloomsbury Publishing Plc

First published in Great Britain 2019 by Red Globe Press
Reprinted by Bloomsbury Academic 2022

ISBN: HB: 978-1-137-52947-3
       PB: 978-1-137-52946-6

To find out more about our authors and books visit www.bloomsbury.com and sign up for
our newsletters.

To Ulli

Contents

List of Tables, Figures and Maps

Tables

Figures

Map

Acknowledgements

This book is the culmination of a long intellectual journey. I cannot put a precise date on its birth, except to say that it was conceived gradually, sometime in spring or summer 2010, when, following the unfolding Greek sovereign debt crisis drama and like numerous other observers, I began to think, to fear, that the process of European political integration with which my generation had grown up was perhaps not as robust and irreversible as most of the literature and scholarship on the topic had long led us to believe. Little did I realize at that time that this was only the first of several crises with which the EU would be confronted in the following decade. Or that my research object would thus become a constantly moving and shifting target.

My thinking on the fundamental issue – to what extent and under what conditions it is conceivable that the European Union (EU) may *dis*integrate – has been influenced by exchanges I have had with many colleagues around the globe during the intervening decade. I owe the greatest debt in this regard to Willie Paterson, co-editor of this series, a colleague and friend of meanwhile 40 years, who has been an unfailing and indefatigable source of encouragement and moral support for this project, commented helpfully on my draft chapters, drawn my attention and facilitated my access to innumerable papers, books and articles relevant to my research, and put me in touch with many other colleagues with similar research interests. I am thankful too to the other series co-editor, Neill Nugent, for having read my draft chapters carefully and supplied numerous useful comments and proposals as to how they could be improved. I have also benefited from regular and numerous exchanges with my former INSEAD colleague Jonathan Story and with Simon Bulmer. I am gratified that this book will appear almost simultaneously with Simon's and Willie's own book on the role of Germany in the EU. In addition, I would like to thank not only Jonathan Story, but also Fritz Scharpf, former director of the Max Planck Institute for the Study of Societies in Cologne, for having carefully read and commented on my draft chapter on the Eurozone Crisis. In France, I have also learned from discussions with my regular lunchtime companion, Christian Lequesne, political science professor at CERI/Sciences-Po in Paris; in Singapore from those that I have had with Jørgen Ørstrøm Møller, research fellow at the Institute of Southeast Asian Studies and former Danish Permanent Representative to the EU; and, at INSEAD and elsewhere, with Fraser Cameron, director of the EU Asia Centre, Brussels.

Initially at least, perhaps for normative reasons, not too many political scientists, least of all scholars of the EU, seemed willing to contemplate the possibility that European political integration might prove reversible. To this small band of 'disintegrationists', for want of a more elegant term, I count

Jan Zielonka, Hans Vollaard, Annegret Eppler, Henrik Scheller and Stefan Auer. I have profited also from my exchanges with them, at conferences and in a research seminar at INSEAD in Fontainebleau. It occasionally requires courage to ask questions that others are not asking or would rather not ask.

I might not have finished writing this book or at least I would have taken rather longer to write it if I had not had the immeasurably good fortune of being able to spend four months across the academic years 2016/17 and 2017/18 as a Robert Schuman Fellow and Distinguished Scholar at the Robert Schuman Centre for Advanced Studies (RSCAS) at the European University Institute (EUI) in Florence. For this possibility, I am immensely grateful to Ulrich Krotz, Professor of International Relations at the RSCAS and the EUI's Department of Social and Political Sciences. I am equally thankful to the director of the RSCAS, Brigid Laffan, and other colleagues at the RSCAS, including Goei Mei Lan and Ingo Linsenmann, for their support and forbearance and having made me feel so much at home during my stay at the enchanting Villa Schifanoia. My visits there, on the hillside between downtown Florence and Fiesole, will remain an unforgettable memory. At the RSCAS and EUI I also had useful conversations for my project with – among others – Stefano Bartolini, Gerda Falkner, Philipp Genschel, Adrienne Hérit-ier, Richard Maher and Tim Oliver.

Towards the end of this project, I conducted a series of interviews in Berlin with civil servants working in several ministries of the German federal government, including the Federal Chancellor's Office, the Foreign Office, the Office of the Federal President, the Federal Ministry of Finance and the Federal Ministry of Internal Affairs. I would like to thank all these persons for agreeing to be interviewed and sharing their time and observations with me. All asked that they should remain anonymous. Where I have cited them in the book, I refer therefore to 'interview, Berlin, 2018'. I am also grateful to Josef Janning, director of the Berlin office of the European Council on Foreign Relations, and to Hanns Maull, research fellow at the *Stiftung Wissenschaft und Politik* (SWP), for having been able to meet and talk to them while in Berlin. I am especially thankful to Hanns Maull for having organized a very enjoyable 'round-table' at which I could exchange views on my research with him and several of his SWP colleagues.

As my book was developing, I had the opportunity to present parts of it as papers at numerous academic conferences and seminars: at two seminars that I gave in 2018, at the kind invitation of Joachim Schild, at the University of Trier; at Ulrich Krotz's 'Europe in the World' seminar series at the RSCAS in Florence in 2016; at the World Congress of the International Political Science Association (IPSA) in Poznan also in 2016; at the Council of European Studies' Conference of Europeanists in Paris in 2015; at the annual conference of the University Association for Contemporary European Studies (UACES) in Bilbao in 2015; at the University of Utrecht, at the kind invitation of Femke van Esch, in 2014; at the annual conference of the New Zealand Political Science Association the same year; at a conference organized by Simon Bulmer at the University of Sheffield in 2013; and at the European Institute at the

University of Sussex in 2012. I thank the other paper-presenters and participants in these conferences and seminars for the comments and feedback they made on my papers.

My first attempts to address the topic of this book were actually made, however, far from Europe, 'down under' in Australia. The first paper I presented about the prospects of European disintegration was at the Monash European and EU Centre in Melbourne in March 2011. The first paper that I published was in the Briefing Paper series of the Centre for European Studies at ANU (Australian National University) in Canberra, in October 2011, following a month-long stay at the centre in February–March 2011. I am grateful to the director of the ANU centre, Jacqueline Lo, for having invited me for this stay as well as to Pascaline Winand, then director of the Monash centre, to which I made two very enjoyable and useful visits in 2009 and 2013.

I also wish to thank Andrew Malvern and his predecessors at Red Globe Press, Steven Kennedy and Stephen Wenham, for their advice and above all their patience and forbearance, as successive deadlines for the submission of the manuscript of this book had to be extended. I also benefited from and am grateful for the assistance and guidance I received in preparing the book from Lauren Ferreira.

I would like to thank my assistant at INSEAD, Virginie Frisch, who provided invaluable support by preparing most of the tables and maps for publication in this book. For those on the Eurozone and the painstaking research required to compile some of them, I am grateful to a former research fellow in the INSEAD Department of Economics and Political Science, Diogo Machado. I thank INSEAD itself for a research grant that permitted me to travel to Berlin for the interviews that I conducted there.

The person to whom I am most indebted, however, is my wife, Ulrike. She has supported me unfailingly and unflinchingly during this project, through thick and thin, and in sickness and in health. So it is to her, with all my thanks, that I dedicate this book.

No matter how much I have profited from exchanges with colleagues, above all those mentioned above, the responsibility for the contents of this book and whatever shortcomings and defects it contains is mine alone. Believing as I do that European political integration has played an important role assuring the peace among the EU's member states, I have derived no joy from witnessing the trials and tribulations that the EU has experienced during the last decade and I derive none from the thought that, under certain conditions, it could well *dis*integrate. But it behoves social scientists to see things not just how they would like them to be, but as they are or might be. To recognize that things are going wrong and to where this could lead is an indispensable precondition to putting them right.

Douglas Webber
Paris, July 2018

List of Abbreviations

AA	Association Agreement
ACI	Actor-Centred Institutionalism
AfD	*Alternative für Deutschland* – Alternative for Germany
APEC	Asia-Pacific Economic Cooperation
ARD	*Arbeitsgemeinschaft öffentlich-rechtlichen Rundfunkanstalten der Bundesrepublik Deutschland* – Consortium of the Public Broadcasters in the Federal Republic of Germany
BDA	*Bundesvereinigung der Deutschen Arbeitgeberverbände* – Confederation of German Employers' Associations
BDI	*Bundesverband Deutscher Industrie* – Federation of German Industry
CAP	Common Agricultural Policy
CDU	*Christlich Demokratische Union Deutschlands* – German Christian Democratic Union
CFSP	Common Foreign and Security Policy
CIS	Community of Independent States
COREPER	Committee of Permanent Representatives
CSU	*Christlich-Soziale Union in Bayern* – Bavarian Christian Social Union
DIW	*Deutsches Institut für Wirtschaftsforschung* – German Institute of Economic Research
EaP	Eastern Partnership
EASO	European Asylum Support Office
EBU	European Banking Union
EEA	European Economic Area
ECB	European Central Bank
ECBG	European Coast and Border Guard
ECJ	European Court of Justice
ECSC	European Coal and Steel Community
EDC	European Defence Community
EEA	European Economic Area
EEAS	European External Action Service
EEC	European Economic Community
EEU	Eurasian Economic Union
EFSF	European Financial Stability Facility
EFTA	European Free Trade Area
EMS	European Monetary System
EMU	Economic and Monetary Union
EP	European Parliament

EPC	European Political Cooperation
EPP	European People's Party
ERM	Exchange Rate Mechanism
ESM	European Stability Mechanism
ESMT	European School of Management and Technology
EU	European Union
EUI	European University Institute
FDP	*Freie Demokratische Partei* – Free Democratic Party
FPÖ	*Freiheitliche Partei Österreichs* – Austrian Freedom Party
GATT	General Agreement on Tariffs and Trade
GDP	Gross Domestic Product
GFC	Global Financial Crisis
G20	Group of 20
HI	Historical Institutionalism
IGC	Intergovernmental Conference
IMF	International Monetary Fund
IPSA	International Political Science Association
IR	International Relations
JHA	Justice and Home Affairs
KGB	Committee for State Security (USSR)
MP	Member of Parliament
NATO	North Atlantic Treaty Organization
OECD	Organization for Economic Cooperation and Development
OHCHR	Office of the (United Nations) High Commissioner for Human Rights
OMT	Outright Monetary Transactions
OSCE	Organization for Security and Cooperation in Europe
ÖVP	*Österreichische Volkspartei* – Austrian People's Party
PEGIDA	*Patriotische Europäer Gegen die Islamisierung des Abendlands* – Patriotic Europeans Against the Islamization of the West
SDR	Special Drawing Rights
SIS	Schengen Information System
SPD	*Sozialdemokratische Partei Deutschlands* – German Social Democratic Party
SRF	Single Resolution Fund
SRM	Single Resolution Mechanism
TUC	Trade Union Congress
UK	United Kingdom
UKIP	United Kingdom Independence Party
UN	United Nations
UNHCR	United Nations High Commissioner for Refugees
USA	United States of America
USSR	Union of Soviet Socialist Republics
WTO	World Trade Organization

Chapter 1

Is This Time Different?

I have come to learn that my belief, a belief shared by many of my generation, that the path of European integration was irreversible, was a fallacy. No, Europe's future is not set in stone.

(Frank-Walter Steinmeier, German president, 2017)

Introduction

Observers of the European Union (EU) could be forgiven for thinking that the EU is in a state of permanent crisis. Since late 2009, when a newly elected Greek government announced that the country's budget deficit was far higher than had previously been revealed, the EU has been managing a Eurozone (sovereign debt) crisis, which has occasionally seemed more acute and sometimes subsided. Since 2014, when popular protests overthrew the Ukrainian president, Russia invaded Crimea and armed conflict broke out between Russian-supported separatists and the Ukrainian army in the eastern regions of the country, the EU has been dealing with a 'Ukraine Crisis' involving it in a confrontation with its largest and most powerful neighbouring state. In 2015, after the 'Arab Spring' that broke out in 2011 culminated in large-scale political violence and conflict in North Africa and the Middle East, especially in Syria, the sudden and rapid growth in the number of persons seeking to flee conflict zones in this region and migrate to Europe – by land or by sea – added a Refugee Crisis to the pre-existing ones and jeopardized the Schengen Area of borderless travel. While the EU was grappling with these crises, a fourth one developed over British membership of the EU after Prime Minister Cameron scheduled a popular referendum over the issue for June 2016. The referendum produced a 52 per cent majority in favour of withdrawal that the British government aimed to carry out by March 2019. The withdrawal of a member state, one of its three biggest, from the EU would be unprecedented.

The apparent pervasiveness and quasi-permanence of crises in the EU's recent history raises the question of whether in this context crisis has not become an overworked concept evoked too readily and unthinkingly to refer to a situation in which two or more actors vie with one another over the 'right' course of action on issues where they represent (even diametrically) opposed interests. However, if one conceives of crisis as a 'situation that has reached an extremely difficult or dangerous point; a time of great disagreement,

1

uncertainty or suffering' (*Cambridge Dictionary*) or as a 'vitally important or decisive stage in the progress of anything; a turning-point; a state of affairs in which a decisive change for better or worse is imminent, applied especially to times of difficulty, insecurity and suspense' (*Oxford English Dictionary*), to describe the EU as being in a (multidimensional) crisis seems justified. The issue is not so much whether the EU is in a crisis (or crises) but rather what will be the consequences or implications of this crisis for the EU and the process of political integration that has unfolded in Europe over the last six-and-a-half decades.

If the history and, still more, the historiography of the EU tell us anything, it is that the EU is a highly resilient entity and that European political integration is a process that has never been rolled back (see, e.g., Schimmelfennig 2016: 189). First, the number of member states has grown continually: from the 6 pioneer members of the European Coal and Steel Community (ECSC) in 1950 and the European Economic Community (EEC) in 1957, to 9 in 1973, 10 in 1981, 12 in 1986, 15 in 1995, 25 in 2004, 27 in 2007 and 28 in 2013. Hitherto, no member has withdrawn from the EU, although Greenland, then a Danish territory, opted to leave it in 1982. Second, there is so far no issue area in which the member states have taken back decision-making competences that they had previously granted to the EU under the European treaties. Third, no reduction has hitherto occurred in the powers of the EU's organs – the Commission, the European Court of Justice (ECJ), the European Parliament (EP), the European Central Bank (ECB) – vis-à-vis the member states as these are specified in the European treaties. In short, European political integration has proven to be a unidirectional process that, while it occasionally may have marked time, has so far never unwound.

This is not to say, of course, that European political integration has not been a (at times bitterly) contested or controversial process. Rather, its resilience has been proven by its capacity to manage, resist and digest crises without being derailed from its fundamental course. The intellectual founder of the EU, Jean Monnet, is famous for his repeatedly cited remark that Europe 'will be forged in crises and will be the sum of the solutions adopted for those crises' (as cited in Barroso 2011: 2). Monnet's assertion has been a source of comfort for proponents of European integration, whom it has reassured that the EU would not only survive crises, but also grow stronger through them. In the remainder of this introductory chapter I shall review the major crises that the EU has faced and surmounted during more than half a century up until 2009 and compare these with the multidimensional crisis that it has been confronting since then. I shall identify several reasons why the magnitude of the contemporary crisis exceeds that of earlier crises and argue that it is therefore dangerous to conclude from the EU's past resilience to crises that 'this time' will not be any different. I will subsequently define the concepts of integration and disintegration that underpin the subsequent analysis and outline the structure of the book.

Past crises of European integration

Regardless of how their role and impact are understood, it is indisputable that crises – times of great disagreement or uncertainty in which major changes of direction appear imminent – have been pervasive in the history of European integration. Before the Eurozone Crisis almost every decade since the 1950s had witnessed a crisis that generated (as it transpired, ultimately unjustified) fears that the integration process would be durably impaired or damaged.

The European Defence Community crisis (1950–54)

Crises have, in fact, accompanied the European integration process from the outset. Arguably the first concerned the European Defence Community (EDC) project, which was launched by the French government in 1950 only a few months after the ECSC had been proposed. Unlike the ECSC, the EDC failed to get off the ground. The intensification of the Cold War manifested by the outbreak of the Korean War raised the pressure in non-Communist Europe to rearm Germany. The original EDC project was aimed at bringing this about but in a way that would preclude the development of an autonomous (West) German military capacity. While it was backed by the other five ECSC member states, support for it in France subsequently dwindled. The UK refused to join the organization and, as French armed forces became increasingly engaged in military action in French colonies, the provisions of the EDC seemed less and less likely to ensure the subordination of German armed forces to the EDC. Parliamentary elections in 1952 significantly strengthened the representation of the left- (Communist) and right-wing (Gaullist) parties hostile to German rearmament and led to the replacement of a 'pro-European' coalition by a government that viewed the EDC more coolly. When the project was finally voted down in the French Parliament in August 1954, government ministers abstained. Although, by this time, this outcome had been widely foreseen, the shock waves provoked by the defeat of the EDC in France were nonetheless considerable. Monnet himself did not think that the collapse of the EDC meant the premature end of European integration (Monnet 1988: 503). But he seems to have been more optimistic than most of his contemporaries. The German Economics Minister Ludwig Erhard claimed that the 'integration tide is no longer running high' and that 'thoughts of European collaboration' might have to be abandoned (Görtemaker 2008: 33). According to Parsons (2006: 116), 'almost everyone thought the community adventure was over. Not even the strongest community advocates would have believed that they stood on the verge of the decisive triumph of the supranational format.' While the EDC's collapse put a definitive end to plans to create a European army for at least several decades, it did not spell the end of West European military cooperation involving West Germany. The British Prime Minister Eden subsequently seized an initiative that led to the signature no more than two months later of the Paris Agreements, under which West Germany was brought into the pre-existing Treaty of Brussels and the North

Atlantic Treaty Organization (NATO), undertook not to produce nuclear, biological or chemical weapons and could begin to rearm. Moreover, within a year of the EDC's failure, the original six ECSC member states had started negotiations over the creation of a common market and atomic energy community that culminated in the adoption of the Treaty of Rome in 1957.

The Empty Chair Crisis (1965–66)

If the launching of the EEC was followed by several 'honeymoon years' (Marjolin as cited in Ludlow 2006: 2), the 1960s were to witness a series of crises related to the stance on issues of European integration adopted by the French president Charles de Gaulle, who returned to power in France only shortly after the Rome Treaty entered into force. The first of these was precipitated by de Gaulle's unilateral decision in January 1963 to reject the UK's entry application – which the other five members supported. The most serious (Ludlow 2006: 70) occurred when, hostile to a package of 'audacious' proposals made by the European Commission that would have strengthened the European Parliament's and its own powers at the expense of the member states, de Gaulle withdrew France from the Council of Ministers. The Commission calculated that France could be persuaded to accept a more 'supranational' Europe in exchange for higher agricultural subsidies, but de Gaulle opposed a proposed extension of the powers of the EEC's supranational organs (the Commission and the Parliament) as well as the scheduled transition from unanimous to qualified majority voting in the Council, by which in future France could be outvoted. After more than six months, during which both sides overestimated the likelihood that the other would capitulate, this crisis was finally resolved by the Luxembourg Compromise, in which France and the five other member states essentially agreed to disagree, but to carry on regardless. The confrontation was prolonged by the fact that both sides were certain that the other could not afford to allow the EU to collapse and would therefore make concessions. In the end, although no changes were made to the Rome Treaty, France nonetheless returned to the Council. According to Ludlow (2006: 115), all the protagonists, France included, had more to gain from the EU's survival than from its collapse. The crisis was thus never existential and its resolution proved the organization's 'institutional resilience' (Ludlow 2006: 204–205, 218). According to a widespread view, it created a 'national veto over all key EC decisions and for almost two decades it stalled progress in many important areas of Community policy' (Teasdale 1993: 567). The notion that the integration process, piloted by the Commission, was unstoppable was called into doubt. Still, the crisis did not prevent the achievement of a customs union between the member states significantly more rapidly than expected. And generally, while it may have helped to entrench the norm that the Council decides by consensus, at least on highly contentious issues, it did not destroy the EU's capacity to make decisions (Golub 1999, 2006). Shortly after de Gaulle's resignation as French president in 1969, The Hague

Summit of heads of the EU governments agreed to launch negotiations for British accession to the EU as well as over 'economic and monetary union'.

The British Budgetary Crisis (1979–84)

The issue of accession to the EU was politically more strongly contested in the UK, which declined to join first the ECSC and then the EEC, than in the six pioneer member states. When the British government changed its mind and applied for membership in the early 1960s, de Gaulle's opposition kept the UK out as long as he was in office (until 1969). The financial terms of the UK's accession and membership was one of the most contentious issues in the accession negotiations and in the British debate and was thus one of the items that the Labour government 'renegotiated' before the UK voted to remain in the EU in what was its first popular referendum in 1975 (Griffiths 2006: 176–178). As a proportionally large importer of products, especially food, from outside the EU and as it had a relatively small agricultural sector, the UK paid a larger net share of the EU budget relative to the size of its economy than other members, despite being poorer than most. However, even the revised formula for the UK's contribution to the EU budget remained controversial. When she came to power in 1979, the Conservative prime minister Margaret Thatcher insisted that 'I want my money back', that is, that the UK's contribution to the EU budget be reduced once again.

The 'British Budgetary Question' was a major contributing factor to a growing atmosphere of stagnation and crisis in the EU in the early 1980s. This period 'marked the apogee of Europessimism' (Moravcsik 1991). *The Economist* magazine, for example, diagnosed the community as being in such an advanced state of decay that it published a front-page cover with a tombstone carrying the words: 'EC, RIP'. Several meetings of the European Council tackled but failed to resolve the conflict. Thatcher considered withholding the British contribution to the budget in 1984 to press her case, but she refrained from doing so because of fears that it would be found to be contravening EU law and opposition to such a move among 'pro-European' Conservative MPs (Moravcsik 1991; Thatcher 1993: 559; Wall 2008: 26–33). She had nonetheless a strong bargaining position, in as far as the UK could veto an increase in the EU's budget that was essential to finance the EU's activities following the imminent accession to the EU of Spain and Portugal. At the same time, however, other leaders' impatience with Thatcher's intransigence over this issue provoked threats that France and Germany would launch a 'two-speed' Europe project in which the UK risked being sidelined (Attali 1993: 640–642, 658–660; Moravcsik 1991; Thatcher 1993: 540; Young 1998: 322). Finally, at the Council meeting in Fontainebleau in June 1984, having been offered a marginally better deal than at the preceding summit, a 'more conciliatory' Thatcher determined that the time had come to settle (Denman 1996: 262; Moravcsik 1991; Thatcher 1993: 545). The Fontainebleau accord marked a turning-point in the European integration process, which was relaunched and galvanized over the next three years with the negotiation and adoption of the Single European Act reforming the EU institutions and liberalizing the internal market. Once again, the EU had proven its capacity to survive and bounce back from crises.

The Crisis of the European Monetary System (1992–93)

The European Monetary System (EMS) had its origins in the turbulence that accompanied the collapse of the Bretton Woods international monetary system and the oil-price crisis of the early 1970s. Aimed at stabilizing exchange rates between the participating states, it was not the first such project, but the oil-price crisis and the EU member states' divergent responses to it had derailed a prior initiative to forge closer European monetary cooperation (see Chapter 3). It was primarily a product of the close collaboration of the German Chancellor Helmut Schmidt and the French President Valéry Giscard d'Estaing, who conceived it with minimal involvement of and to a certain extent against the resistance of their respective finance and economics ministries and central banks (Schmidt 1990: 219–233). The system of fixed but adjustable exchange rates was designed by its creators to promote monetary and economic policy convergence and economic integration between member states and to lay the foundations, in the longer term, for a common or single European currency (Schmidt 1990: 230–231).

Launched in 1979, the EMS survived a first major test in the early 1980s, when, having initially pursued a highly expansionary economic policy, a newly elected left-wing government in France shifted towards a policy of economic *rigueur* and accepted the constraints the system imposed. Without the convergence of economic policy and performance that the EMS promoted during the 1980s, it is inconceivable that the single currency project would have been born in the latter part of the decade. However, while the end of the Cold War and the process of German unification were to accelerate the adoption of this project, the consequences of this process – specifically, of the policies that were pursued to bridge the divergence of living standards between West and East Germany – threatened in the early 1990s to destroy the EMS and thus, indirectly, the single currency project as well. The German Bundesbank raised interest rates to combat a perceived threat of rising inflation arising from a burgeoning government budget deficit. As actors in the international foreign exchange markets began increasingly to doubt whether other EMS members, whose economies were not benefiting from the unification 'boom', would be politically able to follow suit, the existing exchange-rate parities came under growing pressure and looked increasingly unsustainable. This uncertainty was compounded by the negative outcome of the Danish referendum on the Maastricht Treaty in June 1992 and President Mitterrand's subsequent decision to call a referendum on the treaty in France. Shortly before the French referendum, fevered speculation in the foreign exchange markets forced the Italian and British governments to withdraw the lira and pound from the EMS.

They had exhausted their means of defending their respective currencies and the Bundesbank had refused to support them any longer (Milesi 1998: 36–40). The same fate beckoned for the French franc, even after the referendum in France approved the Maastricht Treaty, albeit by the slim margin of 51 per cent. With the survival of the EMS and the single currency project seemingly at stake, German Chancellor Helmut Kohl prevailed upon the Bundesbank to intervene to protect the existing exchange-rate parities between Germany and France and calm the foreign exchange markets (Kohl 2007: 505–506; Milesi 1998: 41–45; Védrine 1996: 574).

The EMS's reprieve proved, however, to be no more than temporary. In spring 1993, a new right-of-centre government came into office in France and began to press the German authorities to lower interest rates so that France could do likewise and stimulate the French economy without precipitating a run on the franc and destabilizing the EMS. As the Bundesbank resisted this pressure, a new wave of speculation against the franc developed. This time, it could not be repulsed using the same solution that had worked the year before: 'Not even massive interventions by the two central banks could hold back the floodwaters of speculation' (Gillingham 2003: 292). Having been unable to agree on anything else, the member states, rather than allowing the EMS to collapse completely, decided to enlarge the fluctuation bands within the system from 2.25 to 15 per cent (Milesi 1998: 51–67).

This second act of the EMS crisis provoked doubts among Euro advocates and sceptics alike as to whether the timetable for the adoption of the single currency set out in the Maastricht Treaty could be kept. Some prominent German economists judged that the crisis had destroyed the project altogether: The Deutsche Mark had been rescued and the Euro was dead. Although the treaty provided that the Euro would be launched at the latest in 1999 comprising the EU member states that then met the stability-oriented convergence criteria, relating to inflation rates and levels of public indebtedness stipulated in the treaty, only tiny Luxembourg actually met these criteria in mid-1993. Given the centrality of the Franco-German relationship to this project and the EU, it was certainly highly unlikely that the Euro would see the light of day if French and German monetary and economic policies followed different trajectories, as the new, enlarged bands of fluctuation in the EMS suggested might transpire.

As we know with the benefit of hindsight, however, this scenario did not materialize. Calm quickly returned to the foreign exchange markets after the fluctuation bands in the EMS had been widened. Within months most of the currencies still in the EMS were back within or close to the old, narrower bands (Sandholtz 1996: 95). The exchange rate between the mark and the franc remained very stable for the remainder of the 1990s. And, facilitated, in the case of some member states, by a creative interpretation of the Maastricht convergence criteria, the Euro was ultimately launched with 11 of the 15 EU member states in 1999. As during previous crises, dire prognoses of the imminent collapse of European integration were misplaced. The EMS crisis too proved to be transient and the integration process again to be resilient.

The Constitutional Treaty Crisis (2005–09)

The Single European Act, which came into force in 1987, was the first to revise the Treaty of Rome. In contrast, in a shorter subsequent period of hardly more than 20 years, no fewer than five attempts were undertaken to change the European treaties. The first of these led to the Maastricht Treaty, of which the most important component concerned the single currency, the Euro. The creation of the single currency involved arguably the hitherto single most significant transfer of sovereignty from the member states to the EU and was correspondingly politically strongly contested in numerous member states. The UK negotiated an 'opt-out' from the single currency at Maastricht, Denmark initially rejected the treaty in a popular referendum and approved it only after it too had negotiated a similar arrangement and a French referendum on the treaty produced a razor-thin majority (see the section 'The crisis of the European Monetary System 1992–93' above). The next two treaties – those of Amsterdam (1997) and Nice (2001) – were intended to reform the EU's institutions, particularly to facilitate decision-making after the Central and Eastern European enlargement of the EU (which occurred in 2004). General dissatisfaction with both the provisions of these treaties and the process by which they were negotiated led the heads of government in the European Council in 2001 to propose that a new treaty be drafted by a 'European Convention' comprising representatives of the European and national Parliaments as well as of the governments themselves. This format was to contribute to making the EU 'more democratic [and] transparent' and to bring it 'closer to its citizens' (European Council 2001: 2, 3).

Although the document that emerged from this process was entitled a 'Constitutional Treaty', it was hardly any more far-reaching in its provisions than its immediate predecessors. Initially none of the three biggest member states envisaged submitting it to a popular referendum for ratification (Wall 2008: 176). However, the British prime minister Blair succumbed to domestic political pressure to call a referendum and made it politically difficult for the French president Chirac not to do the same (Qvortrup 2006: 89–90). In all, some 13 of 25 member states scheduled a referendum on the Constitutional Treaty. While, in the first of these, Spain voted overwhelmingly (by 77 per cent) to approve the treaty, in the second and third, by majorities of 55 and 61.5 per cent respectively, two of the six pioneer member states, France and the Netherlands, rejected it.

Some EU observers saw the rejection of the treaty as no big deal. The 'European constitutional compromise' that had meanwhile emerged amounted to a 'stable political equilibrium' that was unlikely to be upset by any 'major functional challenges, autonomous institutional evolution, or demands for democratic accountability' (Moravcsik 2005: 376). But others were less sanguine in their analysis of the implications of the French and Dutch no votes and argued that they heralded the arrival of a new crisis of European integration. One noted, for example, that 'many analysts have rightly said that the EU is undergoing one of the deepest crises of its history' (Schwall-Düren 2006: 1). Another went further, claiming that the votes confronted the EU with a 'crisis of unprecedented seriousness' (Cohen-Tanugi 2005: 55).

The defeat of the Constitutional Treaty itself was, however, a symptom rather than a cause of this crisis. It did not spell the 'end of the union'. Rather it reflected and deepened a 'profound crisis in the process of European unification' provoked primarily by the EU's 'poor economic performance and uncertain long-term prospects' (Cohen-Tanugi 2005: 59).

In retrospect, this 'constitutional crisis' was not very damaging to the integration process. The EU decided to give itself a year to 'reflect' on the defeat of the treaty and determine how to proceed. Having been rejected by two pioneer member states, including the one that had initially launched the integration process, and given the nature of its provisions, it could not be saved by means of supplementary protocols, declarations or 'opt-outs' as had occurred with Denmark in respect of the Maastricht Treaty and later Ireland with the Nice Treaty. In effect, however, a similar outcome was achieved. Shorn of some of its more controversial, but especially symbolic provisions, the Constitutional Treaty was resurrected as the Lisbon Treaty, which came into force in 2009 after it had been approved in a second referendum in Ireland, the only member state to call a referendum to ratify it. During this period, for all the talk of a 'deep' or 'unprecedented' crisis, the EU was not paralyzed, but continued to conduct business pretty much as usual.

Is the contemporary crisis of the EU different?

Crises are thus clearly nothing new in and for the EU. It has arguably spent much – perhaps as much as a third – of its history in crisis. Analogous to the Empty Chair Crisis of 1965–66, the short-lived British boycott of the Council over the ban on exports of British beef to other member states in the late 1990s might also be analysed as a 'crisis'. The issue of how to respond to the wars in the former Yugoslavia in the 1990s might equally be regarded as having constituted a crisis for the EU (Dinan 2017: 26–27). The entire decade of the 1970s, from the break-up of the Bretton Woods monetary system to the first and second oil-price hikes, might be labelled as a period of crisis for the EU in which currency instability and widely divergent economic performance threatened free trade between the member states and the survival of the Common Agricultural Policy (see, e.g., Dinan 2017). What is clear, however, in any case is that, over a period of meanwhile six decades, the EU has regularly confronted and survived crises that numerous political practitioners and observers said at the time imperilled or would destroy it. As true as it may be that the EU has not actually 'moved forward' through crises (Parsons and Matthijs 2015; see also Dinan 2017), it is certainly the case that they have hitherto *not prevented* closer political integration. On all (vertical, horizontal and sectoral) dimensions of integration, the EU has proved on the contrary to be highly resilient to crises.

History would therefore suggest that fears that the contemporary crisis will provoke partial or complete political *dis*integration in the EU are ill-founded and exaggerated. To dismiss such fears, though, would be warranted only if it can be assumed that this crisis is no different from its predecessors. The contemporary crisis arguably exhibits several traits, of which some can be observed in past crises, but which no past crisis replicates in their entirety. It is therefore highly plausible that 'this time' will be different.

The first of these traits is the *multidimensional character* of the contemporary crisis, which in fact comprises several crises and which I will therefore label the *quadruple crisis*. The original crisis, which had its debut in October 2009, concerned sovereign debt in the Eurozone. The tides of the *Eurozone Crisis* then ebbed and flowed over a period of six years, reaching high points in 2010, 2012 and 2015 at which the survival of the zone, at least in its current make-up, seemed questionable. While these tides were shifting, without having been banished, the *Ukraine Crisis* broke and escalated in late 2013 and 2014, with Russia invading and annexing Crimea in March 2014 and armed conflict breaking out between the Ukrainian military and separatist militias that seized and retained control of parts of south-eastern Ukraine. The EU was challenged to find a common response to Russian or Russian-supported military intervention in Ukraine. The French and German governments were closely involved in the negotiation of the 'Minsk Accords' that included a ceasefire between the protagonists in the conflict. However, no lasting solution to the conflict was found in the following four years and sporadic violence continued on its front line.

To these two crises came a third when in late summer 2015 there was a large, sharp and sudden increase in the number of persons fleeing to Europe from war and conflict zones in the Middle East and North Africa. This *Refugee Crisis* provoked strongly divergent responses among EU member states. As numerous member states resorted to unilateral measures to control or stop the influx of refugees, this also became a *Schengen crisis*, jeopardizing borderless travel within the 26-country area named after a small town in Luxembourg located on the country's borders with France and Germany. Almost simultaneously, following the Conservative Party's election victory with an outright majority in the British Parliament in May 2015 and Prime Minister Cameron's pledge to conduct a referendum on the UK's EU membership, the path was set for the *Brexit Crisis* unleashed by the vote of 23 June 2016.

No political crisis ever exists entirely in a vacuum. Political systems are always handling a multiplicity of issues that generate conflicts with varying degrees of intensity. The EU faced the EMS crisis in the early 1990s, for example, while it was also divided by intense conflicts over the General Agreement on Tariffs and Trade (GATT) Uruguay Round trade liberalization negotiations and the wars in the former Yugoslavia. Similarly, the Empty Chair Crisis in the mid-1960s was arguably an act in a more prolonged drama opposing de Gaulle's France to the five other member states over the issues of British accession and the distribution of power between the EU's supranational organs and the governments of the member states. At no other time in the last six decades, however, was the EU confronted by *as many* simultaneous crises as in the period since 2009.

The second trait that distinguishes the current crisis from most of its predecessors is its *longevity* or *duration*. To specify when a given crisis has 'begun' and 'ended' is an inherently subjective exercise. There are no objective criteria by which it can be precisely determined at which point a political issue or conflict becomes a 'crisis', that is, reaches a moment of great uncertainty, at which a major change of direction could occur. Thus the British budgetary 'question' (as it is often labelled) occupied the EU regularly over a period of at least a decade, bearing in mind that it was one of the central issues in the renegotiation of the terms of British accession that occurred prior to the 1975 referendum. But it arguably did not develop into a crisis – a highly conflictual issue that threatened to provoke major changes in the EU – until 1983–84, when it became the foremost item on the agenda of successive European Council meetings. Such an exercise is or would also be complicated by the fact that, over time, the intensity of a crisis may fluctuate. This was the case with the British budgetary crisis, with the Ukraine Crisis and, even more so, with the Eurozone Crisis, which some observers declared to be over in the period between 2012, when the ECB governor Mario Draghi pledged that the bank would do 'whatever it takes' to save the Euro, and 2015, when Greece elected a radical left-wing, anti-austerity government.

With and despite these caveats, a strong case can be made for classifying the contemporary crisis, dating as it does from October 2009, as the most protracted the EU has confronted. Compared with this, the Empty Chair Crisis of 1965–66 and the EMS crisis, which spanned a period of 15 months between June 1992 and August 1993, were short-lived. Other past crises lasted longer than these: the EDC crisis lasted at most roughly four years, from the announcement of the Pleven Plan in 1950 to the negative vote of the French Parliament in 1954; the British budgetary crisis for five years, if it is dated from the election of Margaret Thatcher's Conservative government in 1979; and the crisis over the Constitutional Treaty for a maximum of just over four years, if it is viewed as having been unleashed by the lost referenda in France and the Netherlands in June 2005 and resolved by the positive outcome of the second referendum over the Lisbon Treaty in Ireland in October 2009. The *uniquely protracted* character of the contemporary crisis points also to its being simultaneously the *most intractable* that the EU has had to manage – as well as to the danger that its disintegrative impact may be stronger than that of previous crises.

That the European integration process has historically been mainly an elite-driven process belongs to the conventional wisdom of EU scholarship. The third specificity of the current crisis is that, in contrast, it has involved an unprecedented *mass politicization* of this process (see also Hooghe and Marks 2008; Parsons and Matthijs 2015: 211, 223–224, 226). Of the earlier crises, only that concerning the EDC involved a comparable mobilization of the mass public and then only in France (Kaelble 2013). Up to the 1990s, EU crises were otherwise confined to and managed within the political elites – of Brussels and the member states. Domestic political incentives and constraints may have shaped elite behaviour to some extent, but there was hardly any direct mass participation in these crises. In most of the member states, the party system was dominated by 'pro-European' political movements spanning the ideological spectrum from the moderate Left to the moderate Right and the party-political mobilization of 'anti-European' sentiment was very limited. Following the end of the Cold War and the adoption of the Maastricht Treaty, the hitherto prevalent 'permissive consensus' in this regard began to wane (see Chapter 2). To legitimize the transfer of decision-making powers in core areas of national sovereignty such as the currency, political leaders have felt obliged to resort more frequently than in the past to popular referenda. These fostered the mass politicization of European integration, but the EU's political elites typically managed – at first – to navigate their way around the obstacles thrown into their path temporarily by negative referendum outcomes. Since the outbreak of the GFC, however, the mass politicization of European integration has begun to manifest itself in at least two additional ways that aggravate the current crisis. First, especially during the Eurozone Crisis, distributional conflicts between different groups of member states have intensified and 'anti-European' parties have been founded and prospered in numerous member states, rendering the mediation of conflicts between governments increasingly difficult. Second, as the EU has become increasingly associated with the imposition of economic austerity in southern European 'debtor' states, the EU and its policies have become the target – notably but not only in Greece – of popular demonstrations, protests and strikes.

The final trait of the contemporary crisis that differentiates it from most if not all past crises relates to *the costs of inaction* (see also Parsons and Matthijs 2015: 211, 223–224). The crisis involving the collapse of the EDC, for example, was resolved by enabling West German rearmament in the NATO. While it cut off the prospective development of a European army and increased Western Europe's security dependence on the USA, it arguably facilitated closer European integration in other, politically less sensitive issue areas. The fallout from a failure to reach agreement over the British budgetary contribution would have been contained because in such a scenario the budget for the previous year would have applied. It would have been more serious if the British government had decided not to transfer its contribution to the EU, but it had ruled out this course of action because of the expectation that the ECJ would have determined this to be illegal and a substantial proportion of 'pro-European' Conservative MPs was opposed to it (Thatcher 1993: 539). If the Constitutional/Lisbon Treaty had definitively failed, the EU would have continued to operate on the basis of the existing treaties. How this would have affected the EU's functioning is uncertain, but the impact would very likely have been gradual and limited (conceivably, for example, by impeding decision-making through the maintenance of unanimous voting in issue areas that the proposed treaties would have subjected to qualified majority voting). There was never any danger of imminent European disintegration.

The Empty Chair and EMS crises are in this regard slightly different. The failure to reach an accord whereby France resumed its seat in the Council of Ministers could have destroyed the EU in its infancy, as France was its most powerful and therefore least dispensable member state, although the five other member states might have tried to offset the impact of a French withdrawal by replacing it with the UK, whose accession they in any case strongly supported. We know in retrospect, however, that, just like the British government withholding its contribution to the EU budget in the early 1980s, in practice French withdrawal from the EU was never a very likely scenario (see the section 'The Empty Chair Crisis (1965–66)' above).

In the EMS crisis in 1992–93, in contrast, the costs of non-agreement and inaction would have been significant, in as far as in this scenario the EMS would certainly have collapsed and the EU would in this issue area have disintegrated. Simultaneously, the credibility of the single currency project would have been destroyed, at least for the time being, in just the same way that the monetary instability that accompanied the first oil-price crisis in the early 1970s had destroyed the initial project for economic and monetary union in the EU. With this, the foundations of the Franco-German bargain, whereby France consented to German reunification in return for Germany's pledge to deepen European integration, would have collapsed, with all the uncertainty that this would have implied for the EU's future. The EMS crisis was also unprecedented in as far as it revealed a set of actors outside the EU's political elites – the firms acting on the international foreign exchange markets – that could precipitate European disintegration in the absence of an accord as to how the crisis should be managed. The stakes of the EMS crisis were nonetheless not as far-reaching as in the contemporary crisis, as the latter's (multidimensional) scope is much wider and the financial, economic and political fallout from the collapse of an actual single currency would be much vaster and more negative than that of a project and timetable to introduce this currency.

The contemporary crisis of the EU is thus different, perhaps even very different: It is unique and unprecedented in its gravity because it exhibits a combination of four traits of which no more than a half characterized any of the earlier crises of European integration. To forecast based on the EU's survival of past crises that it will also resist disintegrative pressures and surmount the contemporary one would therefore be naïvely optimistic. Warnings expressed during the crisis that the 'European integration project' is in 'greater danger today than ever before' or that the EU 'can fall apart' were by no means groundless (Fischer 2014: 160; the Luxembourg foreign minister Jean Asselborn, quoted in *Der Spiegel* 2015a). The goal of this book is to describe the extent to which the EU has integrated or *dis*integrated in these crises and to advance a coherent explanation of the observable patterns of political integration and disintegration that can help us understand the conditions, if any, under which the integration process that has developed in Europe since the middle of the last century may be reversed.

Political integration and disintegration: concepts

For the purposes of this analysis, I conceive its dependent variable, political (dis)integration, as a multidimensional phenomenon. It comprises, first, the expansion or reduction of the range of issue areas in which the EU exercises policy-making competences and, within specific issue areas, an expansion or reduction of the scope of existing common policies. This I label *sectoral political (dis)integration*. Sectoral (dis)integration equates roughly with what has sometimes been defined as the *scope* of (dis)integration (see, e.g., Börzel 2005). The second dimension concerns the expansion or reduction of the formal (i.e. treaty-based) competences and effective authority of the EU's supranational political organs vis-à-vis the EU's intergovernmental organs and/or those of the member states. I label this dimension, which is occasionally called the *level* of (dis)integration (Börzel 2005), *vertical* political (dis)integration. This enables me to distinguish it from my third dimension, that of the expansion or reduction of the number of EU member states, which I define as *horizontal* political (dis)integration. Horizontal and sectoral political (dis)integration may also be seen as two – respectively, geographical and functional – components of the scope of integration. Political disintegration can thus occur as a consequence of a member state withdrawing – completely or partially – from the EU, as a consequence of a loss in the power or authority of supranational organs vis-à-vis the member states and/or the EU's intergovernmental organs, and the collapse of common policies or elements of such policies through their 're-nationalization' by the member states.

Plan of the book

The absence – at least before the contemporary crisis – of any tangible European political disintegration makes difficult the task of identifying the conditions under which it might take place. Unsurprisingly, given that the historical trend has been in the opposite direction, there are many theories of European integration, but few if any of *dis*integration (Zielonka 2014). For this reason, in the following chapter, I review competing theoretical perspectives on European integration, turning them on their head to discover under what conditions their proponents might have expected disintegration to occur. Extending this survey to include a range of theories from international economic and political relations and comparative politics, I find that most approaches fall to a greater or lesser extent into two categories, the one essentially 'optimistic' and the other essentially 'pessimistic' concerning the future of the EU and European political integration. For the theoretical 'optimists', political disintegration in Europe is close to being inconceivable. For the theoretical 'pessimists', the mounting political pressures to reduce the level and scope of integration should prove increasingly difficult for member states to resist. From this perspective, the quadruple crisis that has beset the EU since 2009 ought really to have been the 'perfect storm' that swept away at least a significant part of the existing 'system'.

In fact, however, the quadruple crisis has produced a range of outcomes in respect of political (dis)integration, ranging from closer political integration to partial disintegration. Neither of the general approaches to the analysis of (dis)integration can account for this divergent pattern of integration outcomes. To solve this puzzle is the main objective of this book. I propose an explanation of this pattern based on the hegemonic stability theory of international political economy, whose core claim is that the dominance of one country is a necessary condition of the stability of international (for the present purpose, regional) economic and political systems. Revising hegemonic stability theory, I argue that, before the quadruple crisis, France and Germany, which have been closely linked in a uniquely intensive bilateral relationship, formed a 'hegemonic coalition' in the EU that, while it did not dominate the EU's 'everyday politics', exercised a very strong influence over key decisions and integration projects in the EU's pre-2010 history. They did not always agree: for example, French opposition delayed the UK's accession to the EU, which Germany supported, by a good decade. But, as the following case studies will show, France and Germany, acting together, were the primary architects of the closer political integration that developed, prior to 2010, in respect of monetary, foreign and security and justice and home affairs policies in the EU. This applies especially to the period from 1982 to 1995, when Helmut Kohl was the German chancellor and François Mitterrand the French president and which saw the launching of the Euro, the Common Foreign and Security Policy (CFSP) and the Schengen Area of borderless travel.

During the quadruple crisis, however, the balance of power in this relationship has shifted decisively in favour of Germany. Practically, therefore, the question during this period has been whether Germany, largely alone, is capable and willing to provide stabilizing hegemonic leadership to the EU and, under the weight of the burgeoning crisis, to prevent its possible disintegration. The defining traits of such leadership would consist of playing a dominant role in the process by which these crises were managed, exercising a dominant influence over the rules that were adopted to address them, ensuring that the burdens of the crises and the rules chosen to address them were fairly distributed among member states, and mobilizing members' support for or acquiescence in these rules.

Chapters 3–6 of the book explore, in rough chronological order, the principal crises that have dominated the EU's agenda during the last decade: the Eurozone Crisis, the Ukraine Crisis, the Schengen and Refugee Crisis, and the Brexit Crisis. The former three crises constitute cases of sectoral (dis)integration and the Brexit Crisis one of horizontal (dis)integration. The *Eurozone Crisis*, the subject of the third chapter, has (hitherto at least) resulted in closer political integration. At first glance at least, this outcome seems at odds with the expectations of hegemony stability theory. With cross-issue variations, Germany largely dominated the fiscal politics of the crisis, but it pursued policies that in many respects ran counter to those that a stabilizing hegemonic power would have followed, placing the burdens of crisis-management overwhelmingly on the member states that had to be 'bailed out'. In line with the 'optimistic' theories of European integration, the fact that the Eurozone nonetheless became politically more closely integrated during the crisis is partly attributable to the level of interdependence between 'creditor' and 'debtor' states and the conviction of the governments among both groups of states that the price of allowing the Euro to collapse would be prohibitive and that this scenario should therefore be avoided. Had things been left entirely to the member governments, however, it is nonetheless very conceivable that, at some point in the crisis, especially in 2012, the rapidly rising interest rates that southern European governments were having to pay on their bonds would have precipitated the collapse of the Euro. A more critical factor in the survival of the Euro, in case of doubt, was the intervention of the ECB, which rapidly – and lastingly – calmed nervous international financial markets with the assurance that, within its legal powers, it would do 'whatever it takes' to defend the single currency. In this crisis, the ECB, the kind of international agency with 'real authority' that existed neither in the 1930s nor at the time that Kindleberger was analysing the causes of the Great Depression, assumed a stabilizing leadership role that Germany had largely abdicated. In monetary policy at least, Germany was not the Eurozone's stabilizing hegemon. Rather the ECB was.

The outcomes of the other three crises, however, closely followed the bargaining power exercised and kinds of strategies pursued in them by Germany. There was no supranational actor that could play a role in these crises comparable to that played in the Eurozone Crisis by the ECB. In the *Ukraine Crisis*, Berlin played the role of an ideal-typical stabilizing hegemonic leader. Playing a leading role in determining the stance that the EU adopted in the crisis versus Russia, it sought and maintained a very close relationship with France, one of the EU's two major military powers. It informed and consulted closely with other member states about its contacts with the Russian government. It also bore in absolute terms by far the largest and in relative terms a proportionately large share of the burdens of the economic and financial sanctions imposed by the EU on Russia. It succeeded in mobilizing and retaining the support of the other members, despite numerous prognoses to the effect that the sanctions policy was about to collapse. As the existing treaties provided sufficient instruments for the application of sanctions on Russia, there was, unlike in the Eurozone Crisis, no pressure or need in this crisis to forge closer political integration to hold the EU together.

Compared with the Ukraine Crisis, Germany was significantly less successful in providing stabilizing hegemonic leadership in the *Schengen and Refugee Crisis*. It did not – perhaps could not – consult or coordinate with other member states, except for Austria, before Chancellor Merkel decided in September 2015 not to oppose the entry into Germany of hundreds of thousands of refugees and migrants, many of whom had already landed in or traversed other EU member states. Subsequent bilateral efforts to persuade other member states to take in some of these migrants failed. Several member states refused to fulfil their legal obligations under a German-initiated Council decision to redistribute a limited proportion of refugees mainly from Greece and Italy, defying a ruling of the ECJ. Germany tried to lead, but numerous member states refused to follow it. In effect, refugee policy in the EU was, to a significant extent, re-nationalized. At the same time, to limit the influx of refugees and address fears that these could include some prospective terrorists, several member states reinstated border controls on some of their borders with other members of the Schengen Area. The imposition of these controls did not break the letter (as opposed perhaps to the spirit) of EU law, as the legal basis on which they were justified was regularly changed so that the maximum period for which the controls could be maintained was never exceeded. In effect, however, on some Schengen-internal borders uncontrolled traffic had practically been suspended indefinitely.

Germany tried to provide stabilizing leadership to the EU in the Schengen/Refugee Crisis, but it failed. In the *Brexit Crisis*, its efforts to provide such leadership were far more limited than in either this or the Ukraine Crisis. The relatively low profile that it maintained on Brexit reflected in part its recognition of the limits of its influence over other member states, given that some of these strongly opposed British demands for controls on the free movement of labour and persons between member states and such controls could be imposed only if all members agreed to change the EU treaties. But it was attributable probably no less to the government's conviction that to accede to British demands on this issue could prove to be the 'thin end of the wedge', encouraging other members to raise similar demands relating to the 'four freedoms' that, if granted, could undermine the integrity of the Single Market and – consequently – the EU, whose survival was an overriding goal of German European policy.

In Chapter 7, 'Conclusions', I argue that the overall record of German leadership of the EU during the quadruple crisis is thus very mixed. While it is overall indisputably the EU's most powerful member state and has compelling geopolitical as well as economic motives to preserve the EU, its capacity to play the role of a stabilizing hegemonic power in the EU is nonetheless limited. It is a 'hobbled hegemon'. If the survival of the EU should depend on stabilizing German leadership, the prospects for European political integration are not favourable. The breakthrough of the national-populist party, the Alternative for Germany (Alternative für Deutschland – AfD), in the 2017 federal elections also showed that Germany was no longer exceptional in its resistance to Euroscepticism and may in future no longer be as willing as it has been historically to promote closer European integration.

If German leadership cannot guarantee the future of European political integration, the fate of this process will depend on whether other, more inclusive forms of stabilizing leadership may emerge to fill the vacuum created by Berlin's incapacity or in future conceivably unwillingness to assume this role, at least by itself. I then assess the prospects for the emergence of other possible EU leadership coalitions. I identify three conceivable 'hegemonic coalitions'. One, the most inclusive but also the least likely to materialize, given the existing balance of domestic political power in Poland, would be a 'Weimar coalition', comprising France, Germany and Poland, respectively the three biggest member states from Southern, Northern and Central and Eastern Europe. The second would be a 'Hanseatic coalition', consisting of Germany and a group of eight, mainly small and rich, free-trade-oriented member states from Northern Europe. The third such coalition and the most likely to materialize would be a revived Franco-German relationship.

The election in France in May 2017 of a new, strongly pro-European French president, the centrist Emmanuel Macron, and the continuation in office in Berlin after the 2017 elections of a (much weakened) Grand Coalition government created a window of opportunity for a rejuvenated Franco-German 'tandem' to provide the EU with stabilizing hegemonic leadership. This window could, however, be shut, at the latest in scheduled elections in the two countries in 2021 and 2022. It was not certain whether the two governments would try to seize this chance or whether if they should try, given the rising tide of Euroscepticism in the EU, they would succeed. The absence of stabilizing hegemonic leadership in the EU may not matter unduly for the prospects of the EU and European political integration in normal political times. But it does matter in crises if the EU is 'leaderless'. If existing crises should re-escalate or new ones break out, they could then result in greater European political disintegration than has occurred since the Eurozone Crisis broke out in 2009–10.

Chapter 2

Explaining European Integration and Disintegration

Introduction

The crisis that the EU has been confronting since 2009 is uniquely profound in the history of European political integration. The fact that the EU surmounted numerous previous crises was thus no guarantee that it would emerge no less highly politically integrated from the current one. Historically, far more regional organizations have collapsed than survived (Mattli 1999: 12). Even states, typically far more cohesive entities, can disintegrate. Indeed, some of the EU's own member states, notably the UK and Spain, are exposed to strong disintegrative pressures. It would be myopic and naïve simply to assume that the EU will avert the fate that has befallen so many other regional organizations and even some states.

How, though, can we try to assess the likelihood that the EU will *disintegrate*? In this chapter, I tackle this task in four steps. First, I shall review the (hitherto sparse) literature on European disintegration. Second, I shall discuss existing theories of international relations (IR), comparative politics and European integration and what they can tell us about the likelihood of disintegration. Turning these on their head, I identify the conditions under which they would expect *disintegration to occur* and assess the extent to which these conditions currently prevail. Third, I argue that general theories of European (dis)integration – whether 'optimistic' or 'pessimistic' – are too broad and insufficiently fine-grained or differentiating to explain the divergent outcomes of the crises that the EU has traversed during the last decade, from closer (sectoral) integration in the case of the Eurozone Crisis to (partial horizontal) disintegration in the case of 'Brexit'. Both kinds of approach are overly deterministic and pay too little attention to the decision-making processes by which crises are managed in the EU. Fourth, I set out an explanation of this pattern of (dis)integration outcomes that addresses this *lacuna* in these approaches and is rooted in the theory of hegemonic stability. I describe how during the last decade of crisis, shedding its traditional post-World War II 'leadership avoidance reflex', Germany has increasingly emerged as the EU's hegemonic power. However, while, primarily for geopolitical motives, Germany wants as far as possible to hold the EU together and is meanwhile by far the EU's most powerful member state, it confronts significant constraints in exercising this role. It is in many respects a constrained or 'hobbled' hegemon. How 'well' or 'badly' it performs this role varies across crises, given their divergent traits, and so, consequently, do the outcomes of crises, as determined by whether the crises have resulted in closer political integration, the maintenance of the integration 'status quo' or in political *dis*integration. This analysis implies that the future of the EU is much more contingent and uncertain than 'optimistic' theories would have us believe – but at the same time also slightly less bleak than other, more 'pessimistic' theories suggest. It also tells us that, short of a significant change in the distribution of power between member states, the EU's fate will depend far more heavily than on anything else on what is decided – or not decided – in Berlin.

European disintegration: the existing literature

As if in the German expression *'nicht sein kann, was nicht sein darf'* ('what shouldn't happen can't happen') or perhaps because of their theoretically inspired confidence in its robustness, the proliferation and intensification of crises in the EU did not at first provoke a great deal of reflection among scholars as to whether European political integration was in the process or on the verge of being reversed. Before 2015, only a handful of them had explicitly addressed the issue. Two of the first political scientists to raise the alarm were Wurzel and Hayward (2012). They characterized the EU's prospects as 'unpromising with the danger of returning to the pleasures and poisons of the past: beggar my neighbour protectionism and competitive devaluation; closing national borders to unwelcome immigrants; subordination to international institutions and external powers' (2012: 326). But they did not articulate a very clear explanation for this trend towards 'disunion', except that it had to do with a growing divergence between elite and mass opinion over European integration and an institutional structure that promoted 'leaderlessness' and prevented the EU changing direction quickly when this was necessary. Three years previously, Taylor (2008) had speculated about *The End of European Integration*. However, despite the title of his study, Taylor did not anticipate the EU's disintegration as much as its stagnation. His argument was rather that the process of 'ever closer union' had run its course and that rather than becoming a kind of federal state, the EU was mutating into an ordinary international organization. If this did not involve disintegration as the concept is defined here, it nonetheless implied that in future the EU would become less rather than more important for the member states or, as he expressed it, the British vision of Europe would triumph over the German (Taylor 2008: 1–2). Taylor identified the driving forces of this trend as the end of the Cold War, the post-Communist enlargement and declining public support for integration, especially in the UK, France and Germany.

The post-Communist enlargement also occupies a – in fact *the* – central position in Zielonka's analysis of the EU's future (2006, 2014). Zielonka argues that the accession of states from Central and Eastern Europe has greatly increased the EU's diversity. This precludes the EU ever developing into a 'Westphalian'-style federal state characterized by a 'concentration of power, hierarchy, sovereignty, and clear-cut identity'. Increasingly, the EU will instead resemble a 'neo-medieval empire' with 'overlapping authorities, divided sovereignty, diversified institutional arrangements, and multiple identities' (Zielonka 2006: 15). He is very explicit, however, that this scenario 'does not need to herald the end of European integration'. Indeed, a neo-medieval empire seemed 'better suited' than a Westphalian state to meeting 'some of the basic aims of integration' (Zielonka 2006: 190). The EU as we know it would emerge 'significantly weakened' from the contemporary crisis, surviving only in a 'more modest form, deprived gradually of major legal powers and political prominence'. In the neo-medieval scenario he paints, not the nation states, but rather other political actors – cities, regions and non-government organizations – would be strengthened at the EU's expense (Zielonka 2014: x–xi). The waning of the EU would not lead to 'chaos or disintegration' but to what Zielonka labels 'polyphonic integration' that would be more respectful of 'diversity and pluralism' and at the same time more legitimate, resilient and 'capable of getting things done' than the EU (Zielonka 2014: xi–xiii).

More pessimistic than Zielonka, Krastev (2017) believes that European disintegration 'has left Brussels's station' and fears that this process 'will doom the continent to disarray and global irrelevance' (Krastev 2017: 10). He argues that, with the collapse of the Soviet Union, the geopolitical rationale for European unity 'vanished', creating an existential void that even Vladimir Putin's Russia cannot fill (Krastev 2017: 6). Most of all, however, the EU is threatened by a mass rebellion against the EU's elites, of which the Refugee Crisis ('Europe's 9/11') and the political fallout that has accompanied it are the primary manifestations (Krastev 2017: 13–14, 19). Like Zielonka, he sees the post-Communist enlargement as a centrifugal force in the EU, in as far as it is the 'east-wide divide that re-emerged after the Refugee Crisis' that threatens its survival (Krastev 2017: 44). At the roots of this divide lie the divergent historical experiences of the member states on different sides of the former Iron Curtain (Krastev 2017: 44–59). The outcomes of referenda, 'pivotal elections', major terrorist attacks in Europe or the arrival of a new wave of refugees on Europe's periphery – any of these events could bring the EU 'to the edge of collapse'. If the EU's disintegration is not inevitable, it is nonetheless 'one of the most likely outcomes' (Krastev 2017: 108–109).

In analysing the threat of European disintegration, Vollaard (2014), for his part, casts his analytical net wider than either Taylor, Zielonka or Krastev. Whereas the latter see the challenges facing the EU as having been dramatically magnified by the end of the Cold War and the post-Communist enlargement(s), Vollaard views the threat of disintegration as being rooted in the fundamental structural traits of the EU as a multinational polity. He explores the prospective impact on the EU of the contemporary crisis by applying the approach of Bartolini, who synthesizes Hirschman's micro- and Rokkan's macro-analytic framework to try to explain the formation of political systems (Bartolini 2005). Interestingly, however, although, in contrast to Bartolini, Vollaard is writing after the outbreak of the Eurozone Crisis, he is less pessimistic than his intellectual mentor as to the EU's future (see the section 'Comparative-political analysis and postfunctionalism: an optimist(?) and some pessimists' below). Although the weak scope for the effective expression of 'voice' in the EU increases pressure and demands for 'exit', Eurosceptic dissatisfaction 'has not and will probably not lead to full exits from the EU because of a lack of credible alternatives and a low belief in national efficacy' (Vollaard 2014: 14). The UK might leave, but other member states are more likely to seek 'partial exits within the EU, such as opt-outs, low compliance and less budgetary solidarity or by voicing for exit of malfunctioning member states' (Vollaard 2014: 14). Rather than Europe collapsing (back) into a system of sovereign states, the EU is 'much more likely to become a truncated union due to a full British exit and manifold partial exits' (Vollaard 2014: 14). Vollaard thus envisages the emergence of a more differentiated EU rather than its (full-scale) disintegration.

The conditions of European disintegration: competing theoretical perspectives

Given the relative paucity of theoretically grounded analyses of European disintegration, the most fruitful way of trying to work out what impact the contemporary crisis will have on the EU's future may be to ask to what extent there has been any change in the variables that have fuelled the integration process in the past. This section will explore competing theories of European integration, IR and comparative politics, comparing the explanations they offer for this process and evaluating to what extent the variables that each theory identifies as having driven this process are still present, have waned or have disappeared. The two most pessimistic sets of approaches form 'bookends' to the discussion, those in between are presented roughly in order from the most pessimistic to the most optimistic in respect of the EU's survival prospects.

Neo-realism: the arch-pessimists

The contemporary crisis of the EU should have surprised neo-realist IR theorists less than the exponents of most theorists of European integration. Within months of the fall of the Berlin Wall, the American neo-realist John Mearsheimer portrayed Europe's future in extremely bleak terms. According to him, if the Cold War ended and the Soviet army withdrew from Eastern Europe and American and British troops from continental Western Europe – steps he thought were highly likely – the prospects for major crises and war in Europe would 'increase markedly' (Mearsheimer 1990: 6). Relations among the EU states, he argued, 'will be fundamentally altered. Without a common Soviet threat and without the American night watchman, West European states will begin viewing each other with greater fear and suspicion, as they did for centuries before the onset of the Cold War' (Mearsheimer 1990: 47). Mearsheimer attributed the failure of this scenario to materialize in the decade following his prognosis to the fact that, contrary to his original expectations, NATO had survived and, albeit in reduced numbers, the USA had kept its troops in Europe (Mearsheimer 2001). Still sure at the turn of the century that the USA would eventually withdraw its troops from Europe, provoking 'more intense security competition among the European powers', Mearsheimer later became less certain that this scenario would materialize, while continuing to argue that the US military presence is still the main reason for Europe's peacefulness (Mearsheimer 2001, 2010).

From a neo-realist perspective, European disintegration would hence most probably result from an American military withdrawal from Europe and a collapse of NATO. However, despite a significant reduction in the scale of the US military presence in Europe, sporadic tensions in the transatlantic military relationship, and uncertainty as to its future role, which the election of Donald Trump as US president on a neo-isolationist platform in 2016 greatly compounded, NATO has hitherto survived the end of the Cold War and even expanded. Moreover, uncertainty as to the durability or reliability of the American commitment to European military security has not hitherto led to less security and defence cooperation between EU member states, even if at the level of operational capabilities the EU's progress has been limited and on some important issues, notably relating to military intervention in North Africa and the Middle East, the member states have often been divided (see Chapter 4). Contrary to what Mearsheimer anticipated, growing distrust among Europe's big powers over 'hard' security issues has not provoked Europe's contemporary crisis. This side of the dissolution of NATO that Mearsheimer initially anticipated, but has not yet occurred, neo-realism does not yield any reason to fear that the EU might disintegrate for the time being. The most pessimistic theory concerning the long-run viability of the EU is based on a scenario that failed hitherto to materialize.

[handwritten margin note: NATO collapse needed for EU disintegration]

Traditional intergovernmentalism: the moderate pessimists

Of the theories developed to explain European integration, traditional intergovernmentalism is the one most similar to IR's neo-realism. As for neo-realists, so also for intergovernmentalists such as Stanley Hoffmann, nation states – not supranational organs like the European Commission – were still the key European actors, could have divergent interests and in areas of 'high' (i.e. security and foreign) politics would resist the forfeiture of policy-making powers to supranational entities much more strongly than in those of low (i.e. trade and economic) politics. Continuing integration was by no means preordained and the authority of supranational institutions remained 'limited, conditional, dependent and reversible' (Hoffmann 1966, in Eilstrup-Sangiovanni 2006: 156). The core of Hoffmann's analysis was replicated in Moravcsik's 'intergovernmentalist institutionalist' approach (Moravcsik 1991), but this, the 'early' Moravcsik diverges from Hoffmann by weighting differently the role of international-systemic and domestic-political variables and 'high' and 'low' politics in determining the stance of national governments on European issues. For Moravcsik, integration is thus contingent on the degree of convergence of the preferences or interests of the governments of key member states shaped by the requirements of domestic politics, not on the structure of the international system as in neo-realism. Whether such convergence would be reproduced in the future as it had occurred in respect of the Single European Act in the 1980s was an open question. However, in as far as two of the 'big three' governments (i.e. the French and German) could credibly threaten to exclude the third (i.e. the British) from the integration process and thus coerce it into staying on board, a bilateral Franco-German accord could suffice to keep the integration process on the rails.

Traditional intergovernmentalism thus focuses our attention on the evolution and degree of convergence of the stances of the French, German and British governments as determinants of the future of European integration. Trends in this trilateral relationship since the end of the Cold War most certainly do not augur well for the EU's future. Even before the referendum in June 2016 produced a majority in favour of 'Brexit', the UK had become increasingly marginalized in and disengaged from the EU (Krotz and Maher 2016). Growing British Euroscepticism made Franco-German threats to exclude the UK from the integration process increasingly hollow – not because such threats could not be implemented (they were), but rather because the British government proved increasingly impervious to them. Not least because of British opposition to it, closer integration increasingly assumed a differentiated pattern, with a subgroup of 'avant-garde' member states launching a project and (some or most of) the others subsequently acceding to it.

To the extent that such projects developed centripetal effects that drew more and more other member states to participate in them, they testified to the continuing capacity of the French and German governments, when they work together, to promote closer integration. Especially where the two governments have formed 'opposing poles' in the EU around which other member states could coalesce, the Franco-German 'tandem' has often exercised a decisive influence in the EU (see Krotz and Schild 2013; Schild 2010; Webber 1999a). However, given their occasionally divergent interests, they have not always been able to reach the bilateral compromises that were the prerequisites of such influence. Moreover, since the outbreak of the Eurozone Crisis, France has grown much weaker than Germany and has not played as prominent a role in managing the EU's crises as it might have done in earlier eras. In the absence of credible alternative leading coalitions, a larger, more diverse EU has had to fly increasingly on a single – German – engine (see the section 'The balance of power in the Franco-German relationship has shifted gradually but decisively towards Germany' below). Implying as it does that states are not structurally constrained to acquiesce in ever greater regional political integration and always possess other options, traditional intergovernmentalism would view a significant weakening, let alone breakdown, of Franco-German cooperation as a grave menace to European integration.

International relations institutionalism: the cautious optimists

Institutionalist theories of international relations (IR) are cautiously optimistic as to the prospects for European integration, although IR institutionalists agree with neo-realists that states are the principal actors in European regional as in world politics. They do not share the neo-functionalist precept that international or regional organizations ('regimes') like the EU can be influential actors in their own right. However, in contrast to neo-realists, IR institutionalists argue that such organizations can achieve a high level of durability or permanence by helping states to overcome collective action problems, carrying out functions that these cannot, notably 'facilitating the making and keeping of agreements through the provision of information and reductions in transaction costs', monitoring compliance, reducing uncertainty and stabilizing expectations (Keohane 1993: 274, 284, 288; Keohane and Nye 1993: 2–5). Even so, 'without a basis *either of hegemonic dominance or common interests*, international institutions cannot long survive' (Keohane 1993: 295; emphasis my own). IR institutionalists were nonetheless optimistic, as the Cold War ended, that the EU would flourish in the future. Keohane argued that 'since common interests are likely to persist, and the institutions of the European Community are well-entrenched ... the EC will remain a durable and important entity'. He foresaw correctly that it would be 'larger and have a greater impact on its members' policies in the year 2000 than it was when the Berlin Wall came down in November 1989' (Keohane 1993: 291).

From an IR institutionalist perspective, the critical questions relating to the EU's future are thus whether especially in the enlarged EU there are sufficiently pervasive common interests that link member states and whether, much as for traditional intergovernmentalists, the 'most powerful states' (Keohane and Nye 1993: 18) continue to support the integration process. The institutionalist literature does not specify how the evolution of the incidence of common interests in the EU could be determined, other than in a post hoc fashion, according to whether and with what degree of ease or difficulty the EU has managed to make decisions. Although, other things being equal, growing economic and other forms of interdependence may exert a countervailing effect, the post-Cold War enlargements have surely increased the EU's socio-economic, cultural and political heterogeneity and thus diminished the scope of common interests among the member states. If common interests among member states should indeed be declining, then IR institutionalists would expect the risk of European disintegration to have risen.

The other critical issue for IR institutionalists is whether the 'hegemonic' or most powerful states still support and, in as far as they are EU members, are willing to be constrained by the EU. If this category includes the USA, as it evidently does for Keohane and Nye (1993: 16–19), prospects for European integration may be less bright than they were before the end of the Cold War. As shown, for example, by occasionally expressed US reservations concerning European aspirations to develop a military intervention capacity independent of NATO, American support for European integration has

[handwritten margin note: Sounds Liberal?]

grown more ambivalent since the turn of the century and threatened with Donald Trump as president to turn into outright opposition. As the Iraq conflict already indicated, the USA continues to exercise considerable leverage over (non-Russian) Europe and transatlantic conflicts normally also generate conflicts among EU member states. Among the 'big three' EU members, as noted above, divergences of interest grew between the UK, on the one hand, and France and Germany, on the other. If at first these conflicts did not stall the integration process, but rather produced an increasingly differentiated EU, the 2016 Brexit vote showed that ultimately they could not be mediated. From an IR institutionalist as well as a traditional intergovernmentalist perspective, the EU's post-Brexit future would ride first and foremost on the Franco-German relationship and the extent to which the governments in Berlin and Paris perceived that they had a common interest in the EU's survival.

If common interests should be waning and big powers should become less supportive of European integration, IR institutionalist theory would predict integration to wane, albeit it in a lengthy drawn-out process. For, even in the absence of common interests, Keohane explains (1993: 295), 'organizational inertia, considerations of reputation, and connections to domestic politics mean that institutions often persist even when the conditions for their creation have disappeared'. In this scenario, European disintegration would be a slow process of attrition, in which ever greater difficulties in adopting new legislation would go hand in hand with 'an erosion of the existing *acquis* through creeping non-compliance and "institutional hypocrisy"' (Elena A. Iankova and Peter J. Katzenstein, quoted in Scharpf 2006: 858).

Constructivism: the agnostics

Constructivist analyses of the EU emphasize the role of actors', especially political leaders', subjective and intersubjective beliefs as drivers of the integration process (Eilstrup-Sangiovanni 2006: 393). Not objective structures, circumstances and interests, whether in international or domestic politics, but rather ideas, norms, identities and cultures are the critical explanatory variables. Sociological or social constructivists thus credit European institutions with having a 'socializing' effect that favours the pursuit of integration (Checkel 2006) as opposed to other hypothetically possible political agendas. This effect is exercised, however, on those actors – for example, civil servants – participating directly in the EU policy process. There is no guarantee that EU organs will socialize the mass publics of the member states in 'pro-European' beliefs – these have not grown in the past in line with growing levels of economic and social interaction across member states' borders (Kuhn 2011). How far outcomes are determined by 'constructivist' variables may in any case vary according to the extent to which 'objective pressures' are indeterminate in respect of strategic or policy choices (Parsons 2003: 51). It is because these geopolitical and economic pressures were indeterminate in France in the 1950s that entrepreneurial leaders from different political camps could put Europe on a course towards the 'quasi-federal' political entity that exists today (Parsons 2003: 47).

Constructivist theories seem themselves, however, to be indeterminate as regards the *contents* of the norms that develop at the European level. While they identify processes of societal mobilization and social learning as being central to the emergence of new European norms, nothing in the literature suggests that these must necessarily be favourable to (greater) European integration (see, e.g., Hooghe and Marks 2008). If 'social learning' is most likely to occur under conditions of crisis or policy failure, constructivism does not provide any certainty that member governments will 'learn' that the crisis of the Euro, for example, can be solved only or best by bringing about closer integration as opposed to dismantling the single currency. Moreover, if crises or policy failures lead to changes in prevalent ideas or norms, then not these ideas or norms but rather changing material circumstances are what must be analysed to understand what is driving integration – or disintegration – processes (Moravcsik, as cited in Eilstrup-Sangiovanni 2006: 403). If, in general, constructivism points to the importance of political leaders' ideas and beliefs as determinants of the prospects for integration and thus to the rise of EU-critical political parties in many member states as possible harbingers of European disintegration, the constructivist literature does not specify the circumstances under which 'pro-' or 'anti-European' beliefs are likely to predominate. They cannot therefore shed very much light on whether the EU is likely to disintegrate.

Actor-centred institutionalism: the implicit pessimists

While it is not a theory of European integration as such, but one of decision-making, actor-centred institutionalism (ACI), associated principally with Scharpf (1988, 2000, 2006), implies that there is a high risk of *disintegration*. ACI focuses on how formal and informal decision-making rules and institutional structures constrain policy choices. Scharpf distinguishes three modes of governance or decision-making in the EU: intergovernmental, joint-decision and supranational-hierarchical. In issue areas where the intergovernmental mode prevails, the EU is likely gradually to lose its capacity for policy innovation, as each member government has a right of veto over decisions. In those subject to the joint-decision mode, in which the Commission has the monopoly of legislative initiative, there is greater – but only marginally greater – scope for devising side-payments and package deals to mediate conflicts of interest between member governments, but on politically salient issues these mechanisms have been 'overwhelmed by the increase in numbers of member states and in their heterogeneity' (Scharpf 2006: 851). In contrast, in the supranational-hierarchical mode, feasible on issues of 'negative' (i.e. market-liberalizing) integration, such actors as the Commission, the ECJ and the ECB can override the opposition of minorities or even majorities among the member governments. Intergovernmental and joint-decision governance modes are likely to lead to bad policy choices or increasingly dysfunctional policies because the practical requirement of unanimity prevents policies being adapted to new conditions. In contrast, supranational-hierarchical governance facilitates decision-making, but, as the principal actors in this mode are politically unaccountable, there is a risk that the limits of the 'permissive consensus' may be exceeded and the legitimacy bases of national welfare states undermined (Scharpf 2006: 857). Policy choices in the former two modes of governance may be legitimate, but they are unlikely to be effective; those in the latter may be effective, but they are unlikely to be legitimate. By fostering either 'bad', in the sense of increasingly ineffective, policies or illegitimate ones, all three modes, however, seem likely to produce outcomes that tend to work more in the direction of disintegration than closer integration, all the more so as legal and economic constraints increasingly prevent member governments from acting unilaterally in issue areas where intergovernmental and joint-decision governance modes stymie EU initiatives.

In the extent to which it emphasizes the veto power of member governments over EU decisions, ACI shares a good deal with traditional intergovernmentalist analyses of European integration. What distinguishes it from the latter is the way in which it links the dominant modes of policy-making in the EU to choices and outcomes that are likely – directly or indirectly – to have negative consequences for the integration process. Scharpf's analysis casts doubt particularly on whether, as neo-functionalist perspectives imply, EU-level policy solutions are likely to be 'better', in the sense of more effective or efficient, than national ones (see Majone 2009: 103–106). However, it is also difficult to validate empirically. The increase in the number and diversity of member states following the end of the Cold War did not seem to diminish the EU's overall capacity to take decisions (Hagemann and De Clerck-Sachsse 2007). Decision-makers have developed a wide range of – informal – practices to circumvent vetoes and avert paralysis in the EU (Héritier 1999, 2017). But the *volume* of the EU's decisional outputs says by itself very little about the *effectiveness or legitimacy* of EU policy which is central to ACI analysis. Moreover, as we shall see in the following chapters, the kind of intergovernmental decision-making that for the most part predominated in the EU's crisis management processes was, for ACI, the type potentially most vulnerable to deadlock and paralysis.

Sociological and historical institutionalism: the (slightly qualified) optimists

'New institutionalists' argue that, alongside macro-historical forces and human agency, institutions ('relatively enduring collections of rules and organized practices, embedded in structures of meaning and resources that are relatively invariant in the face of turnover of individuals and changing external circumstances') exercise an independent effect on political outcomes (Olsen 2009: 9; see also March and Olsen 1989). While accepting that institutions can change or even collapse in processes of 'de-institutionalization', they do not specify the conditions under which such scenarios may materialize (Olsen 2009: 10–11, 25). However, criticizing traditional intergovernmentalism, historical-institutionalist (HI) scholars of European integration argue that, over time, the capacity of member governments to control supranational organs such as the Commission and the ECJ has declined and integration has become increasingly irreversible. Pierson (1998) identifies several variables that explain how 'gaps' in the capacity of member governments to control supranational actors emerge: these actors' partial autonomy, the restricted time horizons of political decision-makers in the member states, unanticipated consequences, and shifts in the preferences of the heads of member governments. Once such gaps have emerged, member governments face a well-nigh impossible task trying to close them again, as supranational actors resist them, the treaty-rooted institutional barriers to reversing the gaps are high, governments that do or would otherwise champion such changes are constrained by 'massive sunk costs', and the high and rising price of exit, which makes any threat to leave the EU as a weapon to influence its policies increasingly implausible: 'While the governments of "sovereign" member-states remain free to tear up treaties and walk away at any time, the constantly increasing costs of exit in the densely integrated European polity have rendered this option virtually unthinkable' (Pierson 1998: 47).

In the logic of historical institutionalism (HI), the EU's growing longevity should make it increasingly immune to disintegration or collapse. While HI scholars generally focus on constraints and the '"stickiness" of historically evolved institutional arrangements' and provide 'explanations of continuity rather than change', they nonetheless recognize that critical junctures or crises can bring about 'relatively abrupt institutional change' (Thelen and Steinmo 1992: 15). Krasner has applied the biological concept of 'punctuated equilibrium' to characterize a pattern in which long periods of stasis are interrupted by 'short bursts of rapid institutional change' (Krasner 1984: 242–243). He quotes the evolutionary biologist Gould to the effect that rapid change occurs when a 'stable structure is stressed beyond its buffering capacity to resist and absorb' (Krasner 1984: 242–243). However, HI scholarship does not provide any criteria with which we could identify a 'crisis' or the conditions under which what they define as a crisis would provoke abrupt or radical changes, such as a reversal or collapse of European integration. It is difficult therefore to judge whether from an HI perspective the EU is now in a crisis that could precipitate fundamental institutional change in the EU or even its demise. Still, in as far as they admit the theoretical possibility of radical change, albeit under exceptional circumstances, HI analysis is implicitly more circumspect about the prospects for European integration than contemporary neo-functionalist-cum-transactionalist and liberal intergovernmentalist theories.

Neo-functionalism, transactionalism and liberal intergovernmentalism: the unequivocal optimists

Neo-functionalism and transactionalism, associated respectively with Haas (1958) and Deutsch (1957), both provide fundamentally optimistic theoretical perspectives on European integration. For neo-functionalists, political integration arises from processes of functional and political 'spill-over', whereby integration in one sector produces pressures for integration in related sectors and non-governmental actors in nation states transfer their loyalty to supranational organs and coalesce with them to promote political integration. For transactionalists, politically integrated regions (in Deutsch's terminology, 'pluralistic security communities') could develop on the foundation of growing levels of cross-border transactions and communication. While these theories suggested that there was a certain inexorability about regional political integration, at least where the socio-economic processes on which they focused were present, the trials and tribulations of the EU in the 1960s and 1970s taught Haas and other neo-functionalist 'old hands' that other scenarios than ever closer political integration were conceivable. In the first half of the 1970s, Haas declared regional integration theory altogether to be 'obsolescent' and like-minded scholars declared that not only 'spill-over', but also 'spill-back' was possible (Haas 1976; Lindberg and Scheingold 1970; Schmitter 1971).

More recent neofunctionalist-cum-transactionalist theorizing, as exemplified in the work of Stone Sweet and Sandholtz (1997), is much less ambivalent. In this perspective, European integration – the growth of European-level governmental structures and formal and informal rules – is the more or less inexorable outcome of growing volumes of transnational exchange that force national governments to acquiesce in the transfer of more and more policy-making competences to the European level: 'As transnational exchange rises, so does the societal demand for supranational rules and organizational capacity to regulate' (Stone Sweet and Sandholtz 1997: 306). Once the pressures created by growing transnational exchange have led to the foundation of European governmental structures, similar to the process of spill-over described by Haas, a self-sustaining dynamic of institutionalization – a process by which 'rules are created, applied, and interpreted by those who live under them' – kicks in, locking member governments ever more tightly into the EU (Stone Sweet and Sandholtz 1997: 310). Institutionalization makes it unlikely that even a profound economic crisis, which would likely reduce levels of transnational economic exchange in Europe, could undermine European integration. Sandholtz and Stone Sweet thus argue that transnational interactions

> will not drive the evolution of the EU forever ... EU rules are increasingly dense; ambiguities and conflicts among rules are inevitable. Actors facing those ambiguities and conflicts in EU rules will want authoritative clarifications. The result will be to reinforce EU organizations as arbiters of existing rules as well as generators of new ones ... The EU polity itself generates needs that will be met by enhanced supranational governance.
>
> (Sandholtz and Stone Sweet 1999: 152–153)

Nor was it likely that any other kind of crisis would result in institutionalized cooperation in the EU being 'rolled back' (Stone Sweet et al. 2001: 27–28).

From his liberal intergovernmentalist perspective, (the later) Moravcsik reached conclusions that are less guarded about the EU's prospects than those in his earlier work and he is hardly any less confident about them than the neo-functionalist-cum-transactionalists. Before the financial and sovereign debt crises, he concluded that the EU had developed a 'mature' constitutional order or 'constitutional settlement' that was unlikely to be undermined by any new challenges to its 'functional effectiveness, institutional stability or normative legitimacy' (Moravcsik 2008). In his view, the financial and sovereign debt crises did not jeopardize European integration. Rather they 'boosted the European project' and made Europe 'stronger than ever' (Moravcsik 2009). He remained certain that the 'Cassandras ... predicting the collapse of the euro, if not the European Union itself' would be proved wrong (Moravcsik 2010). Similar to Stone Sweet and Sandholtz, Moravcsik argued that 'increasing transborder flows of goods, services, factors, or pollutants create "international policy externalities" among nations, which in turn create incentives for policy coordination' (Moravcsik 1993: 485). In contrast to Stone Sweet and Sandholtz, however, for Moravcsik member governments remain decisive EU actors, autonomous of the EU's supranational organs, whose authority is relatively limited. As their vulnerability to negative externalities varies greatly, member governments do not all inevitably support cooperation to liberalize trade and provide public goods; so continuing political integration is not to be taken for granted (Moravcsik 1993: 486). Nonetheless, growing economic interdependence seems increasingly to foreclose other, unilateral policy options and to compel member governments to forge or acquiesce in closer integration. This is clear in Moravcsik's analysis of both the Eurozone and Brexit crises. In respect of the former, he argued that EU members, because they 'inhabit the world's most economically interdependent continent ... have no choice but to cooperate' and that France and Germany must support Greece financially 'to avoid a disastrous loss of confidence in French and German banks and bonds' (Moravcsik 2010: 25–28). As for Brexit, given the extent of its interdependence with the other member states, the UK would not leave the EU under 'any circumstances', regardless of the result of the 2016 referendum. A vote to leave would not end in Brexit, but rather in the renegotiation of the UK's current membership terms (Moravcsik 2016).

Comparative-political analysis and postfunctionalism: an optimist(?) and some pessimists

Regional integration and IR theories are not the sole possible sources of theoretically guided analyses of the EU's durability. Since the adoption of the Maastricht Treaty at the latest, the EU may be regarded as a kind of federal state or a case of 'centre formation' whose dynamics theoretical perspectives from comparative politics could help us to understand (Bartolini 2005; Kelemen 2007: 52; McKay 1999b: 179). One way of assessing its survival prospects is to analyse the extent to which it fulfils the preconditions of survival of federal or other emergent political systems.

Most federations, Jonathan Lemco has argued, fail (as quoted in Kelemen 2007: 53). *Multinational* federations, of which the EU is certainly an example, may be more prone to failure than others (Kelemen 2007: 61). Kelemen none-theless concluded optimistically in 2007 that 'rumours of the EU's impending demise are greatly exaggerated' and that the EU is 'built to last' (Kelemen 2007: 53, 65). In Kelemen's analysis, judicial, partisan (party-political) and socio-cultural safeguards are required to prevent federal states from fall-ing apart. The judicial safeguards in the EU are strong, given the 'powerful' position of the ECJ and the effectiveness of decentralized enforcement of its jurisprudence, which is secured through the preliminary rulings procedure and governments' reluctance to disobey their own judiciaries – in as far at least as these accept the ECJ's supremacy on issues of EU law (Kelemen 2007: 57). By Kelemen's own analysis, however, the other two safeguards against the col-lapse of federal systems are weaker in the EU. As regards partisan safeguards, he notes that although the power and discipline of party groups in the EP have been growing, these remain 'too weak to restrain behaviour by national par-ties that might imperil the Union' (Kelemen 2007: 58). His relative confidence that the EU will not be vulnerable to collapse as a consequence of centrifugal dynamics unleashed by party-political competition in the member states rests on his forecast that the gradual transfer of authority from the national to the EU level will be accompanied by a commensurate strengthening of the role and power of European-level parties vis-à-vis their national counterparts. Hitherto, however, the former process has easily outpaced the latter and it is still not evident that European-level political party groups can 'discipline' or 'moderate' the positions taken by their national member parties on EU issues. By socio-cultural safeguards, Kelemen means that the stability of federal insti-tutions 'must be grounded in a shared sense of identity and political culture of federalism' (Kelemen 2007: 59). Here he notes that although there is no consensus among EU scholars as to how much common identity is necessary to 'underpin the EU', there has not been any substantial increase in European identity in recent decades (Kelemen 2007: 59). He therefore judged that 'for the EU to resist centrifugal pressures over the long run, the EU citizens and leaders may need to develop a stronger sense of common, albeit hybrid (i.e. national and European), identity' (Kelemen 2007: 61).

Overall, Kelemen's analysis thus points towards a more circumspect assessment of the EU's durability than his own overall conclusion suggests. McKay's analyses of the preconditions of sustainable federalism and the EU point unambiguously in this direction (McKay 1999a, 1999b, 2004). For McKay, the principal bulwarks against federal states falling apart are provided by formal and informal institutional constraints and norms that 'contain central power and preserve regional autonomy' (as, for example, in Switzerland) as well as by a party system in which political parties are organ-ized in such a way as to be able to mediate and broker conflicts between the centre and the periphery (McKay 2004: 180). While the EU probably meets the first condition, it does not in his view meet the second. Given that in the EU 'all the parties are regional [i.e. national] and all are decentralized', McKay is uncertain whether the Euro will prove sustainable 'in the longer term', fearing that it could generate acute distributional conflicts and mobilize strong populist sentiments and political parties (McKay 2004: 182).

Applying and combining Hirschman's micro-level and Rokkan's macro-level analytical frameworks to the formation of new polities or 'centres', Bartolini (2005) develops a fairly similar argument. For Bartolini, the consolidation of a strong new 'centre' presupposes the development of coinciding economic, coercion and administrative-legal boundaries, 'system building', through which 'enlarged loyalties, identities, and social solidarities' are generated, and 'political structuring', a process through which 'Europarties, interest Eurogroups, and social Euromovements' displace territorially (i.e. nationally – DW) organized actors as 'structures of representation' (Bartolini 2005: 386, 394). Perhaps unsurprisingly given its remorseless territorial expansion, the EU lacks the mutually reinforcing boundaries required for it to become a well-entrenched 'centre'. The prospects for 'European-level system building and political structuring' are correspondingly 'uncertain, if not gloomy' (Bartolini 2005: 386). Bartolini's pessimism is graphically expressed in his judgement that 'system building' in the EU could break down in 'phases of mass mobilization and democratization' like the Ottoman, Habsburg and Russian/Soviet empires (Bartolini 2005: 387).

In their postfunctionalist theory of European integration, Hooghe and Marks (2008) suggest that since the adoption of the Maastricht Treaty in the early 1990s the kinds of scenarios portrayed by McKay and Bartolini have begun to materialize. Transactionalists, neo-functionalists, liberal intergovernmentalists and historical institutionalists emphasize the extent and tightness of the structural economic and other constraints under which member state governments make choices relating to European integration, such that they can barely deviate from a preset path leading towards closer integration. McKay and Bartolini and Hooghe and Marks, in contrast, argue for the ultimate primacy of politics, specifically domestic politics. The post-Cold War period has witnessed the mass politicization of EU-related issues, the emergence of a new national/international cleavage in the domestic politics of member states, the growth of Euroscepticism and greater party-political competition and polarization over European integration. Hooghe and Marks do not go as far as to forecast the collapse of the EU as a consequence of these trends. However, they do anticipate that, since domestic politics has become 'more tightly coupled with European outcomes' and the 'permissive consensus' over integration that once prevailed in the member states has given way to a 'constraining dissensus', conflict mediation in the EU will become more difficult and there will be 'downward pressure on the level and scope of integration' (Hooghe and Marks 2008: 21).

General theories and divergent crisis outcomes

Ploughing the theoretical field of European integration thus yields a diverse harvest of variables whose presence could have a disintegrative impact on the EU (see Table 2.1). If these variables are used as a basis for developing prognoses as to the likelihood of European disintegration, the competing theoretical perspectives divide roughly into three groups.

Table 2.1 Will the EU disintegrate? Theoretical overview

Theory	Main independent variable(s)	(Potential) disintegrator	Theory-based prognosis
Realism (Mearsheimer)	Distribution of military power	European multipolarity after collapse of NATO	Disintegration unlikely as long as USA keeps military presence
Traditional intergovernmentalism (Hoffmann; early Moravcsik)	Preferences/interests of big three EU powers	Divergence of interests of big three powers	Disintegration unlikely provided France and Germany cooperate
International relations institutionalism (Keohane)	Cooperation-facilitating role of institutions (EU)	Decline of members' common interests and hegemonic dominance/will	Disintegration increasingly conceivable
Constructivism	Ideas, norms, identities	Growth of 'Eurosceptic' norms and identities	Indeterminate
Actor-centred institutionalism (Scharpf)	(Formal and informal) decision-making rules	Incapacity of political system to adopt new policies, adapt old ones to new circumstances	Disintegration increasingly conceivable as gap between necessary and politically feasible policies grows
Historical (and sociological) institutionalism (Pierson; Thelen and Steinmo; Olsen)	Ever-tighter institutional constraints	(Generally externally induced) crises or critical junctures	Disintegration likely only in very exceptional circumstances
Liberal intergovernmentalism (late Moravcsik)	Big three powers and economic interdependence	Declining economic interdependence and divergent big three economic interests	Disintegration very unlikely – interdependence remains very strong
Neo-functionalism/transactionalism (Stone Sweet and Sandholtz)	Spill-over/transnational exchange and society	Decline of transnational exchange and society; de-institutionalization	Disintegration virtually excluded – institutionalization prevents even crisis-induced collapse
Comparative-political analysis (Kelemen; McKay; Bartolini); postfunctionalism (Hooghe and Marks)	Transfer of decision-making powers from national to EU level	Politicization, with weakness of common identity and pan-European political parties	Strong risk of disintegration

Short of an unanticipated process of de-institutionalization, a collapse of economic interdependence and levels of other forms of transnational exchange in Europe, or a deep crisis that destroys the EU's 'very sticky' institutional arrangements, neo-functionalists, transactionalists, liberal inter-governmentalists and historical-institutionalists all downplay the risk of European disintegration.

Occupying the theoretical middle ground, IR institutionalism and tradi-tional intergovernmentalism are implicitly or explicitly more circumspect about the EU's future. Viewed from these perspectives, European integra-tion is a more contingent phenomenon, resting on the scope of member states' common interests, which has arguably narrowed following successive waves of enlargement, and/or on the extent of the convergence of interests among the EU's three big powers. The latter diminished even prior to the Brexit referendum as the UK grew increasingly hostile to closer integration, leaving the EU's fate – in these perspectives – increasingly dependent on Franco-German cooperation – that itself may be weakened by an increasingly asymmetrical bilateral relationship (see the section 'The balance of power in the Franco-German relationship has shifted gradually but decisively towards Germany' on page 45 of this text).

Comparative-political analyses and postfunctionalism see danger for the EU in the mass politicization of European integration, at least so long as there is no sufficiently strong and widely shared common European identity and there are no sufficiently strong, integrative pan-European political parties to underpin the kind of federal state into which the (increasingly amorphous) EU has increasingly developed. They are deeply sceptical as to the future of European integration.

None of these competing theoretical perspectives on European integration, however, provides a really satisfactory explanation of the (at least provi-sional) outcomes of the quadruple crisis that has rocked the EU since 2010. As we shall see in the next chapter, one, the Eurozone Crisis, has resulted in closer (sectoral) political integration. A second, the Ukraine Crisis, has wit-nessed no change in the level of political integration. A third, the Schengen or Refugee Crisis, has provoked a limited degree of (sectoral) political *dis*inte-gration. The fourth, 'Brexit', on the other hand, represents a very significant case of (horizontal) political disintegration. The general character of the con-trasting theoretical perspectives reviewed above makes it difficult for them to account for this pattern of divergent crisis outcomes in respect of political integration. On the one hand, the 'optimistic' ones failed to foresee the mass politicization and political polarization over EU issues that postfunctionalists rightly diagnose as a growing threat to European integration and they overes-timated the EU's capacity to resist the challenges that these processes posed. On the other, given the magnitude and multiplicity of the crises that the EU has confronted since 2009, political integration has proven less 'reversible' overall than postfunctionalists probably would have imagined if they had foreseen them. A shared shortcoming of both 'optimistic' and 'pessimistic' integration theories is the relatively scant attention that they pay to crisis decision-making processes and the balance of power within the EU. For the 'optimists', EU decision-makers are the prisoners of external socio-economic and other constraints that tightly limit the range of choices they can make and the extent to which they can deviate from the preset path of integration. For the 'pessimists', at least the decision-makers that come from member state governments are buffeted by increasingly powerful and irresistible domestic-political winds that push them to oppose integration and/or pull them increasingly apart. A more fine-grained approach than either set of perspectives can provide – one that analyses in greater depth how decision-makers, especially those from the EU's most powerful member state(s) have managed the EU's crises – is required to explain the crises' divergent outcomes.

What the 'optimists' got right and wrong

Ironically, with the benefit of hindsight, the theoretical controversy and debate about European integration waned in the decade or so that preceded the EU's quadruple crisis. EU scholars increasingly came to regard it no longer as a form of international organization, but rather as a 'normal political system' (Kreppel 2012: 639; see also Hix and Høyland 2011). Moravcsik's (2008) view that the EU had reached a 'stable' constitutional settlement was probably shared by many other EU scholars then. Already by this time, however, the tectonic plates of EU politics had begun to shift in ways that would cast the EU's future into doubt. Until the early 1990s, the political landscape of most of the EU member states, especially the six founders, had been dominated by 'pro-European' (i.e. 'pro-integrationist') political parties of the moderate Left and Right and centre – Social and Christian Democrats and Liberals. The domination of this broad political centre is one key factor that made the political circumstances of post-World War II non-Communist Europe uniquely favourable to regional political integration and provided the bedrock of the 'permissive consensus' (Lindberg and Scheingold 1970) that during several decades facilitated this process (Webber 2017). The negotiation and adoption of the Maastricht Treaty in the early 1990s was in this regard a turning point, after which European integration became politically more contested and, increasingly, the 'permissive consensus' gave way to a 'constraining dissensus' (Hooghe and Marks 2008: 5, 7, 21; see also Eichenberg and Dalton 2007; Majone 2009; Taylor 2008). The growing political contestation of European integration was recognizable on several dimensions. European issues became more often topics of public political debates. Public opinion towards the EU became more divided and on balance more critical. Apart from elections, the adoption of the Maastricht Treaty and several other treaties, which in some countries had to be and in others in any case were put to public referenda, provided their opponents with opportunities to mobilize politically against closer integration. New 'anti-European' movements and parties were founded and/or some existing ones, such as the British Conservative Party, became increasingly 'anti-European'. In some member states, such parties have won political office, whether alone or as senior or junior coalition partners. In others, their growth has made it politically increasingly risky for the established, 'pro-European' parties to ignore the political attitudes they mobilize and represent.

All of these trends – which scholars of 'politicization' (e.g., De Wilde et al. 2016; Hutter et al. 2016) have analysed comprehensively – were visible to a greater or lesser extent before the quadruple crisis. The politicization of European integration has not been a uniform or unilinear process. Grande and Kriesi (2016: 280) observe a pattern of '*punctuated politicisation*, characterized by significant variation over time, across countries and political arenas'. De Wilde and colleagues (2016: 15) conclude similarly that there are 'differentiated forms, degrees and manifestations of politicisation depending on the time, setting and location in which it unfolds'. Overall, however, European integration has become politically more salient and contested and polarizing over time. Moreover, these trends have strengthened during the crisis years. Thus, in 2012, at the height of the Eurozone Crisis, trust in the EU among member states' citizens plunged to its 'lowest-ever level' (Eurobarometer 2012a: 13). In autumn 2012, no more than 30 per cent, compared with 50 per cent prior to the Global Financial Crisis (GFC), had a 'positive' image of the EU (Eurobarometer 2012b: 13). In the period from 2010 to 2018, support for the old established 'pro-European' parties plummeted in many member states and that for new 'anti-European' parties, whether of the Left or, especially, the Right, soared (Webber 2017: 348–349). Elections and popular referenda by themselves could no longer accommodate the mass political mobilization against the EU in those member states hit hardest by the Eurozone Crisis and subjected to the toughest austerity policies. Opposition to the EU took to the streets. According to one estimate, no less than 30 per cent of the Greek population participated in some way in anti-austerity actions between 2010 and 2013 (Rüdig and Karyotis 2013). These actions included 27 general strikes, large-scale demonstrations, sit-ins, arson attacks on public buildings, widespread destruction of private property, and attacks against the Parliament and MPs. Some 11 per cent of Spaniards took part, according to another estimate, in the protest movement organized by the Indignados (Kriesi 2016). Austerity measures in Portugal likewise provoked 'huge demonstrations' (Kriesi 2016). Other protest movements, such as the German PEGIDA (*Patriotische Europäer gegen die Islamisierung des Abendlands* – Patriotic Europeans Against the Islamization of the West), were galvanized by the Refugee Crisis.

Contrary to what was initially anticipated by transactionalists such as Deutsch and neo-functionalists such as Haas, rising volumes of transnational exchange in Europe failed to produce a corresponding growth of a common European political identity (see Stone Sweet and Sandholtz 1998: 6; also Kuhn 2011). The 'Europeans' among the citizens of the member states – those who have 'deep economic and social ties with their counterparts across Europe' and benefit from Europe 'materially and culturally' – may account for no more than 10 to 15 per cent of the EU population (Fligstein 2008: 250). In Fligstein's estimate, they are overwhelmed by two much larger groups of citizens with either a 'shallower' relationship to Europe (40 per cent or more) or virtually none (another 40 per cent or more). This relative paucity of 'Europeans' among EU citizens in turn has made popular support for the EU and the integration process contingent upon the evolution of the economic conjuncture and other short-term variables. As, in the post-Maastricht era, the EU has become increasingly associated with economic or other crises, this support has waned and, compared with nation states bound together by stronger shared identities, the EU has become more vulnerable to disintegrative pressures (Taylor 2008: 26–35).

The 'optimistic' theories of European integration all have their roots in the pre-Maastricht era of the 'permissive (elite) consensus' and arguably reflect the specificity of the temporal and geographical context in which they were developed. A broader longitudinal perspective, taking account of the events in pre-World War II Europe, might have suggested that in economic crises international exchange between economically closely interconnected states may well be disrupted by political backlash and radicalization. Equally, a broader latitudinal perspective might have indicated that the uniquely high level of political integration in Europe was not the inevitable corollary of high levels of intra-regional trade (Börzel and Risse 2016: 629; Webber 2017). Levels of intra-regional trade in some other regions have begun to approach those in Europe – among the 21 members of the Asia-Pacific Economic Cooperation (APEC), for example, they are higher (Hsiao et al. 2009; WTO 2012: 13, 23, 32). But in no other region has a level of political integration developed comparable to Europe's (on Asia, see, e.g., Katzenstein 1997).

It is only in the post-Maastricht period of a 'constraining (mass) dissensus' and especially that of the quadruple crisis post-2009 that the robustness of liberal intergovernmentalist, neo-functionalist, transactionalist and historical institutionalist theories of political integration has begun genuinely to be tested. The impending withdrawal of the UK from the EU and the partial, albeit limited, disintegration in Schengen and refugee policy point to these theories having overestimated the extent to which European integration is entrenched and irreversible. The case above all of Brexit highlights how domestic political dynamics can in fact overwhelm and sweep aside the supposedly immovable constraints imposed by ties of economic interdependence, 'dense' patterns of cross-border exchange, the 'constantly increasing costs of exit', complex treaty provisions militating against radical political change and so on.

The above said, the outcome of the Eurozone Crisis seems to bear out the contention, explicitly or implicitly common to all these perspectives, that European political integration – specifically the single currency – has created such high levels of financial interdependence between member states sharing the Euro that the costs of exiting from the Eurozone are both economically and politically prohibitive. As we shall see in the following chapter, despite being forced to implement occasionally draconian austerity measures as a price for obtaining financial aid, none of the bailed-out states, not even Greece under a government led by the radical Left, was ultimately prepared to take the risk of abandoning the euro. Nor, in the final analysis, did the 'creditor' states, led by Germany, want to run the (geopolitical as well as economic and financial) risks of letting them go or forcing them out. The perceived costs of leaving or expelling a member state from the Eurozone may, however, be uniquely high. The (again, perceived) costs of defection from common institutions or policies in the Schengen/refugee and Brexit crises were less forbidding. Moreover, it is conceivable, as will be discussed in Chapter 3, that the survival and closer political integration of the Eurozone is attributable more to other factors than the punitively high costs of disintegration of the Eurozone as viewed by the member states.

What the pessimists got right and wrong

The strengths and weaknesses of the 'pessimistic' theories of European integration are a mirror image of those of their 'optimistic' counterparts. They appear to offer a compelling explanation of what political *dis*integration has occurred, but they cannot easily account for the fact that disintegration has hitherto remained limited and partial rather than unfolding on a much larger scale than has been the case. The pioneer postfunctionalists' (Hooghe's and Marks') analysis from 2008 proved extraordinarily prescient. Starting with the Eurozone Crisis, the trends that they identified – mass politicization of European integration, the emergence of identity politics and a new national/international cleavage in member states' politics, and sharper EU-political polarization – rapidly gathered momentum, all the more so as new crises started to pile on top of the first. In the absence of a strong common European identity and strong pan-European political parties, distributional conflicts between member states intensified and more or new demands to renationalize common policies or secede altogether from the EU were raised. For postfunctionalism, the quadruple crisis constituted something akin to the 'perfect storm'. Economic recession, mass unemployment, politically highly contested austerity policies in some member states, opposition to the provision of financial aid to 'debtor' by 'creditor' states, rapidly growing mass immigration from the predominantly Muslim Middle East into Europe, large-scale terrorist attacks by persons of whom some had been able to cross uncontrolled borders between Schengen member states – combined, these conditions might have been thought to be ideal for the generation of irresistible 'downward pressure on the level and scope' of European integration. But the postfunctionalist scenario has materialized only partly. Why has the quadruple crisis, this perfect storm, not swept away a bigger part of the edifice of the EU, as the postfunctionalists would very likely have anticipated if they had seen this burgeoning crisis coming? There could be no more convincing evidence of the limits imposed on political voluntarism by membership at least of the Eurozone than the sight of a radical Leftist government in Greece accepting conditions for the provision of financial aid to keep the country in the single currency that were as tough as, if not tougher than, those accepted by its predecessors and that involved even the curtailment of trade union rights.

The processes of politicization and political polarization that accompanied the EU's quadruple crisis may have been *necessary* conditions of the political disintegration that has occurred, but they have not been *sufficient* ones, otherwise disintegration would have been much more generalized.

The missing explanatory variable: (stabilizing) hegemonic leadership

> Nobody else can do it. I will probably be the first Polish foreign minister in history to say this, but here it is: I fear German power less than I am beginning to fear its inactivity. You have become Europe's indispensable nation. You may not fail to lead: not dominate, but to lead ...
>
> (Sikorski 2011)

The shared weakness of 'optimistic' and 'pessimistic' theories of European integration that makes it impossible for them to explain the pattern of crisis outcomes is their relative neglect of the decision-making processes by which the EU's crises were managed. Whereas the 'optimists' see EU decision-makers bound up in a broad web of socio-economic and institutional constraints that keep them, irrespective of their will, on the path of integration, the 'pessimists' see them as being exposed to growing (and antagonistic) domestic-political pressures that make them either increasingly unable or unwilling to do what is required to avert *dis*integration, albeit they may try to overcome tightening political constraints and shrinking 'win-sets' by falling back on any of a variety of tactics, including, for example, differentiated integration, the conclusion of accords outside the EU treaties and the delegation of powers to non-majoritarian institutions, that enable them to escape such pressures and keep 'the show on the road' (see Grande and Kriesi 2016: 296).

By analysing in greater depth how the EU managed its quadruple crisis, I aim in this book to provide a solution to the puzzle of divergent outcomes that eludes both 'optimistic' and 'pessimistic' integration theories. In doing so, I focus on the (divergent) roles that the EU's most powerful member state, Germany, has played in managing – or not managing – these crises, applying the hegemonic stability theory of international political economy first expounded by the economic historian Charles Kindleberger (1973). In its original version, hegemonic stability theory posits that the overwhelming dominance of one country is a necessary (but not sufficient) condition for the maintenance of an open and stable world (in the present context, regional) economy (Kindleberger 1973; Milner 1998). Hegemonic stability theory derives the indispensability of hegemonic leadership for economic openness and stability from public-goods theory, holding that only large states have a material incentive to supply non-excludable 'collective' goods rather than to 'free-ride', as they may be able to 'capture a share of the benefit of the public good larger than the entire cost of providing it' (Snidal 1985: 581). Its original exponent, Kindleberger (1973: 28), argued that the international economic and monetary system required a hegemonic power, 'a country which is prepared ... under some system of rules that it has internalized, to set standards of conduct for other countries; and to seek to get others to follow them, to take on an undue share of the burdens of the system, and in particular to take on its support in adversity' by acting as a market and lender of last resort. In his meanwhile legendary analysis, the Great Depression occurred in the 1930s because the UK was no longer capable of performing and the USA was not yet willing to perform such a role.

Hegemonic stability theory was subsequently extended and applied by IR scholars and political economists to broader issues of international political as well as economic stability (see especially Gilpin 1981, 1987, 2001). In the course of the years, it has been severely criticized (by, e.g., Lake 1993; Snidal 1985). But it has also found numerous – theoretical and empirical – defenders (e.g., Chase-Dunn et al. 2000; Gilpin 2001: 93–97; Gowa 1989; Hubbard 2010; Webb and Krasner 1989). Much of the debate about hegemony, within or beyond the academic sphere, has been clouded by the negative connotations of the concept, not least when it is linked, in the European context, with Germany. The unease and discomfort that the concept evokes when applied to Germany, both in Germany and among other EU member states, are understandable in the light of Germany's role in the two world wars of the twentieth century and the Holocaust and precisely because European integration was conceived as a process to preclude a reassertion of German domination over Europe.

Such inhibitions tend to rest, however, on an implicit (more negative) definition of the concept of hegemony than that which underlies the academic debate. Schroeder (2004: 298–299), for example, draws a sharp distinction between the concept of 'empire', the 'possession and exercise of political control over foreigners' and that of 'hegemony', the 'possession and exercise of clear, acknowledged leadership and superior influence by one power within a community of units *not* under a single authority'. A hegemonic power is for him 'first among equals ... one without whom no final decision can be reached within the system, whose task and responsibility it is to see that necessary decisions are reached'. Empire, which is about ruling other states, is incompatible with the modern international system based on territorial sovereignty. Hegemony, though, is. The hegemonic power's function is 'essentially to manage, to maintain some degree of order and decision-making capacity within a system of dispersed authority' (Schroeder 2004: 299).

Clark (2011: 236) stresses that hegemony is a relational phenomenon that cannot simply be read off from a specific quantitative distribution of material resources. For him, similar to Schroeder, hegemonic leadership involves reconciling the 'particular needs and interests of the leading power' with those of other states in the system (Clark 2011: 33). It must rest in part at least on the consent of the 'followers' and be seen by them as legitimate, in respect of either (decisional) inputs or outputs or both (Clark 2011: 57–58). By implication, however, and more explicitly for some hegemonic stability theorists (e.g., Gilpin 1987: 73), the 'needs and interests' of citizens of the hegemonic power (assuming this is liberal-democratic) must also be accommodated, for fear that they will otherwise reject the perceived costs of leadership.

In any case, for Clark (2011: 68, 242) the concentration or inequalities of power are an 'inescapable constituent of contemporary order', a 'fundamental part of the fabric of international relations'. The institutionalization of hegemonic leadership may be 'the least-worst solution for the management of international order', as it locates the issue of inequality 'within a formalized institutional setting that constrains the actions of the strong, not only those of the weak' and moreover 'exploits the capabilities of the strong for collective action, by underwriting a measure of central authority otherwise lacking' in an anarchical international society (Clark 2011: 242). In a comprehensive review of the historical evolution of the concept of hegemony, Anderson (2017: 3–11, 25–50) identifies similar ideas in pre- and early post-World War II German contributions on hegemony, which, in contrast to empire, 'precludes direct rule of one state over another' (31), involves a 'combination of coercion and consent' (31), or is 'guided balance', maintained by a power that is 'cautious and respected, not merely feared' and that, while watching over the balance in the system, controls and directs the 'dynamics of its parts' (45). While Kindleberger himself did not like the label of hegemony, he recognized that the kind of leadership he deemed to be necessary to stabilize the international economic system involved 'strong elements of both arm-twisting and bribery' (1981: 243). What endangered the system was 'not too much power ... but too little, not an excess of domination, but a superfluity of would-be free-riders ... No place for the buck to stop' (1981: 253). In effect hegemonic leadership might seem to be a poor system, 'but like democracy, honesty and stable marriages, [it] is better than the available alternatives' (1981: 252).

The main claims of hegemonic stability theorists may thus be summarized (roughly) as follows: hegemonic leadership is required to provide important public goods (notably stability) in international systems. Inequalities in the distribution of power, which are pervasive, are a necessary but not a sufficient condition of hegemonic leadership. The hegemonic power must have an interest wider than mere short-term material interest maximization in supporting the system. Given that it does not rule other states directly, its leadership requires the consent of 'follower' states that may be secured by enabling them to participate in the making of decisions or ensuring that these decisions adequately accommodate their interests. In liberal-democratic states, the hegemon's citizens must also acquiesce in the costs as well as enjoy benefits of such leadership. Evidently, the reconciliation of the conflicting interests of hegemons and 'follower' states is a task at which the hegemon may fail. Moreover, in as far as, over time, distributions of power in the international system change, the basis of a hegemon's superior position may be undermined and the system itself will then tend to become unstable and subject to entropy and decline (Gilpin 1987: 78–79; Kindleberger 1981: 250).

Although the literature on hegemony and hegemonic stability theory pertains overwhelmingly to the international (world) system and is notably focused on the world role of the USA, there is no a priori reason why hegemony – its presence or absence – cannot equally be analysed at the level of regional systems, such as Europe. Whereas Clark (2011: 236) observes that there is no 'fully substantiated historical case' of hegemony (but that this does not constitute a reason to reject the relevance of hegemony as a concept), some scholars claim to have sighted it at the regional level, including in Europe. For Cohen (1998), for example, the presence of a hegemonic power is one of two conditions of the survival of multinational monetary unions. Similarly for Mattli (1999) a hegemon is a condition of 'successful' regional integration, as defined by the extent to which the participating states have managed to 'match their stated integration goals'. In the tow of hegemonic stability theory and echoing Kindleberger fairly closely, Mattli (1999: 42) viewed a 'benevolent leading power' as fulfilling two critical functions: that of a 'focal point in the coordination of rules, regulations and policies' and, through providing financial aid, 'easing tensions that arise from the inequitable distribution of the gains from integration'. The EU's hegemon was, in his view, already at the turn of the century, Germany.

The application of hegemonic stability theory to the EU raises several complex and difficult issues. One of these is whether and under what conditions, in this uniquely densely politically integrated regional organization, which was conceived to avert the domination of the region by a single state and in which member states have ceded so many policy-making powers to central political organs, it is possible to conceive of a single state as a hegemon. A second, at least if the answer to this first question is 'yes', is whether hegemony if it exists can be exercised only by a single state or whether some form of shared, dual or 'cooperative' hegemony is conceivable. A third is whether the role of a hegemonic power within the same space may vary from one issue area to another. Below I answer all these questions in the affirmative, while arguing that, over time, the distribution of power between the leading states in the EU has shifted decisively so that, by the time the quadruple crisis broke, Germany was far more powerful than any other member state.

In the EU, (most) crises are the hour of the member states, especially France and Germany

Already in his analysis of the causes of the Great Depression, Kindleberger (1973: 308) identified the 'effective cession of economic sovereignty to international institutions' to institutions with 'real authority and sovereignty' as an alternative to the exercise of hegemony by a single state – while lamenting that, of all conceivable alternatives, this was the one 'least likely' to materialize. Given the extent to which EU member states have delegated powers to supranational organs and pooled decision-making (Hooghe and Marks 2014: 6), this condition is more likely to be met, however, in the EU than in any other regional or international organization. It may indeed be fulfilled in the 'everyday politics' of the EU. Thus the Commission's policy initiation powers, the EP's co-decision powers, and the ECJ's powers in adjudicating disputes over the implementation of EU law all militate against the exercise of hegemony by a member state, as do the multilateral character of the Council and European Council in which the member governments are represented and the decision-making rules and norms that govern them. Compromise and consensus, not the diktat of a single member, have been the rule in EU decision-making (Achen 2006: 297; Naurin and Wallace 2008: 8–11; Schneider et al. 2006: 213).

As hegemonic stability theorists have suggested, however, *crises* are managed by different logics and processes than 'everyday politics' (Kindleberger 1986a: 11, 1986b; see also Gilpin 1987). Normal 'regime maintenance' is not the stuff of hegemonic powers, but crisis management is (Gilpin 1987: 79). As we shall see in the following chapters, the EU's supranational organs were, for the most part, marginal actors in the quadruple crisis that the EU confronted from 2009 onwards. By and large, they did not possess the requisite legal powers (given the limited scale and flexibility of the EU budget) financial resources or democratic political legitimacy to be able to play a major role in their management. Rather the crises were managed predominantly through processes of intergovernmental negotiation in which inequalities in the distribution of power between member states were significantly less mitigated than in the 'everyday politics' of the EU. The one exception to this rule concerns the Eurozone Crisis, in which the supranational ECB played a key crisis management role – to the point where, without its intervention, the Eurozone may actually have collapsed. Of all the EU's supranational organs, the ECB is the one that most closely corresponds to Kindleberger's ideal of a powerful, autonomous international actor. While it may not possess much democratic legitimacy, it did possess the requisite legal powers and financial resources to address the Eurozone Crisis.

The EU is unique not only in respect of the level and scope of political integration among its member states, but also in the degree to which the integration process has been shaped by the cooperation between two of its biggest member states, France and Germany. Kindleberger (1973: 308) saw a duopolistic distribution of power as a recipe for deadlock and paralysis. Clark (2011: 60–65), in contrast, distinguishes between 'singular' and 'collective' hegemony, an example of the latter being the Concert of Powers in Europe through much of the nineteenth century – prior to the first German unification. The role that the Franco-German 'tandem' has played in the history of the EU suggests in line with Clark that collective – in this case, 'dual' – hegemony is conceivable (Werner Link, cited in Schönberger 2013: 27). Since the early days of European integration and especially since the adoption of the Élysée Treaty in 1962, the two states on either side of the Rhine have developed a uniquely intensive bilateral relationship in international relations – one that Krotz and Schild (2013) have well labelled 'embedded bilateralism' (see also Webber 1999a). They are each other's closest partners in the EU (ECFR 2017; Naurin and Lindahl 2008). They have not always agreed or found common positions on major issues and, when they have not, such as on the issue of British accession in the 1960s, this has typically put a strong brake on European integration. But no crisis or conflict has hitherto succeeded in durably derailing the Franco-German relationship. Moreover, when, departing from divergent positions, they have managed to reach bilateral agreements, these have regularly formed the basis of an EU-wide accord, in as far as the two states have stood for 'opposed' ('northern' and 'southern') poles in the EU, divided in particular but not only by attitudes to the appropriate roles of the market and the state in the allocation of resources and management of the economy (see Webber 1999a: 127).

Empirical analyses of EU decision-making do not show that 'everyday' EU decisions are disproportionately strongly influenced by France and/or Germany (see, e.g., Golub 2013; Schneider 2008: 287; Thomson 2008: 249–251, 255). If this had been the case and the smaller member states had constantly been on the losing end of conflicts with Bonn/Berlin and Paris, the divisive impact on the EU would likely have provoked its explosion. Hegemonic leadership, as discussed earlier in the chapter, in any case demands the 'balancing out' of the demands of leading and other states in the interests of cohesion. A rather different story arises, though, from the analysis of the 'constitutive politics' or the 'history-making' decisions of the EU, including the negotiation of new treaties (see Krotz and Schild 2013; Moravcsik 1991, 1998; Pedersen 1998). To be sure, even in this sphere France and Germany have not played a uniformly central and determining role (Mazzucelli et al. 2007; Paterson 2008: 107). But, as subsequent chapters will trace, the two states were the primary driving forces behind the launching of the Euro, the Schengen Area and the CFSP – as well as other 'flagship' EU projects, from the Common Agricultural Policy and the EMS to the Single European Act (Krotz and Schild 2013; Moravcsik 1991; Webber 1999a). The role played by the EU's most powerful state(s) in managing the EU's contemporary crises is functionally equivalent to that which they have played at earlier critical turning points in the history of European integration.

The balance of power in the Franco-German relationship has shifted gradually but decisively towards Germany

The balance of power in this bilateral relationship, however, has by no means been stable. The dominant power in the EU in its first decades was indisputably France, one of the victorious World War II allies, a nuclear power as of the 1960s, and a permanent member of the United Nations Security Council. (West) Germany's status was unequivocally subordinate to that of France. Not only was Germany burdened by the legacy of World War II and the Holocaust, but it was also divided. The Federal Republic was the West's front-line state in the Cold War, dependent for its security on its allies. France was, with the USA and the UK, a co-guarantor of the security of West Berlin and, with the same states and the Soviet Union, retained a veto power in international law over the future status of 'Germany as a whole'. French president Charles de Gaulle's rejection of two British EU entry bids in the 1960s was partly motivated by his desire to ensure that the UK could not contest France's primacy. As recently as 2000, Siedentop, for example, saw France as the EU's hegemonic power (2000: 113ff.). Not only was the EU a French creation, 'the major initiatives ... have been French and served French interests' (115).

France had constructed a 'European edifice which reflected the French vision of Europe, French habits and French interests' (136). Behind the formal rules governing the EU decision-making process, the French had 'imposed their will to an extraordinary extent' (221). In contrast, Germany had not been the 'motive force. At most Germany has co-operated or acquiesced in what is basically a French design' (139).

Outwardly at least, successive German leaders were long concerned to acknowledge France's primacy in the EU. The first post-World War II chancellor Konrad Adenauer bequeathed the advice to his political descendant Helmut Kohl that the German chancellor should 'bow three times a day' to the French flag, the tricolour (as quoted in Schwarz 2012: 357). Similarly, Helmut Schmidt, chancellor from 1974 to 1982, argued that, although initiatives, compromise proposals and 'often enough financial concessions' might (have to) come from Bonn, Germany had to avoid being seen as a leading power in the EU and rather let France take the lead: 'We can't take any step without France' (Schmidt 1990: 173, 297).

Despite all German efforts to downplay its EU role to the benefit of France, the balance of power between the two states has tilted strongly in Germany's favour since the era of de Gaulle, who reputedly 'half-joked' that in the EU Germany was the horse and France the 'coachman driving the carriage' (Siedentop 2000: 139–140). Four phases can be identified in this process. The first can be seen in the successive conflicts in Western Europe and the North Atlantic in the late 1960s and early 1970s over currency realignment, specifically over a revaluation of the Deutsche Mark. The launching – in the late 1970s – of the EMS may have been the first major case of German leadership in the EU (Ludlow 1982: 290–291). This trend reflected the relative strength of the West German economy and the relative success with which Germany rode out the oil-price crises of the early and late 1970s. When de Gaulle's successor as French president, Georges Pompidou, opened the way to the UK's accession to the EU in 1971, he may have been motivated partly by the belief that the UK could help France to balance growing German power in Western Europe (Brandt 1993: 453).

The second – and most important – phase in this process is marked by the end of the Cold War and German reunification from 1989 to 1991. The implications of this geopolitical transformation for the balance of power between France and Germany were obvious – which is why this prospect caused consternation among French political elites (see Chapter 3). Once German reunification had been concluded, France no longer possessed any of the trump cards in its relations with Germany that it had done as long as Germany was divided, West Germany was a front-line state in the Cold War, and the wartime Western allies guaranteed the security of West Berlin. Compared with France (and other EU member states), Germany was bigger and more secure than hitherto, albeit cast back into the role of a geopolitically 'central power' in Europe (Schwarz 1994), a role which in the past had been a recurrent source of tension, instability, conflict and war.

The third phase, which is an indirect consequence of the second, relates to the post-Cold War enlargement of the EU towards the former Communist states in Central and Eastern Europe. This process was accompanied much less enthusiastically by France than by Germany, which was keen to help create 'Western countries' (i.e. prosperous, stable liberal democracies) on its eastern frontiers. The Eastern enlargement moved the political as well as geographical centre-point of the EU eastwards. Overall, the new member states (which included Austria, Finland and Sweden in the first post-Cold War accession wave) were economically much more closely tied to Germany than to France and cultivated closer relations with the former than the latter in the EU (ECFR 2017; Naurin and Lindahl 2008). Within cooperation networks in the Council, Germany occupied a more singular and central position after the post-Cold War enlargements than before, given that, compared with France, it had tighter links to northern and eastern subgroups of member states (Naurin and Lindahl 2008). An EU which had earlier gravitated in respect of Council networks around a Franco-German core looked more like one that gravitated around Germany alone.

The fourth phase commences with the outbreak of the GFC, followed by the Eurozone Crisis, in 2008–09. Already before the GFC, France's credibility as an advocate of European integration had been damaged by the defeat of the proposed Constitutional Treaty in a referendum in 2005. Its credibility in respect of economic policy also suffered as a consequence of its relative political immobilism and incapacity to reform the French labour market and welfare state, while Germany's was enhanced by the adoption and perceived success of the sweeping reforms that it undertook in these areas under a 'red-green' federal coalition government between 2003 and 2005. By almost all economic indicators, especially the government's budgetary position, Germany was in better shape than France as the Eurozone Crisis unfolded. Germany moved decisively 'centre stage' in the crisis (Paterson 2011). For display purposes, the façade of the Franco-German relationship was maintained, as it arguably suited the French government to be seen to be more powerful than it was and the German not to be seen to be trying to run the EU by itself but to co-opt France in the hope that it would bring on board the member states, notably in southern Europe, typically more closely aligned with Paris than Berlin. The reality – overall – was nonetheless that, as his French counterpart confessed to Greek finance minister Yanis Varoufakis, 'France is not what it used to be' (Varoufakis 2017: 190). A relationship that had at the outset been asymmetrical in favour of France had meanwhile been transformed into one asymmetrical in favour of Germany.

The emergence of Germany at the outbreak of the Eurozone Crisis as the EU's 'indispensable nation' (Sikorski) put the fate of the organization in the hands of the state with not only the strongest capacity to shape it, but also, among the larger members at least, of its most unequivocal champion. At the outset of the integration process, there had not been a 'pro-European' consensus in German politics, in particular because of fears that the integration of West Germany into a Western international organization would render a prospective future reunification with East Germany more difficult. By the 1960s, however, a broad 'pro-European' consensus in favour of European integration had developed. Indeed, the promotion of this process became synonymous with the national interest and a virtual raison d'être of the Federal Republic. The dominant political parties in West Germany – the Christian and Social Democrats and the (smaller) liberal Free Democratic Party (FDP) – all subscribed to this consensus, as did, when they broke through in the party system in the 1980s, the Greens.

Germany's commitment to regional political integration – along with that, more ambivalent, of France – has been far stronger than that of (actual or putative) hegemonic powers in other regions. Together with the predominance in Europe of the 'pro-European' parties from the moderate Left to the moderate Right in the member states' party systems, this may explain why Europe is politically much more integrated than any other region (Webber 2017). Germany's strong 'pro-Europeanism' has been sustained by two principal factors. First, the German economy, with its strong export orientation, is heavily dependent for its prosperity on unhindered access to the markets of other European countries – far more so than other hegemonic powers are on their neighbouring countries (see, e.g., Moravcsik 1998: 495). Thus, in 2016, some 58.6 per cent of German exports went to other EU member states and overall 68 per cent to Europe as a whole (Statista 2017). Particularly since the end of the Cold War and the development of cross-border production networks extending into former Communist Central and East European countries, German firms have also become increasingly dependent on the free movement of regional production factors secured by the EU's single market.

Second, and, judging by the rhetoric of successive German political leaders, more importantly, German support for European integration and the EU has fundamental geopolitical motives, according to which, given its history, geography and relative size, Germany must be bound into a strong regional organization to reassure its neighbouring states and avert the risk of diplomatic isolation and a potentially catastrophic revival of traditional 'balance-of-power' politics in Europe. This theme ran like a constant thread through the foreign policy thinking of post-World War II (West) German leaders. For Adenauer, European integration should bind France and Germany together in such a way that France would not pursue a 'negative' East European policy and seek to cooperate with the Soviet Union to create a counterweight to any new hegemonic aspirations that Germany might develop in Europe (Schwarz 1992: 41). Following German reunification, the former Chancellor Schmidt (1993) argued that

> in terms of population, Germany today is one and a half times as big as France or England, twice as big as Poland, five times as big as Holland, eight times as big as Belgium. In all of these countries there are worries concerning the prospective economic power of Germany; in addition to this, there are the awful memories of the Hitler era. If our country does not want to isolate itself, if Europe is not to return to a policy of forming coalitions as

a counterweight to Germany, then we Germans need to be integrated into an EU that functions effectively.

In the same vein, his successor Kohl reasoned that the 'political unification of Europe is decisive for Germany's future in peace and freedom. As the country with the most neighbours in Europe, we Germans, more than any other nation, have a vital interest in preventing a reversion to the power-political rivalries of former times, to national egoisms and shifting coalitions' (Kohl 1993).

The negative reactions that the prospect of German reunification provoked among a clear majority of other EU leaders in 1989 bore eloquent testimony to the persistence of fears elsewhere in Europe that a reunified Germany might strive to dominate Europe (Kohl 1996: 194–198). For none other than the pioneer neo-functionalist Haas (1964: 78), German reunification and other states' reaction to it was the one political factor that could bring the 'whole process' of European integration to a 'dead stop':

> The interest of Germany's neighbors in complete integration is in large measure the result of their fear of a strong Germany and their continued desire to enmesh the Federal Republic in a web of interdependencies. A Germany of over seventy million people and Europe's greatest concentration of industrial might ... would quickly rekindle the older fears and trigger once more the old stereotypes, whether warranted ... or not. The continued sway of the spill-over process, therefore, does rest on the indefinite division of Germany and on the tacit recognition of that status in the minds of West German leaders.

To assuage its neighbours' fears of prospective German domination, German diplomacy went to great lengths in this period to stress the state's continuing commitment to European integration, which Kohl regularly described as the 'other side of the coin' to German unification.

Germany thus possessed very compelling motives as far as possible not to allow Europe to *dis*integrate. The EU's deepening crisis from 2009 onwards created a dilemma for its political elite. On the one hand, its long-standing 'leadership avoidance reflex' (as reflected in the aforegoing remarks of Adenauer, Kohl and Schmidt) inclined it to shy away from occupying the 'centre stage' (Paterson 2011). On the other, it became increasingly clear as the crisis unfolded that, with the UK (even before the Brexit vote) increasingly isolated on the fringes of Europe, France economically and politically weakened and, apart from the ECB, the EU's supranational organs severely constrained in their action, either Germany had to 'lead' or the EU ran a high risk of collapsing. Thus cross-pressured, Germany, in one analysis, assumed the role of a 'reluctant hegemon' in the EU (Paterson 2011). Not only foreign academics and foreign politicians like Sikorski, but also German commentators began increasingly to acknowledge and argue that German leadership – stabilizing, that is, hegemonic, leadership – was essential for the EU's survival (see, e.g., Brattberg and Pires de Lima 2015; Hoffmann 2016; Matthijs and Blyth 2011; Münkler 2015a, 2015b; Schönberger 2012, 2013). Münkler, for example, cast Germany in the role of the 'power at the centre' (*Die Macht in der Mitte*). Closely echoing Kindleberger's original conception of the role of a hegemonic power, he described Germany's challenge as being to 'hold Europe together, to counter-act the centrifugal forces that will continually emerge, to reduce divergences of interest and to balance things out' (*Ausgleichsprozesse moderieren*) (Münkler 2015a: 8). The times in which Germany could 'lead from behind' France were meanwhile over, the German historian and political scientist argued (2015a: 44). Nothing happened any more in the EU without Germany's agreement or support. As there was no way past Germany, all calls for change were directed towards it (2015a: 44–45).

There can be no doubt that, at this juncture, Germany could deploy a greater volume of power resources in the mission of 'stabilizing' the EU than any other single member state. Although it was not the EU's most powerful member state in respect of *all* relevant resources, notably military power, its 'aggregate structural power' (Tallberg 2008) well exceeded that of any other contender. Above all the size of its economy, which reflected the fact that Germany has not only one of the highest per capita GDPs but also the largest population of any member state, together with its financial strength, reflected in the relatively healthy state of public finances, provided it with very strong potential bargaining power in the EU. Germany accounted for some 16 per cent of the EU's population, made up (at nominal prices) 20.5 per cent of the EU and about 27 per cent of the Eurozone economy and was exceptional among all but a couple of very small Eurozone members in having a smaller cumulative state debt compared with the size of its economy in 2015 than in the last pre-crisis year 2009. In addition, Germany's relative economic success during the Eurozone Crisis arguably gave it a significant degree of 'soft power' – in the face of this crisis, no other member state could point to an alternative economic 'model' that had performed better. Germany could also complement its material and soft power in the EU by expanding its representation in the EU's supranational organs. Thus, during the period from 1999 to 2015, the proportion of top positions occupied by German nationals in European Commission *cabinets* and directorates-general and in the directorates-general, committees and parliamentary groups in the EP rose to exceed that of any other member state – while France's 'foothold' in these positions receded (Mandra 2015). Finally, Germany's political stability and 'pro-European' elite political consensus enhanced its credibility among its EU partners, in as far as the government could be relied upon both to safeguard existing levels of integration and to deliver upon any commitments it made during EU crisis negotiations. Overall, no other putative or conceivable EU 'leader' could rival Germany's potential bargaining power during the crisis years.

Germany is, however, in numerous respects, a 'hobbled' hegemon

This said, it was by no means certain that Germany would alone be powerful enough to provide hegemonic leadership to the EU. Measured by its overall power resources relative to the other states in its region, it does not possess the same potential to dominate Europe east of Russia as other (actual or putative) hegemons may do their regions – whether, for example, it is the USA in North America, Russia in the Community of Independent States (CIS), China in East Asia, India in South Asia, or South Africa in southern Africa. It is for this reason that not only historically but also today Germany has occasionally been labelled a 'semi-hegemonic power' in Europe – too big to be just one state among others, but not big enough to be able to perform the role of a fully fledged regional hegemon (see, e.g., Kundnani 2014: 5–6).

Several other factors – structural and normative – in any case constrain the exercise of German hegemony in the EU and make it an at least partially 'hobbled' hegemon. One of these is the structure of the German political system, in which decision-making powers are highly fragmented and key EU decisions require extensive negotiations and a broad consensus to be reached between government and opposition, federal and state governments and legislative and judicial organs. This trait, the product of the Basic Law, the 'constitution' of the Federal Republic adopted in 1949, strengthens Germany's capacity to *veto* EU-level initiatives, but weakens the capacity of the federal government to take the kind of swift and decisive action required of hegemonic powers to combat financial and other kinds of crises. Indeed, the crisis-era jurisprudence of the Federal Constitutional Court (*Bundesverfassungsgericht*) was to impose additional constraints on the federal government in this regard. Second, the strongly export-oriented structure of the German economy, of which the quasi-permanent trade surplus that it maintains with most other EU member states is one manifestation and consequence, makes it difficult for Germany to play one of a stabilizing hegemon's key functions – namely to provide economically ailing Eurozone member states with a 'market of last resort'. To these structural constraints came two significant normative ones. One of these, German political leaders' traditional post-World War II 'leadership avoidance reflex', weakened as, during the crisis years (see the preceding section), the German political elite increasingly recognized that, without German leadership, the EU could indeed disintegrate. In certain issue areas, it nonetheless remained tenacious, notably in respect of the deployment of military force abroad, as exemplified by the decisions to steer clear of any military engagement in the post-2011 civil and other wars in North Africa and the Middle East. The other – which the Eurozone Crisis challenged, but which remained powerful – pertained to the predominance among German elites of Ordoliberal economic thinking, which, with its strong emphasis on sound money and fiscal rectitude, was antithetical to the Keynesian notions of combating financial crises by easy monetary policies and deficit-spending that underpinned Kindleberger's conception of the role of a hegemonic power in stabilizing the international economy (Brunnermeier et al. 2016). The adoption of a 'balanced budget' amendment to the Basic Law with the support of not only Christian but also Social Democrats on the eve of the Eurozone Crisis in 2009 in fact suggested that as an economic doctrine Ordoliberalism was more deeply entrenched in Germany than ever before – the SPD (*Sozialdemokratische Partei Deutschlands* – German Social Democratic Party) was no longer the 'Keynesian' party that it had become in the mid-1960s.

While Germany had very compelling motives to try to hold the EU together and significantly greater power resources that it could deploy to this end than any other single member state, numerous structural and normative constraints thus circumscribed Berlin's *capacity* to act as the EU's (stabilizing) hegemon. Moreover, as the EU's crises unfolded, not only Germany's capacity but also its *willingness* to assume the burdens of hegemonic leadership became less unequivocal. The successive 'bail-outs' of several Eurozone members, first and foremost Greece, catalysed 'Eurosceptical' opinion among the German public. Germany had long been the EU's principal 'paymaster' and lubricated the integration process by acquiescing in higher transfer payments to poorer member states as a condition of their acceptance of market liberalization and monetary integration (Lange 1992; Moravcsik 1991: 43, 48). Prior to the introduction of the Euro, German budgetary contributions to the EU were nonetheless modest compared with the material and other rewards that Germany gained from the market access and political stability that the EU provided. The Eurozone Crisis, however, magnified the scale of Germany's financial exposure to the EU, understood as the prospective costs of a collapse of the Eurozone and the non-repayment of loans made to bailed-out members. In this conjuncture and conceivably also reflecting generational changes in the German political elite, political leaders' European discourse grew less idealistic and more interest-based and the long-standing 'pro-European' consensus began to show signs of erosion (Becker and Maurer 2009; Bulmer and Paterson 2010, 2011; Paterson 2011; Schieder 2011). 'Anti-European' or 'Eurosceptical' currents emerged or grew stronger in the 'old' political parties, notably in the Bavarian CSU (*Christlich-Soziale Union in Bayern* – Bavarian Christian Social Union) and the liberal FDP (*Freie Demokratische Partei* – Free Democratic Party) (Schieder 2011). The most powerful manifestation of the growth of German 'Euroscepticism', however, was the launching in 2013 of a new party, the AfD, which was originally founded to campaign for Germany's abandonment of the Euro, but, in the midst of the Refugee Crisis, developed into a national-populist movement more concerned with issues of race, religion and immigration than monetary or currency ones. To the extent that, as Münkler argues (2015a, 2015b), a European hegemon requires a more 'EU-friendly' public opinion than that in other member states to be able to play its role, a growing public backlash against European integration in Germany could destroy the domestic political foundations of (stabilizing) hegemonic leadership. Up to 2017 at least, Germany though remained the rock of relative economic and political stability in the EU that it had been since the mid-1970s – the 'fortress' which, for example, the *New Left Review* had called it, referring to the old Federal Republic, in the title of one of its issues as long ago as 1976.

Hegemonic leadership and (dis)integration outcomes vary by crisis

As Clark (2011: 237) notes, hegemonic powers need not play the same role across different issue areas or, by implication, different crises. The nature of crises may vary along numerous dimensions that affect the choices made and strategies followed by the hegemon (and other states). These include inter alia the intensity of the time pressures under which decisions must be taken, the formal rules or informal norms according to which decisions must be made, the configuration or constellation of relevant political actors, the degree of polarization of such actors' interests and preferences, the level of mass politicization, and, not least, the distribution of power resources and hence bargaining power. Depending on these variables, the scope for agency – for the exercise of what may be termed 'statecraft' – may be more or less limited. Compared with 'everyday politics', in crises decisions must also be taken under conditions of greater uncertainty and the consequences of the decisions taken – or not taken – may be both more far-reaching and more difficult to calculate. In the case of Germany, the likelihood of variations in crisis strategies is all the greater, as EU policy-making has historically been more strongly 'sectorized' and less centrally coordinated than in other member states (Bulmer and Paterson 1987). All this means that the hegemon's efforts to manage crises may be more – or less – effective at stabilizing the system (in this case, the EU) and that, as measured by their success or failure in achieving this goal, the outcomes of crises may also vary.

Conclusion

The theoretical analysis of European political integration has always reflected and followed real-world trends and developments – but with an (occasionally significant) time lag (see Saurugger 2014: 3, 249). Although the contemporary crisis of the EU is now almost a decade old, there has still not been very much theorizing of the conditions of European *dis*integration. In the search for variables that might be useful in assessing the risks of disintegration, I have turned existing theories of integration on their head and tried to identify the conditions – if any – under which they would anticipate a reversal of this process as well as surveyed various potentially relevant theories of IR and comparative politics. Most of these theories fall into one or the other of two groups, one fundamentally 'optimistic' and the other 'pessimistic' as to the future of the EU and European political integration. The 'optimistic' theories view member state governments in the EU increasingly as the prisoners of all manner of socio-economic and institutional constraints that, regardless of their political will, leaves them no choice but to acquiesce in ever closer integration. The 'pessimistic' ones, in contrast, emphasize the primacy of politics over economics. They see member state governments as being exposed to increasingly irresistible domestic political pressures to reduce existing levels of integration, if not to withdraw entirely from the EU.

Neither of these contrasting approaches, however, provides a satisfactory explanation of the pattern of (dis)integration outcomes that has emerged from the EU's crises: closer political integration in the Eurozone Crisis, the maintenance of the integration status quo in the Ukraine Crisis, limited disintegration in the Schengen/Refugee Crisis, and more sweeping disintegration with the UK's choice to leave the EU altogether at the referendum staged in 2016. There has been more political disintegration than the theoretical 'optimists' implied was conceivable, as illustrated by Moravcsik's (2016) refusal to believe in the possibility of Brexit. But at the same time there has been less disintegration than the theoretical 'pessimists' would have expected, given that the four crises from their perspective collectively represented something akin to a 'perfect storm' of events conducive to the EU's collapse. To be sure, the mass politicization of European integration – the heightened political salience, public contestation and political polarization around EU issues – that constitutes the core of such theories is a *necessary* condition of political disintegration. But it is not a *sufficient* one. To understand the pattern of (dis)integration that emerged from the quadruple crisis, it is essential to look more closely than do either 'optimistic' or 'pessimistic' theories at crisis decision-making processes in the EU.

Relative to these theories, I provide a more fine-grained, differentiating account of (dis)integration outcomes, one that is rooted in hegemonic stability theory. The core idea of hegemonic stability theory is that the dominance of one country is a necessary (although not sufficient) condition of the maintenance of a stable international politico-economic system. Hegemons, however, are not imperial powers. As argued earlier in this chapter, they are 'first among equals', exercising leadership and influence within a 'community of units *not* under a single authority' (Schroeder 2004: 298–299). They play a pre-eminent role in setting the rules on which the system is based, bear a disproportionate burden of the costs of maintaining and stabilizing the system, and mobilize support for it among other – 'follower' – member states. They must accommodate the interests of the latter for their leadership to be accepted and legitimate, while ensuring that their own publics are willing to bear whatever costs are involved in leadership. Hegemonic leadership involves consent as well as coercion – or what Kindleberger described more colourfully as 'bribery and arm-twisting'. It may not manifest itself in normal political times, but it may be critical for the stability or survival of the system in times of crisis. Obviously, stabilizing hegemonic leadership may not be forthcoming. Even if there is a putative hegemonic power, it may not be willing to provide such leadership – as was the case for the USA in the interwar international economy – or other states may resist the hegemon's leadership ambitions. In this scenario, however, the system is imperilled and may collapse, as, of course, occurred with the Great Depression in the 1930s.

For much of the EU's history, France and Germany provided it with dual hegemonic leadership. This does not mean that Paris and Bonn/Berlin 'ran' the EU's affairs on a daily basis. But it does mean that they exercised a pre-eminent influence over most of the 'history-making' decisions that set the trajectory and direction taken by the integration process. The quadruple crisis intervened, however, at a juncture when the balance of power in this uniquely intensive bilateral relationship was already changing. With France no longer 'what it used to be' (Varoufakis 2017: 190, see page 47), Germany increasingly emerged, more or less by default, as what the Polish foreign minister labelled the EU's 'indispensable' power. But, although, principally because of the size and strength of its economy, Germany stood head and shoulders above all the other member states and had compelling motives to preserve the EU, its exercise of hegemonic leadership was subject to significant constraints, making it an at least partially 'hobbled' hegemon. It could by no means be taken for granted that it could or would provide the stabilizing hegemonic leadership that the EU required in its quadruple crisis.

We shall see in fact in the following chapters that the German government played this role to quite varying degrees and, in respect of the impact on political integration in the EU, with significantly divergent outcomes. In three out of the four crises, the more effectively it played this role, the less 'damage' was done to the level of political integration in the issue area. The other crisis, however, the Eurozone Crisis, represents a deviant case. If the Eurozone emerged politically more integrated from the crisis than it had been previously, this was not attributable to the policies of the German government – which arguably served more to aggravate than to alleviate the crisis. In line with the expectations of the theoretical 'optimists', the (for Germany at least, the geopolitical as much as economic and financial) costs of exiting the Euro or allowing it to collapse looked to be too prohibitive for 'creditor' and 'debtor' states alike. Probably more important for the survival of the Euro, however, was the fact that, in monetary policy at least, the member states (see the section 'In the EU, (most) crises are the hour of the member states, especially France and Germany,' page 43) had already ceded 'real authority and sovereignty' to an international institution, the ECB, so that a hegemonic state was redundant. But for a decisive, stabilizing intervention by the ECB at the height of the Eurozone Crisis, it is conceivable that the Eurozone would have collapsed. This – in terms of the outcome, exceptional – crisis is analysed in the next chapter.

Chapter 3

The Eurozone Crisis

Introduction

The Eurozone Crisis is the oldest of the EU's multiple crises. Its debut may be dated from October 2009, when a newly elected Greek government revealed that the government budget deficit that it inherited from its predecessor for that year would amount to 12.7 per cent of GDP rather than 6.7 per cent. During the following years, sovereign debt crises exploded in several other member states on the EU's southern and western peripheries, including Ireland, Portugal, Spain and Cyprus, all of which suffered major economic recessions and growth in unemployment. The Eurozone survived these crises. Indeed, in 2018, it had three more member states than the 16 it had in 2009 (Estonia, Latvia and Lithuania). Moreover, it exhibited a higher level of political integration than in 2009, in as far as a Eurozone-wide bail-out fund, comparable in principle to the International Monetary Fund (IMF), had been created, banking regulation had been shifted from the national to the EU level, and new steps had been taken to coordinate member states' fiscal policies and restrict their budget deficits. Nonetheless, at several points post-2009, the Eurozone was on the verge of collapsing, at least in its existing composition, most recently in mid-2015, when Greece's ejection from the Eurozone ('Grexit') (once again) became a very real prospect. The threat of a partial, if not complete, collapse of the Eurozone had not necessarily been banished permanently. Even the departing president of the Eurogroup of finance ministers, the former Dutch finance minister Jeroen Dijsselbloem, warned in 2018 that the Eurozone was still not 'shock resilient' (as quoted in *Financial Times* 2018a; for similar warnings, see also Enderlein et al. 2016: 10 and King 2016: 232–238, 338–347). Following the formation in Rome of a coalition government of populist parties of the centre and extreme right after elections in May 2018, Italy loomed as the prospective location for a new round of the crisis (Wolf 2018). Discarding extremely EU-critical pre-election rhetoric, the new government initially pledged to respect the EU's fiscal rules. If it should nonetheless feel compelled to try to redeem its constituent parties' pledges to cut taxes and introduce a basic universal income, it would be bound to come into conflict with these rules, potentially precipitating a sharp rise in Italian bond yields that could culminate in the Eurozone's third-biggest economy needing to be bailed out – a task that would not be feasible without a major increase in the scale of financial aid provided in earlier rounds of the crisis involving far smaller economies.

This chapter analyses the pre-history, creation and pre-crisis evolution of the Euro and the Eurozone, as well as the post-2009 crisis. It emphasizes the extent to which the single currency was the product of the Franco-German relationship. In respect of monetary policy, the preferences of the two states diverged widely. This helps to explain why, in its original design, as laid down in the Maastricht Treaty, the Euro was an 'incomplete contract', whose defects the GFC that broke out in the USA in 2008 rapidly exposed. The GFC could be likened to a tornado that traversed the Atlantic and struck an only half-built European monetary 'house' that had to be secured and repaired while the tornado was still raging. The magnitude of this task was exacerbated by deep disagreements between the house's occupants over how the house ought to be kept upright and rebuilt. These disagreements pitted particularly the Eurozone's 'debtor' and 'creditor' member states against each other. Under ordinary circumstances in the EU, the intense distributional conflicts unleashed by this crisis might have been a recipe for political dead-lock, however, the circumstances of the Eurozone Crisis were anything but ordinary. None of the main protagonists in the conflicts over its management ultimately viewed doing nothing as a feasible option, as, in this scenario, reactions among actors on the international bond market would have torn the Eurozone apart by driving up debtor states' bond yields to the point where these would have been bankrupted with prospectively calamitous socio-economic, and possibly political, consequences. As, however, a lack of agreement and hence inaction would have been more costly for debtor than for creditor states, the latter were able to exercise a much stronger influence over the terms of intervention than the former, and the debtor states had to bear a far heavier share of the burden of adjustment.

As the Eurozone's biggest economy and financially strongest and therefore most creditworthy member, Germany was an indispensable participant and lynchpin of all efforts to 'save the euro'. As the crisis unfolded and its economic pre-eminence vis-à-vis France became increasingly marked, it became the single most influential actor in Eurozone Crisis policy. Its influence nonetheless varied from issue to issue, depending upon the constellation of actors and their preferences, the problem-constellation (especially the degree of acuteness of the crisis), and the nature of the politico-institutional setting in which the issue was being managed. Domestic political constraints – relating to politico-institutional structures, parties' electoral (vote-maximizing) con-siderations and dominant economic ideologies – prevented Germany from playing the role of a *stabilizing* hegemonic power. Rather its crisis-manage-ment strategy, not unfairly characterized as one of providing as little financial aid as possible as late as possible and under the strictest possible conditions, may have prolonged and deepened the Eurozone Crisis, intensified the polit-ical polarization over how it should be managed and increased rather than reduced the threat of European monetary-political disintegration. In the Eurozone Crisis, the main stabilizing actor was rather the ECB, a European institution with an exceptional degree of 'real authority' (Kindleberger 1973) vis-à-vis Eurozone member states.

The next section of this chapter explores the pre-history of the Euro, including the creation and impact of the European Monetary System (EMS) and the conditions that prompted the first initiatives to create a single European currency in the mid- and late 1980s. The third section focuses on the adoption of the single currency project at Maastricht in 1991, how this was accelerated by the prospect of German reunification, how and by whom its provisions were determined, and on the politically determined 'defects' in its design that made it vulnerable to contagion from the GFC. The fourth and largest section deals with the post-2009 crisis itself. This provides a chronological analysis of the negotiations over the main issues in the Eurozone conflict, describing how these unfolded, as well as the motives shaping the stances taken by the principal protagonists and explaining key outcomes. The conclusion draws together the threads of the preceding analysis and assesses the relative power of the protagonists in the Eurozone Crisis and the extent to which, in different dimensions, Germany played the role of a stabilizing hegemon.

The pre-history of the Euro

The launching of the Euro in 1999 was preceded by three decades of debate and negotiations about monetary cooperation and integration in the EU. The first proposals came from the European Commission in the 1960s as a response to changes in exchange rates between member states that threatened to distort farm support prices and undermine the recently launched Common Agricultural Policy (CAP) (Marsh 2009: 38–39). They revealed a pattern of cleavages separating France and Germany and their respective allies that has arguably persisted to the present day, with the former claiming that monetary integration would bring about economic convergence and the latter that monetary integration could only work if economic convergence had been forged beforehand (Marsh 2009: 39–40). No very significant efforts were made in this direction, however, until in 1969 Georges Pompidou succeeded de Gaulle as French president and German elections led to a change of government with the Social Democrat Willy Brandt as the new Chancellor.

The change of government in Bonn coincided with the growth of German economic superiority in the EU and growing instability in the international monetary system – which was to peak in the early 1970s with the collapse of the fixed exchange rate system of Bretton Woods. Already then, two paramount motives guiding French and German policy on issues of monetary cooperation and integration were evident. For France, this was to 'rebalance international monetary power', especially as between France and Germany (as well as to reduce dependence on the US dollar) (Dyson and Featherston 1999: 1–11). For Germany, it was to promote European political integration – not least as a means of assuaging fears that Germany was becoming too powerful or inclined to prioritize deepening its relations with Eastern Europe at the cost of its adhesion to the Western alliance. In this context Brandt's acceptance of Pompidou's proposal for a European monetary union, made at the 1969 summit at The Hague, was designed as a complement to the new government's *Ostpolitik*, intended to reassure West Germany's allies of its continued commitment to Western integration while it was pursuing a policy of *détente* with the states of Communist Central and Eastern Europe, including East Germany.

The Hague summit decision culminated in the Werner Plan for European monetary union, named after the then Luxembourg prime minister. However, whereas Werner proposed to implement his plan over a decade, the form in which it was adopted – thanks in no small measure to German opposition – contained no timetable (Marsh 2009: 55). The 'snake' – a system aiming at limiting exchange-rate fluctuations among its members within a small band – was launched in 1972, but when France decided to withdraw from this system and devalue the franc in 1974, the Werner Plan was in effect destroyed. The collapse of the 'snake' and the Werner Plan turned out though to be no more than a temporary delay in attempts to forge closer European monetary cooperation. Working together with a small number of advisers, outside the normal channels in their respective bureaucracies, German Chancellor Schmidt and French president Valéry Giscard d'Estaing combined to launch the EMS, which all the then EU member states except the UK joined. The comparative role of the two leaders in conceiving the EMS is disputed. Schmidt himself said that the idea arose out of a discussion between Giscard and himself (Schmidt 1990: 221). The author of the most comprehensive analysis of the topic, in contrast, describes it as the first major case of German leadership in the EU (Ludlow 1982: 290–291; see also Connolly 1995). Giscard's and Schmidt's motives were in any case similar. Giscard's goal was to avoid Europe being 'dominated by one country' (i.e. Germany) and ensuring that France and Germany would have comparable influence (Marsh 2009: 69; Schmidt 1990: 229–230). Schmidt saw the EMS as a stepping stone to a single currency that would pre-empt German economic domination of Europe and the formation of balancing coalitions that would lead to Germany's diplomatic isolation (Marsh 2009: 69). The core of the EMS was similar to that of the 'snake' – exchange rates between member states should fluctuate only within a narrow band. However, the fiercely independent German Bundesbank successfully resisted any obligation to intervene on foreign exchange markets to buy the currencies of any other member of the system to protect their value on the grounds that this would be incompatible with its political independence and legal obligation to safeguard the value of the Deutsche Mark (Connolly 1995: 5–7; Ludlow 1982; Marsh 2009: 82–87; Schmidt 1990: 223–224, 228). Schmidt and Giscard had to abandon their proposal to establish a European Monetary Fund that could have assisted the Eurozone in managing the post-2010 sovereign debt crisis (Ludlow 2010b: 7). Ultimately, Germany made few concessions to France on the architecture of the system, which consequently required members running current account deficits to deflate, rather than those running surpluses, such as Germany, to reflate.

The Euro: origins, adoption and launching

After having pursued an expansionary economic policy for his first two years in office and precipitated a current account crisis, the Socialist French president Mitterrand decided in 1983 to stay in the EMS and accept the constraints that the system imposed. Subsequently, monetary union – the adoption of a single European currency – appeared increasingly to Mitterrand and other French policy-makers as the principal means of changing a monetary order in which (West) Germany in effect exported its policy priorities to other members of the system (Marsh 2009: 7–8). The Deutsche Mark, Mitterrand reasoned, was the source of Germany's power, its 'nuclear weapon', as he said (Aeschemann and Riché 1996: 91; Guigou 2000: 76; Schabert 2002: 332–334; Schwarz 2012: 431). In addition, there was a strategic dimension to Mitterrand's thinking on this issue. The strong opposition in West Germany to the stationing of US medium-range missiles in the country in the late 1970s and early 1980s – a decision that Mitterrand supported in a speech to the German Parliament in March 1983 – raised doubts in France as to the reliability of its anchorage in the West. He argued that only closer European integration could prevent (West) Germany from oscillating between East and West. Given its geographic location, it had other options (as quoted in Schabert 2002: 329–331).

Mitterrand first discussed the idea of monetary union with his counterpart, the German Chancellor Helmut Kohl, in autumn 1985 (Guigou 2000). Kohl reportedly agreed with Mitterrand in principle, but stressed the strong attachment of Germans to the Deutsche Mark, implying that for him the project would involve a high level of domestic political risk. There was no significant movement on the issue until, in early 1988, the French finance minister Balladur published a memorandum pleading for a reform of the EMS, arguing that it operated asymmetrically, with the member whose currency was 'at the lower end of the permitted range' having to bear the cost, while 'any country whose policies are too rigorous' did not have to adjust (as quoted in Marsh 2009: 116).

Balladur's memorandum drew an immediate and positive response from the German foreign minister Genscher. Genscher's thinking, however, was shaped far more strongly by geopolitical and strategic considerations than monetary or economic ones. He sensed that with the rise of the Reform Communist Mikhail Gorbachev to the leadership of the USSR hitherto unprecedented opportunities to overcome the Cold War division of Germany and Europe could arise (Genscher 1995: 375, 387). Closer East–West relations in Europe had to be accompanied by closer (West) European integration. Not just in Paris, but elsewhere, the Federal Republic's stance would be scrutinized very closely for signs that it was beginning to go its 'own way', all the more so once German reunification became an issue. Genscher thought that if any uncertainty as to the Federal Republic's commitment to the EU should develop, this would have 'disastrous consequences', as, for reunification, Germany would need its partners, first and foremost France (Genscher 1995: 387). Monetary union had to be viewed in a 'new light', as it had become a major French priority and for Mitterrand the 'litmus test' of the Federal Republic's attitude to European integration (Genscher 1995: 387, 390). Genscher coordinated his action on monetary union very closely with his French counterpart, Dumas, agreeing with him that it was preferable from a tactical point of view for Germany to take the public lead on the issue (Dyson and Featherstone 1999: 169; Schwarz 2012: 434–435).

Chancellor Kohl's attitude towards monetary union remained more ambivalent than Genscher's. Supportive in principle, he feared the prospective domestic political reactions to the project in Germany. Kohl is said to have agreed to a single currency and the harmonization of taxation on savings before the EU leaders' June 1988 summit in exchange for Mitterrand's acceptance of free capital movement in the EU (Guigou 2000: 74). This summit commissioned the Delors Report on monetary union that was accepted by EU leaders a year later at Madrid. Around this time, Kohl allegedly told the council of the Bundesbank that on monetary union, 'we must make a concession to France; you have to accept this as you have to accept the weather', prompting a council member to remark that 'we thought that, if need be, he'd sell the Bundesbank for this purpose' (as quoted in Balkhausen 1992: 70).

Whether and in what form monetary union would actually materialize remained an open question. At this point, Delors himself believed it would be four or five years before an intergovernmental conference (IGC) would be convened to negotiate the details of such a union (Dyson and Featherstone 1999: 751). The Italian member of the committee, Tommaso Padia-Schioppa, thought little would come of the report and the Bundesbank president, Karl-Otto Pöhl, also a committee member, saw it as something that 'might come in the next 100 years' (as quoted in Marsh 2009: 123). Any number of reasons could have been found to postpone its implementation (Dyson and Featherstone 1999: 757).

We cannot be sure whether without the prospect of German reunification this monetary union project would have failed like the Werner Plan. Certainly, however, this prospect accelerated the process of its adoption and implementation. When, at the Madrid EU summit in June 1989, Mitterrand implored him to support monetary union, Kohl still resisted, arguing that 'abandoning the Mark is a big sacrifice for Germans. Public opinion is not ready for it yet' (as quoted in Védrine 1996: 419–420). As late as October 1989, the month before the Berlin Wall fell, Kohl opposed Mitterrand making reference to monetary union in his speech as Council president to the European Parliament. The German business community did not want it and – again – Germany was not 'ready for it' (Guigou 2000: 77–78). The date at which Kohl was prepared to agree to the convening of an IGC shifted within a short period of time from the beginning of 1990 to the end of 1990 'at the earliest' (Schabert 2002: 383ff). Citing 'domestic political considerations', by which he obviously meant the scheduled December 1990 federal elections in Germany, he opposed setting any date for the launching of an IGC at the EU summit in Strasbourg in December 1989 (Genscher 1995: 679–680; Schabert 2002: 409).

Kohl's prevarication persuaded Mitterrand that the German Chancellor wanted to avoid committing himself to monetary union. His mistrust in Kohl's intentions were strengthened by Kohl's 10-Point Plan speech on

German unity, of which Mitterrand was not notified in advance, less than three weeks after the fall of the Berlin Wall. In talks with Genscher, he ratcheted up the diplomatic pressure on Kohl by painting the spectre of a return to the Europe of 1913 and a 'reversal of alliances' (i.e. a coalition of France and Russia against Germany) if German reunification and European integration did not develop at a similar pace (Bozo 2009: 126; Genscher 1995: 678; Schabert 2002: 420–421). The manifest threat of a deep crisis in Franco-German relations (which would have complicated the process of German reunification) appears to have been decisive in persuading Kohl to acquiesce in Mitterrand's demand shortly before the Strasbourg summit (Attali 1993: 350–354; Bozo 2009: 130; Guigou 2000: 79; Marsh 2009: 137). Kohl explained to the US secretary of state Baker that he was aware that the prospect of a 'bigger Germany' was a nightmare for some people, given that it was already Europe's strongest economy. What more could he do in this situation, he asked rhetorically, than to accept monetary union? He had taken this decision 'against German interests', noting that Pöhl, for example, had opposed it. But it was a 'politically important step', as Germany 'needs friends' and could not allow any mistrust to build up against it in Europe (Küsters and Hofmann 1998: 638).

Like the EU summit decision in Strasbourg, the subsequent IGC negotiations, as well as the Maastricht Treaty summit, were dominated by the bilateral Franco-German relationship (Dyson and Featherstone 1999: 4–5, 758–759; Mazzucelli 1997: 140–141). As often in other issue areas, the two governments entered the negotiations with policy positions 'much closer to several other partners than with each other' (Dyson and Featherstone 1999: 758). They tried to mediate these differences in a series of bilateral meetings, including six secret meetings not divulged to other member states (see also Mazzucelli 1997: 126; Quatremer and Klau 1999: 188–191). Working closely with his French counterpart, Trichet, the state secretary in the German Finance Ministry, Köhler, played a particularly influential role in the negotiations, as other participants acknowledged that 'ultimately his government had the one veto that mattered' (Mazzucelli 1997: 126). In exchange for Germany's acquiescence in monetary union as such, Mitterrand accepted that this should follow a German design – particularly that, like the Bundesbank, the future European Central Bank should be politically independent, committed primarily to maintaining price stability, and not allowed to lend to member governments (Bozo 2009: 53). Of the final accord on monetary union, some 80 per cent may have been agreed by the first half of 1991 (Mazzucelli 1997: 132). A critical unresolved issue was the implementation timetable for what became the euro. Mitterrand and the Italian prime minister Andreotti decided to push for 1999 as the last possible starting date for monetary union. Kohl decided alone to accept this deadline to the 'great consternation' of other members of the German delegation – his finance minister, the latter's state secretary and the president of the Bundesbank (Connolly 1995: 119; Mazzucelli 1997: 175; Schwarz 2012: 700–701). In exchange, the French delegation is said to have pledged to support the strict application of the convergence criteria when deciding which member states would accede to the single currency (Mazzucelli 1997: 185).

Despite the Maastricht accord, the single currency project could still have failed. A referendum that Mitterrand called on the treaty in France yielded only a very narrow majority in its favour. In 1992–93, partly as a consequence of the uncertainty provoked by this and another referendum on the treaty in Denmark, the EMS teetered on the verge of a collapse that might have destroyed the project as the crisis of 1973–74 had derailed the Werner Plan (see Chapter 1). The 'alliance at the very top' between Kohl and Mitterrand was critical in keeping France in the system in 1993 after the British pound had been catapulted from it the previous year (Marsh 2009: 162–175). If the EMS had collapsed altogether, it is at least questionable whether the single currency project would have survived.

The monetary union provisions of the Maastricht Treaty, like many EU accords, were in any case an 'incomplete contract' (Héritier 2016: 3; see also Dyson and Featherstone 1999: 783; Jones et al. 2016: 1017). Reflecting the dominant Ordoliberal orientation of economic policy in Germany, it implicitly placed the burden of adjustment in case of divergent economic performance on the member states running current account deficits – which would have to devalue 'internally', that is, reduce wages and government spending and/or raise taxes. The smooth functioning of such processes presupposed a degree of wage and price flexibility within and labour mobility between member states that did not exist in the EU, given the structure of industrial relations institutions and linguistic – among other – constraints on labour mobility.

At the same time, the monetary union decided at Maastricht lacked several attributes that typically underpin and help to stabilize other (almost all national) monetary unions (Copelovitch et al. 2016: 817–824; McNamara 2015: 25–30, 37–42). First, as demanded by Germany, the treaty banned the monetary financing of member governments by the prospective European Central Bank. The latter could not therefore (legally) play the role of lender-of-last-resort performed by most other central banks in economic crises.

Second, there was no provision for the pursuit of a common fiscal policy, which, once the single currency was launched, would remain under the control of the member governments, creating incentives for profligate governments to 'free-ride' on others and complicating the task of coordinating fiscal and monetary policies. In lieu of such a policy, a Stability Pact was negotiated in 1996 to try to institutionalize the Maastricht debt and deficit criteria after the launching of the single currency. These negotiations too were dominated by the French and German governments – which several years later would cooperate to ease the criteria and undermine the pact's credibility (Quatremer and Klau 1999: 132–139).

Third, little provision was made for the kind and volumes of fiscal transfers between richer and poorer regions or regions affected asymmetrically by economic trends that are typical in national states. At the insistence of the poorer EU member states (Spain, Greece, Portugal and Ireland), whose governments threatened otherwise not to sign the treaty, the EU's regional development budget ('Structural Funds') was boosted (Lange 1992; Mazzucelli 1997: 112–113). At still less than half of 1 per cent of the EU's combined GDP, the scale of this budget, however, was very small.

Fourth, no provision was made for an EU-wide system of financial regulation that would have involved a set of security guarantees for bank depositors and resolution funds for financially troubled banks (McNamara 2015: 28). Moreover, managing this only 'tenuously' embedded monetary union in a crisis was bound to be extraordinarily difficult in a highly decentralized political system with many competing political authorities (McNamara 2015: 37). None other than Kohl himself argued that the 'idea of sustaining an economic and monetary union over time without political union is a fallacy' (as quoted in Issing 2016). But the 'political union' that was championed by Kohl and Germany, and negotiated in parallel with the Economic and Monetary Union (EMU), did not Europeanize political authority in the Maastricht Treaty to the same degree as the treaty Europeanized the member states' money (Mazzucelli 1997: 79, 137–138, 148, 180; Schwarz 2012: 690–698).

These 'design defects' of the Euro were fairly widely recognized before the current crisis. At least some key political actors, however, were confident that if and when they became manifest, the EU would integrate more closely and they would be resolved. Kohl, for example, acknowledged that the political union agreed at Maastricht fell far short of what he had wanted, but future 'developments' would sweep aside obstacles to closer integration: 'A dynamic process has been launched that we never had before in history' (as quoted in Schwarz 2012: 698). He argued two decades later that if he had insisted on everything that he thought was desirable and necessary in the long term, the single currency would never have been adopted. 'I made concessions that I still think today are defensible. I think the notion of "design defects" is completely wrong. We didn't go as far as would have been desirable, that is true. But more was not possible and the direction was right and that is what counts' (Kohl 2011: 16). The then president of the European Commission, Romano Prodi, argued in 2001 that although this was politically impossible for the time being, 'someday' there would be a crisis that would force the EU to introduce a new set of economic policy instruments (as quoted in Barber and Norman 2001). In contrast, some scholars were less sanguine as to the likely impact of a possible future crisis – warning, for example, of the destructive prospect that people could be asked to 'make sacrifices for others with whom there was a weak sense of identity' and that the single currency consequently might unleash a 'political storm' that could wreck the EU (Dyson and Featherstone 1999: 796, 801; McKay 1999). The announcement of the almost 100 per cent increase in the projected Greek government deficit in 2009 was the event that unleashed this kind of storm. It did not wreck the EU in the following years, but it came close to doing so on several occasions.

The Eurozone Crisis

The crisis in the Eurozone may be explained as a consequence of the uneasy and difficult co-existence within it of at least two 'varieties of capitalism', distinguished by their markedly divergent 'institutional infrastructures' (Hall 2014; see also Johnston et al. 2014 and Gambarotto and Solari 2015). Whereas the northern European member states possess institutions that facilitate a high level of coordination of wage bargaining that militates against inflation and fosters export-led growth, such institutions are lacking or weak in the southern European states, where growth is led rather by domestic demand and, prior to monetary union, declining competitiveness caused by relatively higher price inflation was offset by currency devaluations. During the first decade of the euro, members of the former group accumulated growing current account surpluses and the latter group growing deficits that were financed to a large extent by loans from northern European financial institutions at the same interest rates as in the north – rates that, given higher inflation in the southern states, were effectively lower there than in the north. Despite the ostensible ban on the monetary financing of Eurozone members by the ECB in the Maastricht Treaty, financial market actors seemed to assume that, in a crisis, regardless of the treaty provisions, the ECB and/or the other member states would nonetheless come to the aid of a member state that threatened to go bankrupt. At the heart of the Eurozone Crisis as it unfolded was the issue of whether, to what extent and under what conditions, the ECB and other member states would furnish this support to crisis-stricken members – first Greece, then Ireland, Portugal, Spain and Cyprus. At the same time, while this storm or tornado was raging, the Eurozone had collectively to decide what could or should be done to secure and repair the half-built euro 'house' so that it could survive.

Between May 2010 and 2015, the financial aid provided to these five Eurozone member states amounted to €537bn, of which €439bn came from Eurozone members and €98bn from the IMF (see Tables 3.1 and 3.2). The principal cleavage in the conflicts over the successive bail-out accords and the recasting of the Eurozone's architecture was to run between these 'debtor' states, on the one hand, and a group of northern European 'creditor' states, on the other. The latter group by no means represented all the 'creditor' states, as, among these, France and Italy frequently aligned themselves with the crisis-struck countries and pressed for more rapid and large-scale intervention to assist them. Among the northern European 'creditor' states, Germany was the one that exercised the strongest influence over the course and outcome of these conflicts. The author of the most comprehensive analysis of the conflict over the first Greek bail-out adopted in May 2010 concluded that the German Chancellor Angela Merkel 'has dominated the story from beginning to end' (Ludlow 2010b: 3). As we shall see below, this judgment may also be applied, albeit to varying extents, to most subsequent episodes of the Eurozone Crisis.

Table 3.1 Bail-outs: ultimate EU donors (EUR billion)

EU Donor	Cyprus Financial Assistance	Greece 1st program	Greece 2nd program	Greece Bridge loan	Greece 3rd program	Spain Financial Assistance	Ireland Financial Assistance	Portugal Financial Assistance	Hungary BoP	Latvia BoP	Romania 1st BoP	Romania 2nd BoP	Romania 3rd BoP	Total
AT	0.26	1.73	4.16	0.17	2.38	1.14	1.23	1.57	0.20	0.08	0.25	0.01	0.01	13.19
BE	0.33	2.33	5.42	0.22	2.97	1.43	1.78	2.24	0.34	0.12	0.45	0.02	0.02	17.68
BG	0.00	0.05	0.08	0.02	0.00	0.00	0.14	0.16	0.04	0.01	0.05	0.00	0.00	0.57
CY	0.02	0.12	0.02	0.01	0.17	0.08	0.04	0.05	0.01	0.00	0.02	0.00	0.00	0.54
CZ	0.00	0.08	0.12	0.08	0.00	0.00	0.34	0.38	0.10	0.04	0.12	0.00	0.00	1.27
DE	2.49	16.40	39.85	1.59	23.19	11.14	11.34	14.58	1.75	0.74	2.05	0.06	0.05	125.20
DK	0.01	0.16	0.22	0.14	0.00	0.00	0.99	0.67	0.17	0.07	0.22	0.01	0.01	2.66
EE	0.02	0.01	0.37	0.01	0.16	0.08	0.09	0.12	0.01	0.01	0.01	0.00	0.00	0.89
EL	0.26	0.09	0.13	0.11	2.41	1.16	0.44	0.50	0.13	0.05	0.15	0.00	0.00	5.43
ES	1.08	6.99	17.19	0.61	10.17	4.88	4.50	5.85	0.62	0.28	0.74	0.02	0.02	52.95
FI	0.17	1.11	2.67	0.11	1.54	0.74	0.79	1.01	0.13	0.05	0.16	0.01	0.01	8.49
FR	1.87	12.30	29.90	1.20	17.41	8.36	8.53	10.96	1.32	0.56	1.59	0.05	0.05	94.10
HR	0.00	0.03	0.04	0.02	0.00	0.00	0.11	0.12	0.03	0.01	0.04	0.00	0.00	0.41
HU	0.00	0.09	0.12	0.05	0.00	0.00	0.26	0.30	0.08	0.03	0.10	0.01	0.01	1.06
IE	0.15	0.45	0.15	0.09	1.36	0.65	17.88	0.44	0.11	0.04	0.13	0.00	0.00	21.47

IT	1.63	10.67	26.09	0.88	15.30	7.35	6.82	8.87	0.97	0.42	1.20	0.03	0.03	30.27
LT	0.04	0.02	0.02	0.02	0.35	0.17	0.08	0.09	0.02	0.01	0.03	0.00	0.00	0.84
LU	0.02	0.18	0.40	0.01	0.21	0.10	0.13	0.17	0.03	0.01	0.03	0.00	0.00	1.30
LV	0.03	0.01	0.02	0.01	0.24	0.11	0.06	0.07	0.02	0.01	0.02	0.00	0.00	0.59
MT	0.01	0.06	0.14	0.00	0.06	0.03	0.04	0.05	0.01	0.00	0.01	0.02	0.00	0.41
NL	0.53	3.63	8.64	0.39	4.88	2.35	2.76	3.50	0.49	0.19	0.60	0.02	0.02	28.02
PL	0.01	0.14	0.20	0.22	0.00	0.00	0.82	0.92	0.23	0.10	0.26	0.01	0.00	2.90
PT	0.23	1.19	0.12	0.10	2.14	1.03	0.40	0.46	0.11	0.05	0.13	0.00	0.00	5.97
RO	0.00	0.09	0.12	0.08	0.00	0.00	0.35	0.40	0.10	0.04	0.12	0.00	0.00	1.31
SE	0.01	0.20	0.28	0.24	0.00	0.00	1.54	1.07	0.27	0.11	0.32	0.01	0.01	4.06
SI	0.04	0.27	0.70	0.02	0.37	0.18	0.18	0.23	0.03	0.01	0.03	0.00	0.00	2.04
SK	0.08	0.04	1.45	0.04	0.70	0.34	0.35	0.46	0.05	0.02	0.05	0.00	0.00	3.56
UK	0.05	0.91	1.26	0.70	0.00	0.00	6.93	3.56	0.93	0.36	1.23	0.05	0.05	16.02
Total	9.32	59.35	139.88	7.16	86.00	41.30	68.92	58.80	8.29	3.43	10.13	0.34	0.29	493.20

Notes: In addition to direct bilateral contributions, countries' contributions to bailouts was calculated through their participation for the EU Budget (which is funded through the European Commission the EFSM and BoP programs), EFSF, ESM, IMF, World Bank groups, EBRD, EIB. Only actual and scheduled disbursements were considered, whenever officially reduced these were not included (last update – December 2015).

Sources: INSEAD's calculations based on European Commission and IMF country reports, EFSF, ESM, World Bank groups, EBRD, EIB. Reports found here at https://www.imf.org/external/np/sec/memdir/members.aspx and https://ec.europa.eu/info/business-economy-euro/economic-and-fiscal-policy-coordination/eu-financial-assistance_en.

Table 3.2 *Bail-outs: funds (EUR billion)*

Funder	Cyprus Financial Assistance	Greece 1st program	Greece 2nd program	Greece Bridge loan	Greece 3rd program	Spain Financial Assistance	Ireland Financial Assistance	Portugal Financial Assistance	Hungary BoP	Latvia BoP	Romania 1st BoP	Romania 2nd BoP	Romania 3rd BoP	Total
EFSM				7.16			21.7	24.3						53.16
EFSF			130.9				17.7	26						174.6
ESM	9				86	41.3								136.3
IMF	1	20.1	28				22.5	26.5	8.7	1.1	11.96			119.86
GLF		52.9												52.9
BoP									5.5	2.9	5			13.4
World Bank										0.4	1	1.15	1	3.55
EBRD										0.1				0.1
EIB											1			1
Ireland							17.5							17.5
UK							3.8							3.8
Sweden							0.6							0.6
Denmark							0.4							0.4
Total	10	73	158.9	7.16	86	41.3	84.2	76.8	14.2	4.5	18.96	1.15	1	577.17

Notes: GLS – Greek Loan Facility, BoP – Balance of Payments Program.
Only actual and scheduled disbursements were considered, whenever officially reduced these were not included (last update – December 2015).

Sources: European Commission and IMF country reports (https://ec.europa.eu/info/business-economy-euro/economic-and-fiscal-policy-coordination/eu-financial-assistance_en).

The dominant role played by Germany in managing the crisis had little to do with its institutional power resources: Germany has the same representation as the three other most populous member states in the Council of Ministers, the same as all others in the European Council, and the same number of votes – one – on the governing board of the ECB as all other Eurozone member states, Cyprus, Malta and Luxembourg included. It has to do first and foremost with the fact that its economy is by far the largest in the Eurozone, accounting for about 27 per cent of its combined GDP. Without a German contribution commensurate to the relative size of its economy, it would have been much more difficult, if not impossible, to mobilize sufficient financial aid to rescue the crisis-stricken states. In the Eurozone, as Merkel reputedly remarked to French president Sarkozy, '*I am the bank*' (Buisson 2016: 404; emphasis added by present author). Vis-à-vis the other large Eurozone economies, France and Italy, German dominance was strengthened by the fact that the government's budgetary situation gave it greater scope to provide financial aid without prejudicing its creditworthiness on government bond markets.

Germany's interests in the Eurozone Crisis were, however, ambivalent and conflicted. The argument has been made that the austerity policies it championed served the *economic* interests of German business, for which other countries in the Eurozone formed a 'regional production platform' in which the lower wage and other costs promoted by austerity would boost German firms' world-market competitiveness (Germann 2017: 9–15). But the empirical evidence that this motivated German policy-makers' stance is flimsy (Germann 2017: 14–15). If anything, German manufacturing-industrial organizations, concerned about a possible collapse of the Eurozone, exercised a moderating influence on government policy during the crisis (see below). However, as financial aid for Greece and the other crisis-hit countries proved very unpopular in Germany, *electoral-political* motives encouraged the government to oppose it. *Ideologically*, the idea of 'bailing out' other Eurozone states conflicted with the 'Ordoliberal' principles of economic and monetary policy that predominated in academic, financial and political circles in Germany, especially on the political Right, which was in government in Berlin throughout the entire crisis. Providing financial aid was also *legally* uncertain and contestable, in the light of the provisions of the Maastricht Treaty and the judgments that the German Federal Constitutional Court had issued on both this and the Lisbon Treaty. The court's rulings raised the spectre of its declaring German participation in any bail-out actions as illegal (Ludlow 2010b: 10). *Tactically*, considerations of moral hazard favoured the adoption of a tough anti-bail-out stance, on the grounds that otherwise the states receiving financial aid would not take the unpalatable decisions required for them (from an Ordoliberal perspective) to bring about a sustained economic recovery and they would thus remain permanently dependent on financial transfers.

At the same time, in determining its policy, the government had to weigh up the risk that, if a Eurozone member state were to be forced to declare bankruptcy, the whole Eurozone might collapse as well as the economic, financial and political consequences and implications that such a scenario could have for Germany. *Politically*, these could include the risk of a major fallout with its European partners, especially France, and, in the worst case, the collapse of the EU and Germany's diplomatic isolation in Europe (see Chapter 2). The grand bargain on which, for France and many other EU member states, German reunification had been based, would have been destroyed. *Economically*, these could include a significant appreciation of a new German currency against the currencies of its European trading partners, posing problems for export-oriented German companies. *Financially*, these could include major losses for German banks that had invested in the government bonds of Greece and the other crisis-hit Eurozone member states. The exposure of German banks to Greece in 2009 amounted to €43bn and to the other three states that were subsequently assisted to €381bn (Bank for International Settlements statistics, as cited in Ludlow 2010a: 5). Among the banks of the other states, only the French – with an overall total of €385bn, including €75.5bn for Greece – was comparably exposed to these four Eurozone members. The German and French banks' exposure to Greek government bonds in March 2010 amounted to €17 and €20bn respectively (Legrain 2014: 78–79).

The analysis of the distribution of costs and benefits of providing financial aid to other Eurozone states was in any case a political exercise to be undertaken by the federal government – the results of which could vary, depending on its party-political composition. The Greek government's announcement of a far higher deficit than previously projected in October 2009 followed a change of government in Berlin the previous month. For the four previous years, this had been a centrist coalition of Christian and Social Democrats. In February 2009, the Social Democratic finance minister Steinbrück had declared that, although the EU treaties did not foresee any help for insolvent countries, 'in reality the other states would have to rescue those running to difficulty'. If there was a risk of the Eurozone breaking up, 'we would have to take action' (as quoted in *Financial Times* 2009). The September 2009 elections brought about a change of government with the liberal FDP joining Merkel's Christian Democrats. In contrast to the SPD, the FDP was to be more resistant to German participation in Eurozone bail-outs than the Christian Democrats, arguably altering the 'political axis of the entire euro area' (Bastasin 2015: 125). As well as between the parties of the governing coalition, government policy had to be negotiated between different governmental organs, notably between Merkel's office and the Federal Finance Ministry, which was headed throughout the crisis by the next most influential figure in the Christian Democratic Union (CDU)/Christian Social Union (CSU), Wolfgang Schäuble, whose stance on some issues would diverge from Merkel's.

The first Greek bail-out and the European Financial Stability Facility (EFSF)

Divergences between Merkel and Schäuble were evident from the outset of the Eurozone Crisis. In February 2010, Merkel disavowed an accord reached in the Eurogroup that pledged support for Greece 'if needed, to safeguard financial stability in the euro area as a whole' (as cited in Ludlow 2010a: 22). The threat of a summit failure, which could have unleashed a new wave of speculation and driven Greek bond yields still higher, prompted the Council president, Herman Van Rompuy, to convene a last-minute pre-summit meeting between Merkel, the French president Nicolas Sarkozy, and the Greek prime minister George Papandreou at which he brokered an agreement, then ratified by the European Council, that made no specific reference to aid for Greece, but rather noted that the Greek government had not requested any financial support, while affirming that the Eurozone member states would 'take determined action, if needed, to safeguard financial stability in the euro area as a whole' (as cited in Ludlow 2010a: 21). Sarkozy worried that if the Eurozone were not to help Greece, the contagion would spread to Italy and the survival of the euro would be endangered (*Le Monde* 2017b). He may have been especially perturbed by the heavy exposure of French banks, whose combined loans to southern European governments amounted to €729bn (Varoufakis 2017: 24). He demanded that the EU 'put some billions immediately on the table' then 'fix the details' (Bastasin 2015: 167–168). But Merkel insisted that no action should be taken 'without a plan' (Bastasin 2015: 167–168). At this point, according to Sarkozy, she 'didn't want to give a cent' to help Greece (*Le Monde* 2017b).

Despite an intensifying Greek sovereign debt crisis, it then took three more months for the Eurozone members to agree on a first bail-out package for Greece. The length of this interregnum was primarily attributable to Merkel's and the German government's prevarication. Germany 'held the initiative', because without it, 'there was nothing remotely credible that the rest of the euro area could do to calm the markets or indeed anybody else' (Ludlow 2010b: 13–14). The terms of the intervention to aid Greece were largely determined in bilateral negotiations between Berlin and Paris, and largely corresponded to Merkel's demands: the IMF would have a major role in the intervention and aid was to be provided only as a last resort, at 'non-concessional' interest rates and subject to 'strong conditionality' (as quoted in Ludlow 2010b: 18–19). In contrast, the French input was largely symbolic and France was 'manifestly Germany's junior partner' (Ludlow 2010b: 21–22, 50).

At the decisive summit in May 2010, reflecting a cleavage that was to typify the entire Eurozone Crisis, the Council was divided between a French-led 'olive-belt' group comprising also Italy, Portugal and Spain, and a German-led group of northern European Eurozone members including also the Netherlands and Finland, and – on this occasion – the ECB president Trichet (Bastasin 2015: 207; Ludlow 2010b: 31–32). Merkel was successful in shielding the ECB from demands led by Sarkozy to purchase government bonds (on the secondary market) so that it could more easily do so without giving the impression that it was ceding to political pressure. She also ensured that the new European Financial Stability Fund (EFSF) was created as an intergovernmental organ in which each member state would have a right of veto rather than as one that would be controlled by the European Commission (Ludlow 2010b: 35–37). Concern to safeguard the fund as well as possible against prospective challenges in the Federal Constitutional Court may have been the predominant motive for Merkel's insistence on this design for the EFSF. However, given the extent of mass, media and elite opposition to financial aid for Greece in Germany (opinion polls suggested as many as 86 per cent of Germans were opposed to it), she may also have wished to postpone her acquiescence in a Greek bail-out until after elections in the biggest German state, North Rhine-Westphalia, on 9 May (Ludlow 2010b: 2, 14, 27, 41). The summit deal was not in fact done until the following day, with Germany the last Eurozone member state to agree to it (Bastasin 2015: 214). However, faced with the growing pressures from international financial markets to find a solution for the Greek crisis, the government and the German Parliament had approved German participation in the Greek bail-out in the days preceding the state elections, at which Merkel's CDU (*Christlich Demokratische Union* – Christian Democratic Union) experienced a severe defeat, its share of the vote slumping from 44 to 34 per cent. Simultaneously with the summit, the ECB governing board decided by a majority to buy Portuguese and Irish as well as Greek government bonds on the secondary market. Apparently, no consideration was given to an alternative solution of writing off the Greek government's debt and compensating Eurozone banks for their losses on Greek bonds through direct subsidies from their respective governments, although this may have 'worked out cheaper than continuing to lend on an open-ended basis to an insolvent Greece' (Legrain 2014: 80). Conceivably, as was the case later with Ireland, other governments were 'scared to death not just by their banks but by their publics, who don't want to hear that public money is required for bank recapitalization' (Barry Eichengreen, as quoted in Blustein 2017: 176–177).

The Fiscal Compact

Primarily at Merkel's behest, the European Council had decided in March 2010 that, to prevent a recurrence of the Greek crisis, the EU's existing rules should be strengthened and complemented and its capacity to act in times of crisis enhanced (Ludlow 2010b: 18–21). A task force chaired by the Council president Van Rompuy was created to draw up proposals. The terms of reference for the group's work 'reflected the German government's priorities' (Ludlow 2010c: 7). Over the following 18 months, this initiative was to culminate in the adoption of a range of measures designed to align the fiscal policies of member states and curb their budget deficits, notably in that of the Fiscal Compact, agreed by all members except the UK and the Czech Republic in December 2011.

The work of Van Rompuy's group was marked by the characteristic cleavage between a northern bloc comprising Germany, Austria, Finland, the Netherlands, Sweden and the UK, and a southern one led by France, but including also Greece, Ireland, Italy, Portugal and Spain (Ludlow 2010c: 9). The pre-eminence of Germany and France within these respective 'camps' among the Eurozone member states was illustrated by the bilateral agreement on crisis strategy reached by Merkel and Sarkozy in talks at the Normandy beach resort of Deauville in October 2010. Disavowing her allies, along with the Commission and the ECB, Merkel gave up her prior insistence on sanctions against governments running too high budget deficits being imposed automatically, while Sarkozy conceded her demand for the imposition of 'haircuts' (financial losses) on private holders of government bonds in the case of bail-outs (Bastasin 2015: 236–239; Legrain 2014: 127–128; Ludlow 2010c: 11–12). Despite the ECB president's vehement opposition to 'haircuts', both proposals were adopted at the European Council's subsequent meeting. The financial markets reacted to the accord over 'haircuts' with a sharp rise in the yields on southern European and Irish government bonds (Legrain 2014: 128–129; Ludlow 2011: 7). Merkel dominated the summit itself 'from beginning to end' (Ludlow 2010c: 1). She was forced to make some significant concessions, especially by dropping a demand that governments running too high budget deficits should be stripped of their voting rights in the Council. But concerned that this could otherwise be judged illegal by the German Federal Constitutional Court, she insisted – successfully – that the EFSF be transformed into a permanent organization (the European Stability Mechanism – ESM) based on an amended European treaty (Ludlow 2010c: 1, 9–10). Other government leaders were reputedly 'willing without exception to give her what she wanted, because they were all aware that she had taken considerable risks in defence of the euro' (a senior member of the European Council, quoted in Ludlow 2010c: 27).

In early 2011, the German government launched a complementary project – initially labelled the 'competitiveness pact' – with a broader set of objectives, ranging from the abolition of wage indexation, raising pension ages, creating a common base for corporate taxation and inserting public debt 'brakes' in member states' constitutions. Merkel secured Sarkozy's backing for this project. Not long before, the French president had remarked that 'all my efforts are directed towards adapting France to a system that works. The German system' (as quoted from a television interview in November 2010, in *Spiegel-Online* 2011a). Implying much more extensive EU intervention in the industrial relations and social welfare systems than had hitherto been the case, and widely viewed as an attempt to 'Germanize' Europe, the project encountered strong opposition from other member states (Bastasin 2012: 259). Adopted in a diluted form by the Eurozone and several other member states at the March 2011 European Council meeting, it was an intergovernmental accord outside EU law and relied on the so-called 'open method of coordination', that is, on the voluntary acquiescence of member states. It was later classified as 'dormant' by the European Commission's own think tank (Wikipedia 2017b). New attempts to reform the EMU had to await a fresh intensification of the Eurozone Crisis towards the end of 2011.

By the middle of 2011, Ireland (November 2010) and Portugal (May 2011) had been bailed out and, the first bail-out having failed to turn around the Greek economy and government finances, a second, bigger Greek bail-out had been negotiated. However, financial market actors continued to worry about the capacity of the Greek government to finance its debt and became increasingly nervous about the sustainability of government finances in Spain and Italy, driving up bond yields in both these countries whose fate, given the greater size of their economies, would have a far greater impact on the Eurozone than that of the three smaller members. As, towards the end of the year, the crisis came to a new climax, the English-speaking financial and economic press was warning that an act of 'supreme collective will' was required to save the euro (*The Economist* 2011a), that the Eurozone could 'break up within weeks' (*The Economist* 2011b) or that it had 'only days to avoid collapse' (Munchau 2011).

The resurgence of the Eurozone Crisis re-energized the German government's efforts to reform the EMU, as well as boosting its bargaining power vis-à-vis other Eurozone members. Opposition to further financial aid for Greece and other crisis-affected Eurozone members had meanwhile grown in Germany – as well as in other 'creditor' states, including France, the Netherlands, Finland and Slovakia (*Financial Times* 2011a, 2011b; *Libération* 2011; *Spiegel-Online* 2011b). Backed by a majority public opinion, the two smaller parties in Merkel's coalition – the FDP and the CDU's Bavarian sister party, the Christian Social Union (CSU) – initially opposed German participation in any further Eurozone bail-outs. The leaders of both suggested that Greece might be expelled from the Eurozone (*Zeit Online* 2011). The critics of financial aid in the FDP managed to force a referendum of party members on the issue – it failed, but 44 per cent of the participants opposed such aid (Kietz 2013: 37–38).

The growing dissension within the governing coalition raised questions as to whether Merkel could secure a Parliamentary majority in favour of further contributions to Eurozone bail-outs. Parliamentary backing for such a policy had become imperative following a ruling to this effect by the German Federal Constitutional Court in September 2011 (*Bundesverfassungsgericht* 2011). Merkel could rely in the German Bundestag on the support of the main opposition party, the SPD, which, after having abstained in the vote on the first Greek bail-out package and despite criticizing Merkel for a policy tailored to domestic political and intraparty political considerations, supported further aid in 2011 'out of an overarching sense of responsibility' for the EU (Steinbrück, as quoted in *Das Parlament* 2011a). If, however, she had lost her 'Chancellor's majority' in the Bundestag, her authority would have been significantly damaged. She defended further financial aid in the Bundestag with the argument that Germany had profited from the euro 'like no other country', that in the long term Germany could 'not be successful unless Europe too is doing well', and that if the Euro should collapse, then so too would the EU (*Das Parlament* 2011b). The head of the CDU/CSU Parliamentary group argued similarly that it was in Germany's interest to help countries that had run into difficulties and to 'prevent contagion'. Such aid would also help to 'stabilize German banks', which supplied capital to German small and medium-sized firms (*Mittelstand*) (Volker Kauder, as quoted in *Das Parlament* 2011a). Merkel won her 'Chancellor's majority' in the Bundestag for the transformation of the temporary EFSF into the ESM in October 2011. Nonetheless, the breadth and depth of opposition to her policy within her coalition conceivably compelled her to pursue a tough line on the conditions attached to further financial aid and on the additional measures that should be taken to stabilize the Eurozone. As one commentator observed at the time: 'It was very clear to all Europeans that the Bundestag was binding not only the Chancellor's manoeuvring room, but that of the European Council over-all' (Bastasin 2015: 332).

The run-up to the October 2011 EU crisis summit was marked by 'violent disagreements' between the German and French governments (*Spiegel Online* 2011c). Officials were quoted as warning that the issues were 'so complex', the time 'so short' and the differences between Paris and Berlin 'so large' that a credible deal could prove 'out of reach' (*Financial Times* 2011c). On the major issues of further private-sector 'haircuts' on Greek debt, the financial volume of the ESM and whether it should be able to support banks and buy sovereign bonds, the two governments were opposed. This summit was notable for the emergence of the 'Frankfurt Round' (Merkel, Sarkozy and the heads of the IMF, the ECB, the Commission and the Council) as an actor in the Eurozone Crisis (*Spiegel-Online* 2011d). Among the six, the German and French leaders were 'the principals' (Ludlow 2011: 4–5). The English-, French- and German-language press were united in their assessment that the summit was 'primarily a success for the German Chancellor' (*Les Echos* 2011; Ludlow 2011: 5; Peel 2011; *Spiegel-Online* 2011e). Merkel resisted demands, led by Sarkozy, that Germany increase its guarantee for the EFSF and that the EFSF be granted a bank licence so that the ECB could lend to it. Against the opposition of both Sarkozy and the ECB, she also persuaded the European Council (and Greece's creditor banks) to accept a 50 per cent 'haircut' on loans to Greece – as part, however, of a larger deal which contained enough 'sweeteners' for private creditors that more than four-fifths of them accepted it (Kalaitzake 2017: 16–20).

Merkel also withstood joint Franco-American pressure to commit more German resources to combat the Eurozone Crisis at the Cannes G20 summit shortly afterwards. The G20 meeting took place as Greece was 'imploding politically' and Italy, 'a country too big to bail out' under current circumstances, appeared 'just days away from being cut off from global financial markets' (Spiegel 2014). The Obama administration was increasingly frustrated and worried about the resurgent crisis and convinced that, as in the USA in 2008–09, only 'a huge wall of public money' would calm international financial markets (Spiegel 2014). The Eurozone had to be saved in its analysis because 'otherwise we'll enter into a depression in Europe, and this will impact the economy of the US and my [Obama's] re-election' (Spiegel 2014). The Obama administration and the French government conceived a plan that they hoped would be acceptable to Germany, while building a 'firewall' that would convince government bond traders that no other Eurozone members would have to default as Greece had had – partially – to do. According to the plan, the Eurozone would increase the volume of its bail-out fund by €140bn by creating new 'special drawing rights' (SDR) for it, identical to those that existed for the IMF. SDR, however, were controlled and managed by IMF members' central banks – in Germany therefore by the Bundesbank, which opposed the Franco-American proposal. Merkel refused to overrule the Bundesbank, protesting 'that is not fair. I cannot decide in lieu of the Bundesbank … I'm not going to commit suicide' (as quoted in Spiegel 2014).

Merkel rejected the Franco-American plan less out of principle than with the argument that this would have required her to make a politically very risky concession without having secured any quid pro quo. The quid pro quo would have been in the form of the Italian government asking for financial support for the IMF and in exchange for this agreeing to implement an austerity programme. Still led – at the Cannes G20 summit – by Silvio Berlusconi, the Italian government refused to agree to more than being 'monitored' by the IMF. The Cannes summit thus failed. Within a week, Italian bond yields would rise to almost 7.5 per cent and Greece's to more than 33 per cent, a level 'almost without precedent for a developed country' (Spiegel 2014). Sarkozy saw his nightmare scenario of a collapse of the Eurozone beginning to materialize (*Le Monde* 2017b).

That, over the next six weeks, this scenario was nonetheless averted – and Merkel's and the German government's crisis management strategy prevailed within the Eurozone, at least for the time being – was conceivably facilitated by important changes of government in three member states caught up in the crisis: Greece, Italy and Spain. In Spain, the centre-left Socialist party lost Parliamentary elections and was replaced in government by the centre-right Popular party. In the other two countries, elected prime ministers were ousted and succeeded – without elections – by technocrats. The change of political leadership in Greece was precipitated by a decision of the prime minister George Papandreou to submit the new bail-out accord reached at the European Council meeting – an accord that involved deep cuts in pensions and public-sector wages and bonuses as well as tax increases – to a popular referendum. Papandreou explained his decision by referring to the opposition to the accord, not only within his own party, but also that of the leader of the conservative opposition (Ludlow 2011: 37). Enraged by Papandreou's decision, Sarkozy, with Merkel's support, insisted that any such referendum should only be on whether Greece wanted to remain in the Eurozone – for which acceptance of the bail-out accord would be a prerequisite (Spiegel 2014). Within days, Papandreou was forced to resign, in one view 'bundled out of office by Merkel and Sarkozy' (Legrain 2014: 154). Whether Merkel and Sarkozy played any direct role in Papandreou's fall is unproven. Certainly, however, the European Commission president José Manuel Barroso appears to have played a prominent role in engineering the change of leadership in Athens by persuading the leader of the main opposition party to support a 'national unity' government to be led by the Greek former ECB vice-president Lucas Papademos. In the case of Italy, Merkel and Sarkozy made no secret of the fact that they had no confidence in the willingness and capacity of Berlusconi to address the burgeoning crisis of government finances. The

Italian president Giorgio Napolitano was the key actor who orchestrated Berlusconi's replacement, also by a technocrat, the former EU Commissioner Mario Monti, who initially enjoyed the Parliamentary backing of Berlusconi's centre-right as well as Italy's main centre-left political party. But Merkel had allegedly called Napolitano to ask him to do what he could to 'nudge Berlusconi off the stage' (as quoted in Brunnermeier et al. 2016: 246).

The composition of the European Council that met in December 2011 was thus more amenable to Merkel's strategy for Eurozone reform than it had been less than two months previously. The Brussels ambassador of one of the member states commented on her initiative with the observation that 'If that is what Germany wants, that is what we will have to do. That is the way the Union works nowadays' (as quoted in Ludlow 2012a: 9). This summit was preceded by a 'comprehensive' bilateral Franco-German agreement (*Financial Times* 2011e). Merkel made two concessions, accepting that the ESM be created a year earlier than planned and, more importantly, that there would be no more private-sector 'haircuts' of the kind that had been imposed on Greece. Sarkozy made more, however, to her and the overall package that was adopted by the Council was 'the equivalent of a German dream' (Bastasin 2015: 342). The volume of aid that could be dispersed by the ESM was not increased (a proposal that, apart from Germany, only Finland opposed), the ESM was not to be given a banking licence, there was to be no mutualization of debts or eurobonds as had been widely mooted, including by the Council president Van Rompuy, and there was no commitment from the ECB to honour fiscal restraint in the Eurozone by the larger-scale purchase of government bonds (Bastasin 2015: 342; Ludlow 2012a: 24–27; Wolf 2011). Moreover, Sarkozy and the Council agreed to her proposal to adopt a treaty for a Fiscal Compact to strengthen fiscal discipline in the EU – something that 'everybody except the German Chancellor' had been unenthusiastic about if not hostile to less than two months before (Ludlow 2012a: 6). The compact contained balanced budget and debt brake rules that required signatory states to maintain budget deficits below 3 per cent and overall debt levels below 60 per cent of GDP respectively and provided for the imposition of financial sanctions against members failing to meet their obligations under the treaty, whose implementation the Commission would monitor. Fines decided by the Commission under the 'Excessive Deficit Procedure' could be overturned only if they were opposed by a qualified (two-thirds) majority of the Council. While the accord strengthened the enforcement powers of the Commission, it was sidelined in the negotiations that led to its adoption. Commission officials were quoted as being increasingly disillusioned and anxious about the EU's future: 'They can see this train-wreck happening, but they can't do anything about it. They're the Commission and it's all in the hands of Merkel and Sarkozy' (Brussels lobbyist, as quoted in *Financial Times* 2011f).

Owing to the opposition of the British prime minister David Cameron, the Fiscal Compact was not adopted as an EU treaty. Cameron made his acceptance of such a treaty conditional upon the other member states' acquiescence in several demands, particularly that all votes on financial services issues in the

Council should be subject to unanimity, thus giving the British government a formal veto over all legislation affecting the financial sector in the City of London. None of the principal protagonists in the summit – neither Merkel, nor Sarkozy, nor Van Rompuy, nor Cameron himself – appear to have viewed an agreement involving the UK as feasible, in part because if a change in the EU treaties had been proposed, Eurosceptic MPs in Cameron's Conservative Party would have raised demands going far beyond Cameron's. Hence the Fiscal Compact was adopted as an intergovernmental treaty outside the EU.

'Whatever it takes': saving Spain and Italy and ECB monetary policy

The adoption of the Fiscal Compact did not, however, bring about a durable resolution of the Eurozone Crisis. Within the next year, the crisis was to flare up again, to be stabilized – as subsequent events were to prove, only temporarily – by a hitherto unprecedented intervention by the ECB and its new president, Mario Draghi. In this phase of the crisis, Germany did not dominate Eurozone Crisis policy to quite the same extent as it had done during the previous two years, making concessions that, in particular, Chancellor Merkel judged were necessary to avert a collapse of the Eurozone that she feared would have incalculable – negative – consequences. The – political – cost of these concessions was a growth of domestic opposition to the provision of further financial aid to Eurozone debtor states, as manifested by an increase in the number of opponents to such aid in her own Parliamentary group and, in 2013, the foundation of a new political party aiming to abolish the euro, the AfD (see Chapter 2).

The next turning point in the crisis was the adoption of a second bail-out accord for Greece in February 2012. Worth €159bn (see Table 3.1 above), this aid package was more than twice the size of the first. Initiating a pattern that was to become increasingly visible as the Greek crisis unfolded, finance minister Schäuble reputedly argued in favour of allowing – or forcing – Greece to default, while Merkel estimated this step to be too risky (*Financial Times* 2012c). Along with allies in the Netherlands and Finland, Schäuble seems to have reasoned that, with the EFSF/ESM in place, a Greek default would not prove contagious for the rest of the Eurozone (*Financial Times* 2012b). While conceding that the Greek government had repeatedly failed to keep its side of the bargain under which the first bail-out had been agreed, Merkel told the German Parliament that the benefits of additional aid nonetheless outweighed the costs, for 'nobody can estimate what would be the consequences for everybody, also for the people in Germany, of a disorderly default by Greece' (as quoted in *Das Parlament* 2012). She stressed the (severe) conditions attached to the aid and that it was granted under the (constraining) terms of the Fiscal Compact (see above). Nonetheless, there was a significant increase – from five to 23 CDU/CSU and from one to ten FDP MPs – in the number of dissidents in her Parliamentary majority, although the significance of this shift was relativized by the fact that the opposition Social Democrats sided with Merkel and her government on the issue. While they were critical of the Chancellor's 'always too late and too little' crisis policy, they voted with the Chancellor in line with the party's pro-European tradition and because it was in Germany's economic and political interest to save the euro, whose very existence was now at stake (Steinbrück, as quoted in *Das Parlament* 2012). This 'Grand Coalition' on Eurozone issues became the norm in Germany, safeguarding Merkel against any danger of a Parliamentary defeat over her management of the crisis.

Not only financial market turbulence that endangered the survival of the euro, but also the shifting balance of political forces in the Eurozone forced the German government to make some concessions that it had hitherto opposed. In May 2012, Sarkozy was defeated in the French presidential elections by the Socialist candidate, François Hollande. This heralded the at least temporary demise of 'Merkozy', the close coordination of Eurozone Crisis policy between Berlin and Paris (Schoeller 2018). Hollande had insisted in his campaign that France would not ratify the Fiscal Compact if it were not revised to include additional provisions to promote economic growth. After his election victory, a coalition emerged in the European Council between him and the Italian and Spanish prime ministers, although both the latter were ideologically closer to Merkel than to Hollande. As the Eurozone Crisis increasingly threatened to envelop their countries as well, they put growing pressure on her to acquiesce in the provision of more financial aid on easier terms to crisis-stricken euro member states. Having immediately launched some measures to liberalize the Italian labour market, the new Italian prime minister Monti warned Merkel – prophetically, in the light of later election results – that sooner or later Italians would need to see tangible benefits from their sacrifices or else they might 'flee into the arms of populists' (*Financial Times* 2012a). With his impeccable pro-European credentials, Monti had the ideal profile to ask for help from Eurozone creditor countries. As one commentator asked: 'If not him, who?' (Wolf 2012). At the G20 summit at Los Cabos in June 2012, the Italian and US governments ambushed Merkel and tried – unsuccessfully – to persuade her that the ECB should be empowered – without conditionality – to buy the bonds of governments under attack on the financial markets (Ludlow 2012c: 6–7; Spiegel 2014). Some ten days later, at the next European Council meeting, Monti and his Spanish counterpart Mario Rajoy, with Hollande's informal blessing, refused to ratify the 'Compact for Growth and Jobs' that had been negotiated to accommodate Hollande unless Merkel also agreed to authorize the ESM to directly recapitalize banks (Ludlow 2012c: 10–11). Merkel had had to agree to the compact as well as to support the introduction of an EU-wide financial transaction tax to secure the support she needed from the SPD and Greens in the German Parliament for the ratification of the Fiscal Compact.

For the Chancellor, direct bank recapitalization by the ESM represented a greater concession than the French-inspired growth and jobs compact, which, to a large extent, was 'no more than a repackaging of existing commitments and proposals' (Ludlow 2012c: 1). It was scarcely a diplomatic defeat for her, however, as in exchange she successfully insisted that Eurozone members receiving financial aid for their banks fulfil the requirements contained in the Fiscal Compact and – to ensure the usage of this aid could be monitored – that a single supervisory regime for Eurozone banks be created. Similarly, any Eurozone members seeking financial aid from the EFSF/ESM in the interim, such as Spain and Italy, would have to adhere to the Eurozone's fiscal rules and meet conditions laid down in a 'Memorandum of Understanding' – without necessarily being forced, however, to adopt austerity policies comparable to those to which Greece, Ireland and Portugal had had previously to accept or being monitored by the 'Troika' (ECB, IMF and European Commission) responsible for overseeing the implementation of these policies. An in-depth analysis of the summit concluded that there was 'little or no evidence' to confirm the thesis that Chancellor Merkel's 'dominance' of the European Council had been broken (Ludlow 2012c: 27). But, in as far as she had to make some concessions to the coalition of Italy and Spain, her dominance was less marked than in the conflict over the Fiscal Compact.

The June 2012 European Council accord nonetheless did not suffice to quell the resurgent Eurozone Crisis. On the contrary, the yield on Spanish and Italian government bonds and the spread between these and German bonds began to rise again sharply (see Figure 3.1). The hitherto biggest turning point in the Eurozone Crisis came rather with a public pronouncement, in late July, by the ECB president Draghi, that the ECB was ready to 'do whatever it takes' to protect the euro, adding: 'And believe me, it will be enough' (*Financial Times* 2012d). Draghi's speech reportedly followed a 'multiplication of contacts' between the ECB president and 'leaders' in the Eurozone in the preceding days, although he did not forewarn Merkel, Hollande or indeed the ECB Governing Council that he was going to make these specific remarks, which he inserted in handwriting into his prepared text (Brunnermeier et al. 2016: 315, 354; *Le Monde* 2012a; interviews, Berlin, 2018). Not knowing about the announcement in advance enabled the German government to avoid being blamed for it by domestic critics (interviews, Berlin, 2018). Draghi followed up this statement in September 2012 by having the ECB's governing council adopt a new plan (Outright Monetary Transactions – OMT) authorizing the bank to buy government bonds on the secondary market, provided the governments seeking such support accepted 'strict conditions', whose fulfilment it would closely monitor (Draghi, as quoted in *Spiegel Online* 2012c).

The ECB's initiative provoked divergent reactions in Germany. It was opposed by the Bundesbank president Jens Weidmann, who in the end and alone abstained in the ECB governing council's vote on the issue and for whom such measures would be 'tantamount to financing governments by printing banknotes' (as quoted in *Financial Times* 2012h). Prominent German economists, such as the head of the Ifo Institute for Economic Research, Hans-Werner Sinn, shared the Bundesbank's critical attitude and pleaded for the abandonment of the euro by the members that had received financial aid (as quoted in *Le Monde* 2012b). On the other hand, the German representative on the ECB's executive board, Jörg Asmussen, a Social Democrat, supported the policy (*Financial Times* 2012f), as did organized German manufacturing industry. Along with the peak organizations of French, Italian and Spanish business, the Federation of German Industry (*Bundesverband Deutscher Industrie* – BDI) and the Confederation of German Employers' Associations (*Bundesvereinigung der Deutschen Arbeitgeberverbände* – BDA) signed a declaration calling for the ECB to take 'urgent and decisive action' to shore up the euro, including by intervening in secondary bond markets to help Eurozone members being aided by the ESM and having accepted 'restructuring programmes' (as quoted in *Financial Times* 2012g). German business leaders reputedly feared negative consequences for German exports should the Eurozone collapse and Germany be forced to revert to a national currency (*Spiegel-Online* 2012b). Publicly, albeit cautiously, stressing that countries aided by the ECB would have to meet 'preconditions' and carry out reforms, finance minister Schäuble likewise backed the ECB (*Financial Times* 2012e). So too – in a joint statement with Hollande – did Chancellor Merkel.

The most likely explanation for Merkel's stance was the fear that, in the absence of such a pledge by the ECB, the yield on Spanish and Italian government bonds would have continued to rise, the financial capacity of the ESM (to which the two governments would then have had to turn for aid) would not have sufficed to rescue these two countries – much larger than those that had so far been rescued – and, contrary to her conception of Germany's economic and political interests, the Eurozone would have collapsed (*The New York Times* 2012). A Finance Ministry study had concluded in June 2012 that a Eurozone collapse involving the re-introduction of a new German currency would lead to a 10 per cent fall in German GDP and a rise of unemployment to 5 million (*Spiegel Online* 2012a). The conditionality attached to ECB bond buying enabled her – to some extent at least – to protect herself and her government against domestic German criticism of the ECB's initiative. That the politically independent ECB should have assumed a larger share of the heavy lifting to avert a potential collapse of the Eurozone was opportune for Merkel, as it reduced the pressure for an increase in the financial resources of the ESM – to which the German government would have had to agree and for which it would have been correspondingly more difficult for it to avoid political responsibility. The potential domestic political costs of her stance were reduced by the fact that the opposition SPD – while attacking her more ECB-critical coalition partners, the FDP and the CSU – gave her its backing. The SPD chairman, Sigmar Gabriel, argued at this time that government and opposition should seek the largest possible consensus in European policy: 'You don't have to sit together in the government to make a common policy in important questions' (*Süddeutsche Zeitung* 2012).

Draghi's London speech was an 'absolutely decisive moment' in the history of the Eurozone Crisis (interview, Berlin, 2018). It averted the increasingly acute danger of a collapse of the Eurozone and created more time for other reforms to be adopted to stabilize it. Alone, the prospect of ECB intervention succeeded in calming the situation on the bond markets and easing the financial pressure on the Italian and Spanish governments. Bond spreads for Eurozone members – which had grown dramatically in 2011 and the first half of 2012 – thereafter declined rapidly (see Figure 3.1).

Figure 3.1   *Long-term government bond yields, 2007–16*

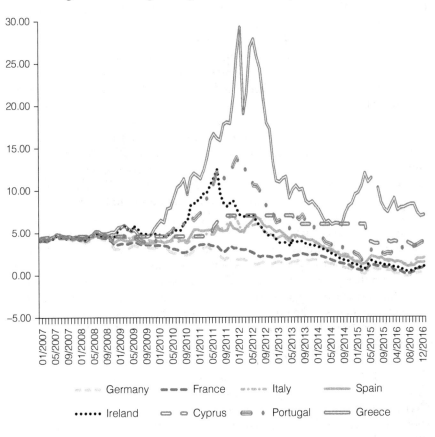

Note: Long-term government bond yields are calculated as monthly averages (non-seasonally adjusted data). They refer to central government bond yields on the secondary market, gross of tax, with a residual maturity of around ten years. The bond or the bonds of the basket have to be replaced regularly to avoid any maturity drift. This definition is used in the convergence criteria of the Economic and Monetary Union for long-term interest rates, as required under Article 121 of the Treaty of Amsterdam and the Protocol on the convergence criteria. Data are presented in raw form. Data is not available for Greece July 2015.

Source: ECB.

The intensity of the Eurozone Crisis was also reduced by two further developments in September 2012. First, pro-European political parties in the Netherlands, normally a close ally of Germany in the Eurozone, fared significantly better than had been anticipated in Dutch Parliamentary elections, easing the pressure on the Dutch government to take a hard line on Eurozone Crisis issues. Second, and more important, the German constitutional court ruled that German participation in the ESM was not incompatible with the German Basic Law. Some 37,000 German citizens had backed the lawsuit, making it the 'biggest protest ever brought before the court' (*Financial Times* 2012i). The jurisprudence of the court had been a continual constraint on German government policy since the outbreak of the Eurozone Crisis (as well as being conceivably a motive that the government could advance to justify a stance which it found in any case politically opportune). Already in 2009, the court, while validating the EU's Lisbon Treaty, had set out limits to the scope of European political integration. This was one of numerous 'yes, but ...' judgments in which the court stopped short of declaring specific EU decisions (or German participation in their implementation) as being unconstitutional, provided certain conditions, particularly the safeguarding of the budgetary powers of the German Parliament, were fulfilled. As, in this case, the Parliament had already given this approval, there was no longer any obstacle to the ESM being launched.

The Cyprus bail-out

Only a fresh financial crisis on the EU's south-eastern periphery, this time in Cyprus, was – briefly – to destabilize the Eurozone between September 2012 and the resurgence of the Greek crisis with the election of a new, radical-leftist government in January 2015. The conflict over the Cyprus bail-out was shaped by widespread perceptions in the Eurozone that Cyprus was a financial haven for wealthy Russian oligarchs. The German government again acquiesced in a bail-out, on the grounds that, in the unanimous view of the ECB, the IMF and the European Commission, even the bankruptcy of so small a member as Cyprus could jeopardize the 'integrity' of the Eurozone (Schäuble as quoted in *Das Parlament* 2013). Anxious, however, to avert the impression that German taxpayers should subsidize wealthy Russians, the government reverted to a stance that it had taken at Deauville in 2010, but had abandoned a year later. Led by the SPD, a cross-party consensus developed to insist that the rescue package had to contain a 'bail-in' of Cypriot banks' creditors (*Financial Times* 2013a; Reuters 2013). On this issue, Berlin refused to blink (Reuters 2013). If Germany was the most fervent advocate of a 'bail-in', however, it was by no means alone. Not only the other 'usual suspects' in Eurozone Crisis conflicts – the Dutch and Finnish governments – but also most other southern European Eurozone members – Italy, Spain and Portugal as well as France – pursued a hard line versus the Cypriot government. Other than in numerous other Eurozone Crisis issues, on this occasion there was 'no north-south divide' (Eurogroup chairman, Dijsselbloem, quoted in *Financial Times* 2013b). As agreed by Merkel in coordination with Hollande and the Council president Van Rompuy, the detailed negotiations themselves were conducted by the heads of the ECB, Draghi, the IMF, Christine Lagarde and the European Commission, Barroso and, above all, Van Rompuy himself (Ludlow 2013a: 6). The rescue package itself, however, reflected the preferences of the German Finance Ministry and the IMF more than those of the Commission (Ludlow 2013a: 4).

European Banking Union

The North–South cleavage absent in the conflict over the Cyprus bail-out was extremely visible, on the other hand, in the negotiations that took place over the creation of the European Banking Union (EBU) between 2012 and 2014. The momentum for the EBU came from the recognition that 'banking nationalism', specifically the strong pressure on national governments to rescue their domestic banks in the case of their imminent collapse in a financial crisis and the explosive increase in government budget deficits that such action provoked, could bankrupt states and destroy the Eurozone. The decision in principle to launch it was taken at the June 2012 Council meeting (see above), at which Merkel insisted on the creation of a single supervisory mechanism, so that the monitoring of the usage of future financial aid made to banks by the ESM would be undertaken by a European rather than national regulatory agencies – which the German government believed would be less likely to supervise their banks effectively. Berlin was backed in this conflict by a small group of northern European member states, notably the Netherlands and Finland within the Eurozone, but faced a bloc of mainly southern member states that had a strong interest in spreading the cost of managing banking crises across the entire Eurozone and that also had the strong support of the ECB and the European Commission (Epstein and Rhodes 2016a: 215, 2016b: 5).

French support for an EBU may have been a 'key change' in the actor constellation on this issue. At the outset of the crisis, the French government had opposed European banking regulation and supervision. Its position changed, however, as the crisis spread from the smaller southern European states to Spain and Italy in 2012 and the height of French banks' exposure to Spanish and Italian bank debt became clear (Epstein and Rhodes 2016b: 5; Krampf 2014: 313). France's loss of its triple *A* rating on government debt in early 2012 may also have expedited this shift by raising the likelihood that France too might require financial aid if the crisis were to worsen. There was no joint Franco-German approach to EBU – whereby the divergence between the two states was heightened by the transition in the French presidency in May 2012 from Sarkozy to the Socialist Hollande, who had criticized Sarkozy's 'subservience' to Germany in his campaign and pledged to strike a tougher stance vis-à-vis Merkel (Schild 2017b). At his first (informal) European Council meeting just after his election, Hollande pleaded in favour of an EBU (Ludlow 2012b: 10). The Commission had already proposed EU directives on bank resolution and deposit insurance before the June 2012 Council meeting at which the decision in favour of EBU was taken and the ECB president Draghi and the German representative on the ECB executive board, Asmussen, had also advocated a Europeanization of banking supervision and resolution (Ludlow 2012b: 7).

Roughly half of the process of building the institutions of a 'complete' EBU had arguably been accomplished by 2016 (Wolff 2016); banking supervision had been fully Europeanized. In contrast, however, banking resolution and its funding was 'only half-way done', although scheduled to be completed by 2024, and bank deposit insurance remained national, with no agreement having been reached on a European scheme (Wolff 2016). Verdicts as to who 'won' the conflict over EBU and the strength of the German imprint on its provisions diverge widely. Thus, Howarth and Quaglia (2016) conclude that, at German insistence, only an EBU 'light' was adopted, validating an intergovernmentalist interpretation of the conflict. Schild argues that, because for an EBU German financial support was indispensable, Berlin occupied a 'strong bargaining position' that enabled it to 'keep the upper hand on a number of issues with strong distributive implications', while nonetheless making some 'significant concessions' (Schild 2017b: 4, 11–12). In a more radical judgment, Munchau (*Financial Times* 2013f) claims that Germany got an 'all-for-nothing deal' and won a – for the EU – thoroughly atypical 'game, set and match victory'. Epstein and Rhodes argue, in contrast and in neo-functionalist terms, that the EBU represents 'truly radical change' and that, despite securing 'some concessions along the way', the German government was outflanked and defeated by a 'coalition of supranational institutions, member state governments and private actors in the banking sector' (Epstein and Rhodes 2016b: 2, 18).

In assessing to what extent Germany dominated and shaped the conflict over EBU, it is important not only to determine how far the decisions taken corresponded to 'German' preferences or interests, but also to consider *which* German actors' preferences and interests should provide the base-line for such an analysis and to what extent (and why) these preferences evolved as the Eurozone Crisis unfolded. Owing not least to the relatively high horizontal and vertical fragmentation of the German political system, the coordination of German European policy is notoriously underdeveloped, so that there may be no single, united German position on EU issues (Bulmer and Paterson 1987). This was the case in the conflict over EBU as on other issues related to the Eurozone Crisis. Thus, for the Bundesbank, for example, a bastion of a hard-line Ordoliberalism, which opposed a transfer of any powers relating to the financial sector from the national to the EU level, as well as any financial transfers from 'creditor' to 'debtor' states in the Eurozone, the agreements reached on EBU certainly represented a defeat, as they did also for German savings banks. But they were not a defeat for Chancellor Merkel, by virtue of her office the authoritative interpreter of German European policy preferences and interests. By 2012, compared with the beginning of the crisis, Merkel's position had shifted 'significantly' (Ludlow 2012d: 50). One argument is that she was forced to 'recalculate' German preferences by the increasingly perilous situation in Spain and Italy, two Eurozone members to which, like their French counterparts, German banks were heavily exposed and whose financial collapse would also have jeopardized the euro's survival, making them thus 'too big to fail' (Krampf 2014: 313). This process had begun, however, earlier. In summer 2011, with her European policy advisers, Merkel had settled on a revised crisis strategy. She accepted that the centralization or supra-nationalization of economic policies – the ideal solution to the Eurozone's ills – was politically infeasible. In lieu of this, in exchange for the provision of greater financial aid to crisis-stricken members of the Eurozone, rules would have to be adopted and implemented to bring about a closer coordination of member states' policies (Walker 2013). It was evident already at the extraordinary European Council meeting in May 2012 that Merkel was prepared to accept closer European financial-political integration on these terms (Ludlow 2012b: 11–12). Moreover, it was the Chancellor herself who, at the subsequent June summit, as a quid pro quo for empowering the ESM to directly recapitalize banks, insisted on the Europeanization of banking supervision, a trade-off to which Schäuble had also given his blessing in a meeting shortly before the summit (*Financial Times* 2013e; Schild 2017b: 5). The main concession Merkel made at this summit was to acquiesce in aid to recapitalize Spanish banks without requiring the Spanish government to implement an austerity programme comparable to those that had been demanded of the governments of the Eurozone members that had previously received financial aid.

The agreement ultimately reached over EBU in the Council was preceded by intensive bilateral Franco-German negotiations (*Financial Times* 2013d; *Le Monde* 2013a, 2013c, 2013d). Merkel did not try to slow down the adoption of the Single Resolution Mechanism (SRM) and the Single Resolution Fund (SRF) (Ludlow 2013b: 33). Hollande and she pushed together for their adoption before the end of the period of the European Parliament ending in 2014. Replicating what had happened with the Maastricht Treaty, France secured an EBU, but largely on German terms. The government in Berlin conceded the gradual mutualization of a Single Resolution fund over a decade, but successfully insisted that bank shareholders and creditors be 'bailed in' to cover resolution costs before tapping the European fund, that the proportion of the costs to be borne by the latter be limited to no more than 5 per cent and that the board authorized to resolve banks be comprised of national rather than EU officials (*Le Monde* 2013b; Schild 2017b: 7–8). Both the SRM and the ESM were created as intergovernmental organizations to assuage Germany, which, along with France and Italy, secured a right of veto over decisions by the ESM to grant financial aid – which in any case, under the treaty terms, would be 'subject to strict conditionality', specified in a memorandum of understanding agreed between the ESM and the recipient country. By 2018, thanks primarily to the German government's opposition, the third pillar of the EBU, a joint deposit insurance fund, had still not been adopted (Schild 2017b: 8–9).

Although the adoption of the EBU undoubtedly represented a defeat for the Bundesbank and the champions of Ordoliberal economic orthodoxy in Germany, it thus bore a very strong imprint of the German government, as incarnated by Chancellor Merkel. Certainly, the mutating Eurozone Crisis brought about changes in its preferences and led to its acquiescence in numerous measures that, when the crisis first broke, it preferred or would have preferred to avoid, but that led to closer European political integration. However, this trend – which in itself vindicates a 'neo-functionalist' reading of the crisis and its impact – was channelled along a path that was closely guided and tightly constrained by Germany. To what extent it succeeds in maintaining control over the EBU would be revealed in the application and implementation of the policy instruments created since 2010. In the first banking crisis to develop since the entry into force of the EBU, the Italian government opted for a taxpayer-financed national bail-out of one of the country's largest banks, preferring to avoid the political backlash it would likely have provoked if it had had recourse to the provisions of the EBU and had consequently had to 'bail-in' thousands of the bank's small-scale savers (*Le Monde* 2017a).

The third Greek bail-out

The erstwhile final episode of the Eurozone Crisis was played out in the first half of 2015, following the victory in Greek elections in January 2015 of the radical-leftist party, Syriza, which, like the majority of Greeks, wanted to keep Greece in the Eurozone, but was fiercely opposed to a continuation of the austerity policies that preceding governments had had to follow as a condition of financial aid since 2010. These policies had not brought about an economic recovery in Greece. On the contrary, since 2010, unemployment had doubled, poverty had become much more widespread and public financial deficits and debt were still very high (see Tables 3.3, 3.4 and 3.5). The failure of austerity policies in Greece had fostered political radicalization and polarization, manifested not only in the rapid rise of Syriza, but also, to a lesser extent, of the extreme-right.

Table 3.3   *Unemployment rate (unemployed as % of the total active population)*

Country	2008	2009	2010	2011	2012	2013	2014	2015
Austria	4.1	5.3	4.8	4.6	4.9	5.4	5.6	5.7
Belgium	7.0	7.9	8.3	7.2	7.6	8.4	8.5	8.5
Cyprus	3.7	5.4	6.3	7.9	11.9	15.9	16.1	15.0
Estonia	5.5	13.5	16.7	12.3	10.0	8.6	7.4	6.2
Finland	6.4	8.2	8.4	7.8	7.7	8.2	8.7	9.4
France	7.4	9.1	9.3	9.2	9.8	10.3	10.3	10.4
Germany	7.4	7.6	7.0	5.8	5.4	5.2	5.0	4.6
Greece	7.8	9.6	12.7	17.9	24.5	27.5	26.5	24.9
Ireland	6.4	12.0	13.9	14.7	14.7	13.1	11.3	9.4
Italy	6.7	7.7	8.4	8.4	10.7	12.1	12.7	11.9
Latvia	7.7	17.5	19.5	16.2	15.0	11.9	10.8	9.9
Lithuania	5.8	13.8	17.8	15.4	13.4	11.8	10.7	9.1
Luxembourg	4.9	5.1	4.6	4.8	5.1	5.9	6.0	6.5
Malta	6.0	6.9	6.9	6.4	6.3	6.4	5.8	5.4
Netherlands	3.7	4.4	5.0	5.0	5.8	7.3	7.4	6.9
Portugal	8.8	10.7	12.0	12.9	15.8	16.4	14.1	12.6
Slovakia	9.6	12.1	14.5	13.7	14.0	14.2	13.2	11.5
Slovenia	4.4	5.9	7.3	8.2	8.9	10.1	9.7	9.0
Spain	11.3	17.9	19.9	21.4	24.8	26.1	24.5	22.1
Euro area	7.6	9.6	10.2	10.2	11.4	12.0	11.6	10.9

Source: author's compilation using data from the European Commission, AMECO database.

Table 3.4   *Government deficit (% of GDP at current prices) net lending (+) or net borrowing (-)*

Country	2008	2009	2010	2011	2012	2013	2014	2015
Austria	−1.5	−5.4	−4.5	−2.6	−2.2	−1.4	−2.7	−1.0
Belgium	−1.1	−5.4	−4.0	−4.1	−4.2	−3.0	−3.1	−2.5
Cyprus	0.9	−5.4	−4.7	−5.7	−5.8	−4.9	−8.8	−1.1
Estonia	−2.7	−2.2	0.2	1.2	−0.3	−0.2	0.7	0.1
Finland	4.2	−2.5	−2.6	−1.0	−2.2	−2.6	−3.2	−2.7
France	−3.2	−7.2	−6.8	−5.1	−4.8	−4.0	−4.0	−3.5
Germany	−0.2	−3.2	−4.2	−1.0	0.0	−0.2	0.3	0.7
Greece	−10.2	−15.1	−11.2	−10.3	−8.8	−13.2	−3.6	−7.5
Ireland	−7.0	−13.8	−32.1	−12.6	−8.0	−5.7	−3.7	−1.9
Italy	−2.7	−5.3	−4.2	−3.7	−2.9	−2.7	−3.0	−2.6
Latvia	−4.1	−9.1	−8.5	−3.4	−0.8	−0.9	−1.6	−1.3
Lithuania	−3.1	−9.1	−6.9	−8.9	−3.1	−2.6	−0.7	−0.2
Luxembourg	3.4	−0.7	−0.7	0.5	0.3	1.0	1.5	1.6
Malta	−4.2	−3.3	−3.2	−2.6	−3.7	−2.6	−2.0	−1.3
Netherlands	0.2	−5.4	−5.0	−4.3	−3.9	−2.4	−2.3	−1.9
Portugal	−3.8	−9.8	−11.2	−7.4	−5.7	−4.8	−7.2	−4.4
Slovakia	−2.4	−7.8	−7.5	−4.3	−4.3	−2.7	−2.7	−2.7
Slovenia	−1.4	−5.9	−5.6	−6.7	−4.1	−15.0	−5.0	−2.7
Spain	−4.4	−11.0	−9.4	−9.6	−10.5	−7.0	−6.0	−5.1
Euro area	−2.2	−6.3	−6.2	−4.2	−3.6	−3.0	−2.6	−2.1

Source: author's compilation using data from the European Commission, AMECO database.

The inevitable confrontation between the new Greek government and its creditors was accelerated by the fact that the second Greek bail-out was due to expire at the end of February 2015 and the terms of any further financial aid to Greece had to be negotiated afresh. The prospectively high costs of non-agreement over a new rescue package for Greece were underlined by the ECB's declaration that in this scenario it would no longer act as a lender of last resort to Greek banks. Already, before Syriza's election victory, the German government had let it be known that, with the new institutions, such as ESM, that had been created since 2010, the risk of contagion from a Greek exit from the Eurozone could be contained and that the other Eurozone members could abandon Greece if a new government made 'unacceptable demands' (*Financial Times* 2015a, 2015b; Kalaitzake 2017: 19).

Table 3.5   *General government consolidated gross debt (% of GDP at current prices)*

Country	2008	2009	2010	2011	2012	2013	2014	2015
Austria	68.5	79.7	82.4	82.2	82.0	81.3	84.4	85.5
Belgium	92.5	99.6	99.7	102.3	104.1	105.4	106.5	105.8
Cyprus	44.7	53.4	55.8	65.2	79.3	102.2	107.1	107.5
Estonia	4.5	7.0	6.6	5.9	9.7	10.2	10.7	10.1
Finland	32.7	41.7	47.1	48.5	53.9	56.5	60.2	63.5
France	68.1	79.0	81.7	85.2	89.5	92.3	95.3	96.2
Germany	64.9	72.4	81.0	78.3	79.9	77.5	74.9	71.2
Greece	109.4	126.7	146.2	172.1	159.6	177.4	179.7	177.4
Ireland	42.4	61.7	86.3	109.6	119.5	119.5	105.2	78.6
Italy	102.4	112.5	115.4	116.5	123.3	129.0	131.9	132.3
Latvia	18.7	36.6	47.4	42.8	41.3	39.0	40.7	36.3
Lithuania	14.6	29.0	36.2	37.2	39.8	38.7	40.5	42.7
Luxembourg	15.1	16.0	19.9	18.8	21.8	23.5	22.7	22.1
Malta	62.7	67.8	67.6	70.4	68.0	68.7	64.3	60.8
Netherlands	54.5	56.5	59.0	61.7	66.4	67.7	67.9	65.1
Portugal	71.7	83.6	96.2	111.4	126.2	129.0	130.6	129.0
Slovakia	28.1	35.9	40.7	43.2	52.2	54.7	53.6	52.5
Slovenia	21.8	34.6	38.4	46.6	53.9	71.0	80.9	83.1
Spain	39.4	52.7	60.1	69.5	85.7	95.4	100.4	99.8
Euro area	68.5	78.3	84.0	86.7	91.4	93.7	94.4	92.6

Source: author's compilation using data from the European Commission, AMECO database.

The vice-chancellor and head of the SPD, Gabriel, stressed Germany was not 'vulnerable to blackmail' and any new Greek government would 'have to stick to the agreements made by its predecessor' (as quoted in *The New York Times* 2015a). While the SPD still wanted to keep Greece in the Eurozone, however, finance minister Schäuble took a tougher line in talks in February over a temporary extension of the second bail-out, suggesting he was willing to contemplate a 'Grexit' if the new government did not stick to the bail-out conditions (Galbraith 2016: 64–65). As in the previous Greek bail-out talks, the French government's stance was more accommodating. Hollande stressed that the engagements made by previous governments in Athens would have to be respected (as quoted in *The New York Times* 2015a). But the French finance minister Michel Sapin dismissed the prospect of a 'Grexit', arguing that while Greece would have to carry out more reforms, it had already carried out a lot and 'we will have to show solidarity in the Eurozone' (as quoted in *Financial Times* 2015c).

A first meeting between the new Greek finance minister, Yanis Varoufakis, and the president of the Eurogroup (of finance ministers of Eurozone member states), the Dutch minister, Jeroen Dijsselbloem, went extremely badly. Dijsselbloem reputedly responded to Varoufakis's proposal to 'rethink the whole [austerity] programme' by saying that if Greece were to insist on this, the ECB would close down Greek banks (Varoufakis 2016). Greece and the other Eurozone members nonetheless reached an agreement providing for an extension of the existing bail-out arrangements until the end of June 2015, including the maintenance of financial support for the Greek banking system by the ECB, a week before these would have expired. This interim accord gave the government some flexibility to change the mixture of existing austerity policies, but committed it to pursue the same budget deficit targets to which its predecessors had agreed and to honour Greece's financial obligations to its creditors, who in turn conceded some curtailment of the 'intrusive, overbearing presence of troika bureaucrats in the Athens ministries' (Galbraith 2016: 11). The Eurogroup (finance ministers') meeting at which the accord was reached was preceded by 'last-minute preparatory talks' between Varoufakis and Schäuble (*The Guardian* 2015). According to the Greek side, the accord was facilitated by a split in the German government, in which Merkel arbitrated a conflict between the more hard-line Schäuble and her smaller Social Democratic coalition partner in the latter's – meaning also in Greece's – favour (Galbraith 2016: 64–65; Varoufakis 2017: 274–277).

Five issues put the Syriza government at loggerheads with its creditors, first and foremost the German government, as negotiations over a new bail-out deal unfolded over the following five months: the degree of fiscal austerity (in practice, how big a budget surplus the government should pursue), pensions, labour market regulation (in practice, a weakening of trade unions and wage reductions), privatization and debt relief or restructuring. On the latter issue, the government could count on the support of one member of the troika, the IMF, which had meanwhile determined that Greece's debt burden was unsustainable (Varoufakis 2017: 441, 483). The other Eurozone members refused, however, to broach this issue before a new bail-out agreement had been reached. According to Varoufakis (2016), his counterparts in the Eurogroup also refused to discuss any substantive changes in, or easing of, the conditions of financial aid to Greece. Among the other Eurozone members, attitudes towards the new government in Athens, if anything, hardened over time. Leading German Social Democrats accused it of not wanting to negotiate seriously and Greek ministers of using their time instead to 'give interviews and lectures' (SPD Parliamentary Group chairman Thomas Oppermann, as quoted in *Das Parlament* 2015a).

Varoufakis's strategy seems to have been to 'disobey the edicts of Brussels and Frankfurt', to 'not swerve' and to play for time (*Financial Times* 2016a). He thought Greece's creditors were bluffing. Perceiving divergences of attitude between Merkel and her finance minister, he did not think that the German Chancellor would run the risk of expelling Greece from the Eurozone, although she 'would *never* yield *until she had to*' (Varoufakis 2017: 347, 131, 274–275, 413, 452; author's own emphasis). Even if Greece were to default on all its debts, ECB president Draghi, he believed, would 'never let exit happen. The creditors would have come back to the negotiating table' (Varoufakis, as quoted in *Financial Times* 2016a). Although the ECB, as in February, had threatened to cut off the supply of credit to Greek banks, Varoufakis counted on the ECB's commitment to preserve the Eurozone (and indirectly itself) to facilitate an accord acceptable to his government in the end. For the case that, contrary to his expectations, Greece was indeed ejected from the Eurozone, he had a group of advisers devise a scheme to create a 'parallel payments system', which would have formed the basis of a new Greek currency (Varoufakis 2017: 95–97). Other observers speculated that geopolitical considerations – not to risk economic collapse, political destabilization and heightened Russian influence in a member state located in a politically highly volatile neighbourhood – might dissuade the rest of the Eurozone from running the risk of 'Grexit' (Barber 2015; *The New York Times* 2015b, 2015c). Such considerations allegedly motivated warnings by US president Obama and his Treasury secretary to French and German leaders not to 'let Greece go' (*Politico* 2015; interview, Berlin, 2018).

The negotiations reached a first climax when, angered and frustrated by what he described as other Eurozone members' 'blackmail and ultimatums' (*Politico* 2015), the Greek prime minister Alexander Tsipras announced that the government would stage a popular referendum and ask Greek citizens to reject the bail-out terms on offer. He conceived the referendum as an 'additional tool' in the negotiating process, designed to persuade Greece's creditors to offer it a less punitive bail-out deal (as quoted in *Le Monde* 2014a). He rejected Hollande's pleas to call the referendum off (Davet and Lhomme 2016b: 510). Other Eurozone members declined Tsipras's request for a temporary extension of the existing bail-out programme, but neither Merkel nor Eurogroup chairman Dijsselbloem precluded further negotiations after the referendum had taken place (Merkel as quoted in *Das Parlament* 2015b). Asked by Tsipras whether, in the event of a 'no' vote in the referendum, Merkel and Draghi would come back and offer the Greek government an accord that included 'our minimum demands of debt relief and an end to self-reinforcing austerity', Varoufakis said that there was a '100 per cent probability' of their doing so '*if they acted rationally*', but that the 'more sensible probability' was 'around fifty-fifty' (Varoufakis 2017: 458; author's own emphasis). However, he thought the risk was worth taking, as a 'new bail-out would be worse than Grexit, however painful Grexit might be' (Varoufakis 2017: 458).

The referendum yielded a strong (61 per cent) majority in favour of the government's stance. It quickly became clear, however, that, despite this result, Tsipras and a majority in his cabinet did not want to escalate the conflict and risk Greece's expulsion from the Eurozone. During the previous few months, Varoufakis, who had not been a member of Syriza before being appointed finance minister and, by his own confession, did not have much 'clout' in the party, had become increasingly isolated within the government (Varoufakis 2017: 471; 421–427). Most of his cabinet colleagues proved to be unwilling to renege on Greek debt repayments to try to secure debt relief. Tsipras judged that his finance minister's proposals to create a new currency in the event of an involuntary Grexit – that Varoufakis described as a 'well-planned deterrent' – were 'so vague, it wasn't worth talking about' (*The Guardian* 2017; Varoufakis 2017: 473). According to Varoufakis, the prime minister argued that 'to get something you have to give something'; so he committed Greece to run a budget surplus amounting to 3.5 per cent of Greek GDP in exchange for (the promise of) debt relief (later), while, for Varoufakis, the pursuit of this kind of austerity policy was self-defeating and would make it impossible for Greece to repay its debt (*Le Monde* 2017c). The day after the referendum, realizing in his account that the government was resolved to capitulate in the conflict, the controversial finance minister resigned (Varoufakis 2017: 471–472).

Neither the referendum result nor Varoufakis's political demise brought about any softening of the bargaining position of the other Eurozone member states. On the contrary, the German government's stance hardened. The 'most blistering German condemnation' of Tsipras's referendum decision actually came from SPD leader and vice-chancellor Gabriel, who attacked the Greek PM for having 'pulled down the last bridges over which Europe could have moved to a compromise' (as quoted in *Financial Times* 2015f). He warned that to grant Greece additional financial aid that was not attached to tough conditions would create a precedent that other Eurozone members would be tempted to emulate and culminate in the emergence of an unlimited 'transfer union' that would overwhelm the Eurozone and play into the hands of extreme-right-wing nationalist movements (as quoted in *Das Parlament* 2015b: 6). With both Merkel's and Gabriel's acquiescence, Schäuble proposed following the referendum that Greece be 'offered swift negotiations on a time-out from the Eurozone' and that, to help pay off its debt, it should be required to privatize assets worth €50bn that would be placed in a trust fund located in Luxembourg and controlled by the ESM (Traynor 2015).

This was not the first time that Schäuble had proposed that Greece leave or be expelled from the Eurozone – he had done so, but not publicly, already in 2011 and 2012 (Blustein 2017: 247, 329, 436–437; Papaconstantinou 2016: 219; Varoufakis 2017: 338). Participants in negotiations over financial aid for Greece believe he had concluded that Greece 'had to go' even before Syriza's election victory (Traynor 2015). However, the German finance minister's initiative opened up fissures in the hitherto united front of the other Eurozone members, revealing two rough blocs. By far the larger of the two comprised Germany, all the other northern European members, and the other southern European members that had been bailed out in exchange for implementing austerity programmes and had begun to recover economically. None of the latter governments, least of all the Spanish, which was facing rising radical-leftist opposition, welcomed the prospect of being retrospectively discredited for having accepted more onerous aid conditions than the Greek government was holding out for. Apart from Cyprus, the much smaller bloc, with which the European Commission aligned itself, contained Italy, whose prime minister Matteo Renzi reputedly regarded Schäuble's initiative as an 'untenable exercise in German humiliation of Greece' (Traynor 2015), and, most significantly, France.

The French and German governments had closely coordinated their positions on the 'Grexit' crisis and – up until Tsipras's decision to call a referendum – had shared 'more or less the same line' (*Le Monde* 2015n). According to Varoufakis, neither Hollande nor Sapin had ever opposed Schäuble or made the 'slightest proposition' in the conflict – they had been 'mere spectators' (*Libération* 2017). Now, while Merkel stated that she opposed a 'compromise at any price', Hollande declared his opposition to any 'brutal rupture' within the Eurozone and his resolve to facilitate a solution to the conflict that would keep Greece in the Eurozone (*Le Monde* 2015n). With this goal, the French president tried to persuade Tsipras to moderate his resistance to continued austerity. In part at least, Hollande's stance was motivated by domestic-political considerations: to persuade Tsipras and Syriza to be 'more reasonable' and thus to deradicalize them, while keeping Greece in the Eurozone, served to counter the appeal of both the radical-left and right in France (Davet and Lhomme 2016: 503). The French president's pitch to Tsipras was 'to help me to help you' strike a deal enabling Greece to stay in the Eurozone (Davet and Lhomme 2016b: 504; Blustein 2017: 433). He delegated a team of ten French civil servants to advise the Greek government and help it devise proposals that Germany and its allies in the Eurozone could accept (Blustein 2017: 436; Davet and Lhomme 2016b: 508–509). At the same time, domestic-political considerations were pulling Merkel in the opposite direction to Hollande. Already in February 2015, some 29 backbenchers in her CDU/CSU Parliamentary group had rebelled against a temporary extension of the Greek bail-out programme. Meanwhile, the number of prospective rebels had grown to 'well over 100' (*Spiegel Online* 2015b). If, in her Grand Coalition government, a rebellion of this magnitude would not have threatened her Parliamentary majority, it would nonetheless have damaged her political authority.

The final act in the third Greek bail-out drama was played out in a European Council summit a week after the referendum. A Eurogroup meeting the day before ended in failure, with Schäuble's Grexit proposal still on the table (Traynor 2015). After a plenary session lasting three hours, the Council president, Donald Tusk, convened a smaller meeting comprising Tsipras, Merkel, Hollande and himself in which Hollande and he mediated between the Greek and German leaders (Traynor 2015): for more than ten hours, 'most of the leaders of Europe were mere bystanders to history in the making. They dined. They sipped white wine, made small talk, and napped ... "We'd never seen anything like this," one person said. "Three or four people meeting separately and making decisions, and everyone else with nothing to do, some of them dozing"' (Traynor 2015). Tusk feared that a deal would not be reached because Merkel and Tsipras were 'more concerned about not returning home looking like losers' (Traynor 2015). The last sticking point on which negotiations threatened to fail related to the use and location of the trust fund to be built up by the privatization of state-owned Greek enterprises. An agreement was reached when Merkel agreed that the fund could be located in Athens rather than Luxembourg and that €12.5bn rather than €10bn of the notional €50bn revenues of privatization could be invested in Greece rather than used to pay off Greek debt and aid Greek banks (Traynor 2015). The accord was generally deemed to be tougher than the one on offer when Tsipras walked out of the bail-out negotiations and called the referendum. Tsipras later explained his acceptance of the bail-out terms by saying that his government had been 'put in a corner from which there was no way out. I had no choice' (as quoted in *Financial Times* 2018b). Although his party split over the final accord, with one-sixth of his MPs leaving to form a new, more left-wing political movement, he secured a Parliamentary majority with opposition support and won new elections that he called in September 2015 with an only slightly reduced number of seats. In Berlin, 60, or about one-fifth of the German Chancellor's MPs – by far the highest number since the debut of the Eurozone Crisis – voted against the deal, but, with proportionately wider support for the deal in the SPD Parliamentary group, the accord was ratified with a majority of almost four to one.

Conclusion

The Eurozone Crisis did not lead to European monetary-political disintegration – or at least it had not done so by 2018. It had three more member states than at the outset of the crisis. Vis-à-vis the member states, the powers of the supranational organs concerned with monetary and fiscal policy, the ECB and the European Commission, had been strengthened rather than weakened, even if this shift had taken place principally at the behest of the 'creditor' states and the extent to which *in practice* the Commission could police the fiscal policy behaviour of Eurozone members was uncertain (see final paragraph below). Since 2009, a new organization, the ESM, had been created to bail out crisis-stricken members, banking supervision had been shifted from the member states to the ECB, a Eurozone-wide resolution board and fund had been set up to wind up bankrupt banks, and a comprehensive set of new rules had been adopted to prevent member states running too high government budget deficits. In all (horizontal, vertical and sectoral) dimensions, the EU was politically more highly integrated than it had been when the crisis broke in 2009.

The EU's capacity to resist the threat of monetary- and fiscal-political disintegration over this period is striking. The crisis provoked an unprecedented process of mass politicization; how it was managed became a politically highly salient issue, politically bitterly contested and thus politically highly polarizing in many member states. It nonetheless defied the 'downward pressure on the level and scope of integration' that, other things being equal, post-functionalist theorists would have expected to prevail. It was also hard to reconcile with the predominant understandings of the nature of the EU policy process – which stress the prevalence of rules and norms of consensual decision-making and the EU's consequently high propensity to gridlock, stalemate and minimalist solutions (see, for example, Scharpf 1988). The magnitude of the material stakes involved in the successive 'sub-crises' that confronted the EU from 2009 onwards far exceeded that involved in any previous crisis. The distributional conflicts between 'creditor' and 'debtor' states were correspondingly extremely intense. In the 'debtor' states, the austerity policies that governments were forced to follow as a condition for the receipt of financial aid were deeply unpopular. Among the Eurozone member governments that were forced to submit to fiscal austerity, none avoided a major drop in electoral support and almost all were defeated in the first following elections. The unpopularity of austerity imposed by creditors in Cyprus forced the incumbent Communist president Christofias not to run again for the office in 2013. In Ireland, the governing Fianna Fail suffered a catastrophic defeat, its share of the vote collapsing from 42 to 17 per cent, at elections in 2011. Its successor in government, Fine Gael, which was bound by the terms of the Irish bail-out accord, remained in office after elections in 2016, but only as a minority government and after its voting share had fallen from 36 to 25.5 per cent. In Portugal, at the first elections after the bail-out accord reached in 2011, the then governing Socialist party's vote fell from over 38 to 28 per cent. The Socialist administration was succeeded by a mainstream right-wing government that continued to apply the terms of the bail-out accord – then also fell at the next elections in 2016, when the voting share of the governing party declined from 50.2 to 38.6 per cent. In Greece, the mainstream left-wing Pasok, whose election victory in 2009 immediately preceded the crisis, was literally decimated, after being forced to impose severe austerity policies, at the next elections in 2012. Its successor, the mainstream right-wing New Democracy Party, survived new elections within six weeks of first returning to office in 2012, before losing to the radical left-wing Syriza in 2015. Syriza was re-elected in snap elections called by Tsipras over the terms of the bail-out accord negotiated in July 2015, but these took place barely eight months after Syriza's initial election victory. In sum, governing parties avoided being (severely) punished electorally by their citizens for their complicity in imposing austerity policies only when they were fresh in office and the opposition parties had still not recovered from their prior performance of the same role.

While governing parties in the 'debtor' states on the south-eastern, southern and western peripheries of the Eurozone faced an electoral backlash, the bail-out accords were – to varying degrees – unpopular in the 'creditor' states. In several of these, support for the governing parties declined and that for (sometimes new) 'anti-EU' or 'anti-euro' parties burgeoned – for example, in Austria (Freedom Party), the Netherlands (Freedom Party), Finland (True Finns), and, to a lesser extent at first, in Germany (the AfD). In those 'creditor' countries where Parliamentary majorities had to approve bail-out agreements, these occasionally looked to be in jeopardy, but were ultimately always found.

If political parties are vote-maximizers, as is assumed, for example, in rational-choice theories of political behaviour, and if austerity measures were unpopular in the 'debtor' states and bail-outs unpopular in the 'creditor' states, why, at the successive high points of the Eurozone Crisis, were agreements always found and gridlock – and the partial or complete collapse of the Eurozone – always averted, even if this apparently often involved governments committing almost certain political suicide? The most plausible answer to this question is that both 'debtor' and 'creditor' groups of Eurozone member states calculated – in the last analysis – that the (financial, economic and political) costs of agreement were still lower than those of non-agreement. In this scenario, the ECB would most likely have cut off the provision of credit to banks in the 'debtor' states, which would then have faced sudden financial collapse and a contraction of the economy and rise of unemployment significantly greater than that associated with the austerity policies they were compelled to adopt in exchange for being bailed out. Not even the radical-leftist Syriza government in Greece was prepared in the end to assume this risk, not least perhaps because, despite the strength and intensity of popular opposition to austerity, a large majority of Greeks – 76 per cent of respondents 'at any cost', for example, in a survey conducted in January 2015 – preferred to keep the euro rather than returning to a national currency (Bloomberg 2015).

For the 'creditor' states, the key issue was how high the risk was that the withdrawal or ejection of a member state from the Eurozone would provoke a contagion effect leading to the exit of additional members or the collapse of the Eurozone as a whole. The dilemma confronting their governments is neatly captured in a reported exchange between Chancellor Merkel and the German member of the ECB executive board, Asmussen, and the Bundesbank president, Weidmann, during the negotiations over the second Greek bail-out in 2012. Told by both that if Greece were to exit the Eurozone, Cyprus would probably also leave, Merkel is reputed to have asked them how many other 'dominoes' would fall. When Asmussen replied that there was 'no way of knowing', Merkel said that that was 'too uncertain' (Walker 2013). For Germany, for example, the financial cost of a complete collapse of the Eurozone could have been very high. At the height of the crisis in 2012, according to the calculations of one economic research institute, Germany's 'exposure' in such a scenario – how much it would cost if debts owing to Germany could not be repaid – amounted to some €771bn (Ifo-Institut 2012). After large-scale lending to governments and banks on the Eurozone periphery, banks in both Germany and France would have sustained very heavy losses in the case of a Eurozone collapse. As the crisis broke in 2010, the exposure of German and French banks to their counterparts in Greece, Spain, Portugal and Ireland stood at €127.6bn and €75.7bn respectively (Legrain 2014: 70). To a significant extent, when the German and French governments bailed out these countries in the Eurozone Crisis, they were, indirectly and surreptitiously, bailing out their own banks, to which they had already given considerable, but unpopular, financial aid earlier in the GFC (Legrain 2014: 79–80; Varoufakis as quoted in *Libération* 2017; Varoufakis 2017: 21–27). Indeed, of €216bn aid granted to Greece in the first and second bail-outs, less than 5 per cent reached the Greek fiscal budget, while by far the biggest part went to 'existing creditors in the form of debt repayments and interest payments' (Rocholl and Stahmer 2016: 4, 19). The macro-economic fallout from a Eurozone collapse could have also have been very severe. With the Finance Ministry foreseeing a deep economic recession and a rise of German unemployment to over 5 million in the first year after a hypothetical re-introduction of a new German currency (see above), finance minister Schäuble judged that, compared with co-financing bail-outs, the collapse of the Eurozone would have been much more expensive for Germany (as quoted in *Financial Times* 2013c). All in all, Germany was 'too closely extricated' in the euro and the Eurozone and its crisis to be able to 'get out of it again' (interview, Berlin, 2018).

The history of the Eurozone Crisis up to 2018 thus bore out – to some extent at least – the expectations of 'optimistic' (neo-functionalist, transactionalist and liberal intergovernmentalist) theorists that the impact of the levels of financial and economic interdependence forged by the sharing of a single currency would outweigh that of the centrifugal forces of domestic politics and generate even more powerful centripetal pressures in favour of (albeit asymmetrical) compromise. This is not to say, however, that governments' responses to the Eurozone Crisis were shaped only, or perhaps even primarily, by financial motives. To the financial and economic costs of a Eurozone collapse would have come the – still much less quantifiable – political costs. For Germany, the political stakes were always more important than the financial ones (interview, Berlin, 2018). The collapse of the Eurozone – the EU's most iconic integration project – would almost certainly have had a severely destabilizing impact on the EU. Merkel repeatedly warned that 'if the euro fails, then Europe fails'. The government had to try to hold the Eurozone together so that the EU would not collapse, re-opening the 'German Problem' for which European integration had been designed to provide a permanent solution (see Chapter 2).

In most episodes of the Eurozone Crisis, the German government played the leading role, although only in part that of a (stabilizing) hegemonic power in Kindleberger's conception. But it was not omnipotent. Rather, its influence on the decisions taken or not taken varied by issue. Three main variables shaped the extent to which Berlin dominated Eurozone Crisis policy. The first is *the constellation of actors and their preferences* – Germany's influence was greater, the more allies it found for its stance among the other member states (Schoeller 2017). German initiatives not supported by a significant number of other member states typically failed. This was the case, for example, for the proposal to create a 'Super-Commissioner' for economic and financial affairs, with stronger powers vis-à-vis Eurozone members and greater autonomy than the existing Commissioner vis-à-vis other Commissioners (Schoeller

2017). The 'Competitiveness Pact' conceived by the German government, and subsequently adopted under the 'Open Method of Coordination' in 2011, encountered a not too dissimilar fate and remained a dead letter (see above). Most striking of all was the failure of the 'contractual arrangements' project. Merkel and her government were the principal supporters of this project, which would have involved member states signing legally binding contracts with EU organs committing themselves to implement 'structural reforms' in exchange for financial aid (Bosch 2013; Stierle 2014; *The Economist* 2013a). Included in the Four Presidents' Report in October 2012 and backed in a joint Franco-German paper in June 2013, the project ran into fierce opposition in the European Council, where a 'negative coalition' of rival camps opposed the project for diametrically opposed reasons. The Netherlands and Finland, normally close allies of Germany on Eurozone Crisis issues, opposed any additional financial transfers, while southern member states rejected the idea of 'yet more surveillance and reforms imposed from Brussels' (*The Economist* 2013a). Germany found itself in a 'tiny minority' in negotiations on the issue, backed only by the heads of the Council, Commission and ECB and a few other governments, notably the Danish (Ludlow 2013c: 24, 2013d: 30–37, 48–50). Most governments' reluctance to acquiesce in the project was strengthened by the imminence of European Parliamentary elections in May 2014, as the project was generally regarded as likely to prove unpopular (*The Economist* 2013a). The Council finally decided to defer any decision on the project until late 2014, but it appears subsequently to have been quietly buried.

At the other end of the spectrum in respect of the alignment of preferences as between the German government and other actors were the crises over the bailing out of Cyprus and – especially in 2015 – Greece. On these issues, backed by a broad majority of other member states, as well as the EU organs (and the IMF), Germany was typically the major protagonist and very successful in shaping the terms of any agreements – to the point where in 2015, following the Greek referendum, it forced the Syriza government to accept a tougher accord than the one that it had initially rejected. In between these extremes lay conflicts such as that over the 2012 rescue of Spanish banks, in which, faced by a coalition of the Spanish and Italian governments, implicitly supported by the new French president, Hollande, Merkel had to make more significant concessions than vis-à-vis the smaller peripheral Eurozone members when they needed financial aid.

The second variable is *the problem-constellation*, specifically the intensity or acuteness of the crisis to be managed. Germany's influence was greater the more urgent the need was for corrective collective action to avert a prospectively very negative outcome. Other things being equal, it was more successful in stamping its imprint on decisions when, in the absence of an agreement, another member state or states would have confronted extreme financial and economic hardship. Thus, Berlin's influence was greatest when it came to determining the terms of the bailing out of the 'debtor' states in southern and south-western Europe and when fears of an imminent collapse of the Eurozone were strongest. Thus, whereas it was able largely to dictate the provisions of the Fiscal Compact towards the end of 2011, amid great uncertainty as to the survival of the Eurozone, its push in 2013 in favour of 'contractual arrangements' to promote 'structural reforms' was rebuffed. By this time, following Draghi's London speech, the Eurozone had stabilized once again and, among the leaders of other member states, there was a 'feeling that the crisis was over' and it was therefore easier to oppose Merkel (Ludlow 2013d: 35).

The third variable is *the nature of the politico-institutional setting and the decision-making process, ordinary or extraordinary,* in and through which the issue was handled. Germany's influence was greater when there was no EU treaty basis for a given course of action and the process by which decisions were reached was largely 'intergovernmental', marginalizing the EU's supranational organs. Other things being equal, German bargaining power was most unadulterated on issues where the Eurozone's point of departure was a *tabula rasa*, the Commission was practically sidelined and the European Council was the critical decision-making location and body – as was the case, for example, for the successive bail-outs, the creation of the EFSF and its successor, the ESM, and, owing to the veto of the British prime minister, Cameron, the Fiscal Compact. Where, in contrast, as, for example, in the negotiations over the EBU, the treaties empowered the Commission to exercise its right of initiative and the approval not only of the Council, but also the European Parliament was required, the German government made more significant concessions (Bulmer and Paterson 2017; Epstein and Rhodes 2016a: 224, 2016b: 17). Other significant regulations – notably the 'Six-Pack' and 'Two-Pack' concerning tighter surveillance and closer coordination of member states' fiscal policies – were also adopted without the German government having played a major decision-making role. Perhaps, in these two cases, however, because the thrust of the regulations in any case corresponded closely to German preferences (Laffan and Schlosser 2016).

Overall, with significant cross-issue-area variations, the German government was thus the single most influential actor setting the rules by which the Eurozone Crisis was managed. However, the story of the Eurozone Crisis cannot be told, and its provisional outcome cannot be explained, without reference to a second, not much less critical, actor, the ECB. The ECB is exactly the kind of international institution with 'real authority' that in Kindleberger's view would render single-state hegemony superfluous in international systems but was unlikely to materialize (see Chapter 2). The European treaties protected its independence and equipped it with strong, although by no means unlimited, legal powers to intervene in the crisis. Given these powers, it could circumvent the cumbersome consensual norms and practices that typified other decision-making procedures in the EU and if need be manage the crisis 'hierarchically' (see Scharpf 2006). At the height of the crisis, the ties of economic and financial interdependence and mutual fears of economic doom might not have sufficed to coerce the member states into reaching the agreements required to prevent the Eurozone's collapse. But for the July 2012 intervention by its president Draghi and its subsequent actions to shore up the financial systems in the crisis-stricken member states, it is entirely conceivable that the Eurozone would have collapsed. The ECB did more to stabilize the Eurozone in the crisis than Germany, which, with its persistent insistence on austerity in exchange for financial aid and steadfast refusal to reflate its own economy, arguably exacerbated the crisis.

This said, for the most part, and especially at the beginning of the crisis, the ECB was an ally rather than an adversary of the German government, reinforcing Berlin's insistence on the pursuit of austerity in the crisis-affected Eurozone members, especially by threatening otherwise to cut off the supply of credit to their banks, as happened with Ireland, Italy and Greece (Blustein 2017: 168–169, 178–180, 230–232; Brunnermeier et al. 2016: 331–343; Tokarski 2016). On several issues where it opposed the German government, notably IMF involvement in Eurozone Crisis management and the 'bailing-in' of private sector creditors, the ECB lost (Blustein 2017: 95–101; Brunnermeier et al. 2016: 327–331). Beginning with Draghi's London speech, conflicts began to emerge between the ECB and German monetary and financial as well as academic circles over the ECB's (potential) support for 'debtor' states, which was regarded in these circles as illegal under the terms of the Maastricht Treaty, and over its monetary policy, which was viewed as too accommodating. But Draghi's remarks, although he made them on his own initiative (see above), nonetheless remained within the parameters of German Eurozone policy, which was to combine financial aid with austerity while striving to keep the Eurozone intact. Merkel and Schäuble correspondingly backed Draghi's pronouncement after the event. In line with German government preferences, any ECB financial aid to Eurozone members would be subject to conditionality. Under German pressure, Draghi and the ECB conceded that national central banks would be liable for almost all the losses incurred as a consequence of the ECB buying their governments' bonds rather than these liabilities being mutualized (*Financial Times* 2015d, 2015e). The crucial litmus test of whether the ECB's overall monetary policy diverged from German preferences would be the rate of price inflation in the Eurozone. During the crisis, however, inflation fell to well below the target rate, indicating that 'the ECB has not eased beyond what economic circumstances and its monetary objective mandate' (Henning 2016: 192). Nevertheless, the monetary policy of quantitative easing, involving massive bond-buying, that the ECB launched in 2015, provoked widespread misgivings in Germany, with finance minister Schäuble, for example, blaming its low interest-rate policies, which penalized German savers, for the rising support for the extreme right-wing AfD (*Financial Times* 2016b).

France was much less able to balance German power in the Eurozone Crisis than in earlier EU crises. In time-honoured fashion, there was a great deal of Franco-German coordination, manifested in bilateral summit talks, joint position papers, pre-EU summit consultations and joint participation in critical mini-lateral summit negotiations. The preservation of the 'form' of Franco-German cooperation could not disguise the fact, however, that Berlin provided the engine of Eurozone Crisis management and manned the steering wheel, while for the most part Paris was confined to applying a brake that could slow down the vehicle, but not stop it entirely nor change the direction in which it was moving. Sarkozy thus failed to move Merkel with his insistence, at the outbreak of the Greek crisis, that the Eurozone members should 'put some billions immediately on the table' (as quoted in Bastasin 2015: 167). Despite having strongly criticized German Eurozone policy for its focus on austerity and demanded a renegotiation of the Fiscal Compact, the new president Hollande, once elected in 2012, did not mount a sustained challenge to German primacy. Reputedly, he never intended to do so, having sent an emissary to Berlin before his election to assure Merkel that his discourse was motivated only by electoral-political considerations and was not therefore a guide as to how he would act in office (Morelle 2017: 48). He signed up to the Fiscal Compact after having secured no more than cosmetic changes to it. Faced with Merkel's strong resistance, he appears fairly rapidly to have abandoned the idea of eurobonds, which implied the mutualization of at least a part of Eurozone members' public debts. Left-wing critics of Hollande's 'capitulation' to Merkel accused him of lacking political courage (Morelle 2017: 316–318). Hollande indeed saw his role in the EU as that of a mediator, trying to find the 'point of equilibrium' rather than uncompromisingly championing French interests (as quoted in Davet and Lhomme 2016a: 490). However, his government's and his reluctance to challenge Merkel head-on over Eurozone Crisis policy had more to do with their acceptance that France's relative economic weakness condemned it to playing a secondary role alongside Germany with its superior economic and budgetary power. France, according to the person who became Hollande's secretary-general at the Élysée Palace, could not win against Germany so long as it had not made the same efforts that Germany had at economic reform (Jean-Pierre Jouyet, as quoted in *Financial Times* 2011d). Unilaterally, it could not afford to pursue an expansionary fiscal policy as this would have alarmed international financial markets and provoked a costly increase in French bond yields (finance minister Pierre Moscovici, as quoted in *Financial Times* 2012j; Brunnermeier et al. 2016: 33). Any fiscal stimulus would thus have to have been undertaken at the European level and, by implication, led by Germany (Hollande, as quoted in *Le Monde* 2014h). These may have been the main reasons why, when Sapin first met Varoufakis in 2015, he told his Greek counterpart that 'France is not what it used to be' – and, siding with Germany, offered him no support in his quest for debt relief (Varoufakis 2017: 190).

The *European Commission* was not nearly as influential an actor as the German government or the ECB when it came to shaping Eurozone Crisis policy (Brunnermeier et al. 2016: 17–27; Varoufakis, as quoted in *Le Monde* 2017c; Varoufakis 2017: 258–263). In some ways, this policy enhanced the powers of the Commission (Bauer and Becker 2014; Becker et al. 2016; Nugent and Rhinard 2016). As a member of the 'troika', along with the ECB and the IMF, the Commission shared extensive powers of intervention in the domestic affairs of Eurozone 'debtor' states. The Fiscal Compact and

'Six-Pack' and 'Two-Pack' legislation gave it stronger powers of surveillance, intervention and enforcement over Eurozone members' fiscal policies. However, these instruments were put to the service of a crisis policy of austerity that was made by other actors elsewhere, notably in the European Council and the Eurogroup, in which, respectively, the German Chancellor Merkel and finance minister Schäuble were the most influential members. Aligning itself strategically with Germany, the Commission became in effect an 'instrument for creditors to impose their will on debtors' (Philippe Legrain, as quoted in *Financial Times* 2014a). Between the Commission and the German government Eurozone Crisis management was thus a positive-sum game, in which, however, the Commission was the subordinate player. Schäuble allegedly advised Varoufakis (2017: 407) to 'pay no attention to them': 'It's a mistake to believe anything the Commission tell you. What can they offer you? They talk and talk and talk but it is all just talk'.

The third member of the Eurozone 'troika', the *IMF*, became involved in the management of the crisis only because, against widespread opposition, Merkel insisted on its participation, believing that the Commission in particular was not up to the job because it was 'too cozy with European politicians and too timid about offending them' (Blustein 2017: 65). Once engaged, however, the IMF largely assumed the role of the 'junior partner', generally giving way when confronted with 'strongly held positions among top European policy-makers – Trichet, Merkel and Schäuble in particular' (Blustein 2017: 453). As the crisis evolved, and especially in the conflict over the third Greek bail-out, the IMF and the German government found themselves increasingly at loggerheads over debt relief, which the IMF saw as imperative (Varoufakis 2017: 441, 483), but which Germany strongly opposed.

The informal – and intergovernmental – *Eurogroup*, comprising the finance ministers of the Eurozone member states, may have been as influential an actor, or at least venue for making decisions, in the Eurozone Crisis as any of the three organizations of the 'troika'. This was certainly Varoufakis's view (as quoted in *Le Monde* 2017c). Within the Eurogroup, however, the German finance minister Schäuble, who was in office continuously from 2009 to 2017, was the dominant member, the 'doyen' of the group to whom, when he spoke, 'everybody' listened (Finnish finance minister Alexander Stubbs, quoted in *ARD* 2015). Schäuble was backed, at the political and bureaucratic level, by representatives from allied member states who occupied key functions in the group, such as its chairman, the Dutch finance minister, Dijsselbloem, and the Eurogroup working group chairman, the Austrian, Thomas Wieser. With Finland, these two member states generally shared Germany's approach to how the crisis should be managed – as did also the Central and East European members of the Eurozone. In the Eurogroup negotiations concerning Greece in 2015, Schäuble seems not to have prevailed only when he was opposed by his own Chancellor (Varoufakis 2017: 231–250).

Germany thus played two of the distinguishing roles of a hegemonic power in the Eurozone Crisis. First, it was the single most influential player in setting the rules by which the crisis was managed. Second, supported often by the ECB and the European Commission (as well as the IMF), it tried – hitherto by and large successfully – to get other Eurozone member states to follow its lead. However, it hardly played the third role of a (stabilizing) hegemonic power, namely to shoulder a disproportionate share of the burden of managing the Eurozone Crisis. It did not provide a 'market of last resort' for crisis-stricken Eurozone members. Throughout the crisis, Germany ran a current account surplus varying between 2 and 4 per cent of GDP with the remainder of the Eurozone. Although it sustained an increased government budget deficit of around 3 and 4 per cent of GDP in the immediate aftermath of the GFC in 2009 and 2010, it reduced this to 1 per cent and lower in subsequent years, after the adoption in 2009 of a balanced-budget amendment to the Basic Law (Article 109) that required federal and state governments normally to run a deficit no higher than 0.35 per cent of GDP. There was no fiscal stimulus, nor any above-average increase in wages and salaries, in Germany that could directly or indirectly have boosted economic growth in the crisis-hit Eurozone member states. While the German market remained open to exports from these countries, it did not absorb a higher volume of these than before the crisis, nor was there any significant increase in German consumption of their services.

Germany was certainly an important 'lender of last resort' in the Eurozone Crisis. Proportionate to the size of its economy in the Eurozone, it put up about €125bn (about 25 per cent) of the financial aid made available to bail out the zone's crisis-stricken members up to 2015 (see Table 3.2, page 68). It is important to bear in mind, however, that this aid took the form of loans or, in the case of the ESM, guarantees, not grants. German loans have been repaid with interest, such that, in financial terms, Germany has been a beneficiary of the Eurozone Crisis. Up to 2018, the federal government made a profit of €2.9bn on the financial aid it had provided to Greece (*Spiegel-Online* 2018b). Of the overall loans worth €216bn made to the Greek government in the first and second bail-out programmes, the bulk went to pay interest, to repay debts and to recapitalize Greek banks, while less than 5 per cent went into the Greek fiscal budget (Rocholl and Stahmer 2016: 4, 19). An unquantifiable portion of these loans actually flowed from Greece back to the bailed out countries' original creditors, prominent among which were German, French and other Eurozone banks. Indirectly, the German government benefited even more strongly from the Eurozone Crisis. As a comparatively 'safe haven' in the Eurozone, it was able to issue bonds at significantly lower interest rates than otherwise would have been the case. According to one analysis, for the period 2009 to 2013, the savings to the German government through the crisis-induced reduction of bond yields amounted to about €80bn, a far higher sum than the guarantee pledged at that time by the German government to the ESM (Brinkmann 2014). For the period from 2010 to 2014, the Federal Finance Ministry itself calculated savings from lower bond yields to be almost €40bn (*Zeit-Online* 2013). The Eurozone Crisis would become costly for Germany only if bailed out members were to renege on their debts and/or the Eurozone were to collapse. The same analysis may and has been made equally of the Target2 payments system linking the ECB and its member national central banks, in which by mid-2018 the Bundesbank's claims had reached the unprecedented sum of €976bn (Marsh 2017; Pisani-Ferry 2017; Plickert 2017; *Spiegel-Online* 2018c).

Overall, as SPD chairman Gabriel, then in the opposition in the German Parliament, claimed in 2012, it would be 'wrong to portray Germany all the time as the luggage-carrying donkey' of the EU and the single currency. 'We are not net contributors to the EU, but rather net beneficiaries' (Gabriel 2012: 22706). In the strategies followed to cope with monetary and financial crises in the EU, both before and after the creation of the Euro, there has in fact been a constant thread – the burden of adjustment has always been distributed asymmetrically and been borne disproportionately by the 'deficit' countries. Moreover, whereas for a long period in the history of the EU, living standards between the richer and poorer member states converged, during the Eurozone Crisis – between Eurozone members – they began once again to diverge (see Figure 3.2; *Financial Times* 2017). Unsurprisingly, in autumn 2015, German and bail-out countries' citizens' perceptions of their personal financial situation diverged significantly and in some cases were highly polarized: while 82 per cent of Germans judged their financial situation to be good (and 16 per cent bad), the corresponding figures for the Irish were 71 and 24 per cent, for the Spanish 59 and 40 per cent, for Cypriots 51 and 49 per cent, for the Portuguese 41 and 57 per cent and for the Greeks almost exactly the reverse: 24 and 76 per cent respectively (Eurobarometer 2015).

Figure 3.2   *Economic convergence and divergence between Germany, France and selected other Eurozone member states, 2003–16*

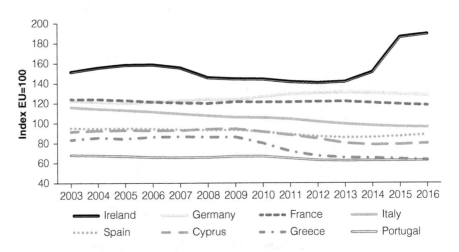

Note: Gross domestic product at 2010 reference levels per head of population. Country indexes constructed with EU average as 100.

Source: European Commission, AMECO database.

'What we did wrong in the last grand coalition,' said Gabriel self-critically in 2018 of the government in which he was first economics and then foreign minister, was that 'we paid too little attention to Europe. We wrote a chapter in European history in which the Germany-centric economic views of Wolfgang Schäuble played too great of a role. That was a mistake' (*Spiegel Online* 2018a). The question is whether the process of socio-economic polarization that Berlin's stance in the Eurozone Crisis promoted will at some stage destroy it, completely or in part. For most of the Eurozone Crisis, the German government's strategy had been to offer 'debtor' states strictly conditional financial aid and to insist on the *adoption* of binding rules to constrain member states' fiscal policies. If it was very successful in achieving these objectives, it was much less certain that, in the longer run, these rules could be effectively *implemented*. Compliance with the terms of the Fiscal Compact proved to be weak (Gros and Alcidi 2014). When it came to the enforcement of new fiscal policy rules vis-à-vis France at least, the Commission choreographed an elaborate charade to enable the government to create the appearance that it was complying with them when both sides knew it was not (Davet and Lhomme 2016: 515–519). In the words of president Hollande: 'You do what you want with the Commission ... It's the privilege of the big countries' (Davet and Lhomme 2016b: 518). Such weaknesses in respect of compliance pointed to limits in the extent of German influence over the management of the Eurozone Crisis. On the one hand, they highlighted the fragility of the governance system devised during the crisis for the Eurozone. On the other, however, they endowed the system with a degree of flexibility without which conflicts would have been more difficult to mediate and hence more explosive.

Chapter 4

The Ukraine Crisis

Introduction

While the Eurozone Crisis was still unfolding, the robustness of the EU and European integration was also tested, from 2011 onwards, by a series of crises in its southern and eastern neighbourhoods. The most direct and acute of these for the EU arose on its eastern periphery, in and over Ukraine, where the decision of President Viktor Yanukovych in November 2013 not to proceed with an Association Agreement (AA) with the EU but rather to join a Russian-sponsored Eurasian Economic Union (EEU) provoked protests and demonstrations that culminated in his overthrow in February 2014. Russian president Vladimir Putin reacted to Ukraine's subsequent westward pivot by invading, occupying and annexing Crimea, which had been part of Ukraine since 1954, and by providing military support to separatist movements in eastern Ukraine that took up arms against the central government in Kiev and still effectively controlled the Donbas region of the country in 2018. This amounted, in the view of one analyst of European security, to 'arguably the most severe crisis of the 21st century in Europe's neighbourhood' (Howorth 2017: 133). The then German foreign minister, Frank-Walter Steinmeier, called it the 'most serious crisis' in Europe since the fall of the Berlin Wall (as quoted in *Der Spiegel* 2014d). It was certainly the bloodiest and most destructive conflict in Europe since the wars in the former Yugoslavia in the 1990s (Davis Cross and Karolewski 2017: 4). By 2017, it had killed more than 10,000 people, wounded another almost 25,000 and made around 1.8 million Ukrainians refugees (*Le Monde* 2017d; OHCHR 2017: 6–7).

The – in post-World War II Europe unprecedented – invasion, occupation and annexation of a part of one country by another was diametrically opposed to the peaceful norms and model of international relations for which the EU had come to stand and which had become a constitutive element of its self-conception and identity as a 'civilian power' (Duchêne 1972). Unleashed as it was by the new Ukrainian government's choice to align itself with the EU instead of Russia, it led to the 'biggest confrontation' between the West, including the EU, and Russia since the end of the Cold War (Davis Cross and Karolewski 2017: 4). Of the world's big powers, Russia is the one geographically closest to the EU. Nuclear-armed, it remains, despite the collapse of the former Soviet Union, a military Great Power. While it is by no means an economic Great Power in overall terms, many EU member states depend heavily on imported Russian oil and gas supplies and conduct significant volumes of trade with Russia in other goods and services. No other state or at least conceivable adversary of the EU possesses a comparable capacity to affect the EU's and its member states' physical and economic security.

The challenge that the Ukraine Crisis posed for the EU was all the more formidable, as in the past the member states had frequently fallen out over their relations with Russia – a pattern that reflected divergences of interest rooted inter alia in geographic location, historical experience, political and cultural orientation, and trade patterns (Natorski and Pomorska 2017: 58–59). For historical reasons, Germany was frequently suspected of wanting to cultivate a special relationship with Russia at its neighbours' expense. In general, despite an overall trend towards a closer coordination and alignment of member states' foreign policies, past external crises had as often as not divided and incapacitated the EU (Krotz 2009: 565). Historical precedents thus pointed to there being a strong risk of the Ukraine Crisis splitting the EU, undermining its efforts to develop and pursue a common foreign policy, and strengthening and accelerating tendencies towards political *dis*integration.

This highly conceivable negative scenario did not, however, materialize. Arguably against the odds, and certainly against the expectations of many seasoned observers of EU foreign policy and EU–Russian relations, the EU succeeded in developing and maintaining a common stance over Ukraine and towards Russian military interventions in the country. How effective this stance was in shaping Russian actions in Ukraine is uncertain. The EU did not persuade or coerce Russia into reversing its annexation of Crimea or suspending its military intervention in Donbas in favour of separatist movements. Whether the measures it adopted and implemented dissuaded or deterred Russia from extending its military intervention to the rest of Ukraine or into other neighbouring states remains an open question. But for more than four years, despite frequent forecasts to the contrary, it managed to stick together. On the one hand, the Ukraine Crisis did not result in any closer foreign-political integration in the EU. There was no greater 'communitarization' of EU foreign policy and no new instruments of a common foreign policy were created by changes of the treaties, ordinary legislative acts or intergovernmental accords reached 'outside' the treaties. The actions taken vis-à-vis Russia rested on the deployment of measures for which the treaties already provided. On the other hand, nor did the crisis provoke any genuinely significant foreign-political *dis*integration with member states defecting and pursuing their own, unilateral Russian policies. At most, in this regard, one could say that, as the crisis intensified, the EU's supranational organs were progressively disempowered, while the leaders and foreign ministers of two of the 'big three' members – France and Germany – became increasingly central players (Howorth 2017: 121, 130; Natorski and Pomorska 2017: 54, 63–64; Seibel 2017: 276; Sjursen and Rosen 2017: 28–30; Youngs 2017: 154–155).

The domination of the EU's handling of the Ukraine Crisis by France (to a lesser) and Germany (to a greater extent) could perhaps be construed as an instance of *vertical* political disintegration, of a weakening of the EU's central and supranational organs to the benefit of the member states' governments. This, however, would be to overlook the fact that the bi- or trilateral management of the EU's big external crises is the historical norm, illustrated by the way in which other such crises – such as the Iranian nuclear programme and the civil wars in Libya and Syria – have also been handled. But it would also be to ignore the extent to which, in devising the EU's and their response to the Ukraine Crisis, the French and German governments strove to craft positions that reconciled and represented not only their interests, but also those of the other member states. What was specific and unique to this external crisis was rather that not France and the *UK*, but instead France and *Germany* were the central EU actors and that, in this tandem, Germany was actually the more influential partner (*Der Spiegel* 2014d; *Eurocomment* 2014c: 9; *Financial Times* 2015g; Orenstein and Kelemen 2017: 96; Stewart 2016). That Germany played a leading role in managing a major international security crisis was unprecedented in the post-World War II period (Krotz and Maher 2016; Speck 2015).

The next section of this chapter assesses the evolution of EU foreign policy in the period before the Ukraine Crisis, exploring particularly the extent to which, in different issue areas, this became integrated and stressing the role played by France and Germany and their relationship in shaping these trends. The remainder of the chapter analyses the Ukraine Crisis and how this was managed by the EU. First the roots and then the outbreak of the crisis are explored. Subsequent sections deal with the EU's response to Russia's annexation of Crimea and covert military intervention in eastern Ukraine, the escalation of the crisis and the role that the EU, led by France and Germany, played in the negotiation of the Minsk accords, the second of which, in early 2015, seemed to contain the armed conflict in the eastern regions of the country. The conclusion assesses the extent to which Germany played the role of a (stabilizing) hegemonic power within the EU in this crisis.

EU foreign policy before the Ukraine Crisis

The EU that confronted (and arguably inadvertently provoked) the Ukraine Crisis exhibited highly divergent degrees of foreign policy integration, depending on the issue area. Formally, it had from the outset a *communitarized* foreign *economic* (external trade) policy. This was a by-product of the decision in the Treaty of Rome to create a customs union between the member states. Based on a mandate adopted by the Council, the Commission negotiated trade agreements with third states that the Council had subsequently to ratify. On external trade issues, the Commission possessed significant capacity to act autonomously of the member states. In some other issue areas, such as foreign *environmental* policy, the EU's powers were gradually expanded, but the member states retained important competences, so that the EU's foreign policies in these domains were formulated and conducted jointly by the Commission and the member states. They were thus partially or *semi-communitarized*. In foreign *security and defence* policy, in contrast, the EU's role for a long time was non-existent or weak. Although, since the end of the Cold War, this has changed to a certain extent, its security and defence powers and role today remain strictly limited and decisions to threaten to or actually to deploy military force against other states (or political movements) are taken by the member states, either unilaterally or in other international alliances, above all NATO. EU foreign security policy has thus been predominantly *intergovernmental*, leaving plenty of scope to member states to pursue their own security policies. In practice the conduct of the EU's foreign policy is marked by an informal division of labour between the member states and EU institutions that 'often deviates from the formal rules' (Delreux and Keukeleire 2017: 1471).

The EU's foreign policy/policies might have developed differently, but for the collapse in 1954 of the EDC project (see Chapter 1). During the Cold War, the defence and security of Western Europe was organized through NATO and thus provided first and foremost by the USA. The Treaty of Rome contained no defence provisions and in as far as the EU subsequently exercised power externally, it was as a 'civilian power' (Duchêne 1972) or a 'market power' (Damro 2012). For most of the 1960s, the original six members were divided in their fundamental security and defence policy orientations between 'Gaullist' France, which wanted Western Europe to organize its own defence, and the five other 'Atlanticist' states. The six made their first gentle steps towards closer foreign policy cooperation in the 1970s, following the launching in 1970, after de Gaulle's resignation as French president, of the European Political Cooperation (EPC). EPC was organized outside of the EU and the Commission, but it fostered increasingly intense interaction between the member states' foreign ministries and a gradual rapprochement of their foreign policies (Keukeleire and MacNaughtan 2008: 44ff.; Mérand 2008: 77–80).

EPC was codified – but not communitarized – in a separate section of the Single European Act in 1987. The decisive impulse towards a 'common' EU foreign policy came rather with the end of the Cold War – the collapse of the Communist bloc and German unification – and the related negotiation and adoption in 1991–92 of the Maastricht Treaty. As with the Euro (Chapter 3) and the Schengen Area (Chapter 5), the principal architects of this shift were the French and German governments, led by Mitterrand and Kohl and their respective foreign ministers, Dumas and Genscher (Mazzucelli 1997: 63–64, 141, 190–191). Compared with monetary-political integration, however, the roles of the two governments were reversed on foreign policy, with Germany more and France less 'integrationist', arguably reflecting the then prevailing balance of power between the two states in these two issue areas (Mazzucelli 1997: 97). While the German government wanted to communitarize EU foreign policy by bringing it fully into the EU treaties, France – successfully – championed the incorporation of the foreign policy provisions of the treaty in a separate, 'second' treaty pillar. Kohl said that the German government had been 'prepared to go further' than this, but that this had not been possible in the 'present situation' (quoted in Deutscher Bundestag 1991: 5801).

The 'Community method' was thus not applied in EU foreign policy-making. Foreign policy decisions were subject to unanimity, although decisions as to how these were implemented could be taken by a qualified majority. Subsequent treaty changes – those adopted at Amsterdam in 1997 and Lisbon a decade later – also brought some significant institutional innovations in EU foreign policy. The Amsterdam Treaty created the post of High Representative for the CFSP, attached to the Council. The Lisbon Treaty strengthened the role of the High Representative by making her simultaneously a vice-president of the Commission and created the European External Action Service (EEAS), providing the EU with a diplomatic service akin to those of the member states.

Maastricht was not only a turning point in respect of EU foreign policy overall. It was also the first EU treaty to contain specific defence provisions. These, too, were largely inspired by Kohl and Mitterrand. Sceptical as to the strength of the USA's long-term commitment to West European security, Kohl began to push for closer military cooperation within the EU in talks with Mitterrand in the 1980s (Attali 1993: 326, 713–714, 814, 872). Both Mitterrand and he were concerned to anchor (as it was at the time, West) Germany 'irreversibly' in the West and thus to pre-empt the possible emergence of a strong and independent German military force (Attali 1993: 814, 1995b: 606). These concerns motivated the two leaders to announce the creation of a joint Franco-German brigade in 1987 (Attali 1995a: 337, 342, 364–365, 407). Circumventing their respective foreign and defence ministries, they proposed shortly before the Maastricht summit that this brigade be transformed into a 50,000-strong army corps open to other member states (*Der Spiegel* 1991). However, although the Eurocorps was launched in 1992, only Belgium, Spain and Luxembourg joined it and it did not become the credible nucleus of a European army. In the wake of the Yugoslavian wars, which had painfully exposed the EU's military impotence, prospects for European defence cooperation outside of NATO were instead revived by an Anglo-French initiative launched at St Malo in 1998. The (at least temporary) meeting of minds of the only two EU member states with a significant military power projection capacity gave rise to a flurry of defence cooperation projects, notably to establish a 60,000-strong 'rapid reaction force' (later, smaller 'battle groups'). Comprising detachments from member states' armed forces, these were intended to intervene in external conflicts. Not least, however, because of divergences between France and the UK, none has so far been deployed (Dempsey 2013). EU military intervention outside of NATO has been largely confined to a range of modest-scale, non-combat training and peace-keeping operations. Despite significant technology-, cost- and security-related pressures militating in favour of closer cooperation or integration, there has been next to no integration of member states' defence policies in the EU (Menon 2014). Where, as in defence policy, there was no or hardly any political integration in the EU in the first place, no crisis, such as that over Ukraine, could provoke political disintegration.

In any case, none of the EU member states proposed a military response to Russian aggression in Ukraine. The closest they came to anything remotely resembling this was to debate whether, with the USA, they should supply the Ukrainian government with defensive weapons to deploy against the armed separatist groups in the Donbas region – a step from which, not least owing to French and German opposition, they refrained. Instead intra-EU negotiations focused almost exclusively on the imposition of diplomatic, travel-related, economic and financial sanctions against Russia. By this time the EU already had a history of more than three decades of the deployment of such sanctions – the 'ultimate coercive foreign policy tool before military force' – as an instrument of foreign policy (Portela 2010: xiv). It had first imposed economic sanctions on third states in the early 1980s – in respect of the USSR after its invasion of Afghanistan and Argentina in connection with its seizure of the Falklands Islands (Portela 2010: 20). As with foreign policy in general and defence policy in particular, the Maastricht Treaty was the first to make specific reference to sanctions as an EU policy instrument and lay out a procedure for their adoption and implementation – although, in so doing, it merely 'formally codified' what had become established practice (Portela 2010: 24). The treaty subjected the adoption of sanctions to a unanimous decision of the European Council and the Council, but it empowered the Council to decide the 'necessary measures' by a qualified majority. Whereas some kinds of sanctions – flight bans, trade restrictions and financial ones – fall within the EU's competence, others, such as those of a diplomatic nature, visa bans and arms embargoes, must be implemented by the member states. Alone in the two decades following the adoption of the Maastricht Treaty, the EU applied sanctions against the governments of ten countries in Asia, Africa, Central Asia, the former Soviet Union and south-eastern Europe – whereby, however, its success rate, as reflected in the sanctions' impact on the behaviour of the governments targeted – was 'low' (Portela 2010: 56, 101). By and large the EU steered clear of imposing sanctions on its main trading partners (Portela 2010: 173).

Most analysts of EU foreign policy concurred, around the eve of the Ukraine Crisis, that this had to a significant extent been 'Brusselsized', in the sense that numerous EU organs were typically involved in the management of foreign policy issues and that there were extensive processes of consultation and coordination over such issues with and between the member states. 'Brusselsization' and coordination were not to be equated, however, with communitarization, let alone foreign policy *integration* (Howorth 2014: 68–69, 214–215; Nugent 2017: 416–417). Foreign policy remained largely an intergovernmental affair, not much could be done, at least not effectively, without the 'firm political and operational support of member states', especially the three most powerful ones, and there had been only a limited convergence of member states' foreign policy identities and 'strategic cultures' (Howorth 2014: 234–241; Keukeleire and MacNaughtan 2008: 296, 330, 334).

In view of the persistence of such divergences and the very limited integration of EU foreign policy, the EU's frequent failure to agree on how to respond to external crises is hardly remarkable. The list of such failures – including in the post-Maastricht era, in which the EU's level of foreign policy ambition rose significantly – is long. The member states initially divided over how to respond to the outbreak of war in former Yugoslavia – before finally uniting in support of a (USA-led) military intervention against the Milosevic government in Serbia in the late 1990s. The US invasion and occupation of Iraq in 2003 provoked deep splits within the EU, with most member states joining the UK in supporting the USA and only a small minority rallying to the opposing camp led by France and Germany. In 2011, supported by a handful of other member states, but not by Germany, France and the UK intervened militarily in Libya to overthrow the regime of Muammar Gaddafi. In Syria in 2013, France was willing to launch air attacks on the Assad regime to punish it for its use of chemical weapons in the civil war, but it was abandoned by its erstwhile UK ally after Prime Minister David Cameron decided to seek parliamentary support for intervention and failed to secure it. When it came in international conflicts to the deployment of sanctions, as opposed to the politically more controversial resort to military force, even if there had been occasional cases of their 'circumvention' by some member states, the EU had hitherto maintained a better record of forging and maintaining a common stance (Portela 2015: 39–61). But no previous crisis in which the EU had adopted sanctions had been comparable to the one in which it would confront its Great Power neighbour, Russia.

The Ukraine Crisis

The Ukraine Crisis had its roots in the shifting balance of power between (a politically increasingly authoritarian) Russia and the West, including the EU, in post-Cold War Europe. Amid the rubble of the former Soviet Union, a popular referendum in Ukraine in December 1991 yielded a majority of over 92 per cent in favour of independence. All the Ukrainian regions, including those with substantial numbers of Russian-speaking citizens, voted to create an independent Ukrainian state. Only in Crimea, where most citizens were Russian-speaking, did fewer than four voters out of five opt for independence, but here too there was a majority for independence, albeit, at 54 per cent, a much smaller one. Contentious security issues arising from the collapse and legacy of the Soviet Union were addressed in three agreements reached in the 1990s. In 1994, the two states signed a memorandum under which nuclear warheads still located in Ukraine were transferred to Russia in exchange for Russia supplying fuel to Ukrainian nuclear power stations, with a third signatory, the USA, compensating Russia for cost of the fuel. The same year Russia, the USA and the UK signed – and France and China endorsed – the Budapest Memorandum, under which, in recognition of Ukraine's forfeiture of its nuclear weapons (and accession to the Nuclear Non-Proliferation Treaty), the five major nuclear powers undertook to 'respect Ukraine's independence and sovereignty' as well as its existing borders (Yekelchyk 2015: 68). In 1997 Russia and Ukraine signed the Partition Treaty, which established two independent naval fleets and divided bases between them. Crimea having been ceded by the USSR to the republic of Ukraine in 1954, the Russian Black Sea fleet was now located 'abroad'. Under the Partition Treaty Russia leased its naval base at Sevastopol in Crimea from Ukraine in exchange for offering Ukraine a discount on its Russian gas imports. In 2010, the Kharkiv Accords, named after the city in eastern Ukraine, extended this arrangement up to 2042.

In the decade and a half following the end of the Cold War, not only the EU, but also NATO enlarged eastwards to include the former Communist states in eastern Central Europe as well as, among the former Soviet republics, the three Baltic states Lithuania, Latvia and Estonia. At the same time, steps were taken to forge closer ties with post-Soviet Russia. These led to the EU–Russia Partnership and Cooperation Agreement, which came into force in 1997, lasted until 2007, and was subsequently renewed annually. In renewing it in 2007, the two sides agreed to aim at forming 'common spaces' relating to economic, security and cultural ties as well as justice and home affairs. A 'Partnership for Modernization', whose goal was to help modernize the Russian economy, was launched while Dimitri Medvedev was Russian president, in 2010.

None of these projects to institutionalize EU–Russian relations could, however, prevent their deterioration during the era, from 1999 onwards, in which Putin dominated Russian politics. Putin signalled and emphasized his opposition to the gradual eastwards expansion of NATO at the Munich Security Conference in 2007, describing it as a 'serious provocation' to Russia and contrary to assurances given to Russia at the time of German unification that NATO would not expand beyond Germany (Putin 2007). Putin's fears in this regard were exacerbated by the occurrence of 'colour revolutions' that brought pro-Western leaders to office in Ukraine and Georgia in 2003–04 and by the NATO summit in April 2008 at Bucharest, which seemed to hold open the prospect of the two states' eventual accession. This would, he said, be seen as a 'direct threat' to Russian security (as quoted in Wikipedia 2017c). When the Georgian government launched a military assault against the Russian-aligned separatist region of South Ossetia in Georgia in summer 2008, Russian armed forces invaded the country to protect both South Ossetia and another breakaway region, Abkhazia, and forced a Georgian retreat. French president Nicolas Sarkozy, then also the chair of the European Council, rapidly negotiated an end to the military confrontation. Russia subsequently recognized the two breakaway regions as independent states. The diplomatic fallout from the (brief) Russian military intervention in a neighbouring state was minimal. In retrospect, the quick restoration of normal ties between Russia and the West may have persuaded Putin that the risks of a confrontation over Ukraine would be manageable (Hacke 2014; Speck 2014b).

If the prospect of Georgia joining NATO had already alarmed Putin, the prospect of Ukraine allying itself with the West was bound to disturb him more deeply. For several reasons, Ukraine's cultural, economic, political and strategic orientation mattered a great deal more for Putin and Russia than that of any other post-Soviet republic. One was historical and cultural: known for his conviction that the collapse of the USSR amounted to the 'greatest geopolitical catastrophe of the 21st century', Putin, like many Russians, viewed the Ukrainian capital, Kiev, where the Russian Orthodox Church was founded, as the cradle of the Russian nation and Russia and Ukraine as a single nation, linked by a common culture, language, religion and mentality (*The Economist* 2013b; Hille 2013; *Le Monde* 2013f). A second was economic. Russia and Ukraine were major trading partners. In 2011, Russia had launched an initiative to create the EEU in which it wanted to integrate numerous post-Soviet republics. As Ukraine was economically the largest of these, its participation in the prospective trading zone was indispensable to its success. If, by contrast, Ukraine were to join or, short of membership, form a customs union with the EU, Russia would have to reckon with significant negative economic consequences as Russian firms would have less favourable terms of access than EU-based ones to the Ukrainian market.

Third, perhaps most importantly, the fate of Ukraine was fundamental for Russian security (George Friedman 2014). As there were no serious topographical obstacles to the invasion of Russia from the West, Ukraine, given its size and geographic location, was critically important to Russia as a buffer state (Kaplan 2014; Ørstrøm Møller 2014b). During World War II, for example, almost a half of the material destruction suffered by the former USSR occurred in Ukraine (Sellier and Sellier 1995: 82–83). Ukraine and Russia shared a highly permeable land border of almost 2000 kilometres. Russia could be no more indifferent to the prospect of Ukraine joining an opposing military alliance – and NATO conceivably stationing troops directly on its borders – than could the USA, for example, to that of Canada or Mexico doing the same thing (Mearsheimer 2014). While neither Ukraine's NATO or EU accession was an issue in 2013–14, the conclusion of an AA had typically constituted a first step to EU accession for post-Communist European states and EU enlargement had hitherto proceeded in close tandem with that of NATO. Aside from their other motives for opposing Ukraine's alignment with the EU, Russian leaders could well have regarded the EU in this context as playing the role of a 'stalking horse for NATO expansion' (Mearsheimer 2014). The Western political and/or military integration of Ukraine would also have jeopardized the stationing of the Russian Black Sea naval fleet in Crimea and thus its access to the Mediterranean Ocean.

A further conceivable motive for Putin to oppose any much closer relationship between the EU and Ukraine concerns the threat of 'liberal-democratic contagion'. The Russian president's preoccupation with events and trends in other post-Soviet republics seems to have increased in the wake of the 'colour revolutions' that brought pro-Western political leaders to office in Georgia and Ukraine in 2003–04. In choosing to integrate with the EU and hence align itself with its political, legal and economic norms, Ukraine would simultaneously be making a decisive step towards entrenching a liberal-democratic political and market-oriented capitalist economic system on Russia's doorstep. In time it could serve as a beacon to Russians in the same way that, during the Cold War, West Germany was to East Germans and, since the end of the Cold War, Poland, which had been as poor as Ukraine in

1990 but was now three or more times richer, had been to Ukrainians. Not only numerous foreign observers of Russian politics, but also some Russians, including the political dissident Alexeï Navalny, believed that, as he expressed it, Putin wanted first and foremost to 'stop a revolution' in Russia that could 'unseat his own corrupt regime' (as quoted in *Le Monde* 2015c; see also Dempsey 2013; Hille 2014; Hockenos 2014; *Le Monde* 2015b; Ørstrøm Møller 2014a; Rachman 2015; Thom 2014; Wolf 2014; Wood 2014). The most frequent remark made in the Kremlin during the protests in Ukraine after the then president Yanukovych abandoned plans to conclude an AA with the EU, according to one report, was indeed: 'Do we want this to happen in Moscow?' (*The Economist* 2014d; see also Freedman 2014).

At any rate, as again many observers of Russia and Ukraine noted at the time, the fate of Ukraine mattered a great deal more to Russia than it did to the EU (*The Economist* 2014a; George Friedman 2014; Mearsheimer 2015; Speck 2014a). Putin himself was later to declare that Russia's interests in 'Crimea and the surrounding region' would 'always outstrip those of Western countries'. Towards the USA, he said, 'You are where? Thousands of kilometres away ... We are right here ... [and] we are ready for the worst possible scenario' (as quoted indirectly in *Financial Times* 2015i). Moreover, the presence of significant proportions of Russian-speakers in Crimea in particular, but also in eastern Ukraine offered Putin a useful pretext to justify Russian intervention in terms of an obligation or mission to protect the rights of Russian minorities abroad.

Overall Putin was certainly right that the EU and its member states, not to mention the USA, were much less preoccupied than Russia with the fate of Ukraine. The principal champions of a closer integration of Ukraine with the EU were the easternmost member states, first and foremost Poland and Sweden. Their respective foreign ministers launched the 'Eastern Partnership' (EaP) aimed at intensifying the EU's relations with a group of post-Soviet republics that had not yet been accepted as candidates for EU or NATO accession. The German foreign minister Frank-Walter Steinmeier had declined a request to co-sponsor the project from his Polish counterpart, Radoslaw Sikorski, who then recruited the Swedish foreign minister Carl Bildt in Steinmeier's place (Speck 2014a, 2014c). Most member states, according to one analyst, 'simply don't care much' about Ukraine (Speck 2014a). This seems also to have applied to France and Germany, which, the same observer argued, never gave the EaP project their full support (Speck 2014c).

In the absence of the member states' engagement, the management of the EU's relations with Ukraine were left largely in the hands of the Commission and the EEAS, especially those of the Enlargement Commissioner and Czech, Štefan Füle, a strong supporter of the project, and the High Representative for the CFSP, the Briton, Catherine Ashton. The Commission conducted negotiations with the Ukrainian government on the basis of a mandate approved by the Council. In Ukraine, even the European Parliament ventured to play the role of a crisis mediator (Nitoiu and Sus 2017). Retrospectively, the Commission was widely accused of having ignored the geopolitical implications and explosiveness of the AA project and 'sleep-walked' into a crisis with Russia – an accusation that a former Enlargement Commissioner, Günter Verheugen, argued applied no less, however, to the member states as well (*Der Spiegel* 2014e, 2015b; House of Lords European Union Committee 2015; Howorth 2017: 127–128; Kuzio 2017: 116). 'Berlin officials' were said to have had some doubts as to the wisdom of the proposed AAs, but their concerns reportedly 'never reached' the Commission's Enlargement DG in Brussels (*Der Spiegel* 2014d). While the EaP and associated AA talks stagnated initially, they were relaunched during the Hungarian and Polish Council presidencies in 2011 (Wilson 2014: 13–14). Having denounced the EaP 'from the outset', Russia launched the EEU with Belarus and Kazakhstan within months of the 2011 EU summit in Warsaw (Freedman 2014). The EEU appeared as 'almost the last possibility of providing a sufficiently substantial context for the exercise of Russian power' (Freedman 2014). However, all the other three plausible 'candidates' for the EEU – Armenia, Moldova and Ukraine – were also in the process of negotiating AAs with the EU. As by far the biggest of the three, Ukraine was undoubtedly an 'essential building block' for Putin's project (Freedman 2014).

In 2013, the Russian government stepped up its efforts to peel the three post-Soviet republics away from the EU and bring them into the EEU. In the case of Armenia, which depended heavily on Russian military support in its conflict with its neighbour, Azerbaijan, and had tense relations with another neighbour, Turkey, it succeeded. Moldova and Ukraine, however, were more resistant to Russian persuasion and coercion. Despite imposing barriers on Moldovan exports to Russia and threatening that this could complicate a settlement of the conflict over the breakaway region of Transnistria, which Russia backed both financially and militarily, the Moldovan government nonetheless went ahead and initialled an AA with the EU in November 2013. When Putin visited Kiev but failed to persuade President Yanukovych to join the EEU in July 2013, Russia also imposed barriers on Ukrainian exports to Russia. As late as October, Yanukovych continued to defend his intention to sign the AA with the EU (Entous and Norman 2014). He seems finally to have capitulated to Russian pressure after a series of meetings in Sochi in early November, withdrawing from it only a few days before it was due to be initialled. Given mounting economic problems in Ukraine and the imminence of presidential elections that were scheduled for 2015, Yanukovych may well have been swayed by President Putin's offer to reduce the price of Russian gas exports to Ukraine and to grant the government a 'no-strings-tied' loan of US$ 15bn (*Financial Times* 2013h; *Le Monde* 2013g; Seibel 2017: 274). The EU was not prepared to match Putin's offer (Entous and Norman 2014; *Financial Times* 2013g; Freedman 2014; *Le Monde* 2013g). Yanukovych's choice to go with Russia may well also have been influenced by the fact that, as a condition for the AA, the EU had insisted on the release from imprisonment of Yanukovych's domestic political rival and former prime minister, Yulia Tymoshenko (Howorth 2017: 127).

The outbreak of the crisis

Neither Yanukovych nor Putin nor the EU had reckoned, however, with the reaction of Ukrainian civil society to the Ukrainian president's about-face. Within only a couple of days, 'close to 100,000' people had turned out to protest against this decision in Kiev, where they occupied the main square. 'In a country that has been largely apathetic for nearly a decade', one commentator argued, 'no one could have expected such a strong reaction to a decision that would not even guarantee Ukraine's full membership in the EU – not even in the future' (*New York Times* 2013b). Not the prospective 'direct economic benefits' of the AA mobilized the protesters as much as a 'set of values that results in the absence of corruption, a strong social safety net …, a stable currency and responsible government'. Everything else was regarded as 'backward – the "dustbin"' (*New York Times* 2013b). Opinion polls revealed that a strong majority of Ukrainians supported the AA, even in eastern Ukraine (*New York Times* 2013b). Meanwhile, public backing for joining the EEU had diminished by half during 2013 – a trend that was widely attributed to resentment among Ukrainians against Russian trade sanctions and threats (*The Economist* 2013b; *Le Monde* 2013e, 2013f; *New York Times* 2013a).

Despite – or because of – the Ukrainian government's increasing resort to force to crush the protests, these continued to escalate. The responsible EU commissioners, Thüle and Ashton, made several trips to Kiev to try to mediate and resolve the crisis (*Der Spiegel* 2013; Kuzio 2017: 107–108). In contrast, the member states – initially – held back. It was only when the crisis came to a climax and Yanukovych seemed to be on the verge of deploying massive physical force to crush the protests that the foreign ministers of the Weimar Triangle (France, Germany and Poland) flew to Kiev and, along with an Russian emissary, tried to forge an agreement between the protesters and the government. After 21 hours of talks, an accord was reached in which Yanukovych agreed to involve his opponents in the government, to curtail his own powers and to stage elections earlier than scheduled. Described in the moment as a 'diplomatic coup' for the German foreign minister Steinmeier (*Der Spiegel* 2014b), the accord collapsed even before the foreign ministers had left Kiev. As the police appeared to withdraw their protection of the president, he fled Ukraine for Russia, leaving his pro-EU opponents to assume political power.

Russian military intervention and the EU's response

The Russian response to the 'pro-European' revolution in Ukraine was swift. Putin appears to have decided to annex Crimea by force within 48 hours of Yanukovych's flight, on the eve of the closing ceremony of the Winter Olympic Games staged by Russia at Sochi (*Financial Times* 2015i). Already the day after, the *Financial Times* quoted a 'senior Russian official' as saying that Russia was 'prepared to fight a war over Crimea' to protect ethnic Russians and its military base there: 'If Ukraine breaks apart, it will trigger a war.' A Russian diplomat warned: 'We will not allow Europe and the US to take Ukraine from us. The states of the former Soviet Union, we are one family

... They think Russia is still as weak as in the early 1990s, but we are not' (*Financial Times* 2014b).

Russian armed forces were certainly far superior to their Ukrainian counterparts. Whereas Russia had undertaken a military build-up in the previous decade, Ukraine's military capacity had declined (Wilson 2014: 112). The new Ukrainian defence minister claimed that Ukraine could mobilize no more than 5000 troops and in practice no longer had an army. It had been 'systematically destroyed by Yanukovych and his entourage' (Wilson 2016). The new interior minister estimated that the Russian army was 'a hundred times stronger' than the Ukrainian (Pond 2014b). The latter offered in any case no resistance to the Russian invasion and occupation of Crimea, where power was seized by no more than '60 men with Kalashnikovs' – although within a week, according to the Ukrainian government, 16,000 Russian soldiers were deployed in Crimea in addition to the 25,000 already stationed there (*Le Monde* 2014b; Wilson 2014: 110).

Neither the EU member states nor the USA (and therefore nor the NATO) contemplated any kind of military reaction to Russia's invasion and annexation of Crimea. In the West, as one security expert observed at the time, 'nobody is willing to go to war over Crimea and Putin knows this' (Jan Techau, quoted in *Financial Times* 2014c). The issue in the EU was rather *whether* it would impose sanctions on Russia, if so, what form would these take and what accompanying measures, if any, should be taken to persuade Putin to reverse his course and promote a peaceful settlement of the conflict (*Le Monde* 2014f, 2015a; Merkel 2014). At the outset, it seemed by no means certain that the EU would adopt any sanctions at all against Russia. It had not done so, for example, when Russia invaded Georgia in 2008 (discussed earlier in this section). Numerous commentators and analysts noted the 'timidity' or 'caution' that characterized the EU's initial response to the events in Ukraine and expressed doubt as to whether it would be willing or able to adopt meaningful sanctions against Russia (*The Economist* 2014c; McNamara 2014; Munchau 2014; Stephens 2014). Under the CFSP provisions of the EU treaties, unanimity was required for any sanctions to be adopted against Russia, so that, in principle, a single member state could block them. If the EU had reached a lowest-common-denominator stance on this issue, as of the end of February 2014 this would likely have meant adopting no sanctions against Russia.

The EU could not take a decision to confront Russia over Ukraine very lightly. Advocates as well as opponents of sanctions recognized that without Russian cooperation and goodwill, which sanctions would jeopardize, some major international conflicts, such as the civil war in Syria, would be harder to resolve (Hacke 2014; Merkel 2014; Steinmeier 2016; Italian Prime Minister Matteo Renzi, as quoted in *Eurocomment* 2014e). Not least, given their dependence in particular on Russian gas and oil imports, numerous other member states had to reckon with significant economic costs should the EU impose sanctions, as these would very likely provoke Russian retaliation. Indeed, Putin counted on this prospect to dissuade the EU from adopting significant sanctions in the first place: 'In a modern world where everything is connected, of course you can cause some damage' with such measures, he said, but 'such damage will be mutual' (as quoted from a press conference in *Financial Times* 2014e).

Russia and the EU member states were asymmetrically economically interdependent to Russia's disadvantage. Whereas, for goods, EU members depended on Russia for no more than 7.3 per cent of their export revenues and 11.9 per cent of their imports in 2012, a record year for EU–Russian trade, the EU accounted for more than half of Russia's international goods trade: 57 per cent of its export revenues and 46.5 per cent of its imports (Eurostat 2013; House of Lords European Union Committee 2015). However, the EU states were heavily dependent on Russia for imported natural gas (39 per cent) and crude oil and oil products (one-third). Six of them – the three Baltic states, Finland, Bulgaria and Slovakia – imported *all* their natural gas from Russia. EU member states were thus more vulnerable to the prospective disruption of trade with Russia by sanctions than macro-trade statistics indicated and, among them, some were a great deal more vulnerable than others.

In absolute terms, Germany was far and away Russia's biggest partner in the EU, accounting for almost a quarter – 23 per cent – of its trade with Russia in 2012: 31 per cent of the bloc's exports to Russia and 19 per cent of its imports (Eurostat 2013). This was more than twice the volume of trade of Russia's next most important trading partner in the EU, the Netherlands. As many as 300,000 German jobs were estimated to depend on trade with Russia (*Der Spiegel* 2014c). More than 6000 German firms were also registered in Russia – ten times as many as, for example, British firms (House of Lords European Union Committee 2015). In short, no EU sanctions regime against Russia could be very effective unless Germany supported and participated in it. Given that it conducted far more trade with Russia than any other EU member state, some observers specifically identified Germany as being likely to oppose economic sanctions (*The Economist* 2014b, 2014c; *Financial Times* 2014d, 2014d; *Le Monde* 2014b, 2014c; McNamara 2014).

Given its geographic location, Germany was also more exposed than the other major member states to the possible negative political and security-related fallout of a conflict with Russia over Ukraine. Moreover, in Berlin, the SPD had just formed a governing coalition with Merkel's Christian Democrats. It had been the main architect of the *Ostpolitik* that, from the early 1970s on, had paved the way for closer and better relations between the West and the then Soviet Union and Communist bloc (Bender 1986). Provider of the foreign minister (Steinmeier again) in the new government, the SPD might have been expected to be very reluctant to acquiesce in decisions that risked provoking a new 'Cold War' with Russia.

Member states' attitudes to imposing sanctions on Russia over Ukraine diverged. The 'doves' on this issue were primarily the southern, south-eastern and central European states: Italy, Austria, the Czech Republic, Cyprus, Greece, Hungary, Malta, Slovakia, Spain and Slovenia (Bechev and Buras

2014; Dempsey 2014; *Eurocomment* 2014d: 47–48; *Le Monde* 2014a; Moret et al. 2016: 12, 17–18; Natorski and Pomorska 2017). Portugal, Bulgaria, Luxembourg and – before the downing of the MH17 aircraft in July 2014 – the Netherlands were also occasionally classified as sanctions 'sceptics' (*Financial Times* 2014g; *Le Monde* 2014d, 2015a). Their reservations were 'almost all economic rather than political' (Eurocomment 2014d: 48). Nonetheless, even ignoring the case of Germany, interstate variations in attitudes towards sanctions did not very closely follow variations in levels of economic dependence on Russia. Rather several of the most 'hawkish' member states on sanctions – mainly northern and north-eastern European states (Poland, the three Baltics, Sweden and Denmark) – belonged to those most economically dependent on Russia. The perceived security threat posed by Russia played a bigger role in determining member states' attitude to sanctions, with those located closer to Russia feeling more threatened and less reluctant to bear the costs of sanctions compared with those further away from Russia. The 'big three' member states fell between the camps of 'doves' and 'hawks', with the UK tending occasionally towards the latter group (Bechev and Buras 2014; interview, Berlin, 2018).

For all their divergences on sanctions, the member states were more easily able to reach a compromise on this issue than on any other conceivable tougher measures against Russia (interview, Berlin, 2018). The EU agreed the main elements of its approach rapidly, within roughly a week of the Russian intervention in Crimea. There was 'no real confrontation', but rather an 'unexpected' degree of consensus (interview, Berlin, 2018; Natorski and Pomorska 2017: 58). While these elements were modified at the margins, in the light of events 'on the ground' in Ukraine, during the following four years, they remained fundamentally intact. First, the EU offered to sign an AA with the new Ukrainian government – the political provisions of the agreement were then signed in March and the economic provisions in June 2014. Second, it pledged (IMF-conditional) financial aid to the new government as well as help to diversify and secure Ukrainian energy supplies. Third, it called on the Russian and Ukrainian governments to start negotiations as quickly as possible to solve the crisis 'including through potential multilateral mechanisms' (European Council 2014a). And, fourth, it approved a calibrated three-stage sanctions strategy that it would pursue vis-à-vis Russia if it did not withdraw from Crimea or it should expand its military intervention in Ukraine. The first of three stages was adopted already by the Foreign Affairs Council on 3 March and involved the suspension of both the EU's talks with Russia over a successor agreement to the 1997 Partnership and Cooperation Agreement – talks that had in fact ground to a halt in 2010 – and member states' bilateral talks with Russia over visa liberalization. The second stage was to comprise the cancellation of the next scheduled EU–Russia Summit and the imposition of travel bans and asset freezes on individuals and 'entities' that the EU judged to have been implicated in the seizure of Crimea. These measures were to be taken if the Russian government refused to negotiate with its Ukrainian counterpart over the crisis or such negotiations failed to 'produce results within a limited time-frame'. The third stage, which would be applied if Russia were to take 'any further steps ... to destabilize the situation in Ukraine', would 'lead to additional and far-reaching consequences for relations in a broad range of economic areas' (European Council 2014a).

The European Council actually toughened the initial draft of its sanctions strategy while it was meeting in Brussels, as on the same day the Crimean Parliament voted to accede to Russia, the Russian Duma endorsed this request and a referendum to ratify the parliamentary vote in Crimea was announced for only ten days later. The strategy adopted, notably the third stage, was 'considerably stronger' than any of the heads of government had considered likely upon their arrival in Brussels (*Eurocomment* 2014a: 7–15).

The capacity of the leaders in the European Council to agree – rapidly – on a crisis strategy that was more than the lowest common denominator of their initial attitudes reflected a level of convergence in their analysis of Russian actions in Ukraine that had not hitherto characterized their relations with Russia. This convergence rested on a combination of – partly interrelated – normative, security and internal-political considerations. In respect of norms, they were united in viewing Russia's invasion and annexation of Crimea as a flagrant contravention of numerous international treaties that Russia had signed (see earlier in this section) and as representing a frontal challenge to the kind of rules-based, peaceful international security order that had developed in post-World War II Europe and of which the EU saw itself as an incarnation and leading promoter and guardian (Sjursen and Rosén 2017). The rights of territorial integrity and national self-determination were defining norms of the EU that, if they were so directly challenged, it could scarcely abandon them without gravely damaging its image and self-conception (Sjursen and Rosén 2017).

Security concerns also motivated the support of at least some member states for sanctions. They viewed these as a (non-military) means of deterrence, fearing, based on historical precedent, that, if Russia were left unchecked, they could be the next targets of its military aggression. Its seizure of Crimea unsettled or threatened to unsettle Russia's entire neighbourhood (George Friedman 2014). The president of Lithuania, Dalia Grybauskaite, warned: 'First it's Ukraine, Moldova will be next and, finally, it can reach the Baltic states and Poland' (as quoted in *Financial Times* 2014f). The British prime minister, Cameron, similarly argued that if the EU did not respond firmly, 'there will be other such problems to come' (as quoted in Sjursen and Rosen 2017: 26–27). These fears were not assuaged, to say the least, when Putin later told his Ukrainian counterpart that, if he so ordered, Russian troops could not only be in Kiev in a matter of two days, but also in Riga, Vilnius, Tallinn, Warsaw or Bucharest (*Der Spiegel* 2014g).

The EU also saw itself as having a 'special responsibility for peace, stability and prosperity in Europe' (European Council 2014a). Given their conception of its role, the member states regarded the option of doing nothing in the face of the events in Ukraine as unacceptable (Sjusen and Rosén 2017). There was at the same time a widespread awareness among them that the Ukraine Crisis would be a litmus test of the credibility of the EU's aspirations to have a common foreign policy. Steinmeier, for example, cautioned that if Russia succeeded in dividing the EU over the crisis, then this would be the end of an EU common foreign policy 'before it ever began' (as quoted in *Eurocomment* 2014b: 30; Sjusen and Rosén 2017: 27–28). From this perspective, how well or badly the EU managed this crisis would determine whether the EU could maintain the existing level of foreign policy integration and thus have implications extending far beyond the specific issue of Ukraine and EU–Russian relations.

The escalation of the crisis

As, in the following weeks, Russia tightened its grip on Crimea and intensified its efforts to destabilize Ukraine, the EU gradually strengthened its sanctions in line with the strategy it had adopted. It activated the second phase of sanctions involving mainly asset freezes and travel bans when, following the 16 March referendum, Russia formalized the annexation of Crimea. The threat of more far-reaching sanctions if Russia should refuse to talk to the Ukrainian government and further destabilize Ukraine did not dissuade Putin from expanding the scope of his military intervention in the eastern part of the country, where separatist groups had taken up arms against the Ukrainian government and declared their own republics in Donetsk and Luhansk (see Map 4.1). On the one hand, with evidence of Russian (physical and logistical) support for the separatist uprisings becoming increasingly incontrovertible, despite Putin's denials, and Moscow continuing to show little inclination to negotiate with Kiev, the pressure on the EU to ratchet up its sanctions rose

MAP 4.1   *Map of Ukraine, 2015*

Note: This map of Ukraine includes data points for the Crimea, although its sovereignty is contested (as of 2018).
Sources: The Economist.

during summer 2014. On the other, the EU struggled to maintain a common front. Reservations among some member states – according to one source (Dempsey 2014) Austria, Italy, Slovakia, and Bulgaria, according to another (Speck 2016: 8) France, Italy, Austria, Slovakia and Greece – delayed the Council deciding to enlarge the list of individuals and companies affected by travel bans and asset freezes. Ultimately, however, the Council did decide to enlarge the list (Natorski and Pomorska 2017: 63; Orenstein and Kelemen 2017: 95).

Within 24 hours of the Council having taken this step, the political context of the EU's sanctions policy was suddenly transformed and the likelihood of the EU splitting over the policy greatly reduced. On 17 July 2014, the civilian passenger aircraft MH17 was shot down by a missile over a separatist-held part of eastern Ukraine, killing 298 people, more than two-thirds of them Dutch. For the politics of the Ukraine Crisis, the downing of MH17, which the separatists may have mistaken for a Ukrainian military aircraft, proved to be the 'proverbial game-changer', a 'turning-point' (Seibel 2017: 277; see also *Financial Times* 2015g; Kuzio 2017: 110; Natorski and Pomorska 2017: 63; Orenstein and Kelemen 2017: 94; Speck 2016: 9). Whatever doubts some member states might have still have had about applying stage-three sanctions on Russia were 'almost literally destroyed' by this event (*Eurocomment* 2014c: 44). There was very little or no doubt concerning the responsibility of the separatists for this attack or that the launcher from which the missile was fired came from the Russian military (*Le Monde* 2014e; Yekelchyk 2015: 150). This event provoked a complete breakdown in any relations of trust between EU leaders and Russia, especially in the relations between Merkel and Putin (Orenstein and Kelemen 2017: 95). This was evident in the language of the EU communiqué declaring the toughening of sanctions against Russia two weeks later: 'The illegal annexation of territory and deliberate destabilization of a neighbouring sovereign country cannot be accepted in twenty-first century Europe. Furthermore, when the violence created spirals out of control and leads to the killing of almost 300 innocent civilians … the situation requires [an] urgent and determined response' (European Council 2014b). Merkel herself is said to have been 'shaken' by what she termed this 'horrendous' event (as quoted in *Financial Times* 2015g).

The aircraft attack not only generated a 'strong sense of solidarity' in the EU (Seibel 2017: 277), but also had a 'galvanizing' impact on public opinion in the member states (Orenstein and Kelemen 2017: 95). Public attitudes towards Russia subsequently became much more critical (Pew Research Centre 2015b). In the Netherlands, which had hitherto accepted sanctions against Russia only reluctantly, 80 per cent of respondents in a public opinion survey said they would support them even if they hurt the Dutch economy (*Financial Times* 2014h). A similar survey in Germany found a majority of 52 per cent in favour of toughening sanctions against Russia even if this should lead to the loss of 'many jobs' (*Der Spiegel* 2014f).

Far more comprehensive than those already in place, the 'third-stage' sanctions adopted by the EU after the downing of flight MH17 affected primarily the financial, oil and defence sectors. The sanctions banned EU firms from issuing or trading in Russian bonds, equity and similar financial instruments with a maturity of at least 90 (later cut to 30) days and from supplying oil industry equipment in Russia as well as goods comprising dual-use (civilian and military) technology and arms or related goods. These sanctions above all had a 'notable crippling effect' on the Russian economy (Yekelchyk 2015: 154). They were viewed, along with falling oil prices, as having caused the Russian economy to shrink and foreign direct investment in the country to have ground to a halt in 2014–15 (Nevskaya 2016; Orenstein and Kelemen 2017: 95). Russia retaliated swiftly by banning agricultural imports from the EU.

The main architects of the initial EU response to the invasion of Crimea – alongside the Council president Herman van Rompuy – were the leaders of the 'big three' member states, Merkel, Hollande and Cameron (who was a strong proponent of the toughening of prospective sanctions that took place at the summit), and the Polish prime minister, Donald Tusk, who represented the third member of the 'Weimar Triangle' that had spearheaded diplomatic efforts to resolve the escalating domestic political crisis in Ukraine just a couple of weeks earlier (*Eurocomment* 2014a: 10–13). From this point on, the Commission and the previously involved Commission members receded from the front line of crisis management. The Commission henceforth played a significant 'back-up' role in the crisis, particularly by undertaking the technical work relating to sanctions, but, unlike the period in which the AA with Ukraine was being negotiated, it was no longer setting the direction of EU policy (*Eurocomment* 2014c: 9, 2014d: 44; Howorth 2017: 130; Natorski and Pomorska 2017: 65; Speck 2016: 6). Similarly, the European Council, under van Rompuy's chairmanship, was an important venue for debates and consensus-building among the heads of government and its president during the crisis, but it was not an influential collective actor as such (*Eurocomment* 2014c: 9; Speck 2016: 6). Rather the Ukraine Crisis was '*Chefsache*', a matter that the chief executives of the member state governments had primarily to deal with (*Eurocomment* 2014a: 9). Among them, Chancellor Merkel was more than the *primus inter pares*. According to one long-time observer of the European Council, reflecting the almost consensual view of numerous others, Merkel was 'always … the leader' in the EU's management of the Ukraine Crisis, in which the EU could do 'virtually nothing of any significance … without the German government's active involvement' (*Eurocomment* 2014c: 9; Krotz and Maher 2016; Natorski and Pomorska 2017; Orenstein and Kelemen 2017: 96–97; Speck 2014a, 2016: 1, 4–5, 10).

Germany's relations with Russia had begun to cool already before the Ukraine Crisis, following Putin's return to the presidency and signs of growing authoritarianism in Russian politics (Forsberg 2016: 23–28). But there had been no sharp break from previous policy, which focused on commercial and economic cooperation (Forsberg 2016: 24). However, Russia's invasion and rapid annexation of Crimea provoked a major shift in German policy in which economic interests were subordinated to security and normative considerations. Merkel put herself at the head of the movement to impose sanctions on Russia if it did not withdraw from Crimea and destabilized other regions of Ukraine, while trying to bring Russia to the negotiating table. Merkel represented this new position with for her atypical passion and emotion; her role in the EU on this issue was 'pivotal' (*Eurocomment* 2014b: 32–33; Youngs 2017: 72). Despite their stronger historical attachment to *détente* with Russia and the former Soviet Union, her Social Democratic coalition partners followed suit, with Steinmeier strongly condemning Russia's actions and making clear that Germany would be prepared to sustain 'economic disadvantages' in opposing them (as quoted in speech to German-Russian Forum, *Eurocomment* 2014b: 30). Regardless of such prospective disadvantages, and despite the negative attitude to sanctions of the German business lobby for trade with the former Communist bloc, the *Ostaussschuss der Deutschen Wirtschaft* (Eastern Committee of German Business), the principal German manufacturing-industrial business organization, the BDI, accepted the primacy of politics on this issue and fell in with the government's sanctions policy (Kerber 2014). There was little in the German response to back the interpretation that Germany was abandoning its European and Western allies in search of a special relationship with Russia (see Kundnani 2015).

The central role that Merkel played in managing the Ukraine Crisis in and for the EU is reflected in the relatively high intensity of her contacts with Putin. Between February 2014 and November 2015, for example, she talked 65 times with the Russian president (including 35 one-on-one conversations), almost twice more often than did the French president Hollande and more than four times more often than President Obama or the British prime minister, Cameron (Speck 2016: 4). Her intensive exchange with Putin did not bring the two leaders any closer together, however. Early in the crisis, she allegedly described him as living 'in another world' (*The Guardian* 2014). She was especially antagonized by what she regarded as Putin's mendacity (as illustrated by his repeated denials of Russian participation in and support for the separatist militias in eastern Ukraine) and his untrustworthiness (as indicated by his failure to implement the commitments he made in the Minsk accords – see the following section) (*Financial Times* 2015g). After some 35 telephone conversations between the two leaders, they met face to face for four hours at the Brisbane G20 summit in November 2014, but the meeting left them, in case of doubt, further apart than ever (*Financial Times* 2015g; *Le Monde* 2014g). *Immediately* after it, Merkel used a speech in Sydney to castigate Russia for its actions, for intimidating other states in Eastern Europe and for threatening to spread conflict more broadly across Europe (*New York Times* 2014). The Social Democrat Steinmeier was hardly any less critical of Russia: there could be no return to 'business as usual' in relations with Russia after what had happened in Ukraine. Germany's 'fundamental trust' in Russia had been eroded and could not be restored overnight. It could not accept that borders in Europe could once again be changed arbitrarily (Steinmeier 2014).

While piloting the EU's approach to the crisis, German leaders did not want to be perceived as representing German interests alone and thus to risk becoming isolated in and from the EU. In dealing with Putin, they wanted to be able and be seen to speak not just for Germany, but also – and legitimately – for the entire EU (*Eurocomment* 2014b: 40; Speck 2014b). Hence, within the EU, they pursued an inclusive style of crisis management: 'We attached great importance to letting our EU partners know what was going on. There were regular briefings. We were very concerned to answer their queries' (interview, Berlin, 2018). This approach bolstered other states' trust in German diplomacy:

> The conduct during the negotiations and intense information-sharing practice, in particular Merkel's efforts to keep the partners on board through not only Brussels channels, but also bilaterally ... somewhat reassured them about Germany 'acting in good faith'. Germany and France, well aware of representing the EU in a very sensitive matter, consulted the positions of other partners and reported back on the progress of talks conducted in the Normandy Format in order to maintain the common EU position on the relation between sanctions and ceasefire. National diplomats were satisfied with the information received and regarded it as solid and unproblematic.
>
> (Natorski and Pomorska 2017: 64)

Confidence in German leadership of the EU on this issue was also developed and maintained by ensuring that the distribution of the burdens of EU sanctions within the EU was relatively equitable. Without such efforts, the accord reached on sanctions would have been more difficult to achieve (Natorski and Pomorska 2017: 63). The sanctions were drafted by the Commission and the EEAS, but then negotiated in the Council (Christie 2016: 54; Youngs 2017: 70–71; interview, Berlin, 2018). In particular the third-stage sanctions package adopted after the shooting-down of MH17 reflected the need to 'spread the burden as equitably as possible between member states and across economic sectors' (*Eurocomment* 2014d: 44; also Bechev and Buras 2014). Thus France, for example, made concessions on arms, Germany on energy technology and the UK in the financial sector (*Eurocomment* 2014d: 44). In the event, member states were nonetheless affected somewhat differently by the EU's sanctions. In absolute terms, the exports of all member states to Russia declined in the wake of sanctions, but there were considerable interstate variations in the magnitude of the decline. In nominal terms, Germany suffered by far the biggest decline in the value of its exports to Russia in the year following the imposition of stage-three sanctions in July 2014, three-and-a-half times more than the next most strongly hit member state, Italy (Giumelli 2017: 1071). In percentage terms, the declines were biggest in Cyprus, Ireland and Malta, with Germany the 9th (and France the 12th) most strongly affected member. If, relative to the size of its economy, Germany was by no means the member state worst hit by sanctions, it could demonstrate that it was willing to bear a large and in proportional terms a fair share of the burdens associated with the imposition of sanctions.

Among the other EU member states, the German government cooperated most closely with France. 'There was a very intensive exchange of views and close coordination with France' on how to manage the crisis (interview, Berlin, 2018). In one observer's judgement, Merkel and Holland were 'practically joined at the hip' on the Ukraine Crisis (Howorth 2017: 130). Indeed, Franco-German bilateralism was more pronounced in the management of this crisis than in any of the others that gripped the EU since 2010. The view in Paris was that the close cooperation between Merkel and Hollande during the Ukraine Crisis 'seriously' reinforced the overall relationship (Davet and Lhomme 2016b: 496). According to Hollande, Merkel saw advantages in managing this crisis bi- rather than unilaterally: 'It's better to do it as a couple than all alone' ('*C'est mieux à deux que tout seul*') (as quoted in Davet and Lhomme 2016b: 496). By working closely with Paris, Germany would provoke or encounter less mistrust among other member states that otherwise might suspect that it was being too 'tough' or 'soft' on or being too strongly swayed by its commercial links with Russia (Davet and Lhomme 2016b: 496–497).Cooperating with France also helped bring on board other member states, especially in southern Europe, that stood traditionally closer to Paris than to Berlin in the EU (interview, Berlin, 2018; Krotz and Maher 2016: 1060–1061; Speck 2016: 5). Indeed, in Hollande's view, 'If I had not been there, she would not have been able to do Ukraine' (Davet and Lhomme: 498b). Nonetheless, in this crisis too, Germany's influence on EU policy was stronger than that of France: Hollande played rather the role of Merkel's 'loyal lieutenant' and was 'rarely if ever an independent actor' (*Eurocomment* 2014c: 9; Krotz and Maher 2016: 1061).

Franco-German diplomacy: the Normandy Format and the Minsk accords

The very close cooperation between the German and French governments over the Ukraine Crisis was most clearly visible in the action undertaken to promote a negotiated settlement of the crisis – the other main component of the EU's Ukraine strategy, apart from applying sanctions to Russia and supporting the government in Kiev. On the diplomatic stage, the other EU member states 'essentially delegated their responsibility' for trying to solve the crisis to France and Germany (Seibel 2017: 276). The German and French foreign ministers initially proposed to create a forum in which talks could be held involving the EU and the USA as well as the governments in Moscow and Kiev (Rinke 2014). Supporting this proposal, Merkel called for the creation of an 'international contact group' (*Eurocomment* 2014a: 6; Merkel 2014). The Russian government agreed to take part in talks instigated by the USA in Geneva in April 2014, but although some measures were agreed there, they had 'no impact on the situation on the ground' (Speck 2016: 10). Separatist militias continued to expand the areas they occupied in eastern Ukraine. Undeterred by their initial failure, the French and German governments launched a fresh initiative aimed at bringing about talks between the two sides during the 70th anniversary celebrations of the D-Day landings in Normandy in early June 2014. Out of this first, informal meeting between Putin and Poroshenko, which Hollande says was his idea, developed the 'Normandy Format', a quadrilateral framework for negotiations over the crisis involving Ukraine, Russia, France and Germany (Davet and Lhomme 2016a, 2016b: 491–498). In meeting Poroshenko, who had been elected president on 25 May, Putin tacitly recognized the new Ukrainian government, with which he had hitherto refused to talk. Hollande's initiative was far from unilateral, however. He planned it in detail and in 'constant concertation' with Merkel (Davet and Lhomme 2016a).

This initial meeting in Normandy opened a dialogue between the protagonists in the Ukraine conflict and created a channel through which future negotiations could be conducted. In the short term, however, it did not make any contribution to pacifying eastern Ukraine, where armed conflict continued to rage. Towards the end of August 2014, Ukrainian armed forces appeared to be on the verge of defeating their separatist opponents in the Donbas region. But, as this prospect became increasingly realistic, the Ukrainian forces suddenly found themselves confronted by a much larger number of far more professional, far better-equipped opponents, suggesting that, to avert a military defeat for the separatist groups, and despite denying having done so, Putin had rapidly increased Russia's military presence in Donbas (*Eurocomment* 2014d: 45–46; *Financial Times* 2015g). Some 4000 Russian soldiers allegedly crossed the border into Ukraine on 24 August alone (*Financial Times* 2015g). In the last four months of 2014, the number of Russian soldiers fighting in Ukraine is estimated to have reached between 8000 and 10,000 and made up roughly a quarter of the rebel forces (*Financial Times* 2015j).

By strengthening the Russian military presence in eastern Ukraine, Putin was in effect telling Poroshenko: 'Whatever you do on the battlefield, Russia will do more; this is a fight you cannot win' (*The Economist* 2014e). Encouraged by Merkel, the Ukrainian president had little choice but to plead for a ceasefire, allegedly persuading Putin to negotiate with the threat that otherwise the Ukrainian government would publish evidence that Russian soldiers had been killed or captured in Ukraine (*Eurocomment* 2014d: 45; *Financial Times* 2015h). Under an accord reached on 5 September at Minsk (Minsk I) and a subsequent 'memorandum', the Organization for Security and Cooperation in Europe (OSCE) was to monitor a ceasefire and oversee its implementation, heavy weapons were to be pulled back from the front line of the conflict, power in the Donbas region was to be decentralized and free local elections held, offensive operations and foreign mercenaries were to be banned, and the Ukrainian–Russian border, over which the Ukrainian government had lost control in the region, was to be monitored. The participants in the Normandy Format did not take part directly in the negotiations themselves, but 'prodded' the direct protagonists in the fighting to negotiate under the aegis of the OSCE (Yekelchyk 2015: 155).

After the adoption of Minsk I, the intensity of fighting in south-eastern Ukraine diminished only temporarily. By early 2015, when the Russian-backed separatist forces wrested control of Donetsk International Airport from the Ukrainian army, the accord had collapsed completely. The Normandy Format members increasingly realized that they had to be 'directly involved in negotiating any prospective settlement' of the conflict (Yekelchyk 2015: 156). However, in late January, new Normandy Format talks also broke down. Once more on the backfoot, Ukrainian forces were increasingly in danger of also losing control of Debaltseve, a major road and rail junction in south-eastern Ukraine. The increasingly perilous position of the Ukrainian armed forces, combined with a growing discussion in the USA about whether it should supply Ukraine with arms, which Merkel thought would only exacerbate the conflict, prompted Berlin and Paris on their own initiative to propose a new peace plan that was discussed again in the Normandy Format in Minsk on 11–12 February 2015 (Speck 2016: 10). This was 'the most serious diplomatic initiative at the highest levels' to resolve the conflict (Seibel 2017: 279). A deepening economic crisis in Russia – that Western sanctions may have exacerbated – arguably disposed Putin to look for a negotiated settlement of the conflict (Yekelchyk 2015: 156). Some 17 hours of talks between the four Normandy leaders and their foreign ministers culminated in the adoption of a new 13-point accord (Minsk II), in which the protagonists in the conflict undertook to do many of the same things that they had pledged to do in Minsk I but to different degrees had not done.

For the EU, the accord was arguably no more than a 'fragile holding operation' (Youngs 2017: 113). Its provisions reflected the balance of military power 'on the ground' in the Donbas region. Poroshenko conceivably signed it only to avert Ukraine's military collapse vis-à-vis Russia (*Le Monde* 2017d). Critics lamented, for example, that Merkel and Hollande had forced Poroshenko to make a 'total capitulation' to Putin and that Russia was no more likely to respect the terms of the new accord than the old one (Ferguson 2015; Thom 2015). Merkel and Hollande appear to have prioritized achieving a ceasefire at all costs, given their belief – or Merkel's at least – that Putin would not let Russia be beaten in a military conflict in Ukraine (Merkel quoted in Ferguson 2015). From this viewpoint, it was prudent to make major concessions to the Ukrainian separatist groups and Putin if it served to stave off the possible military defeat and political collapse of Ukraine as a whole.

The fact that within only a few days of the conclusion of Minsk II accord separatist forces compelled the Ukrainian army to withdraw from Debaltseve did not bode well for the accord's future. And, indeed, Russia and its allies in eastern Ukraine subsequently did little to implement the accord – which for the EU was a condition for its lifting of sanctions. One analysis concluded in 2017 that the accord had 'yet to produce substantial results' and was 'running out of steam', while there was a 'creeping Russian escalation' of the conflict and the situation in the Donbas region was deteriorating (Pothier 2017). However, the level of armed conflict and casualties was much lower in 2017 than it had been prior to Minsk II and the front lines in the conflict had not shifted again since 2014–15 (*Le Monde* 2017d; OHCHR 2017: 6–7). The Ukraine Crisis had become a smouldering or 'simmering' conflict – in other words, one that had subsided, but could once again be reignited or boil over (Pifer 2017).

Conclusion

Measured by the objectives of bringing about the reversal of Russia's annexation of Crimea, an end to Russian support for separatist militias in eastern Ukraine and a negotiated and implemented accord to end armed conflict, the EU's Ukraine Crisis policy failed. Sanctions were not alone responsible for a sharp decline in EU–Russia trade – by more than a third from €326bn in 2013 to €209bn in 2015 – but, along with declining oil prices, they were a significant contributory factor (Giumelli 2017: 1066–1067; Howorth 2017: 132). They may also have had a significant negative impact on the Russian economy. A Russian analysis concluded that Western (i.e. not only EU) sanctions 'significantly affected' the Russian economy and explained about a third of the economy's contraction between 2013 and 2015 (Nevskaya 2016). The IMF estimated that sanctions caused Russian GDP to decline in 2015 by 1.25 per cent (as cited in Christie 2016: 58). Putin himself admitted in 2016 that the sanctions limiting Russia's access to international financial markets were 'severely harming Russia' (as quoted from an interview with the German *Bild-Zeitung*, 11 January 2016, cited in Speck 2016: 1). But they fell 'far short of entailing a complete rupture in economic relations' (Youngs 2017: 98). And they did not persuade the Russian government to reverse the steps it took in the first half of 2014.

It is more difficult to answer the question whether the sanctions persuaded Putin not to expand Russia's military intervention in Ukraine beyond the Donbas region or to annex this region to Russia in the same way as Crimea. Some observers of the conflict have speculated that this was the case (e.g., Dempsey 2014; *Der Spiegel* 2016a; Porter 2017; Speck 2015, 2016: 2; Thomas Friedman 2014; Yekelchyk 2015: 159). All that can be said is that, especially after the mildness of the EU's reactions to Russia's military intervention in Georgia in 2008, Putin and his government probably did not expect as tough an EU response to its intervention in Ukraine as that which materialized (Mendras 2016). According to a Russian think tank, they had wrongly anticipated that Russia's economic ties with the largest EU member states, 'particularly Germany', would protect them from sanctions (as cited in Orenstein and Kelemen 2017: 95–96). Russia allegedly had enough troops massed near the border with Ukraine in April 2014 to invade and occupy the country and knew, given the weakness of Ukrainian armed forces, that they could have done so (Gressel 2015; Pond 2014a). That no such overt invasion took place may, however, have other explanations than the fear of the anticipated consequences of EU-led sanctions. First, Russia was aware that if they were to take this step, it would likely provoke a 'strong counter-insurgency campaign' (Gressel 2015). Outside Crimea at least, its intervention in Ukraine seems to have been highly unpopular (Kuzio 2015). Even most Russian-speakers in eastern Ukraine appear to have been hostile to the idea of being annexed by Russia and in favour of Ukrainian alignment with the EU (Garton Ash 2014; Kuzio 2015; Pew Research Center 2015b: 6–8, 14–15). Second, and relatedly, a prolonged military intervention in Ukraine that met with fierce local resistance would cause large-scale casualties among Russian soldiers and likely prove increasingly unpopular in Russia itself (Speck 2016: 2). That the Russian government feared such a domestic reaction is suggested by the fact that it tried to keep secret the number of Russian troops killed in its intervention in eastern Ukraine. Thus it is possible that the unanticipated adoption of sanctions against Russia by the EU helped to persuade Putin not to extend the scope of Russian military intervention beyond Crimea and eastern Ukraine, but it may not have been the only or indeed the most important factor.

In one, for this study critical, respect, however, the EU's management of the Ukraine Crisis was a 'success story' (Speck 2016). Other than in many other major external crises, the EU succeeded in developing and, over at least the following four years, pursuing a common crisis policy. The stakes for the EU in this crisis were very high. As Steinmeier warned (see the section 'Russian military intervention and the EU's response' above), if the EU had divided over how to deal with Russia, any prospect of the pursuit of a common EU foreign policy would likely have been destroyed and the EU's aspirations in this regard thoroughly discredited. To maintain the unity of the EU was the overriding goal of German policy in the Ukraine Crisis as well as numerous other EU governments (interview, Berlin, 2018; Youngs 2017: 216). There was no trend towards foreign policy disintegration with individual member states parting ways and pursuing their own unilateral policies. Nor was there any shift towards closer foreign policy integration either – the sanctions instruments provided for in the EU treaties sufficed for the EU to manage this crisis. The Ukraine Crisis thus constitutes a 'middle case' between the Eurozone Crisis (Chapter 3), from which the EU emerged politically more closely integrated, on the one hand, and the Schengen and Refugee Crisis (Chapter 5), in which it showed signs of political disintegration, on the other. The process whereby, as the crisis unfolded and intensified, the German and, to a lesser extent, the French government took over the reins of the EU's management of the crisis from the Commission could otherwise be interpreted as evidence of *vertical* political disintegration, but this would be to ignore the extent to which this pattern of crisis management typified the EU's handling of past external crises, including, the conflicts in or concerning Georgia (2008), the Iranian nuclear programme, Libya (2011) and Syria (2013). The management of the Ukraine Crisis by a subgroup of the most powerful EU member states was thus no more than par for the course in the EU's external relations rather than a manifestation of a new trend towards the disempowerment of the EU's supranational actors. What was new and unique about the Ukraine

Crisis was rather that, for the first time, not France or France and the UK, but rather *Germany* played the role of the EU's primary external crisis manager. How novel this role was can be seen by contrasting it with Germany's abstention from any intervention in the conflicts in Libya and concerning the deployment of chemical weapons by the Assad regime in Syria.

Whether, over a much longer period, the EU would be able to maintain a common policy vis-à-vis Russia over Ukraine remained to be seen. This would depend heavily on whether there were significant changes in Russian policy. Numerous member states – for example, Bulgaria (*Le Monde* 2016l) – continued to express unease over the maintenance and utility of the sanctions. The French Senate voted in favour of lifting them (Moret et al. 2016: 12). The French foreign minister, Jean-Yves Le Drian, declared that the sanctions 'can be reversed from the moment when things should progress' – but added that this was not yet the case (*Le Monde* 2017e). In Germany, prime ministers of the east German states, which have relatively strong economic ties with Russia originating from the Cold War period, pressed for the sanctions to be lifted (*Der Spiegel* 2016b). Steinmeier and his (also Social Democratic) successor as German Foreign Minister, Sigmar Gabriel, proposed that sanctions be eased gradually to the extent that Russia fulfilled its parts of the Minsk II accord (*Der Spiegel* 2017; *Financial Times* 2016c). However, Gabriel assured that Germany would not recognize Russia's annexation of Crimea and insisted that, for Germany, Ukraine's territorial integrity and sovereignty were 'non-negotiable' (Federal Foreign Office 2017). Despite frequent prognoses that support for the sanctions in the EU was crumbling, they were renewed regularly, the last time in June 2018, despite the formation in Italy of a new government reputedly hostile to them. The EU's unity proved 'stronger and more resilient than many believed it could be' (Gressel and Wesslau 2017).

The domestic politics of the Ukraine Crisis in the member states made it less difficult than in the other crises for the EU to find and maintain a common position. The Russian military intervention and use of military force in Ukraine – the annexation of Crimea, its military engagement in eastern Ukraine, and the shooting-down of MH17 – provoked a convergence of elite and mass attitudes on the crisis in the member states and helped to generate what proved to be a robust consensus among the governments in favour of sanctions. The shared perception of a common threat to European peace and stability promoted cohesion in the EU in a way comparable perhaps to that fostered by the threat of the Communist bloc during the Cold War. The domestic politics of the Ukraine Crisis thus diverged from that of the Eurozone and Schengen and refugee crises, which generated high levels of political polarization between the member states. It is, of course, questionable whether this consensus would have withstood a concerted bid by the most 'Russia-critical' member states to impose a much more sweeping trade embargo (affecting, for example, imports of Russian oil and gas), but no such proposals were ever seriously advanced. A neo-functionalist, transactionalist or liberal intergovernmentalist analysis of the EU's policy in this crisis might emphasize that the EU's states' dependence on Russia for energy supplies prevented them from taking any meaningful action against Russia over Ukraine and that this explains why the crisis failed to provoke any European disintegration. Indeed, this dependence may account for the fact that the EU's sanctions did not target natural gas or oil supplies. However, this interpretation would underestimate the scope of the EU's sanctions, which did have a significant negative effect on the Russian economy (see earlier in this section) and went well beyond being the lowest common denominator between the member states when the crisis first broke. The consensus forged in the EU over sanctions was not reached because these were harmless, either for the EU or for Russia. Moreover, member states' attitudes on the imposition of sanctions did not vary according to the extent of their energy dependence on Russia, but rather by the extent to which they perceived Russia as a threat to their (physical-military) security.

In as far as there was less political polarization within the EU over the Ukraine than over the other crises, postfunctionalist integration theory would not necessarily have led one to expect that the EU would disintegrate over this issue. However, there were still sufficiently large potential conflicts of interest and preferences between member states to erode and destroy the EU's unity. The EU held together not least because, in this crisis, more than any other that the EU has confronted since 2010, the German government did act as a stabilizing hegemonic power. It was the central actor in the process by which the EU set its rules for managing the crisis and its relations with Russia. Berlin's dominant role in handling this crisis may be attributable to a combination of several factors. One is that, on account of its geographic location, Germany was at least potentially more strongly exposed to the crisis than either of the other 'big three' member states. A second factor, which depended on the EU's reliance on economic sanctions as a means of influencing Russia, is that it was and is by far Russia's largest trading partner among the EU states so that, if it so chose, it could inflict more economic damage on Russia than any other member state. A third is that, given the size of its economy and the strength of the federal government's finances, compared again with other member states, it could provide greater – direct or indirect – financial aid to the 'pro-European' Ukrainian government (Speck 2016: 12). A fourth is that none of the other 'usual suspects' – in particular the UK and the USA – was both willing and able to step up to the plate in this crisis, leaving a vacuum in the EU and the West that only Germany was capable of occupying. Less affected by the crisis than its eastern neighbours and less important to Russia as an economic partner, France was less well-suited than Germany to orchestrate the EU's response as well as 'weakened' by chronic economic stagnation (Speck 2015). The UK had become 'increasingly disconnected from the EU' and 'increasingly irrelevant on the international stage' (respectively Speck 2015 and the British ex-Deputy Commander of NATO, General Shirreff, quoted in Clegg 2016b: 214–215; Krotz and Maher 2016; *The Guardian* 2016). US President Obama was not convinced that the USA had a significant stake in the crisis and correspondingly inclined to allow the

EU to handle it (Chollet 2016: 178–179; Landler 2016: 282; Speck 2016). Finally, of the leaders of the major Western powers, Chancellor Merkel was the one who had the longest experience dealing with and best knew Putin, who had been a KGB officer in the former East Germany and often spoke German with her. Germany had good reason, however, to cooperate closely with France in the crisis, particularly given the historically grounded fears of the (now EU member) states 'in between' Germany and Russia that Berlin and Moscow could deal with each other over their heads and at their expense.

At the same time, Germany also consulted other member states intensively over how to manage the crisis and went to considerable lengths to ensure that the EU's strategy accommodated their – as well as or, in some instances, such as the question of the exclusion of Russia from the G8, instead of German – interests (see, e.g., *The Economist* 2014b; Natorski and Pomorska 2017: 62–64). The template for Germany's inclusive style of managing the crisis within the EU was arguably set by Steinmeier's trip to meet his counterparts from the four Visegrad states early in the crisis – a meeting at which he reassured them that their respective concerns regarding Russia were 'European worries, and therefore our concerns, too' (as quoted in Sjursen and Rosén 2017: 27). Throughout the crisis, other member states appear to have trusted Germany, with France, to manage it in the EU's collective interest. In time-honoured fashion, Berlin's close cooperation with France in this crisis contributed to widening the support for its stance in the EU, especially in Southern Europe, where support for sanctions was weaker than elsewhere. Germany's inclusive approach to managing the crisis was also reflected in the distribution of the costs of sanctions. Inevitably, in as far as it conducted far more trade with Russia than any other member state, Germany bore by far the biggest burden of sanctions in the EU. But, even relative to the size of the economy, it bore a proportionally higher share of their cost than most others. Through the inclusive process by which it handled the Ukraine Crisis and through its acquiescence in a fairly equitable distribution of the burden of sanctions within the EU, Germany succeeded in mobilizing a very high level of 'followership' among the other member states.

Germany's style of management of the Ukraine Crisis thus diverged sharply from the one it followed in the Eurozone Crisis, in which the deficit states had to bear an overwhelming share of the adjustment costs, and in the Schengen and Refugee Crisis, in which it was also to bear a disproportionately large part of the crisis-management costs, but, acting under severe time constraints, followed a unilateral or, at best, bilateral path that led, temporarily at least, to its isolation in the EU. It is to this crisis that we turn next.

Chapter 5

The Schengen and Refugee Crisis

Introduction

Just as, in summer 2015, the Eurozone and Ukraine Crises began to abate, the EU's next crisis was rapidly intensifying. The roots of this new crisis lay primarily in the civil wars and political turmoil unleashed in parts of North Africa and the Middle East by the 'Arab Spring' that had commenced in Tunisia in January 2011. These conflicts provoked the flight of several million refugees, especially from Syria, into surrounding countries and regions, including, increasingly, to Europe. At stake in this crisis was an EU policy that, alongside the Euro, had had a more tangible impact on the lives of many EU citizens than any other, the free movement of persons across borders of the 22 EU and four other member states of the Schengen Area, named after a small town bordering on France and Germany in Luxembourg where five EU members had signed an agreement to abolish mutual border controls in 1985. Conflicts over how to cope with the growing wave of refugees prompted numerous Schengen member states to reinstate border controls in 2015–16. Not only the fate of 'Schengen' was at stake, however. The crisis also jeopardized the level of political integration that the EU had meanwhile achieved in issue areas, such as political asylum, that the abolition of border controls had put on its agenda. It too was seen by many observers as it unfolded as an 'existential crisis' that threatened the very survival of the EU (*Eurocomment* 2015b: 4, 21).

Not too dissimilar from the process of European monetary integration, the three decades following the signature of the Schengen Accord in 1985 had witnessed a steady process of horizontal, vertical and sectoral political integration in respect of border controls and related issues. Five EU member states had signed up to abolish mutual border controls at Schengen in 1985. By 2015, the Schengen Area comprised 26 members with a population of 420 million, 42,600 km of coastal and 7721 km of land borders (see Map 5.1; Sénat 2017: 10). Initially negotiated, adopted and implemented on an intergovernmental basis, outside the European treaties, the Schengen 'acquis' was subsequently brought, step by step, under the roof of the EU, so that the scope of the EU's 'supranational' organs – the European Commission, the EP and the ECJ – to shape policy on border controls was expanded. Several European agencies – Europol, the European Asylum Support Office (EASO) and the European border agency Frontex – were

MAP 5.1   *Schengen Area*

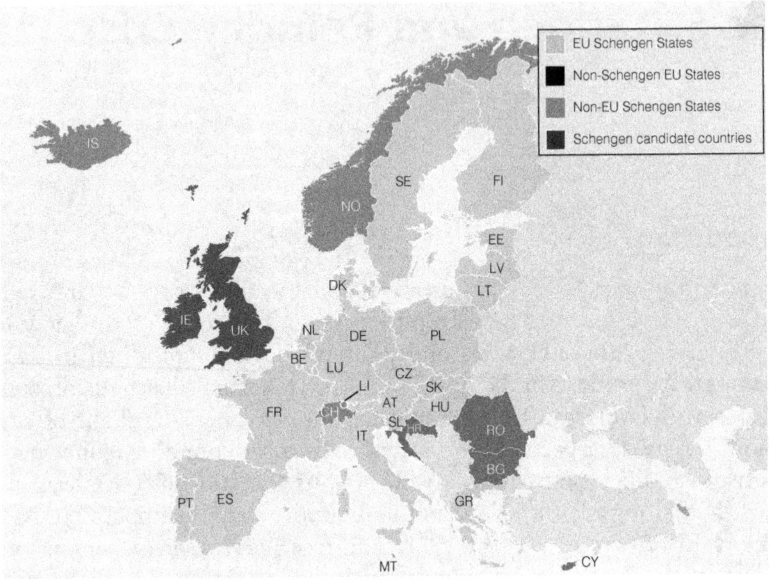

Source: European Commission.

also created to help to coordinate and to assist in the implementation of EU policies. The abolition of border controls between Schengen members also generated strong pressures for them to harmonize their policies, or to adopt common EU policies, on numerous related issues, such as, inter alia, visas for citizens of third countries, the control of the external borders of the Schengen Zone, immigration, refugees and political asylum, cross-border terrorism, and police and judicial cooperation and information exchange – such that the overall area of justice and home affairs had become the 'most expansive and rapidly developing EU policy area' (Monar 2006: 4). In other words, there had been a significant 'spill-over' from border control abolition into adjacent policy domains.

A general restoration of Schengen border controls would have affected people making 1.3 billion border crossings a year, including some 1.7 million cross-border work commuters (*The Economist* 2016c: 18). The border crossings of some 57 million trucks a year would also have been complicated – over a third of road-freight traffic in Schengen crosses a border. One – French – study calculated that the restoration of border controls would impose the equivalent of a 3 per cent tax on intra-Schengen trade and, over a decade, would reduce output in the Schengen area by 0.8 per cent (*Le Monde* 2016d; *The Economist* 2016c). Another – German-sponsored – analysis concluded that the economic cost of such a scenario would be significantly bigger, in the order of 3.5 per cent of Schengen members' output over the same period if the cost of imports rose by 1 per cent and three times this figure if they rose by 3 per cent (*Financial Times* 2016g; *Le Monde* 2016f).

Whatever the direct economic fallout of the disintegration of Schengen, the broader, prospective political implications – at least in the proclaimed views of major protagonists in the crisis – would have been greater. Thus the Commission president Jean-Claude Juncker expressed the fear that in this scenario the Euro too would collapse, as the single currency would not make sense if border controls were restored (*Spiegel-Online* 2015a). At the height of the Refugee Crisis, the Dutch prime minister Mark Rutte foresaw the collapse of the EU as well as Schengen if the EU did not regain control of its external borders (*Financial Times* 2015r). Popular perceptions of the EU in the member states would likely have suffered, as, in 2015 at least, some 25 per cent of citizens rated free movement of persons as the 'most positive result' of the EU, a higher proportion than for any other perceived result of European integration than the maintenance of peace (Eurobarometer survey finding, as published in Ademmer et al. 2015: 4).

The dismantlement of border controls was a highly controversial issue between and within the EU member states. Their EU-wide abolition proved to be politically unfeasible, principally owing – as in the case of the Euro – to British opposition. Again like the Euro, Schengen was thus launched as a project of differentiated integration – in this case, by five of the original six EU member states. Divergent interests between the first seven members delayed the implementation of the original accord by a decade following its initial adoption. Under the weight of the Refugee Crisis in 2015–16, hitherto irreconcilable conflicts broke out between member states open and hostile to receiving (predominantly Muslim) refugees. In part, these conflicts were rooted in divergent calculations of the electoral-political costs and benefits of competing policies. In part, like those in the Eurozone Crisis that separated proponents of Keynesian and German Ordoliberal policy approaches, these also reflected more fundamental ideological divergences between member state governments relating to human rights and mono- versus multiculturalism.

Again as with the Euro, the political force required to bring about the abolition of border controls was supplied by the close cooperation of the French and German governments, although, in this case, not France but rather Germany was the *demandeur* of closer integration. As neighbouring issue areas were increasingly Europeanized, however, the Franco-German relationship became gradually less pivotal. On the German side, *Franco-German bilateralism* gave way increasingly to a practice of *promiscuous bilateralism* in which the German government cooperated with different other partners, depending on the issue. Finally, in 2015–16, Chancellor Merkel shifted to a more *unilateral* mode of crisis management, in which she had no stable partner. No other member state deployed comparable diplomatic efforts to Germany's to shape the EU's response to the Refugee Crisis. But it had only very limited success in this regard. It tried to supply leadership, but it secured relatively little 'followership' from other member states. Because of this failure, it was left to bear a disproportionately high share of the crisis burden in terms of the number of refugees it accepted. Germany secured far less 'followership' among other member states in this crisis than in the Eurozone or Ukraine Crises.

The next sections of this chapter explore the origins, negotiation and adoption of the Schengen Accord and the process of the horizontal, sectoral and vertical integration of 'Schengen' and adjacent policy domains, including political asylum policy, in the EU. Later sections focus on the Schengen/ Refugee Crisis in 2015 and 2016 and analyse the conflicts within the EU over the extent to which it should initially keep its borders open to refugees, over whether and how, once arrived, they should be 'relocated' among member states, and what measures should be taken to limit the ongoing influx. The conclusion assesses how far this crisis has provoked political disintegration in the EU, compares the German government's role in the management of this crisis with that which it has played in others and explains why it was much less able to influence the stance taken by other member states in this crisis.

The pre-history of Schengen

Passports were not always required to travel between European states. The Austrian writer and intellectual, Stefan Zweig, for example, lauded the ease of cross-border travel in Europe prior to World War I: 'The whole world was open to us. We could travel anywhere we liked without passes and permits' (Zweig 2009: 111; Davis and Gift 2014: 1542; Leparmentier 2014). The expansion of border controls after this war reflected security concerns and mirrored the general increase in the scope of state intervention and regulation of the economy and society. The practical importance of state borders reached its zenith in the four decades after 1945 (Zaiotti 2011: 47).

Passport-free travel was not among the foremost concerns of the founding fathers of European integration. The Treaty of Rome referred in Article 3 to the 'abolition of obstacles to the free movement of persons' as an aim of the European Community, but it did not specifically propose to dismantle border controls. Rather the first initiatives in favour of passport-free travel were taken by three subgroups of European states. The oldest, the Common Travel Area between the UK, Ireland and the Channel Islands, actually dates back to the 1920s (Taschner 1997: 12). The Benelux countries introduced passport-free travel within the economic union that they adopted in 1958, the year after the Rome Treaty was agreed (Hreblay 1998: 11–13). In the Nordic Passport Union, four Scandinavian states, Denmark, Finland, Norway and Sweden, abolished passport controls for their citizens in 1952 and for citizens of third countries in 1958. But for a long time the abolition of such controls between all EU member states did not become a significant political issue. The 1974 Paris summit meeting of EU heads of government decided to establish a working group to examine the possibility of establishing a passport union, which 'would involve ... the abolition of passport control' between member states, but this decision long remained a dead letter. Supported by Ireland, the UK insisted that passport controls be maintained for non-EU citizens – and therefore, in practice, for EU citizens as well (Taschner 1997: 15). When, in 1982, the European Commission made a legally non-binding proposal to ease or simplify border controls, the 'lowest common denominator' solution reached by the member governments in the Council rendered it practically meaningless (*Neue Zürcher Zeitung* 1984; Taschner 1997: 15–18).

The negotiation and adoption of Schengen

The prospects for the abolition of border controls in (at least some member states of) the EU were transformed when this cause was adopted in 1984 by the German and French governments. Neither had warmed to the Commission's 1982 proposal – apart from the Benelux governments, the others had all cited national security grounds for resisting it (Taschner 1997: 17). The balance of forces on the issue shifted radically, however, when it was taken up by the chief executives – by the German chancellor Kohl and the French president Mitterrand. Kohl particularly became the chief proponent of dismantling border controls, both within his own government and in the EU.

Kohl's stance on the issue may be attributed to a combination of motives. First, on European issues, other than on those of domestic policy, he was a – pro-European, even federalist – 'conviction politician' (Schwarz 2012: 397–419, 690; see also Baumann 2006: 68–69). As a young person, a sign of his pro-European zeal, he had taken part in a symbolic dismantling of turnpikes on the Franco-German border in his home state, the Rhineland Palatinate. For Kohl, arguably more than for any of his predecessors as Chancellor, European integration was indispensable to the preservation of stability and peace on the continent. His sense of mission in this regard was heightened by his belief that he would be the 'last pro-European Chancellor' (as quoted in Schwarz 2012: 352). Second, he was concerned to counter the impression that European integration chiefly benefited business interests rather than providing anything tangible for citizens (Eisel 2009; Baumann 2006: 69). This concern was undoubtedly all the stronger because the second direct elections to the EP were to take place in June 1984. Not least because of the 'Iron Curtain' that ran through and divided the nation during the Cold War, border controls were unpopular in Germany. All the German political parties campaigned for their abolition – not least the main opposition party, the SPD (*Frankfurter Allgemeine Zeitung* 1984; Rogalla 1983; Vogel 1984). This was an issue on which Kohl certainly did not want to see himself outbid by the opposition. Third, border controls were also disliked by German business interests, which viewed them as a costly hindrance to trade. This was especially the case among transport companies. Given the high volume of goods being transported to and from nearby, but foreign, ports, such as Dutch Rotterdam, delays at the borders with Belgium and the Netherlands were particularly unpopular (Foucher 2016: 3). The visibility of border delays and controls was magnified in early 1984 by a wave of protests among French truck-drivers against a strike of French customs officials and chronically long delays crossing Italy's northern borders (*Der Spiegel* 1984; *Die Zeit* 1984). German and Austrian truck-drivers joined and extended the protests, thus raising public awareness, as the German government's press spokesman expressed it, of 'these stupid borders and these stupid controls' – an unequivocal statement of where the government or at least Kohl stood on this issue (Peter Boenisch, as quoted in *Der Spiegel* 1984). In Germany, however, public opinion and that of business interests were less decisive in shaping this stance than – in this case, Kohl's – political-ideological convictions and the conflict over border control abolition was much less a public one than one conducted within the government (Eisel 2009).

At their bilateral summit in Rambouillet in May 1984, Kohl and Mitterrand agreed in principle to dismantle border controls between France and Germany. It was, in the description of a German participant in later negotiations, a 'clandestine operation' (*Nacht-und-Nebel-Aktion*) that took the relevant government ministries in both Bonn and Paris by complete surprise and provoked anguished protests among security officials (Eisel 2009). Fearing that the security-conscious Interior Ministry and the Foreign Office, in charge of and concerned about visa policy issues, would crush the initiative, Kohl circumvented their prospective opposition to his project by transferring responsibility for negotiating with the French government to the Federal Chancellor's Office (Baumann 2006: 77–79; Eisel 2009; Sturm and Pehle 2005: 336).

Schengen was even more an 'intra-governmental' affair in France than in Germany. French public opinion was passive and did not really provide any support for the project (Lalumière 2006). Within the government bureaucracy, there was considerable hostility to it. The French Interior Ministry raised 'all manner of objections' to it, according to the chief French negotiator of the accord (Lalumière 2006). So too, less for security reasons than out of a concern for customs' officials' jobs, did the Finance and Economics Ministry (Lalumière 2006). The decisive factor driving French support was rather the 'political will' of President Mitterrand (Lalumière 2006). Like Kohl, he too was keen on taking 'concrete and popular' steps to make the EU 'more tangible' in the eyes of citizens (Lalumière quoted in *M le magazine du Monde* 2015). However, Schengen implied greater changes in the status quo in France than in Germany, as it controlled its borders more intensively, including (under the Socialist-Communist government in power since 1981) to combat a flight of capital. Unlike in Germany, there was no party-political consensus in favour of the project – for security reasons, the Conservative opposition was rather opposed to it. Hence Mitterrand did not pursue the project with the same vigour as Kohl.

Schengen was conceived in a period of growing tension and conflict in the EU between the British Conservative government of Margaret Thatcher and most other member states, headed by France and Germany. The principal bone of contention was the British contribution to the EU budget (see Chapter 1). Before the Council meeting held under the French presidency at Fontainebleau in June 1984, Kohl and Mitterrand had threatened to pursue closer political integration among a subgroup of 'willing' member states if this conflict was not resolved. As a lever to soften the Thatcher's opposition, the Franco-German duo raised the spectre of a 'multi-speed' Europe (Attali 1993: 658; Dumas 2007: 213–217; Mitterrand 1984; Schwarz 2012: 406–407). The settlement of the British budgetary conflict at Fontainebleau was followed within less than three weeks by the adoption of a Franco-German accord to dismantle mutual border controls at the frontier city of Saarbrücken. In principle, Kohl could have chosen initially to cooperate in this endeavour with the Benelux countries, as proposed by a German and other Christian Democratic MEPs (Deutsche Gruppe in der Fraktion der Europäischen Volkspartei des Europäischen Parlaments 1984). However, he preferred a bilateral agreement with France, as the symbolic and political 'signal effect' of an accord with a large member state with which Germany had had deeply rooted historical rivalries would be much greater (Eisel 2009). Moreover, he was aware that, once France and Germany had joined together to eliminate border controls, the Benelux states would in any case want to come on board. The Dutch and German transport ministers had already been exploring ways of expediting the movement of goods across their borders. In December 1984, the Benelux governments proposed to Bonn and Paris that the five governments should work towards an agreement to abolish border controls (Zaiotti 2011: 70).

Parallel to these activities, the European Commission decided to launch its own initiative within the EU institutions. According to the prevailing legal interpretation of the Rome Treaty, it had no legal competence in this issue area (Grant 1994: 69). Nonetheless, trying to build on the momentum provided by the Franco-German project, it proposed a regulation with similar provisions to those in the Saarbrücken accord in January 1985, basing it on Article 3 in the treaty (see the section 'The pre-history of Schengen', page 138). Several member states – Greece, Denmark, Ireland and, above all, the UK – rejected the proposal in the Council and the Commission ultimately withdrew it (Epiney 1995: 24; Gehring 1998: 51–52; Sturm and Pehle 2005: 335; Taschner 1997: 20–22). At this point, France, Germany and the Benelux states made good Kohl's and Mitterrand's threat not to let the 'slowest ship set the speed of the convoy', signing their accord at Schengen on 14 June 1985, the same day that the Commission launched the Single Market programme.

Schengen was not well received by the EU's supranational organs. Prevented from influencing it by its intergovernmental character, the EP opposed it 'strenuously', attacking its 'undemocratic nature' and (prospective) effect on immigrants and asylum-seekers (Zaiotti 2011: 77). The Commission even discussed whether it should take a case against the signatory governments to the ECJ, but it decided not to do so (Baumann 2006: 85). In the end, it chose instead to treat the accord as a 'laboratory' for closer integration, hoping that it could 'help to speed up the removal of controls throughout the Community' (Commission official quoted in Bieber 1995: 180–181; Monar 2001: 750–752; Zaiotti 2011: 75). It was included in negotiations about the accord's implementation only three years later and then only with the status of an observer (Zaiotti 2011: 74).

The horizontal, sectoral and vertical political integration of Schengen

Schengen began in 1985 as a border-control-abolition project of five of ten EU member states operating outside of the EU. The implementation of the accord encountered numerous technical and political obstacles. It did not enter into force until a full decade later – during which time the EU's Single Market programme had been put in place, the Cold War had ended, the Soviet Union had collapsed, and Germany had reunified, radically changing the geopolitical context in which the agreement had initially been reached. By 2015, the character of Schengen had been transformed in all three integration-related dimensions. First, its membership had grown from the original five to 26 member states, with three others (Bulgaria, Croatia and Romania) waiting to join it. Second, there was a great deal more vertical political integration of border control and related policies. These had been brought to a very large extent under the roof of the EU. The Commission had the right of policy initiative, the Council could vote by a qualified majority rather than only unanimously to approve Schengen-related decisions, the EP had an equal right of co-decision with the Council, and the ECJ was empowered to adjudicate disputes over the interpretation and application of Schengen-related law. Third, the abolition of border controls had triggered a process leading to the Europeanization of numerous policy domains in the broad area of justice and home affairs, including inter alia visa, political asylum and *external* border control policies and police and judicial cooperation. In this sphere, among the EU actors, national and supranational, both during and after the chancellorship of Kohl, the German government was most central. However, whereas at the outset it collaborated most closely with its traditional French partner, it preferred later to cooperate with different partners, depending on how closely their positions were aligned to Germany's. *Franco-German bilateralism* increasingly made way for a practice of *promiscuous bilateralism*.

The horizontal political integration of Schengen

Schengen fairly quickly developed a powerful snowball effect. States bordering on the Schengen area had strong incentives to join the accord (Gehring 1998). To the extent that, in exchange for abolishing internal border controls, the Schengen Five strengthened or aimed to strengthen controls on external borders, neighbouring states' citizens and firms faced the prospect of longer border waiting times. Depending on the orientation of Schengen members' policies, neighbouring states could also be compelled to deal with higher numbers of political asylum-seekers. As the accord's principal champion, the German government professed to be happy at every application to join it (Eisel 2009).

Not every EU member had the same incentives to join Schengen, however. The costs and benefits of accession to Schengen varied according to states' geographic location. An island, the UK could police its borders more effectively than Schengen non-members on the European continent. Moreover, given that it did not require its citizens to carry identity cards, the security consequences of dismantling border controls were arguably stronger. As Ireland has a land border (Northern Ireland) and far greater border traffic with the UK than other EU member states, it had practically no option but to stay outside Schengen with its neighbour (Eisel interview).

In contrast, EU member states on the European mainland all rallied, sooner or later, to Schengen. Italy was the only one of the six original EU member states that did not take part in Schengen from the outset. This was not because the five founding members wanted to exclude Italy, but rather because Italy was initially rather 'uncertain' about the project (Eisel interview). When it later indicated its interest in participating in it, the five decided not to 'endanger the difficult negotiations' by admitting Italy but instead granted it 'observer' status (Gehring 1998: 58; Taschner 1997: 26). As the original accord was 'more of a working program than a detailed plan of action', the subsequent negotiations proved indeed to be 'complex and slow' (Zaiotti 2011: 70–71). Italy finally joined Schengen in 1990, less than six months after the original five members had concluded the Schengen Implementation Convention (see the following section, 'The vertical and sectoral political integration of Schengen'). In contrast to Italy, Austria would like to have joined the accord right from the outset. It actually signed a bilateral agreement with Germany comparable to the latter's Saarbrücken accord with France just a few weeks after this was reached, in August 1984 (Baumann 2006: 57; Taschner 1997: 25 and 50). Encouraged by the Commission, however, the Schengen Five decided for the time being not to admit any non-EU members to the accord.

Schengen initially posed the same quandary for the Scandinavian states as for Austria. As a member of the Nordic Pass Union, Denmark did not want to join it as long as this would interfere with passport-free travel with its northern neighbours. To a large extent, however, this obstacle was removed by the accession of Austria, Sweden and Finland to the EU in 1995. Austria joined Schengen the same year, within five weeks of its entry into force, while Denmark, Sweden and Finland acceded to the accord all on the same day in 1996 – by which time, of 15 EU member states, only the UK and Ireland remained outside the accord. The incorporation of Schengen into the EU treaties in 1999 left states aspiring to EU membership no option but to adopt the Schengen *acquis*, although their accession required the unanimous approval of existing Schengen members and the Commission. Thus nine of the ten mainly post-Communist states that joined the EU in 2004 were not admitted to the accord until 2008, while, by 2018, none of the three most recent members – Bulgaria, Romania and Croatia – had yet been admitted to Schengen. The four non-EU members admitted as 'associated members' to the Schengen Area after 1995 – Norway, Iceland, Switzerland and Liechtenstein – are required to accept Schengen rules without participating in their negotiation, albeit, in the case of the former two, they may be able to count on the three other Scandinavian full members to defend their interests (Taschner 1997: 27–28). Even the UK was not entirely insusceptible to the snowball effect of Schengen, in as far as it felt compelled to participate in elements of the accord (see the next section).

The vertical and sectoral political integration of Schengen

From the beginning, the German government wanted to bring about the abolition of border controls under the roof of the EU. The negotiation and adoption of the Schengen as an intergovernmental agreement outside the EU reflected Kohl's and Mitterrand's acknowledgement of the fact that 'widespread opposition' to border control abolition made it politically unfeasible in the EU as a whole (Eisel 2009). In these circumstances, they saw no other way than to launch it on a 'parallel track' – an 'unavoidable deviation' from the official pathway (Eisel 2009). The accord was nonetheless conceived so that it could later be 'inserted' into the EU – the deviation, in other words, was to be only temporary (Eisel 2009).

In the end, the journey via this deviation was to take well over a decade. The Schengen Five took five years each to agree as to how to implement the accord and then to put it into force. The Five had agreed from the outset that the abolition of border controls required the adoption of a wide range of 'compensating' measures involving the adoption of common policies or the harmonization of national policies relating to external border controls, the treatment of and visas for third-country nationals, political asylum-seekers and refugees and cross-border crime. The 1985 accord (Article 139) stipulated that it enter into force only once 'preconditions for its implementation have been filled' by the members. Conflicts over policies on sports weapons, drug trafficking, legislative and judicial control of executive agencies responsible for implementing the accord, and whether or under what conditions the police in one member state could cross borders into another in pursuit of suspected criminals held up an agreement over how to implement the accord until 1990. By this time, the fall of the Berlin Wall and the 'Iron Curtain' had led to a major and rapid growth in the number of political asylum-seekers, especially in Germany, where some political actors, especially among the governing Christian Democrats, threatened by the rise of a new anti-immigration party, *Die Republikaner* (The Republicans), got increasingly cold feet about the accord. In France, the election of a conservative government in 1993 also slowed down the implementation of Schengen. The official explanation for the delay was technical, computer-related obstacles encountered in setting up the Schengen Information System (SIS) in French Strasbourg, but the German side suspected the delay was rather attributable to the reservations of the French interior minister (and law-and-order 'hardliner') Charles Pasqua (Eisel 2009).

Faced with a rapidly growing number of political asylum-seekers and unable to take unilateral action to curb them, given the German Basic Law, the German government had a strong incentive to 'Europeanize' this issue. In the approach to the intergovernmental conference that culminated in the Maastricht Treaty, Kohl launched a – very much 'personal' – initiative to extend the powers of the EU into the areas of justice and home affairs (Mazzucelli 1997). While Mitterrand, the other main architect of the treaty, was less enthusiastic about this proposal, he acquiesced in it, in exchange for Kohl's support for a high French priority, the inclusion of stronger social policy provisions than currently existed (Mazzucelli 1997: 137–139). But, supported by the UK, Mitterrand forced Kohl, who would have preferred these issues to be directly and more strongly 'communitarized', to accept that justice and home affairs would constitute a separate pillar of the EU in which intergovernmental cooperation would apply instead of the Community method (Mazzucelli 1997: 137–139, 148–149). As for the substantive treaty provisions themselves, they are said to have been 'all but' written by Kohl himself (Mazzucelli 1997: 198). Kohl viewed them as a 'first step' which he had accepted in the expectation that this was 'the only way that we can quickly make practical progress' and open up the possibility of communitarizing these issue areas (Deutscher Bundestag 1991: 5800).

Kohl and the German (federal) government remained strong advocates of deeper integration in justice and home affairs through the 1990s. They 'heavily supported' the communitarization of the Schengen conventions at the Amsterdam Treaty negotiations in 1997 (Bösche 2006: 57). The newly elected British Labour government acquiesced in this change, previously opposed by British governments, in exchange for being allowed to take part in the SIS. The Amsterdam Treaty also transferred the areas of asylum, immigration and external border control policy from the third pillar to the first, in which the Community method applied (Trauner 2011: 150–151). The 'deepening' of integration in these areas occurred, however, only gradually. For an initial period of five years, decisions in these issue areas could be made only unanimously, the Commission had to share its powers to make proposals with the member states, and the EP had no power of co-decision but only the right to be consulted. Qualified majority voting was vetoed at Amsterdam by the German government at the insistence of the federal states, which were competent for many Schengen-related issues under the Basic Law and, since the adoption of the Maastricht Treaty in 1993, had a right of veto over new European treaties (Bösche 2006: 60–68). German actors were thus simultaneously both supporters and opponents of the communitarization of Schengen.

The Amsterdam Treaty left areas of justice and home affairs policy where member state governments were more sensitive to protect their sovereignty, especially police and judicial cooperation, in the third pillar from Maastricht. The combination of the requirement of unanimity in the Council with widely divergent interests rooted in different traditions in respect of cross-border police cooperation made it more difficult to reach decisions and forge common policies than in the issue areas that the treaty shifted to the first pillar (Kietz and Maurer 2007: 441, 2009: 113–115). Germany belonged with Austria and the Benelux states to a group of EU members increasingly frustrated at the slow rate of progress in forging closer cross-border police cooperation (Kietz and Maurer 2009: 116–118). Given its geographic location and experience with terrorism in the 1970s, it had long had a strong interest and been an agenda-setter in cross-border police cooperation (Bulmer 2011; Kietz and Maurer 2009: 117). By the early 2000s, it had negotiated numerous bi- and multilateral cooperation accords with neighbouring states, notably with Austria and the Netherlands. Its interest in such cooperation was heightened by the fact that, following the collapse of the Communist bloc on its eastern borders, it was one of the EU member states most confronted with and concerned about the growth of transnational crime – no other member had as many borders with other, non-member states as it did (Bulmer 2011: 8; Luif 2007: 8).

This was the context in which the ('red-green') German interior minister Otto Schily launched negotiations that culminated in the adoption in 2005 of a renewed experiment in 'multi-speed' integration, the Prüm Convention, whose main provisions facilitate the exchange of DNA and fingerprint data among members (Barthon de Montbas 2010: 5–6; Kietz and Maurer 2009: 119; Luif 2007: 9). Schily's approach to forging closer cross-border police cooperation was 'very pragmatic and results-oriented' (interview, Berlin, 2010). He decided to push ahead with an 'avantgarde' of member states as he feared, based on the 'tortuous negotiations' and slow pace of progress on this issue in the Interior Ministers' Council, that otherwise nothing would be achieved while he was in office (interview, Berlin, 2010). The Amsterdam and Nice treaties had meanwhile created scope for such a strategy within the EU framework. However, Schily judged the 'enhanced cooperation' provisions of the treaties, which required a minimum of eight member states to launch such a procedure, to be 'too complicated' and in respect of its prospective outcome 'too uncertain' (interview, Berlin, 2010). He did not bother to weigh up whether Germany could win the support of the seven other members required to activate these provisions.

Unlike Kohl with Schengen, however, Schily did not pair up with France for this initiative, but rather with his counterpart in Luxembourg (interview, Berlin, 2010; Niemeier and Zerbst 2007: 537). Initially they sought support for their project from the Netherlands, Belgium and France – the same member states which had launched Schengen (Niemeier and Zerbst 2007: 537). France, however, quickly withdrew from the negotiations, owing to fears that allowing foreign police to pursue suspected criminals across the border into France would conflict with French constitutional law. Its place in the talks was then taken by Austria. In fact, numerous provisions of the Prüm Convention, which Germany drafted, were almost identical with those in a pre-existing bilateral German–Austrian accord (Luif 2007: 13). In contrast, by the time France rejoined the talks in 2005, they had almost been concluded. France accepted the proposed treaty provisions more or less intact, after changing no more than 'half a sentence' (interview, Berlin, 2010). Initially angry at and opposed to the intergovernmental character of the initiative, the Commission subsequently changed its stance, as substantively there was little difference between the German–Luxembourg proposals and its own (Kietz and Maurer 2007: 446, 2009: 131; interview, Berlin, 2010).

Following the convention's adoption as an international treaty, other member states rallied to it even faster than they had to Schengen. Seven states, including Spain, signed the convention in May 2005. Finland, Hungary and Slovenia immediately expressed in joining it, soon to be followed by seven more. Not only the widening, but also the 'communitarization' of Prüm advanced more rapidly than that of Schengen. The convention stipulated that its provisions were to apply only so long as they were compatible with EU law. Moreover, as with Schengen, the signatory states proclaimed their goal of incorporating the convention into EU law – in the case of Prüm, within the following three years (Barthon de Montbas 2010: 2, 3). In fact, after agreeing to scrap the convention's provisions relating to air marshals and hot pursuit across borders, all 27 interior ministers took this step during the German Council presidency in June 2007.

Prior to the adoption of Schengen, border control and related policies – to the extent that they were harmonized at all – had been coordinated through practices of 'purely informal intergovernmentalism' (Peers 2017: 11). In formal-legal terms at least, the balance of power between the member states and the EU's supranational organs was transformed in the following 25 years. By the time of the entry into force of the Lisbon Treaty in 2009, the 'nearly complete application of the Community method' to the issue areas of police cooperation as well as political asylum, migration and external border control policies had been accomplished (Peers 2017: 17). Divergences of interest between member states that otherwise were or would have been irreconcilable were circumvented by recourse, in the cases of Schengen and Prüm, to 'avantgarde' groups initially comprising a minority of member states and, when it came to incorporating the provisions of such accords into the EU treaties, by the use of 'opt-outs' and 'opt-ins' to accommodate dissenting member states such as the UK, Ireland and Denmark.

No other member state had left as strong a 'fingerprint' on this process as Germany (Baumann 2006). For a mixture of motives relating to ideology, domestic politics, economic interests and geographic location, it had been the main driving force of both the Schengen and Prüm accords and the inclusion of justice and home affairs in the EU treaties (Bulmer 2011. It had also spearheaded the creation not only of the European police agency, Europol, of which Kohl had been the first and leading political advocate (Mazzucelli 1997: 148), but also that of Eurojust (the European Union's Judicial Cooperation Unit) (Bulmer 2011) and, alongside Italy, that of the European border control agency, Frontex (Leonard 2009: 376). Over this period, however, its strategy for forging closer political integration in this domain had changed. Initially its 'privileged partner', as in other issue areas, had been France, with which it championed the causes of border control and the inclusion of justice and home affairs in the Maastricht Treaty. Later, in contrast, it became more promiscuous in its choice of partners, pursuing the Prüm accord primarily with Luxembourg and Austria and the creation of Frontex with Italy. France was no longer Germany's reflexive partner of choice.

The level of *substantive* deepening or vertical political integration of border control and related policies that Germany above all had championed was not as far-reaching, however, as the *formal-legal*. The Community method was constrained and 'weakened', resulting in an 'intergovernmental bias' (Wolff 2015: 131); the Commission refrained from 'pushing its luck' and preferred to 'appease member states rather than push through its agenda' and to kowtow to the Council (Zaiotti 2011: 140); the EU's legal output was 'softer' in this than in other issue areas and member governments played a stronger – and supranational actors a weaker – role (Trauner 2011: 152–153). The extent to which, on different issues, the EU has actually succeeded in adopting and implementing common policies has correspondingly varied widely.

Following the inclusion of political asylum policy in the EU's competences in the Amsterdam Treaty, the EU adopted a Temporary Protection Directive that was designed for situations of mass influx of refugees and contained provisions for the voluntary relocation of refugees between member states. Between 2003 and 2005 and 2011 and 2014, efforts were made to set 'common standards' on asylum procedures, reception conditions and status determination (Lavenex 2018: 1203). These directives remained 'relatively vague, leaving a large scope for discretion' to the member states, prompting one observer to label attempts to develop 'fully harmonized asylum standards and procedures' as having failed (Lavenex 2018: 1203; Trauner 2016: 316). Nonetheless, this legislation combined with references in the EU Charter to the right of political asylum and rhetoric about the creation of a 'Common European Asylum System' to give the impression that there was a 'well-developed European asylum policy' and that the EU would be 'well prepared' for future refugee crises (Lavenex 2018: 1203).

The crisis that broke out in summer 2015 very rapidly put both the robustness of the EU's political asylum policy and passport-free travel in the Schengen Area to the test. Fairly suddenly, several Schengen members reinstated controls on some of their borders and the apparently impressive edifice of EU legislation that had been generated largely in response to the abolition of internal border controls looked as if it stood on perilously fragile political foundations.

The origins and debut of the Schengen and Refugee Crisis

The crisis that broke in 2015 and threatened to unwind the Schengen area has its immediate roots in the 'Arab Spring' that began in Tunisia in 2011 and within a few months resulted in the outbreak of a civil war in Syria. Still raging several years later, this war had produced several million refugees by 2015. Apart from those displaced from their homes but living elsewhere in Syria itself, the great majority of the refugees had fled to the neighbouring states of Jordan, Lebanon and Turkey, which accommodated the largest number. At the same time, numerous refugees continued to flee especially Iraq and Afghanistan, where civil wars or civil-war-comparable conditions were much older than in Syria.

Early in the 'Arab Spring' the political turbulence and decline of state authority in North Africa, especially in Libya, where no stable government was established following the overthrow of the regime of Muammar Gaddafi, created a context in which growing numbers of refugees and migrants tried to cross the Mediterranean Sea to Europe. Already in 2011 a sudden spike in the number of refugees arriving in southern Italy provoked tensions in the Schengen Area, with the French government opposing their entry from Italy over their joint land border (Guiraudon 2011). According to the Dublin Convention, which had been adopted simultaneously with the Schengen accord in 1990, the Schengen member state via whose territory a refugee first entered the Schengen Area should register and accommodate him and deal with any application for political asylum. This provision meant that, during the Schengen crisis, initially at least, the burden of managing the influx of refugees and migrants fell principally on two of the area's southern- and south-easternmost members, Italy and Greece. Not only are these two states typically perceived as being the most corrupt and as having the least effective public administrations in the EU outside the post-Communist members (Transparency International 2017; World Bank 2017), but Greece was also the hardest hit and Italy one of the hardest hit by the Eurozone Crisis and they had respectively the highest and second-highest stock of public debt relative to GDP (see Table 3.5).

At the time that the Dublin Convention was adopted, however, Italy and Greece did not foresee that they would become front-line states in a refugee and migration crisis 25 years later. Both were traditionally countries of *emig*ration rather than *immig*ration (*Financial Times* 2015m). In 1990, just after the 'Iron Curtain' between capitalist-democratic Western and Communist Eastern Europe had fallen, the countries on the EU's and Schengen Area's eastern frontiers – notably Germany – were confronted with the biggest influx of refugees and migrants. Up until then, the East European Communist regimes had functioned as the 'external border police'. It had been 'easy to have an open-door policy when almost nobody could come' (Rainer Muenz, migration analyst, quoted in *Financial Times* 2015r). The sudden post-Cold War growth in immigration into Germany provoked an intense controversy that died only after, faced with a sudden surge in support for a new, extreme right-wing political party, the main German political parties agreed to revise the Basic Law to limit the scope for claiming political asylum in the country.

The fallout from the 'Arab Spring' shifted the flow of refugees towards the Schengen Area from its eastern to its southern and south-eastern peripheries. Already in 2014 the number of political asylum-seekers in the EU rose by 44 per cent compared with 2013 (Hirseland 2015: 18). In the first two months of 2015, the number of 'irregular' immigrants entering EU member states exceeded that for the same period in 2014 by 250 per cent. Starting in spring 2015, the flow of refugees and migrants towards the EU and the Schengen Area accelerated sharply once again, now especially via the 'Eastern Mediterranean' route. Several 'push' factors may have contributed to this trend (Faigle et al. 2016; UNHCR 2015). First, the Syrian civil war intensified in this period, leading to an overall increase in the number of refugees and a growing perception among them that they would not be able to return home in the foreseeable future. Second, because of budgetary shortfalls, food rations to refugees based in neighbouring countries were cut. Third, refugees' rights in these countries, including the right to work and children's access to education, began to be curtailed. To what extent the impact of these 'push' factors was heightened by 'pull' factors, specifically the policies of EU and Schengen member states, notably Germany, is and remains politically controversial, with opponents of a liberal refugee and migration policy accusing Chancellor Merkel of having been largely responsible for the trend. This can hardly have been the case, in as far as most of the refugees who arrived in EU member states in 2015 had set off on their journey before she decided to open – and keep open – German borders for them. Merkel did not trigger this influx, although it is conceivable that her decisions intensified it by giving many refugees in countries surrounding Syria the impression that she had 'invited' them to come to Europe (*Eurocomment* 2015a: 7; Faigle et al. 2016).

The EU and its member states had been warned about a likely big increase in the stream of refugees (Braun 2018) (Figure 5.1). In March 2015, the head of Frontex reported that its sources estimated the number of migrants waiting in Libya to cross the Mediterranean to Europe at between 500,000 and 1 million (Aust et al. 2015). In June he told a German parliamentary committee that the number of 'irregular' migrants crossing from Turkey into Greece had risen in 2015 by 550 per cent compared with the previous year (Aust et al. 2015). Significant numbers of asylum-seekers also came from states in the western Balkans. In February 2015, the German Embassy in Kosovo warned Berlin that at current rates as many as 300,000 Kosovars might try to

Figure 5.1   *Illegal border crossings into the EU, 2014–17*

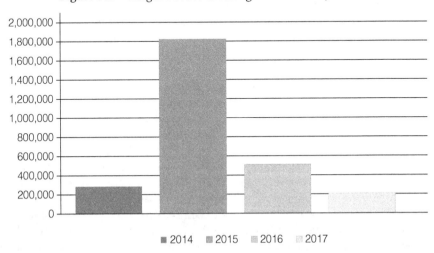

Note: Only around 10 per cent of Syrian refugees sought refuge in Europe. At the end of 2016, there were 2.8 million Syrians in Turkey, over 1 million in Lebanon and 656,000 in Jordan.

Source: created using data from Frontex, *Risk Analysis for 2018*.

migrate to Germany that year (Aust et al. 2015). The German Federal Office for Migration and Refugees regularly updated – and increased – its prognoses as to the likely overall number of asylum-seekers in Germany in 2015: from 250,000 in February 2015 to 400,000 in May (Aust et al. 2015). By the middle of August, the official estimate had risen once again to 650,000–750,000. Still, as Chancellor Merkel herself would later confess, the German government did not see the scale of the challenge facing it until it was 'too late' (Merkel 2018; interview, Berlin, 2018).

The EU had arguably 'kidded itself' for several years that it could 'shut out the world' and that Syria was 'someone else's problem' (Stephens 2015). Astonishingly, in 2015, the European Commission and all the member states but one, the Netherlands, had cut their financial contributions to the United Nations World Food Programme's budget for helping refugees in Syria and the neighbouring countries (*Eurocomment* 2015a: 8). The burgeoning wave of refugees in the first half of 2015 nonetheless prompted it to begin to react. The Dublin Convention had been revised on two occasions since its adoption, once in 2003 and then in 2013. However, despite the increasingly inequitable distribution of the burden of coping with asylum-seekers, other member states, Germany included, resisted the efforts led by Italy to revise these provisions of the convention. In June 2015, the European Commission instead proposed a refugee relocation scheme through which some 40,000 asylum-seekers would have been redistributed among Schengen member states over a two-year period according to a key that assessed their respective refugee-absorption capacities. Although, already at this time, this number paled in comparison with the prospective number of asylum-seekers for 2015 alone, the Commission's project was fiercely resisted by the member states in the Council. Several of the older West European members were reluctant to take in asylum-seekers under the scheme. These included the UK, which had a right to 'opt out' of EU asylum policy, Austria, and Spain. France too opposed the compulsory nature of the scheme that the Commission proposed, while Germany took no clear position on it (Alexander 2017: 91; *Le Monde* 2015d). The strongest opposition to the project came, however, from the newer, Central and East European member states. Some participants in the Council meeting reputedly emerged 'traumatized' from the session by the 'intellectual, cultural and mental gulf' that divided these and the older, West European member states on this issue (Kauffmann 2015). The meeting was deadlocked. Although the deadlock was broken and a decision reached a month later, the number of refugees to be relocated was reduced to just over 32,000 – more than half of whom would have been relocated to Germany or France. More significantly, member states' participation in the scheme was made voluntary instead of compulsory. The 'mountain' EU had moved, but given birth to a 'mouse' (*Le Monde* 2015d). The conflict in the council over this (as it was to turn out, first) refugee relocation scheme provided a foretaste of things to come. As the influx of refugees and migrants arriving especially in Greece escalated in summer 2015, the yawning and widening gap between the (rapidly growing) scale of the challenge facing the EU, on the one hand, and the scale of its (paltry) collective response, on the other, became both increasingly visible and increasingly unsustainable. As inaction in the face of the challenge became a less and less viable option, the question was whether there would be an agreed, collective EU crisis management policy or a host of national, 'beggar-thy-neighbour' responses that could end up destroying borderless travel in the Schengen Area.

The Schengen and Refugee Crisis, 2015–16

The preferences articulated by the member states in the refugee and migration crisis closely mirrored the domestic political constellations and constraints faced by their governments. These in turn were moulded by nationally specific combinations of several variables. The most fundamental of these was the state's geographic location relative to the Middle East and North Africa. This cleavage divided the 'front-line' states, primarily Greece and Italy, from the others. A second divided 'destination' states – the states in which a disproportionately high number of asylum-seekers sought refuge – from the others. In absolute terms, Germany was the principal 'destination' state; relative to population, it was Sweden. A third cleavage separated 'transit' states from the others. These were the states that lay on the route between the 'front-line' and 'destination' states. This group included several EU members, such as Hungary and to a lesser extent Slovenia and Croatia, as well as non-EU members lying between Greece and Hungary, that is, Macedonia and Serbia. Austria was a 'transit' state for refugees seeking asylum in northern Europe as well as a 'destination' state for others. A fourth cleavage arguably also existed, dividing the 'front-line', 'transit' and 'destination' states, those most directly affected by the crisis, on the one hand, from the geographically more distant member states, primarily in northern and north-western Europe, on the other.

The second variable that shaped domestic political preferences concerning this issue was the degree of exposure to immigration and immigrants from other, especially non-European or non-Western, societies and cultures during the post-World War II period. While the degree of exposure to the crisis tended to divide the EU and Schengen Area on a north–south basis, this cleavage divided the member states on an East–West axis. Other things being equal, there was less hostility towards refugees in West European states with a relatively long (sometimes including an imperial-colonial-legacy-related) history of immigration and relatively large numbers of citizens or residents from beyond Europe, and a longer history of political and economic openness towards refugees from the Middle East, North Africa and further afield than in post-Communist Central and East European states that had not shared this history and, since World War II, had in ethnic, linguistic and religious terms remained much more homogeneous (*The Economist* 2015a: 25; Lyman 2015; Rupnik 2015). The sharpness of this East–West cleavage was diluted partly, however, by a third variable: the strength (as defined by their level of voter support or government representation) of political parties and move-ments of the national-populist or extreme right that had often been founded recently and had flourished in numerous states since the outbreak of the GFC. Strong national-populist or extreme right parties or governments in which these parties were represented were to be found not only in post-Communist Europe, notably in Hungary and, after October 2015, in Poland, but also in numerous West or North European states. Thus, in mid-2015, they belonged to the governing coalition in Finland and to the parliamentary majority sup-porting the government in Denmark, while in France (*Front National*) and the UK (United Kingdom Independence Party), with 25 and 27 per cent of the respective popular votes, they had emerged as the biggest parties from the 2014 European parliamentary elections. Defining themselves largely by their opposition to immigration, they had thus become political forces that in their response to the crisis most other political parties could ignore only at their peril. These pressures and constraints were much weaker in member states where the national-populist or extreme right was neither represented in gov-ernment nor (as yet at least) a major political force. This was the situation – in mid-2015 – in Germany and Sweden.

This complex pattern of intra-EU cleavages, underpinned as it was by pro-found divergences of values as well as of material-economic and political interest, fostered a high level of political polarization in the EU over this crisis that, depending on the dimension of the issue, made the mediation of con-flicts very difficult, if not entirely infeasible. This task was made all the more intractable by the consensual orientation of the EU's decision-making rules and norms, which militated against mediating them by (in the case of the EU, qualified) majority votes. The discrepancy between the speed of events (concretely, that of the movement of refugees and migrants towards the EU) and the speed of EU decision-making greatly heightened the likelihood of the member states opting to respond unilaterally to the crisis.

The conflict over the reception of refugees

The crisis came to a climax in August–September 2015 and above all during the first weekend of September. Compared with May–June, the number of 'irregular border crossings' recorded by Frontex in Greece in July and August exploded by 250 per cent from 54,000 to 137,000 (Council of the EU 2015: 2). The Dublin Convention had already largely ceased to exist except on paper. The Greek government allowed a large proportion of the refugees arriving in the country to travel further without being registered, making it impossible for them to be sent back to Greece on their arrival in other Schengen member states. The governments of Macedonia and Serbia, the two non-EU transit states separating Greece from the closest EU and Schengen state to its north, Hungary, decided in June 2015 to grant transit visas to refugees travelling northwards (Lehmann 2015: 8). The number of asylum-seekers in Hungary was to reach 108,000 in the third quarter of 2015, more than double the number in the preceding quarter (Eurostat 2015: 1–3). Its national-populist government under Prime Minister Viktor Orbán had decided already in June to build a fence on the country's border with Serbia to keep out refugees and migrants. Now it decided to expedite the passage of the refugees through Hungary from Budapest to Austria and Germany by putting on special trains to transport them. Some 1200 refugees left stranded by the subsequent closure of Budapest railway station to travellers without Schengen visas then set off by foot on the highway intending to walk from there to Vienna.

Under the Dublin Convention, Austria and Germany could lawfully have turned back asylum-seekers arriving from another Schengen member state. To do this, however, they would have been required to reinstate controls on their respective eastern borders. Emergency border controls would or could have been legal under EU law, which provides for the temporary reintroduction of internal border controls in the event of there being a 'serious threat' to public policy or internal security. Referring to this legal provision, the German authorities had imposed temporary controls on its borders with other Schengen members when a G7 summit had been staged only two months earlier in Bavaria.

In fact, how the German government would respond to the refugees' march towards Austria and Germany had been presaged by an order from the Federal Office for Migration and Refugees to its staff a few days earlier no longer to send back to Greece asylum-seekers who had entered the Schengen Area there. The principal motive for this decision seems to have been practical (*Financial Times* 2015o; Lehmann 2015: 10). A significant proportion (in 2014, one-fifth) of the cases that the – increasingly overburdened – office had to deal with concerned refugees who had made their first application for asylum in another Schengen member state (Hirseland 2015: 21). Moreover, the number of refugees that Germany was sending back to Greece and other Schengen members under the terms of the Dublin Convention was very small, not least because of a series of judgments by the ECJ, the European Court for Human Rights as well as lower-level courts forbidding the return of refugees to the countries through which they first entered the Schengen Area on account of the inhumane conditions under which they would live and be accommodated there (Braun 2018; Lehmann 2015: 9).

Political motives may nonetheless have shaped the German government's response to the crisis more strongly than legal ones, given the ambivalence of the relevant jurisprudence, or practical-administrative ones. At this time, the refugees provoked sympathy rather than anxiety among the German public (Alexander 2017: 46–47). Awareness of and sympathy for their plight – also elsewhere – had been heightened by several incidents in which refugees had died: the capsizing of a boat that drowned an estimated 800 to 900 refugees off Libya in April 2015, the discovery of the bodies of 71 suffocated refugees in a parked lorry near Vienna in late August and, a few days later, the diffusion of the photo of the body of a three-year-old Syrian boy washed up on a beach in Turkey after the boat that he had been aboard had capsized between the Turkish and Greek coasts. Under sudden pressure, late on a

Saturday evening, to react to Orbán's initiative to 'empty' Hungary's refugee camps (Alexander 2017: 58), Chancellor Merkel and her Austrian counterpart, Werner Faymann, improvised a joint response. Faymann did not want to take in all the refugees in Austria or to be held co-responsible for any violence that Hungarian police might use to hold them back if Austria decided not to admit them. He proposed a solution to Merkel whereby Austria and Germany would each take in a half of the refugees on the road – who were now being transported to the Austrian border by a fleet of Hungarian buses (Alexander 2017: 55–56; Aust et al. 2015; Walker and Troianovski 2015). Merkel informed and consulted with two leaders of her coalition partner, the SPD, about how to respond. She failed, however, to reach and inform or consult with the chairman of her Bavarian sister party, the CSU, which subsequently became very critical of her refugee policy (Alexander 2017: 56–57). Nor did she consult beforehand with any other EU governments – an omission that SPD chairman Gabriel described later as her 'biggest mistake' (SPD 2017). Like Faymann, Merkel wanted 'under all circumstances to avoid any violence' on the road between Budapest and Vienna or on the Austro-Hungarian border (Alexander 2017: 56). For 'humanitarian' reasons linked with the 'emergency situation' at the Hungarian border with Austria, she agreed 'exceptionally' to take in the refugees who sought asylum in Germany (Alexander 2017: 60; Deutscher Bundestag 2015: 11614).

After Merkel and Faymann had made their decision, Merkel's European policy adviser spent several hours calling his counterparts in other EU member states trying to persuade them to take in some of the refugees that Germany was now to admit – 12,000 the next day. The French government agreed to take in 1000, the Belgian 250 and the Danish 40, but no other government was spontaneously prepared to take in any of the newly arriving refugees. Merkel herself reputedly called various 'friendly' counterparts among the EU member states personally, but her attempts to persuade them to accept some of the refugees proved futile (Alexander 2017: 61) (Table 5.1).

The refugees' arrival in Germany in the following days elicited a wave of sympathy, enthusiasm and support among the German public, a response that was quickly labelled as the *Willkommenskultur* (literally 'welcome culture'). The broad 'pro-refugee' consensus was reflected in a German parliamentary debate over the issue three days later. The spokespersons of not only the parties of the governing coalition, but also those of the (green and left-wing) opposition parties uniformly backed Merkel's decision (*Deutscher Bundestag* 2015: 11604–11629). In as far as they were critical of the government's stance, leaders of the Left party and the Greens called on it to commit more resources to coping with the influx of refugees (also Alexander 2017: 82). Speakers from both governing and opposition parties described the refugees as an 'opportunity' rather than a 'problem' for an ageing society, such as the German, experiencing or likely to experience growing labour shortages. The chairman of the CDU/CSU parliamentary group, Volker Kauder, recounted that in ten years of coalition government since 2005, it had been rare for the governing parties to be 'so united as to what we should do' as on this issue

Table 5.1   *Political asylum claims in the EU by member state, 2014–17*

Member State	2014	2015	2016	2017	% of all, 2014–17
Germany	202,815	476,620	722,265	198.255	42.0
Italy	64,625	83,540	121,185	126,550	10.4
France	64,310	76,165	76,790	91,070	8.1
Austria	28,065	88,180	39,875	22,160	4.7
Greece	9,435	13,205	49,875	57,020	3.4
UK	33,010	40,410	39,240	33,310	3.8
Hungary	42,775	177,135	28,215	3,115	6.6
Sweden	81,325	162,550	22,330	22,190	7.6
Netherlands	24,535	44,970	19,285	16,090	2.8
Belgium	22,850	44,760	14,250	14,035	2.5
Bulgaria	11,080	20,365	18,990	3,470	1.4
Spain	5,615	14,785	15,570	30,455	1.7
Poland	8,025	12,190	9,780	3,005	0.9
Denmark	14,715	20,970	6,055	3,125	1.2
Finland	3,625	32,345	5,275	4,325	1.2
Cyprus	1,745	2,265	2,840	4,475	0.3
Luxembourg	1,150	2,505	2,065	2,320	0.2
Ireland	1,450	3,275	2,315	2,910	0.3
Malta	1,350	1,845	1,735	1,610	0.2
Romania	1,545	1,260	1,855	4,700	0.2
Slovenia	385	275	1,265	1,435	0.1
Czech Republic	1,155	1,525	1,200	1,140	0.1
Portugal	445	895	710	1,015	0.1
Croatia	450	210	2,150	880	0.1
Lithuania	440	315	415	520	0.04
Latvia	375	330	345	355	0.03
Estonia	155	230	150	180	0.02
Slovakia	330	330	100	150	0.02
EU 28 Total	627,780	1,323,465	1,206,120	649,855	3,807,220

Source: Author's compilation and calculations from Eurostat.

(Deutscher Bundestag 2015: 11625). Several speakers praised the mobilization of German civil society in support of the refugees. Even the parliamentary leader of the CSU – the least 'refugee-friendly' of the parties represented in the Parliament – emphasized that the government had the capacity to cope with the influx of refugees 'not only in a financial respect, but also in respect of the mood of the public' (Deutscher Bundestag 2015: 11629).

The German state and local governments whose administrations had to manage the inflow of refugees had not been consulted by Merkel before she made her decision. In as far as there was a cleavage in German politics over the Refugee Crisis at this moment, this ran more between the federal and state governments than between the federal government and opposition. As, in the following days, the influx of refugees continued to grow (the number of asylum-seekers registered in Germany peaked in November 2015), more and more of them – only five days later 14 out of 16 – protested that their capacity to take in more refugees was exhausted (Alexander 2017: 15; *Politico* 2015). According to their estimates, only 850 more refugees could be accommodated in the available facilities, while over the coming weekend an estimated number of 40,000 refugees would arrive in Germany (Alexander 2017: 15). Under pressure from his state-level counterparts and interior affairs' specialists in his own party, the Christian Democratic Federal Interior Minister, Thomas de Maizière, came down in favour of installing controls on Germany's border with Austria to prevent more asylum-seekers entering Germany. At a summit meeting, leaders of the coalition partners initially approved his proposal and the German federal police force was mobilized to secure the German–Austrian border from the following evening.

In the end, however, the order to seal the border against refugees was not signed or executed. To the consternation of the federal police force, whose very raison d'être as the former Federal Border Protection force was to protect Germany's borders, the government reversed the decision it had taken the previous day (interview, Berlin, 2018). Officials advising the Interior Minister were divided as to whether the closure of Germany's borders would have been lawful (Alexander 2017: 22–23; Braun 2018). While the federal police force thought it was, other divisions of the Federal Interior Ministry thought it was not, as EU law, which broke German law, required each individual claim for political asylum to be examined – a task that could not be carried out at Germany's borders (Braun 2018).

Merkel herself also evidently began to have reservations about the measure. Apart from uncertainty as to whether the closure of German borders to refugees would survive possible legal challenges, her concerns appear to have been twofold. First, along with de Maizière, she was worried about the risk of the refugees dying on the roads of Europe or trying to storm the border and the damage that could be caused by images of Austrian or German police exerting force to turn them back (Alexander 2017: 56; Aust et al. 2015;

Niellsen 2017; Staudinger and Treichler 2015; Walker and Troianovksi 2015; interviews, Berlin, 2018). The Interior Minister allegedly asked the head of the federal police what the police would do if, despite being turned back at the border, refugees nonetheless still tried to cross it. The head of police said that they would form a 'passive wall' to stop them. They would also try to prevent them crossing the border outside the official control points. Asked by the minister how long he thought the police could maintain this effort, he replied 'roughly a week'. Like Merkel, de Maizière doubted whether for days or weeks on end Germans would tolerate the images they would see of police turning back refugees at the country's borders (Braun 2018).

Second, Merkel was worried about the danger that such a measure would unleash a chain reaction whereby, one after the other, the states between Germany and Greece would close their borders to refugees. In this case, each state would have shifted the burden of coping with them on to its immediate southern neighbour, potentially fomenting violent unrest and political instability, including in Greece itself (Alexander 2017: 22–24; Münkler 2016: 6–7; Niellsen 2017; interviews, Berlin, 2018). A fence might work for Hungary, she allegedly told Orbán, referring to his project for its border with Serbia. But she sought answers for 'all Europe' (as quoted in Walker and Troianovski 2015). Her Social Democratic coalition partners followed Merkel's change of heart, allegedly fearing that, because her refugee policy was popular, it would be harmful for them to be blamed for closing German borders. Given the party's history, they were strongly attached to the right of political asylum and they did not want to be seen as being to the 'right' of Merkel on the issue (Alexander 2017: 24; interview, Berlin, 2018). Instead of closing the German border with Austria to all refugees, as had originally been agreed, the government decided to reinstate controls there, but to admit and register all asylum-seekers. The flow of refugees and migrants into Germany was not reduced, but the Schengen Area, temporarily at least, was no longer entirely borderless.

This – the most dramatic – phase of the Refugee Crisis had been managed, over no more than a week, largely trilaterally between the Hungarian, Austrian and German governments. Faced, relative to its size and compared with other EU members, with a heavy burden through the influx of refugees, the Orbán government had confronted its Austrian and German counterparts with the choice of either risking a humanitarian catastrophe on the Austro-Hungarian border or continuing to take in the growing wave of refugees streaming northwards from Turkey and Greece through the Balkans. At short notice and under great time pressure, the Austrian and German governments developed and pursued a joint strategy. Relative to its population, Austria was in any case to receive two and a half times more asylum applicants in the second and third quarters of 2015 than Germany (Eurostat 2015). Austrian public opinion was arguably less 'refugee-friendly' than the German and the parties in its Grand Coalition government had to contend with a stronger national-populist competitor than their German counterparts (Alexander 2017: 221–223). Without the certainty that the great majority of the

refugees would simply transit the country to Germany, the Austrian government would not have kept open its border with Hungary for them. For the
refugees' fate, it was thus Germany's stance that was decisive. Merkel was
adamant that Germany could cope with this challenge (*Wir schaffen das!*
We'll manage this!). But, she argued, there had to be a 'European solution'.
With its engagement and strength, Germany could 'pave the way' for such a
solution, but national policies alone could not provide it (Deutscher Bundestag 2015: 11613).

The intensity of the conflict between the member governments in the Council
over the relocation of (a smaller number of) refugees less than three months earlier and the failure of Merkel's attempt to persuade other heads of government
to take a significant number of the refugees and migrants that were now arriving
in Germany testified to the prospective obstacles to devising a viable 'European
solution' to the crisis. Moreover, in the coming months, the Austrian-German
coalition that was forged on this issue in early September 2015 was to collapse,
leaving Merkel even more isolated in the EU than she had been already.

The conflict over the relocation of refugees

The burgeoning number of refugees entering the Schengen Area had put the
issue of the distribution of asylum-seekers back on the EU's agenda already
before the events of 5–6 September. The Commission tabled proposals in the
second half of August (*Financial Times* 2015k). Backing these, Merkel and
French president François Hollande appealed jointly for a 'more equal distribution of asylum-seekers across the EU' (*Financial Times* 2015l).

The key issue for the fate of the refugee relocation proposals was whether
there had been or would be any significant shift in the balance of forces
among the member states since the conflict over the far more modest measures
adopted by the EU no more than a month earlier. Among some of the Central
and East European governments, the growing influx of refugees in the intervening period had led to a reassessment of positions. A Polish government
official was quoted as saying: 'The atmosphere and the details of what we
are dealing with are much, much different to the last time we discussed it ...
The challenge seems more real'; while another in Hungary conceded that as
'the magnitude of migration has changed, so we have to revisit the situation'
(*Financial Times* 2015n). It nonetheless remained uncertain whether member
states' positions on the issue had changed drastically enough to enable the
Council to approve significantly more far-reaching measures than the very
limited ones that the EU had so recently adopted.

The member governments opposed to refugee relocation did not have
their backs to the financial wall in the way that the states that needed to be
bailed out in the Eurozone Crisis had had and they were correspondingly
less vulnerable to pressure exerted by the Commission and the (German-led)
member states that championed this agenda. The latter had four conceivable
bargaining weapons. The first was the threat that, without such measures,
the Schengen Area would collapse. The German government regularly linked

refugee relocation and 'burden-sharing' to the survival of the Schengen Area. Echoing Merkel and the Christian Democratic Interior Minister, de Maizière, the SPD chairman and Economics Minister, Sigmar Gabriel, described the decision to reinstate controls on the border with Austria as a 'signal' towards other EU member states that, while Germany was willing to assume a dispro-portionate share of the burden, it was not willing to take in all the refugees (SPD 2015). Gabriel argued that the re-erection of borders and destruction of Schengen would affect other countries much more than Germany (*Financial Times* 2015o).

Not only Gabriel and de Maizière, but Hollande too referred to the possi-bility of imposing financial sanctions on the opponents of refugee relocation (*Financial Times* 2015o; *Le Monde* 2015e, 2015i, 2015j; Leparmentier 2015). The dependence of the Central and East European member states on finan-cial transfers – 'structural funds' – from the EU budget and net-contributing members, notably but not only Germany, was the second potential source of bargaining power for the advocates of redistributing refugees. The utility of this resource was limited, however, by the fact that EU structural funds were allocated on a multi-annual, usually seven-year basis, so that these sanctions could not be applied immediately with a view to shifting the Central and East European members' stance on the issue. Merkel herself was more restrained in issuing this threat, while by no means ruling out such punishment: 'I don't want to bring out all the instruments of torture now. We want to find a solu-tion as good friends' (as quoted in *Le Monde* 2015e).

The third potential source of leverage that protagonists of refugee redis-tribution possessed over the Central and Eastern European states was their dependence on the former for support on other for them equally if not more crucial issues. In the context of the Ukraine Crisis that had exploded in 2014, this dependence appears to have been felt especially in the three Baltic states, a diplomat from one of which was quoted as saying: 'If we want international support over Russia, then we need to show solidarity here. It is a touchy issue domestically, but this isn't just a domestic problem' (as quoted in *Financial Times* 2015g). In the end, all three Baltic states were to support refugee relo-cation in the Council.

Otherwise Germany and its allies were reliant on moral suasion or appeals to try to mobilize support for refugee relocation. Merkel argued that the promotion of universal human rights, to which a generous approach to the reception of refugees corresponded, was a part of European identity. If Europe were to fall apart over the Refugee Crisis, it would no longer be the kind of Europe that the EU had historically stood for (*Le Monde* 2015e). Critics highlighted the fact that the governments of countries that had ben-efited from the fall of the Iron Curtain were now constructing new walls to prevent the free movement of people (Hockenos 2015; Kauffmann 2015). This kind of argument cut little ice, however, with Orbán. The Iron Curtain had been 'against us', he argued; the fence that his government was building on the border to Serbia, in contrast, was 'for us' (Drozdiak 2017: 26). More-over, Orbán had an entirely different conception of Europe and European values than Merkel. He conceived Europe as a Christian civilization that had to be protected against a Muslim demographic invasion and Hungary as the principal line of defence in this 'battle' (Chastand and Stolz 2015). Moreover, his refugee policy seems to have enabled him to boost his previously flagging domestic political popularity drastically – in a context in which his most serious political opposition came from the (more) extreme right (Chastand and Stolz 2015).

Three days before a meeting of the Justice and Home Affairs (JHA) Council, the German foreign minister Steinmeier and the foreign minister of Luxembourg, Jean Asselborn, who was also the Council president, met the heads of government of the four Visegrad states in Prague to try to break their opposition to refugee relocation. While the Hungarian and Slovakian governments remained steadfast in their rejection of the proposals, the Polish government announced that, in view of the 'magnitude of the humanitarian catastrophe', it would accept some refugees after all – although not necessarily that it would support a compulsory relocation scheme (Prime Minister Ewa Kopacz, as quoted in *Le Monde* 2015f). One observer noted at the time that the Polish shift 'may well have had some other explanations as well', but 'pressure from Berlin was surely a factor' in bringing it about (*Eurocomment* 2015a: 8). At the 'acrimonious' Council meeting, the Hungarian, Romanian, Slovakian and Czech governments were 'taken to task by their German and French colleagues' for their rejection of refugee relocation. But they maintained their opposition (*Eurocomment* 2015a: 11).

So long as Poland opposed the project there would be no qualified majority in its favour in the Council, so the Luxembourg council president decided not to force a vote on the issue. This preserved the possibility of the Council returning to the issue at a later meeting, by which time the Polish position might have changed. Merkel was dissatisfied with the outcome of this meeting, especially with the failure to agree a relocation scheme, and wanted 'immediate action to remedy the situation' (*Eurocomment* 2015a: 12). The German government tried to line up support for the project before a second meeting of the JHA Council. The governments of Greece and Italy, from which the refugees would be relocated, could be counted on to support it, as could those member states, such as Sweden and Austria, that were receiving relatively large numbers of refugees. Berlin focused in particular on getting its French, Spanish and Polish counterparts on board (Janning 2015b). While it preferred to resolve the conflict consensually if possible, it was willing to push for a vote on the project, not least since the binding nature of the relocation mechanism had 'already been watered down' (Janning 2015b). Germany, one commentator observed, was 'claiming solidarity as a constituent part of the European project and evidently is not willing to wait for everyone to share that view' (Janning 2015b).

The second time around, the JHA Council voted by a qualified majority in favour of a compulsory scheme whereby overall 160,000 refugees would be relocated. The Polish government having meanwhile decided to back the project, opponents of the scheme no longer had a blocking minority in the

Council, even though, at the insistence of the True Finns, a national-populist party in the governing coalition, the Finnish government abstained. The conflict over the issue was by no means ended with the Council vote, however. The Czech government announced it would contests its legality before the ECJ. The Slovakian government said it would not comply with it and that it would rather risk an infringement proceeding against it than to respect 'this diktat of the majority, which was unable to push through its opinion using rational arguments' (Prime Minister Robert Sico, as quoted in *The Atlantic.com* 2015).

By now, in any case, the scale of the refugee relocation project looked very modest compared with the magnitude of the influx of refugees. With 5000 refugees pouring daily into Greece via its islands, a project that *The Economist* argued had looked 'far-sighted' at the outset now looked 'irrelevant' (*The Economist* 2015b: 27). Presciently, the news magazine also described the scheme as 'nightmarishly, perhaps impossibly, hard' to implement. German officials acknowledged that even if states opposed to receiving refugees fell into line, there was no way that they could stop the refugees from returning to their initial host country if they wished (interview, Berlin, 2018). Two years later, fewer than a fifth of a target of 160,000 refugees had been relocated under the scheme, including hardly any to the four Visegrad states. The ECJ dismissed the complaints brought against the decision by the Hungarian and Slovakian governments and supported by Poland, where, in autumn 2015, a new national-conservative government had been elected to office. While the Slovakian government subsequently accepted the verdict, the Hungarian and Polish governments announced they would defy it.

The deep fissures that opened up in the EU in the conflict over refugee relocation closely reflected the contrasting pressures and constraints of domestic politics in the member states. The German government balked at the magnitude of the prospective financial and other burdens involved in managing the continuing influx of refugees. The crisis was not just a challenge for Germany, Merkel now argued, but one for 'all of Europe … Germany can't shoulder this task alone' (speech to the congress of the trade union Verdi, as quoted in *The Guardian* 2015a). The *Willkommenskultur* that had blossomed at the outset of the crisis quickly showed signs of waning (*Le Monde* 2015j). There was massive German support for the idea of refugee relocation – but, among other large West European EU member states (but, understandably, for Italy), public opinion was far more ambivalent (*Le Monde* 2015k). Among the publics of the Central and East European member states, reflecting their distinctive historical experience (see the beginning of this section), public opinion towards the reception of refugees was more hostile (*Le Monde* 2015g). Ministers of their governments justified their opposition to refugee relocation in terms of domestic politics: 'How do you want me to go and explain my decision to my Parliament?', asked, for example, the Slovakian interior minister, referring to a scenario in which he would have supported the project in the JHA Council (*Le Monde* 2015h). A Czech diplomat explained his government's opposition similarly: 'We were either with Orbán or we were with the Germans. And the public were with Orbán, so we had no choice' (Foy and Buckley 2015).

The level and depth of polarization precluded a consensual resolution of the conflict. In contrast to the Eurozone Crisis, the German government found itself in this one in the role of *demandeur*. The bargaining resources which it possessed in the Refugee Crisis – the (not immediately or easily realizable) threat of cutting financial aid to the Central and East European member states, the menace that the Schengen zone might otherwise collapse, the linkage of this issue with others on which these states required German support, and moral suasion – did not suffice to break (most of) these governments' strong opposition to refugee relocation. The German government may, however, have played a significant role in persuading its Polish counterpart to acquiesce in the project. The Polish government's change of stance ultimately facilitated the mediation of the conflict by a (qualified) majority vote in the Council. A German-led coalition had won the upper hand in the EU legislative process, but this proved to be a pyrrhic victory in as far as they could not ensure that the decision, once taken, was subsequently implemented on the ground in the member states.

The conflict over limiting the influx of refugees

The limited scale of the refugee relocation scheme (and the rapidly perceived obstacles to its implementation) underscored the importance of limiting the overall influx of refugees into the EU if the crisis was to be managed by common EU action and without precipitating the collapse of the Schengen Zone. Otherwise there was no feasible way by which the pressures on the EU and Schengen members admitting relatively large numbers of refugees could be eased. The danger that a 'domino effect' could develop and destroy Schengen was illustrated by a series of unilateral decisions by national governments from mid-September onwards to reintroduce at least temporary controls on Schengen-internal borders. After Germany announced the (limited) controls on its border with Austria, the Austrian and Slovakian governments followed suit, imposing tighter checks on refugees. As large numbers of refugees continued to flow into Sweden, the Swedish government reintroduced controls on its border with Denmark. In late November 2015, the Commission president Juncker lamented that the Schengen Accord was 'partly comatose' (*Le Monde* 2015m). By January 2016 as many as seven governments had reimposed Schengen-internal border controls, prompting a German government spokesman too to describe Schengen as being endangered (*Le Monde* 2016a).

The German government's (and its allies') success in securing a decision in favour of refugee relocation in the second September JHA Council meeting conceivably conveyed a misleading impression as to the extent of its influence over other member states in the refugee and Schengen crises. How limited this was could be seen in the almost complete lack of willingness of other governments to admit any of the refugees that had streamed via Hungary and Austria into Germany in the first weekend of September (see the section 'The conflict over the reception of refugees' above). Measured alongside the magnitude of the refugee influx, the commitments made by the member governments that voted for the project were also actually small, although proportional to their assessed capacity to absorb refugees as defined by demographic, economic and labour market variables. Some 40,206 refugees were supposed to be relocated from Italy and Greece to Germany, another 30,783 to France, 19,219 to Spain and 11,946 to Poland. The UK exercised its right not to participate in the scheme under the EU treaties, but it pledged to take in 20,000 Syrian refugees direct from camps in countries neighbouring Syria. Over the next few months Germany's relative isolation in the refugee and Schengen crises was to increase – before, almost single-handedly, it launched a major diplomatic initiative that may – or may not – have made a major contribution to stemming the flow of refugees into the EU in spring 2016 (see later in this section).

German isolation was not least visible in its relationship with France, whose solidarity with Berlin in these crises was strictly limited. Outwardly the rituals and norms of the Franco-German relationship were by and large obeyed. In the communiqués following their meetings they beseeched their fellow political leaders to devise a common response to the crises. President Hollande generally backed Merkel's stance – following her, for example, in abandoning his initial opposition to a compulsory refugee relocation scheme (Alexander 2017: 92).

Nonetheless there were wide substantive Berlin–Paris divergences on how the crisis ought to be managed. These divergences were rooted in the two countries' contrasting economic, financial and political conditions. With the government budget in surplus and unemployment below 5 per cent, there had 'probably never been a better moment in the last 70 years' for Germany to deal with such a crisis (the director of the *Deutsches Institut für Wirtschaftsforschung* – German Institute for Economic Research - DIW, Markus Fratzscher, as quoted in *The Guardian* 2015b). This was far from the case though in France, where the government budget exceeded the 3 per cent of GDP rule for the Eurozone and unemployment, at more than 10 per cent, was double the German level. The contrast between the French and German political landscapes was no less stark, especially in respect of – in this issue area critically important – variations in popular support for anti-immigrant and anti-Islamic parties of the populist or extreme right. In Germany, the AfD had been founded in opposition to the Euro in 2013. After having polled 7 per cent at the European parliamentary elections in 2014, it had been riven by internal disputes and experienced a major decline in popular support. By the beginning of September 2015, most polls estimated its support to have fallen to no more than about 3–4 per cent of German voters (Wikipedia 2017a). In France, again in contrast, the right-wing extremist party the *Front National* was a well-established and formidable political force that, in the 2014 European elections, with 25 per cent of the vote, had emerged as the biggest political force in the country. It was commensurately more difficult for the French government to formulate its refugee and Schengen policy without calculating how this might influence its political support relative to that of the *Front National*. Taking in refugees in France in autumn 2015 was much less popular than in Germany – thus, in one opinion survey, more than twice as many French respondents as in Germany rejected the notion that the country had a duty to take in 'migrants fleeing war and misery' (IFOP poll, cited in *Le Monde* 2015k).

These Franco-German divergences were then exacerbated by the Paris terrorist attacks of 13 November 2015, which brought the internal security dimensions of the refugee and Schengen crises to the fore, especially once it was revealed that several of the terrorists had entered the EU as refugees and, in the absence of border controls, had been able to travel unhindered between France and Belgium. The Socialist government resolved not to be outflanked on the issue by the mainstream and extreme right. The prime minister, Manuel Valls, was the most outspoken exponent of tougher action to curb the influx of refugees, emphasizing, shortly after the Paris attacks, that 'we can't take in so many refugees in Europe any longer – this is not possible'. The EU had to control its borders better, 'otherwise the people will say "It's over with Europe"' (as quoted in *Le Monde* 2015l). This contradicted Merkel's stance, in as far as she refused to set any upper ceiling on the number of refugees that Germany would take in. Valls defended his stance explicitly by referring to the danger that the crisis would strengthen the *Front National* (*Financial Times* 2015j). Valls acknowledged the magnitude of the challenge that Germany was facing and that 'we must help Germany' and he pledged that France would take in the 30,000 refugees it was obliged to accept under the relocation scheme – but no more than that (*Der Spiegel* 2016c; *Le Monde* 2016e). In Germany, he intimated that Merkel's refugee policy had failed – remarks that a German commentator regarded as an 'act of extraordinary hostility' (Davet and Lhomme 2016b: 471–472; Thomas Klau, as quoted in *The Economist* 2016d: 24).

President Hollande did not like Valls having made these remarks in Germany, but substantively he shared his prime minister's stance on the Refugee Crisis: 'He thinks, and I do too, that the French are anxious and they have to be reassured, in particular in relation to migrants and refugees' (as quoted in Davet and Lhomme 2016b: 472). Like other member states, including Germany, France was concerned to take more and stronger action to secure the Schengen Area's external borders. So long as the refugees remained elsewhere, however, Hollande and his government were not exposed to the same pressure to address the crisis as the countries experiencing a large refugee influx. To a large extent they consequently became crisis 'bystanders' (*The Economist* 2016d: 24). German criticism of the French government's relative lack of engagement, however, remained muted. Everyone understood, a German MEP was quoted as saying, that, with the terrorist attacks and the strong *Front National*, France was in a 'special situation', but it should nonetheless have been more involved in managing the crisis (Manfred Weber, as quoted in *Le Monde* 2016g).

As much value as the German government continued to attach to keeping up the appearance of a close Franco-German relationship, it looked more towards other member states to tackle the Refugee Crisis. This was particularly visible in the way in which Merkel promoted a second component of its strategy for addressing the Refugee Crisis – curbing the inflow of refugees entering the Schengen area via the Greek islands from Turkey. The focus on obtaining the support and cooperation of the Turkish government had been proposed by the German (CDU) finance minister, Wolfgang Schäuble (Alexander 2017: 139–141). Merkel was initially reluctant to pursue this option, as she had a notoriously difficult relationship with the Turkish president Recep Tayyib Erdoğan (Alexander 2017: 189–204). Erdoğan's prime minister, Ahmet Davutoğlu, had offered the EU Turkey's assistance to curb the refugee flow already in the first week of September – at a price of €6bn (Alexander 2017: 189). Numerous member states were, however, loath to 'outsource' the control of the influx of refugees into the EU to Turkey. Fearful that Turkish assistance might be bought at the cost of Cyprus and the prospects of the reunification of the island, the government in Nicosia was at the forefront of the opposition (*Eurocomment* 2015d: 11–13). But other governments, including the French and Belgian, were also wary as to the possible terms of such an accord, especially the notion that it might oblige EU member states to take in refugees directly from Turkey (*Eurocomment* 2015b: 16, 2015c: 17, 2015d: 9–10, 18–19). At a meeting of the Committee of Permanent Representatives (COREPER) in late November 2015, the German representative's proposals in this regard were 'shot down' (*Eurocomment* 2015d: 16).

The adoption of Merkel's project for an EU–Turkey refugee accord was also complicated by her growing estrangement over the issue with the Council president (and former Polish prime minister) Donald Tusk. Tusk had been sceptical as to the utility of the refugee relocation scheme launched in September. He thought that it made demands on other EU member states that they 'could not and should not have been expected to deliver' (*Eurocomment* 2015b: 22–26, quote from 23). He expressed his scepticism publicly: 'There is no majority to be won in Europe when it comes to resettlement or the next phase of relocation. And not because of the eastern and central parts of Europe only. But many more countries' (as quoted in *Eurocomment* 2015d: 21). Convinced that it was infeasible as well as undesirable to construct 'Berlin type walls around Fortress Europe', Merkel aimed to *manage* the inflow of refugees (*Eurocomment* 2015d: 5). Tusk's priority was rather to recover control of the external borders of the Schengen area and to *stop* the refugee influx (*Eurocomment* 2015d: 5). Or, as he said himself, referring evidently to Merkel: 'Some European leaders say that this wave of migrants is too big to stop. I'm absolutely sure that … this wave of migrants is too big not to stop' (as quoted in: *Eurocomment* 2015d: 21).

Not being able to rely on Tusk and the Council bureaucracy in respect of the EU's relations with Turkey and faced with widespread resistance among other member states, Merkel launched a diplomatic initiative to circumvent this opposition. The German government organized several informal 'mini-summits' of a subgroup of member states, promptly dubbed a 'coalition of the willing' comprising Austria, Sweden, Finland, the Benelux states and Greece in addition to Germany (*Eurocomment* 2015d: 2, 18–19). The absence of the French president Hollande from the first meeting of this 'coalition' in late November 2015 was explained by the prior obligation he had to participate in the UN climate change conference that France was hosting in Paris. Significantly, however, France was not represented either at subsequent meetings of the group. A German source labelled the group's members as the member states '"most affected" by the Refugee Crisis' (*Eurocomment* 2015d: 18). In any case, the group comprised member states whose governments were at least 'willing' to discuss taking in refugees directly from Turkey in the event of the Turkish government agreeing to curb the influx of refugees via the Greek islands (*Eurocomment* 2015d).

In lieu of the Tusk and the Council, this initiative was backed by the European Commission, which conducted initial talks with the Turkish government over the terms of an accord. Never in the previous 15 years, according to Juncker, had the Commission worked so closely with the German Chancellor as it did on this issue (*Eurocomment* 2015d: 23). Primarily involving granting financial aid for Turkish-based refugees, visa liberalization for Turkish citizens travelling to Europe and the reopening of Turkish EU accession negotiations in exchange for the Turkish government preventing refugees reaching the Greek islands, a provisional accord was reached on 29 November 2015. However, some 11 member governments refused in mid-December to approve the accord, insisting on first seeing more evidence of a reduction of the flow of refugees from Turkey to Greece and rejecting the Commission proposal that there should be a 'voluntary humanitarian admission scheme' under which member states would take in refugees directly from Turkey (*Financial Times* 2015s).

Within the 'coalition of the willing' that the German government conceived as implementing this scheme, the most intensive bilateral relationship linked Germany and Austria, which, in the Refugee Crisis, assumed the role that in other crises had traditionally been played by France (Alexander 2017: 223). However, in Austria presidential elections were to occur in April 2016 and the parties in the Grand Coalition government were facing a strong challenge from the national-populist Freedom Party (*Freiheitliche Partei Österreichs –* FPÖ), which wanted to stop the flow of refugees completely. As the refugee influx showed few signs of abating, the Social Democratic Chancellor Werner Faymann came under growing pressure from his Christian Democratic partner to toughen Austria's stance, all the more so after refugees, mainly from North Africa, were accused of widespread acts of sexual aggression against women in the west German city of Cologne on New Year's Eve 2015 (Alexander 2017: 226). Breaking a pledge he had allegedly made to Merkel, he caved in to this pressure in mid-January 2016 and agreed to introduce a ceiling on the number of refugees in Austria. The pressure from his coalition partner and the public mood in Austria left him no other choice, he explained to the German chancellor, whose attempts to persuade him to stick to his original stance failed (Alexander 2017: 230). He later said that the government's stance changed because it had become evident that Merkel's attempt to find a European solution to the crisis would fail. The German government had calculated, he argued, that if 1 or 2 million more refugees should come, some 300–400,000 of them would remain in Austria, easing the pressure on Germany. But Austria was not willing thus to become 'Germany's waiting-room' (as quoted in *Le Monde* 2016i).

With the Austrian government beginning to distance itself from its German counterpart, Merkel looked increasingly, if not 'totally isolated' in the EU (Gerald Knaus, European Stability Initiative, as quoted in *Le Monde* 2016c). One analysis concluded that all the main components of Merkel's refugee strategy were unravelling – the refugees were still coming, there was little sign of Turkey implementing the accord reached in November and the refugee relocation scheme had so far been a flop. Germany had 'tried to lead in Europe, but others will not follow' (*The Economist* 2016b). Not least following the events in Cologne, Merkel was exposed to many of the same pressures that had caused the Austrian government to change course, especially from her coalition partner, the CSU, but also from the SPD (*Le Monde* 2016b). A series of state elections was imminent in Germany. According to one account at least, her steadfastness in the face of these pressures reflected Schäuble's and her joint fear that if Berlin were to 'shut its borders', this would precipitate not only the end of the Schengen area, but also that of the euro and the Single Market (Dempsey 2016). She carried on trying to forge a group of member states that would take in refugees directly from Turkey. By mid-February 2016, the German government reckoned to have expanded the size of the group from 8 to 12 members, including inter alia the Benelux countries, Sweden, Greece, Portugal, Slovenia and Austria (Alexander 2017: 231–232; *Financial Times* 2016e).

Berlin had, however, miscalculated. Within two days of this assessment having been made, the 'Coalition of the Willing' suddenly collapsed. The Austrian foreign minister Sebastian Kurz had developed an alternative plan for addressing the Refugee Crisis, involving the closure of the Balkans route (Alexander 2017: 219–238). When the Turkish prime minister Davutoğlu called off his participation in a planned EU–Turkish summit because of a terrorist attack in Ankara, the Austrian government cancelled a meeting of the coalition members that it was to host in Brussels, announcing at the same time that it would henceforth accept no more than 80 political asylum claims a day, less than half the number it had previously been receiving (Alexander 2017: 232). More refugees than hitherto were therefore likely to seek asylum in Germany. While a European Council meeting the following day endorsed Merkel's stance that the EU should prioritize an accord with Turkey as a means of addressing the Refugee Crisis, it did not rule out trying to stem the influx by closing the Balkans route. The Austrian vice-chancellor made the collapse of Merkel's coalition unmistakably clear by stating that 'anyone can deduce' that it no longer existed in its original form (*Financial Times* 2016f;

Alexander 2017: 232). German officials were reportedly 'furious that an old ally has broken ranks' (*Financial Times* 2016f). The German Interior Minister de Maizière warned that 'if some countries should try unilaterally ... to put a shared problem on to Germany's back, then this could not be accepted by us without consequences' (as quoted in Alexander 2017: 233). As one commentator noted, however, how Germany could implement such a threat remained unclear. It could hardly threaten to close its own border to Austria, as this would have unleashed exactly the kind of 'domino effect' on the Balkans route that Germany wanted to avert (Alexander 2017: 233). In any case, the threat failed to impress the Austrian government. A week later, it called a summit of Balkan states – Macedonia, Montenegro, Serbia, Croatia, Slovenia, Bosnia-Hercegovina, Kosovo, Romania and Bulgaria – to discuss closing off this route to refugees. Pointedly, neither Germany nor the European Commission was invited, nor Greece, where refugees would continue to enter the EU unless the influx from Turkey via the Greek islands was curbed. In effect, the EU was now pursuing two different, although not necessarily contradictory, policies to manage – or stop – the inflow of refugees.

A new version of the EU–Turkey refugee agreement was scheduled to be adopted in early March 2016. However, the evening before the formal summit the Turkish prime minister Davutoğlu organized a trilateral meeting with Merkel and the Dutch prime minister Mark Rutte, the rotating Council president at the time. At this meeting, Merkel approved Davutoğlu's proposal that for every Syrian returned to Turkey, another Syrian would be resettled (directly) from Turkey to the EU (Alexander 2017: 263–270; Council of the EU 2016). Neither Tusk nor the Commission president Juncker nor indeed the French president Hollande had been invited to take part in the meeting (*Financial Times* 2016h). Merkel subsequently had to face 'massive' criticism in the European Council when it was unexpectedly confronted the next day with the new provision in the proposed accord (Alexander 2017: 271; *Financial Times* 2016h). As member states' participation in the resettlement process was to be voluntary, the number of resettled Syrians was to be limited initially to 72,000, and the number of refugees taken in directly from Syria could be subtracted from the total number of refugees that they were required to accept under the September 2015 relocation scheme, Merkel could convince the other heads of government to accept this part of the accord. If, as pledged, Turkey were to reduce the number of refugees reaching Greece, this would ease the pressure on the Greek–Macedonian border and work as a complement to the Austrian-initiated closure of the Balkans route (Alexander 2017: 272). There was no consensus in the Council, however, in favour of ratifying the draft accord that Merkel and Rutte had negotiated with Davutoğlu. Tusk was particularly critical of the process by which his own draft accord had been pushed aside, equating the German government's approach as being akin to Orwell's animal farm and stressing that 'all animals are equal on my farm' (as quoted in *Financial Times* 2016i). Apart from Cyprus, several member states, including Italy, Belgium, Luxembourg, Spain, Portugal and indeed France, objected to the absence of any provisions concerning press freedom in Turkey or raised concerns about standards in the Turkish asylum system (*Financial Times* 2016j; *Le Monde* 2016j). The accord finally signed by the two sides ten days later was arguably 'less advantageous' for the Turkish government than the one originally 'pre-negotiated' by Merkel and Rutte (*Le Monde* 2016k).

In its original incarnation, the EU–Turkish accord had remained 'basically a dead letter' (*Le Monde* 2016h). In contrast, the new accord seemed to be much more effective in reducing the number of refugees reaching the EU. Starting in March 2016, this number began to fall very rapidly. Whether this trend was attributable to this accord, however, is questionable. Officials in Berlin attributed a greater role in halting the influx to the Austrian-inspired closure of the Balkans route for refugees, which was put in place two weeks before the new EU–Turkish accord entered into force. Already with the closure of the Balkans route, the entry of new refugees into Austria had practically been brought to a standstill (Alexander 2017: 273). In any event, the long-term fate of the EU–Turkey accord remained uncertain, as it was improbable that the EU would redeem several pledges it made to Turkey in exchange for its curbing the influx of refugees into the EU, notably those relating to visa liberalization and EU accession negotiations, not least after the Turkish government's crackdown on political freedom in the country following an abortive coup attempt a few months later.

Conclusion

Unlike the Eurozone Crisis, the Refugee Crisis did not produce a higher level of (horizontal, sectoral or vertical) political integration. It was certainly not a motor of closer political integration according to Monnet's famous or notorious adage. Unlike in the Ukraine Crisis, nor did the pre-existing levels of horizontal, sectoral and vertical integration remain unaffected. Despite numerous warnings and prognoses to this effect at its height, nor did the crisis bring about the complete collapse of the Schengen Area and generalized reinstatement of border controls between its members.

Rather, overall, the crisis provoked limited political disintegration, variable by integration dimensions. There was no *horizontal* disintegration of Schengen. No pre-crisis member of the Schengen Area left it nor was any expelled, although in early 2016 the threat of excluding Greece was raised to increase the pressure on the Greek government to accelerate the erection of 'hotspots' to register refugees arriving in Greece. But there was some *sectoral* disintegration. To be sure, most Schengen members did not reintroduce internal border controls and most travellers inside the area continued to cross borders without being controlled. However, during the Refugee Crisis, Schengen-internal border controls were erected by several member states on borders that were (actual or prospective) entry points for large numbers of refugees. Such controls are legal 'as a last resort' under the Schengen Border Code, which permits them where there are 'serious threats to public policy or internal security', but they are meant normally to last for no more than one month or exceptionally for up to two years. Five Schengen members – Germany, Austria, Denmark, Sweden and Norway – nonetheless still had controls in place in 2018, justifying them by reference to the perceived threat of the 'secondary movement of irregular migrants' (Policy Department for Citizens' Rights and Constitutional Affairs of the European Parliament 2018: 11, 13). 'Important interests of the member states were at stake' in one German official's view (interview, Berlin, 2018). The threat of terrorism and illegal immigration was 'too serious' for them to do otherwise than maintain border controls. The Commission rejected this analysis, arguing that 'deficiencies in the external border management by Greece and the secondary movements resulting from these deficiencies can no longer be invoked to justify reintroduction or prolongation of internal border controls' (Policy Department for Citizens' Rights and Constitutional Affairs of the European Parliament 2018: 12). Nonetheless, faced with the resolve of the member states to maintain the controls anyway, it proposed to relax the code's provisions so that governments could extend them further without running foul of EU law (Policy Department for Citizens' Rights and Constitutional Affairs of the European Parliament 2018: 34–35). A precedent seemed to be in the process of being created whereby, in violation of the principle of borderless travel in Schengen Area, member governments could impose border controls regardless of the Commission and retain them indefinitely.

The weakening of the Commission's authority in this way was also one, but not the only, manifestation of a trend towards *vertical* political disintegration in this crisis. The ECJ's authority was also challenged and damaged. In respect of policy implementation, the most powerful manifestation of this trend was the refusal of two Central and East European member states to take in refugees under the 2015 relocation scheme, even after the ECJ had found against them. Key decisions during the crisis were negotiated primarily in bargaining between the member states. The Commission and the Council president tended to be either ignored, to 'fly in the Chancellor [Merkel's] slipstream' (*Eurocomment* 2015d: 23) or, if they fell out with her, to be sidelined. The high point of this trend was reached and illustrated by the manner in which the second EU–Turkish accord was negotiated – by Chancellor Merkel – in March 2016. The crisis witnessed the 'collapse' of the Common European Asylum System, which meanwhile existed merely 'on paper' (Lavenex 2018: 1203, 1209). These trends were not offset let alone outweighed by the strengthening of Frontex and its reincarnation as the European Coast and Border Guard (ECBG) in 2015 (see Niemann 2018). The ECBG would 'still largely depend on EU member states' border personnel and tools, as well as their capacity to cooperate' (Carrera and den Hertog 2016:16; Servent 2018: 96). The 'Integrated Border Management System' of which the refurbished Frontex was intended to be a part was judged unlikely to replace the 'old intergovernmental and disintegrated model of border control and surveillance' (Policy Department for Citizens' Rights and Constitutional Affairs 2018: 40). Overall there was thus some vertical disintegration and re-nationalization of Schengen and political asylum policies during the crisis.

In justice and home affairs, compared with other issue areas, the role of the EU's supranational organs had remained restrained even after it had been communitarized by the Lisbon Treaty (Servent and Trauner 2014; Wolff 2015). Even so, in more than two decades up to 2015, border control, asylum and other aspects of justice and home affairs policy seem to have obeyed a fairly strong neo-functionalist logic of Europeanization (Monar 2006: 4; Niemann 2016). The Refugee Crisis broke this trend and, to a limited degree, reversed it. The prospective economic costs of a reinstatement of border controls in the Schengen Area were tangible (see the introduction to this chapter). But the costs of the disruption that their reinstatement provoked were not sufficient to dissuade numerous governments from reintroducing them at least partially. The constraints exerted by the ties of economic interdependence on Schengen member states were not quite as powerful as neo-functionalist, transactionalist and liberal intergovernmentalist theories of European integration would have led us to expect.

Rather, in line with the expectations of postfunctionalist integration theories, the – disintegrative – outcome of the crisis could be attributed to the mass politicization of the issue and the political polarization that it provoked among the EU member states' mass publics as well as governments. The Refugee Crisis preoccupied and mobilized EU publics on an unprecedented scale, even exceeding that achieved in the Eurozone Crisis. By spring 2015 'immigration' had become one of the two most important issues facing the EU for more EU citizens – 38 per cent – than any other (European Commission 2015a). In autumn 2015, this percentage rose steeply to 58, more than twice the percentage for the next-most-frequently cited issue, terrorism (European Commission 2015b). Public disapproval of the EU's handling of the Refugee Crisis was massive, albeit with significant variations by member state (Pew Research Center 2016). The combination of the high salience of the issue and the high level of popular dissatisfaction with the management of the crisis created fertile political ground for the growth of (new as well as pre-existing) anti-EU, anti-refugee and/or anti-Muslim political movements and parties in many member states. After the Eurozone Crisis, the refugee crises gave these political forces a second, even more powerful boost. In winter 2015/16, such parties were the largest in terms of polled public support in Austria, France, Greece, Hungary, the Netherlands, Poland and the UK. They were growing fast in Germany, Italy and Sweden. They were the main governing parties in most of Central and Eastern Europe, especially in Poland and Hungary, a minority governing party in Finland and parliamentary supporters of the government in Denmark (Webber 2017: 346–350). The pressure on the existing political parties to accommodate public opinion on the crisis became increasingly intense, all the more so in those countries in which elections were imminent.

The Refugee Crisis became a highly salient and profoundly polarizing and divisive issue, at the European as well as domestic level. It split the member states along several cleavages, based on geographic location, political history, cultural and ethnic diversity, and domestic political constellations (see the section 'The Schengen and Refugee Crisis, 2015–16', beginning on page 152). Attitudes towards refugees were, for example, far more positive in Sweden and Germany than in most other member states, especially in Central and East European member states such as Hungary and Poland, where, compared with the former two countries, the proportion of citizens who regarded refugees as a burden because they 'take our jobs and social benefits' was more than twice as high (Pew Research Center 2016). In as far as the preponderant preference among member states' citizens was to minimize the influx of refugees, there was a strong temptation for them to revert to unilateral, 'beggar-thy-neighbour' policies that could indeed have put a general end to borderless travel in the Schengen Area.

As in the Eurozone and Ukraine Crises, so too in the management of the Refugee Crisis, Chancellor Merkel and the German government assumed the central role. No other member state deployed the same diplomatic effort to shape the EU's response to the crisis, either initially or in relation to the refugee relocation scheme and the negotiation of an accord with Turkey to curb the influx of refugees to Greece. If, at the height of the crisis, in the last four months of 2015, Germany had turned away the refugees trying to enter the country, this would likely have provoked a far more comprehensive reinstatement of border controls than actually occurred. The survival of borderless travel in the Schengen Area turned primarily on its decision. In deciding, however, not to turn back the refugees on its border with Austria then, the German government, as we saw above, was motivated more by domestic and EU-related political considerations than by any calculations of the economic implications of the reinstatement of border controls of the kind that neo-functionalist, transactionalist or liberal intergovernmentalist theories of integration suggest would have been determining for its stance.

In admitting a disproportionately large proportion of refugees that fled to EU states in 2015 and 2016, Germany certainly played one of the defining roles of a stabilizing hegemonic power. Overall, compared with the Eurozone and Ukraine Crises, however, the German government was not nearly as influential in determining the 'rules' by which the crisis was managed. At the outset of the crisis, it was very unsuccessful in persuading other member states to take in a proportion of the refugees that it admitted. While it succeeded in securing the adoption of the relocation scheme that was designed to ease the burden on Greece and Italy as well as, indirectly, on the main destination countries, such as Sweden and Germany itself, it could not, however, compel recalcitrant member states to implement it. It did enjoy greater success as the protagonist of the EU–Turkey accord. But numerous other member states did not regard the refugee-reception provisions of this agreement (see the preceding section) as very burdensome and, in any case, the accord ran parallel with the closure of the Balkans route to refugees – a project that had been sponsored by its erstwhile crisis ally, Austria.

As much as Germany tried to supply leadership in the Refugee Crisis, it thus did not secure very much 'followership' elsewhere in the EU. The Franco-German relationship, the 'motor' that had powered the initial adoption of the Schengen accord in the second half of the 1980s, still existed as a façade in the Refugee Crisis, but it did not amount to much more than that. French president Hollande and his government offered flanking moral and political, but much less substantive, support to Berlin, which in turn accepted the domestic political constraints under which Hollande was operating and refrained from criticizing the low profile the French government kept in the crisis. Franco-German bilateralism gave way to a practice of pragmatic or promiscuous mini- or bilateralism whereby it sought partners among those member states most strongly affected by the crisis and from which it expected or hoped for tangible assistance in dealing with it. Hence, on the issue of the distribution of refugees, it sought to build a coalition of those member states willing to accept a proportion of them. In the middle of the crisis, however, precisely its closest initial partner in this project – Austria – deserted it abruptly in favour of an alternative strategy and coalition. By spring 2016, the only close ally left in the German camp seemed to be the European Commission – which Merkel, however, ignored in her final talks with the Turkish prime minister over the EU–Turkey accord. By this time, Germany truly had become Europe's '*lonely* liberal hegemon' – only more lonely than hegemonic (Benner 2016; emphasis my own).

Germany's bargaining power in the Refugee Crisis was a great deal weaker than in the Eurozone Crisis. Far fewer other member states shared its stance on admitting and relocating refugees and managing their inflow than was the case in the Eurozone Crisis, especially in the conflicts over the Greek bail-outs. Its opponents in the management of the Refugee Crisis were not as vulnerable to German financial or other sanctions – at least not in the short term – as had been the Eurozone members that faced an imminent risk of financial and economic collapse. Whether it concerned the (implicit or explicit) threat of the collapse of the Schengen Area, the withdrawal or curtailment of EU structural funds, or condemnation by the ECJ for non-compliance with EU law, the 'instruments of torture' to which Merkel referred in this context proved relatively blunt. In the Refugee Crisis, once it had admitted several hundred thousand refugees, Germany was – unusually – the member state that was seeking help. Merkel's counterparts were loath to provide this aid, as most of them calculated that they would have to pay a (greater or smaller) political cost for this step. They may have felt all the less inclined to rally to Merkel as she had taken the decision to (keep) open Germany's borders for refugees without having informed or consulted them and, in some cases at least, because they believed she had encouraged them to flee to Europe (*Le Monde* 2016c).

The domestic political, economic and financial context in Germany in mid-2015 was different from – and much more benevolent than – that in most other EU member states. This certainly facilitated Merkel's refugee-political *Sonderweg*. Whereas in other countries the notion of rapidly admitting large numbers of Middle Eastern and other non-European refugees was politically highly contested, there was in Germany, with the *Willkommenskultur*, a broad consensus in favour of a liberal refugee policy. It did not take long, however, for this mood, fuelled by public anger over events such as those at Cologne, to wane and reverse. Merkel's authority was increasingly contested within her own party (e.g., Spahn 2016). Aware of the domestic political risks of her stance, Merkel had begun to change tack in some aspects of refugee policy fairly early in the crisis, as the government tried inter alia to expedite the return of illegally overstaying migrants to their home countries, to cut cash benefits paid to asylum seekers and to reduce the number of countries in relation to which political asylum could be claimed in Germany. But she resisted pressure from the CSU to set an upper ceiling on the number of refugees that Germany would accept. The political salience of this issue may have diminished as the influx of refugees started to wane in spring 2016, but public attitudes towards Merkel's management of the Refugee Crisis remained very critical. More than any other single issue this accounts for the meteoric rise of the AfD in German state elections in 2016 and 2017, for its entry into the German Parliament as the third-biggest party, with 12.6 per cent of the popular vote, in 2017 and for the simultaneous slump in support for Merkel's CDU at the federal elections from 41.5 to 33 per cent. The Refugee Crisis preoccupied more than twice as many voters as any other issue in the 2017 elections (*Berliner Morgenpost* 2017). Contrary to numerous prognoses made at the height of the crisis, Merkel's policy did not cost her her job as chancellor, but it severely weakened her authority and it created a big political vacuum to the right of the CDU/CSU that enabled a national-populist political party to win parliamentary representation in Germany for the first time in over 60 years. The CSU's worries about the emergence of a credible competitor to its right were certainly a major motive for its insisting that Germany turn away refugees already registered in other Schengen member states at its borders. Its stance on this issue precipitated a fierce clash with Merkel over refugee policy that brought the new Grand Coalition government to the brink of collapse in June 2018, only a few months after it had been formed. Merkel opposed the demand because, if implemented, it would, she argued, lead to a 'cascade of border closures throughout the EU' that would destroy Schengen (*Financial Times* 2018d). This conflict was settled only by the negotiation of a fragile compromise in the EU whose prospective effectiveness and viability was widely questioned and that hence failed to allay new fears as to Schengen's future.

Merkel's policy in this crisis appeared to have been shaped by a mixture of factors, including by her experience growing up 'staring at' the wall between the two German states before 1989 (as quoted in Drozdiak 2017: 2–3). In part it was also informed by her conception of a wider European interest, specifically her concern that if Germany would close its borders to the refugees, the ensuing 'domino effect' could destabilize fragile states in the Balkans as well as Greece. It is plausible that, among the EU's leaders at the time, only Merkel was thinking 'beyond the constraints of national politics' (*The Economist* 2016a: 20). Above all, however, she was concerned, however, to 'avoid nasty images' of German police using force to protect the country's borders against refugees (see sources above and interview, Berlin, 2018). Arguably, this fear was stronger among Germany's political elite than in any other state involved in the crisis, given Germany's legacy of the Third Reich.

Having decided at the outset, bilaterally with Austria, to open Germany's borders to the refugees and then, after having initially thought otherwise, to keep them open, Merkel largely failed in her efforts to persuade other member states also to take them in. Along with a few much smaller members, notably Sweden and Austria, Germany consequently bore a disproportionately large share of the burden of managing the Refugee Crisis. By default, Germany became the European 'protection giver of last resort' (Benner 2016). Many were the voices in the first two months of 2016 warning that if the influx of refugees should not be brought under control rapidly ('within two months'), the Schengen Area would collapse (Tusk, quoted in: *Financial Times* 2016d; Dutch prime minister Mark Rutte, quoted in *Politico* 2016). That it did not may be partly attributable to the EU–Turkey accord, of which Merkel was the main architect. But it may have had more to do with the Austrian-sponsored closure of the Balkans route that intervened slightly earlier and conceivably dissuaded many refugees from trying to cross from Turkey to Greece, which they would not then have been able to leave (interview, Berlin, 2018). In this latter case, both Merkel's chancellorship and the Schengen Area may have been rescued by a competing government and strategy.

Whether in the longer term a strategy aimed more at sealing off the EU from refugees than managing their entry could succeed is, however, another question. A German government report in 2017 observed that 'up to 6.6 million people are clustered around the Mediterranean preparing to cross to Europe from Africa' (Michta 2017). The Balkans route having been closed, more refugees were converging once again on Libya with a view to crossing the Central Mediterranean Sea to Italy. Some estimates 'put the number of migrants preparing to enter Europe as high as 8–10 million' (Michta 2017). New, future refugee or migration crises would likely test the robustness of the Schengen Area and borderless travel between its members as or even more severely than that of 2015–16. The crisis that temporarily split the German Grand Coalition and the EU in summer 2018 occurred despite a very big fall in the number of refugees seeking political asylum in the EU in the two previous years. If this number should rise again in the future, the political fallout in the EU may prove to be much more difficult to contain than on this occasion.

Chapter 6

The Brexit Crisis

Introduction

With the outcome of the referendum staged on 23 June 2016 – which produced a 52 per cent majority in favour of the UK's withdrawal from the EU – the fourth crisis confronting the EU reached its provisional climax. The referendum result did not automatically and inevitably terminate the UK's EU membership. However, it set in motion a train of events that would likely lead to this outcome. The prime minister who called the referendum, David Cameron, resigned the following day and was replaced by Theresa May, who, with the phrase 'Brexit means Brexit', committed to withdrawing the UK from the EU. In March 2017, the new prime minister activated Article 50 of the EU treaty, notifying the EU of the government's intention to leave the organization within the next two years and initiating negotiations over the terms of the UK's withdrawal. Scenarios under which the UK ended up remaining in the EU were still conceivable, as some observers speculated (e.g., Moravcsik 2016). Uncertainty as to how to whether, when and, more so, under what conditions the UK would leave the EU was compounded by the result of the June 2017 parliamentary elections, in which the Conservative Party lost its majority and after which the survival of the May government became dependent on the support of the Democratic Unionist Party from Northern Ireland. The range of conceivable fundamental outcomes ranged from '*no Brexit*' to a '*soft Brexit*', in which, in exchange for unhindered access to the EU single market, the UK would likely have to comply with most existing EU rules, contribute to the EU budget and accept the jurisprudence of the ECJ, to a '*hard Brexit*', in which the UK would not be bound by existing EU rules, but would trade with EU member states on the same basis as other states without bilateral trade accords with the EU, and even a '*chaotic Brexit*', in which, after the failure of EU–UK negotiations, the UK would leave the EU without any accord over the terms of their future relationship having been reached. While the May government seemed to be tending towards a rather 'soft Brexit' that would limit the economic disruption that Brexit would provoke, it remained uncertain in summer 2018 whether an accord on the terms of British withdrawal could be found that would be acceptable both to her parliamentary majority and to the remaining 27 EU member states. This uncertainty was exacerbated by the possibility of cross-party coalitions forming on the issue in the British Parliament, the government collapsing and new elections being held. A 'chaotic' Brexit that would involve 'chaos at all Britain's borders' and trucks and flights being grounded was not the least probable of all conceivable scenarios (*Financial Times* 2018c). It was also plausible that, to avoid such a scenario, the UK and the EU would decide at the last minute to postpone the current withdrawal date of 29 March 2019.

No member state had previously chosen to leave the EU. Depending on its broader consequences, the UK's withdrawal from the EU could prove a major turning point in the history of European integration. The goal of this chapter is to explore and explain how the UK came to vote for Brexit. It discusses why the UK initially opted not to join the EU and why it subsequently changed its stance, leading to its accession in 1973. It then explores how and why the UK remained an ambivalent and 'awkward' participant in European integration and, following the end of the Cold War, increasingly became a 'semi-detached' EU member. It focuses subsequently on the accelerating growth and mobilization of Eurosceptic attitudes in the UK manifested by the rapid growth in support for the United Kingdom Independence Party (UKIP) and growing support for Brexit also in the Conservative Party. It argues that trends in British EU policy and notably the decision taken by Prime Minister Cameron to stage the 2016 referendum were driven overwhelmingly by exigencies of domestic politics. Having decided, in response to these pressures, to stage a referendum, Cameron's strategy for winning it relied heavily on his capacity to renegotiate the terms of British membership in a way that would accommodate the main Eurosceptic grievances against the EU and, to achieve this end, on flanking support above all from the most powerful member state, Germany. Germany, however, was unwilling to concede all his demands and it is questionable whether, even if it had been, it would have been able to deliver the support or acquiescence of other member states in these concessions, which would have required changes in the EU treaties. Finally the chapter assesses the likelihood of whether Brexit would trigger a 'contagion' effect propelling other members also to leave the EU – whether, that is, it would provoke a broader process of *horizontal* political *dis*integration.

A history of relentless 'widening'

Brexit halted – and threatened to reverse – a process whereby, during the preceding 60 years, the EU had relentlessly 'widened' to take in more and more member states. At the outset, the ECSC and the EEC had been launched by the same six 'pioneer' members: France, Germany, Italy and the three Benelux states. In the first enlargement, in 1973, the UK joined along with Ireland and Denmark. In the 1980s, the EU expanded to the south and south-east, taking in the three post-right-wing authoritarian states, Greece (1981) and Spain and Portugal (1986). Following the end of the Cold War, its membership more than doubled: from 12 at the time of the adoption of the Maastricht Treaty in 1992 to 28. The first post-Cold War wave of enlargement in 1995 took in three states – Austria, Finland and Sweden – that had been officially neutral during the Cold War. In three subsequent waves, some

11 post-Communist states acceded to the EU, along with the small Mediter-ranean island states of Cyprus and Malta. From 15 in 1995 the number of EU member states grew to 25 in 2004, 27 in 2007 and 28, with the accession of Croatia, in 2013.

The enlargement of the EU – the growing *horizontal* political integration of Europe – was fuelled by several, often mutually reinforcing, factors whose significance varied by the acceding state. The first is that the creation and existence of the EU (as a customs union) caused a 'relative loss of market access' for non-member countries – a loss that was all the greater the more closely the EU's members integrated and reduced mutual obstacles to economic exchange (Mattli 1999: 59–60). The second, conceivably related factor – in the period preceding membership application – is inferior economic performance compared with that of EU member states. Through their impact on the calculations and choices of the governments of the day, both these factors played a role in the accession bids of the UK in the 1960s (see the following section, The UK: from 'splendid isolation' to accession, up to 1973) and Sweden, Finland and Austria in the 1990s (Mattli 1999: 80–94). The choice of the latter three states to join the EU was also greatly facilitated, however, by the end of the Cold War, as a result of which they were no longer constrained in their alliance choices by the need to take account of their proximity to the Communist bloc. The collapse of the latter was, of course, the sine qua non of the EU accession for all but two of the states that joined the EU in this century. For these post-Communist states, EU accession was a fundamental choice about their politico-economic orientation that was motivated not only by economic considerations – the prospects of better conditions of market access and (given their relative poverty) financial aid from the EU's regional budget – but also by security-political considerations and the goal of democratic consolidation. The stabilization of young democratic political systems – alongside improved market access and the prospect of financial aid – also belonged to the motives for the EU accession of the post-right-wing-authoritarian states Greece, Portugal and Spain in the 1980s (see Mattli 1999: 94–95).

Among the long-standing democratic West European states, only Iceland and, through popular referenda, Switzerland and Norway resisted the 'pull' of EU membership. The Swiss approved a free trade accord with the EU by referendum in 1972, but they voted narrowly (50.3 per cent) against joining the European Economic Area (EEA) in 1992 and massively (77 per cent) against opening negotiations over accession to the EU in 2001. Nor-wegians twice voted narrowly against joining the EU – by 53.5 per cent at the time Denmark joined in the early 1970s and by 52 per cent when Sweden and Finland joined in the mid-1990s. Iceland applied to join the EU during a deep financial crisis in 2009, but, having recovered from this while the Eurozone plunged into crisis, it suspended its application in 2013 and withdrew it altogether in 2015. As all three countries had free trade agree-ments with the EU, whether bilaterally (Switzerland) or through the EEA (Norway and Iceland), market access considerations did not push them towards accession.

True, two overseas territories of member states had left the EU. Having previously been a French *département*, Algeria seceded from the EU by breaking away from France in 1962. Antagonized above all by the common fisheries policy, Greenland opted to leave the EU in a referendum in 1982, but as an autonomous territory of Denmark, exploiting the enhanced autonomy previously granted it by the Danish government. Nonetheless, before Brexit, no *state* had left the EU *after* having joined it. For 60 years, Europe had experienced a process of steady horizontal political integration that stalled from time to time either because an existing member state rejected an application (France with the UK in the 1960s) or, as with Norway and Switzerland, a candidate country rejected accession in a popular referendum. The withdrawal of a member state would thus be entirely unprecedented.

The potential implications of Brexit were all the more significant as the UK was far from being 'any' EU member state (see, e.g., Oliver 2016b). It was the third-most populous of the 28 members, accounting in 2016 for around 13 per cent of its population. It was, with a share of 16 per cent in the EU's collective GDP in 2016, the second-biggest economy. Accounting for 27 per cent of all military spending of EU members in 2015, it was, by this definition, the biggest EU military power. With France, the only other EU member state with a comparable military power projection capacity, it was one of only two EU members with a permanent seat on the UN Security Council and nuclear weapons. The implications of Brexit were doubtless bigger for the UK itself than for the then 27 remaining member states. But Brexit also threatened to diminish the EU's (arguably already declining) international weight and influence (Oliver 2016b; Webber 2016).

The UK: from 'splendid isolation' to accession, up to 1973

Although the label 'splendid isolation' is arguably a misnomer for a state that played a leading role in several major European wars, it is nevertheless true that, for centuries up until the middle of the last century, the UK steered clear of permanent engagement on the European continent, preferring to intervene militarily only when continental Europe threatened to fall under the domination of a single hostile power (Lieber 1999: 14; McGowan and Phinnemore 2017: 80). The UK could afford the luxury of 'not interfering except in great emergencies' (early nineteenth-century foreign minister Lord Castlereagh) thanks to geography, the fact that it is separated from the continent by the English Channel, which, despite being no more than 33 km wide at its narrowest point, has helped it to avoid any foreign invasion and occupation since 1066. In this respect, among the major European states, British history is exceptional.

By freeing it from the need to maintain a large standing army and enabling it to develop a correspondingly larger navy, the UK's island status also facilitated its development as a colonial power whose empire, in the early twentieth-century, had reached dimensions far exceeding those of any contemporary competitor. Around 1900, the UK ruled 50 colonies with a total population of 345 million, accounting for a quarter of both the world's population and land area (Lieber 1999: 33). In the wake of World War II, a rapid process of decolonization began to unfold, starting with India, the 'jewel' of the former empire, but the UK still hoped that the British Commonwealth as the successor organization comprising most of its former colonies would constitute a source of leverage in international affairs that no other West European power possessed.

Alongside its island status and its leadership of the Commonwealth, the UK also regarded its prospects for exercising international influence, compared with continental West European states, as strengthened by its close ties to the USA, which had intervened on its side in the two world wars and, in the Cold War, assumed the role of the leader of the non-Communist world and principal manager of the international capitalist economy.

In the early post-World War II period, the British political elite thus saw the UK as a member of three circles, 'the Commonwealth, the Anglo-American special relationship, and a relationship with Europe'. The latter was 'much the least important of the three ... For a great victorious power to abandon its world role, its leadership of the Commonwealth, and its favoured position with the United States in order to throw in its lot with a bombed out, defeated rabble south of the Channel seemed to the British unthinkable' (Denman 1997: 184–185).

The wartime prime minister Winston Churchill's thinking about the UK's relationship with continental Europe was illustrative of the dominant British perspective on the issue. Long before World War II, he had characterized the UK as being '*with*, but not *of* Europe' (as quoted in Young 1998: 13). In a confrontation with the then French resistance leader de Gaulle during the war, he emphasized that every time the UK had to choose between 'Europe and the open sea, it is always the open sea that we shall choose'. Although a driving force in the creation of the Council of Europe in 1948, he wanted this organization to be based on intergovernmental cooperation rather than being supranational. And, while he spoke out for the creation of a 'United States of Europe' based on Franco-German reconciliation in a famous speech in Zurich in 1946, he did not envisage British participation in such a project.

The two main British political parties were united in their opposition to the UK's participation in European political integration in the early post-World War II period. The Labour Party, which governed the UK from 1945 to 1951, was in case of doubt more hostile to the Schuman Plan to create the ECSC than the Conservatives. It feared the ECSC would hamper its efforts to develop the welfare state and manage the British economy. But prospective domestic opposition to the plan also shaped the government's rejection of the plan. The acting prime minister in early June 1950, Herbert Morrison, proclaimed that 'the Durham miners won't wear it' (as quoted in Denman 1997: 188). And Labour made clear that it attached higher priority to the UK's ties to the Commonwealth than to those to continental Europe, declaring that 'in every respect except distance we in Britain are closer to our kinsmen in Australia and New Zealand than we are to Europe' (as quoted in Denman 1997: 188).

Invited to take part in the negotiations that led in 1957 to the Treaty of Rome and the creation of the EEC, the British government, now Conservative, sent a high-level civil servant from the Board of Trade to represent the UK. He left the negotiations in Messina in November 1955 after having reputedly told the representatives of the other six states present that the treaty under discussion 'has no chance of being agreed; if it was agreed, it would have no chance of being ratified; if it was ratified, it would have no chance of being applied; and if it was applied it would be totally unacceptable to Britain' (as quoted in Denman 1997: 198–199). Even the Suez crisis in 1956 did not suffice to alter the government's stance on European integration. While American opposition to Anglo-French military intervention in Egypt strengthened France's commitment to closer European cooperation, it encouraged the UK, in contrast, to 'remake the Washington relationship' (Young 1998: 110). For a second time in the 1950s, the UK thus missed the European boat.

The then British prime minister Harold Macmillan was acutely aware of the prospective negative consequences for the UK once the EEC was formed: 'For the first time since the Napoleonic era ... the major continental powers are united in a positive economic grouping, with considerable political aspects, which ... may have the effect of excluding us both from European markets and from consultation in European policy' (as quoted in Young 1998: 118). Already in the 1950s the continental European economies had grown much faster than the British (Young 1998: 106). The UK reacted by championing the creation of the European Free Trade Area (EFTA) comprising six other, economically much smaller members (Sweden, Norway, Denmark, Switzerland, Austria and Portugal), but EFTA could not be a viable alternative to the EEC, outside of which the UK, in the analysis of a British diplomat at the time, faced 'disaster' (Young 1998: 119).

The British government thus subsequently applied to join the EEC in July 1961. Five of the six EEC members, Germany included, strongly supported British accession. However, French president de Gaulle vetoed the application in January 1963, provoking a deep split with the other members. De Gaulle's decision appears to have had several motives. First, he wanted to consolidate and strengthen the EEC's newly launched Common Agricultural Policy, which was vitally important to France, but which the UK would likely oppose once a member. Second, given the close Anglo-American relationship, he feared the EEC would develop into a political satellite of the USA, undermining his goal of building a 'European Europe'. Third and relatedly, he feared that, given the size of the Commonwealth and the UK's ties with it, British accession would be tantamount to the EEC joining the Commonwealth rather than vice versa (Peyrefitte 1994: 302–304, 333–335). Further, he suspected the UK of wanting to enter the EEC to 'paralyse it from within' (de Gaulle 2000: 1045). Finally he also feared, according to German and British sources at least, that once in the EEC, the UK could contest France's at the time undisputed status as the organization's most powerful member (Brandt 1993: 255; Heath 1998: 228).

De Gaulle's veto unleashed a storm of indignation in Germany as well as in the four other member states and split the German political elite into rival camps of 'Gaullists' and 'Atlanticists'. German Economics Minister Erhard speculated that this step might destroy the young EEC. He was particularly angry that, in vetoing UK accession, France had not honoured the numerous concessions that the German government had made to it in negotiations over the Common Agricultural Policy and financial aid for members' (especially France's) overseas territories (Heath 1998: 233). Jean Monnet and the (German) president of the European Commission Walter Hallstein implored the German chancellor Konrad Adenauer not to approve the draft Élysée Treaty on Franco-German cooperation unless de Gaulle accepted UK accession (Maillard 1995: 221). Although annoyed by de Gaulle's tactics, especially his timing, Adenauer, however, resisted this demand (Maillard 1995: 221–222). More a 'Gaullist' than an 'Atlanticist', the Chancellor was reputedly 'not too troubled' by de Gaulle's veto (Brandt 1993: 255; Kipping 2004: 153). The German Parliament ratified the treaty nonetheless, although not without inserting a preamble into it that, in de Gaulle's (as it turned out, mistaken) view, rendered the treaty largely worthless. In the end, Germany was not prepared to jeopardize its relationship with France or the existence of the EEC for the sake of the UK's accession.

A second British accession bid, launched by a Labour government in 1966, met the same fate as the first. At this point, all the members' foreign ministers, bar the French, were 'bursting with impatience' to get the UK into the EEC (Brandt 1993: 452). This time, though, de Gaulle vetoed UK accession even before any negotiations had begun. From talks with the four other governments, the new British prime minister Harold Wilson and his foreign minister George Brown allegedly formed the 'mistaken impression' that the German government would just need to lay down the line to de Gaulle to overcome his opposition, with Brown telling the then German foreign minister Brandt: 'Willy, you must get us in, so we can take the lead' (Brandt 1993: 453). This arguably amounted to a similar misreading of German interests and power in the EU to that made by the Cameron government before the 2016 referendum (see the section 'The renegotiation of the UK's EU membership terms' below). The five other member states acquiesced in France's insistence that negotiations with the UK could be launched only with the agreement of all six members, with Brandt intervening to head off any confrontation between France and the other four members (Peyrefitte 2000: 274).

De Gaulle's vetoes served – temporarily – to calm the British debate over accession to the EEC. However, the reactions provoked already by the first entry bid hinted at how explosive the issue of the UK's relations with the EU would later become in British domestic politics. In 1962, for example, the Labour Party leader Hugh Gaitskell opposed accession because it would mean 'the end of a thousand years of history', that is, of an independent British state. The cleavages over this issue were to run not only (or even primarily) between government and opposition, but also between rival currents and factions within the main political parties. Unlike in most other EU member states, in the UK there was never a 'permissive consensus' in favour of European political integration. Moreover, the rationale advanced for accession was overwhelmingly economic – that membership would be good for the British economy and therefore for Britons' living standards. In contrast, other than on the continent, the *political* case for European integration – that it promoted political stability and peace – was rarely made, leaving its EU membership vulnerable to a political backlash if its economic benefits failed to materialize (see Clegg 2016b: 191–196; Curtice 2017: 23–24; Korski 2016).

A quarrelsome partner, 1973–90

The external obstacles to UK accession were cleared fairly rapidly after de Gaulle resigned as French president in 1969. His successor, Georges Pompidou, was not persuaded by the other member states to open the door to the UK (Brandt 1993: 453). According to the British ambassador in Paris at the time, the French government did not expect 'any strong pressure from their partners' to admit the UK to the EEC: 'They believe that in the last resort the Germans will acquiesce in what they decide' (Christopher Soames, as quoted in Heath 1998: 364). Pompidou's change of stance from that of de Gaulle was motivated rather by a reappraisal of French interests. In the last few years of the 1960s, Germany's growing economic power had become increasingly manifest (see Chapter 2). Having the UK in the EEC could help France to balance German power. Brandt, German chancellor from 1969 to 1974, used this fear to underline the case for the UK's accession, arguing at the heads of government summit in The Hague in 1969 explicitly that 'he who fears that the economic weight of Germany could have a negative impact on the balance of power in the EU should be for the enlargement' (Brandt 1993: 453; see also Simonian 1985: 80). Brandt eased Pompidou's concerns about the possible negative effects of British accession on France by assuring him that Germany would ensure that the EEC remained adequately financed and that it would not undermine the Common Agricultural Policy (Brandt 1993: 454).

Just as fast as the external barriers to accession diminished, the conflicts and divisions apparent in the early British debates about EU membership, however, resurfaced. The process of parliamentary ratification of accession was bitterly contested. Given the opposition of a minority of its own MPs, the Conservative government that had been in office since 1970 could secure a majority for accession only with the support of 'pro-European' Labour MPs who rebelled against the party line opposing accession on the negotiated terms. Labour returned to government in 1974, pledging to renegotiate these terms and put any new agreement to a popular referendum – a position that constituted a point of equilibrium between the 'pro-' and 'anti-European' currents in the party. For the party leader, Prime Minister Harold Wilson, who had originally opposed demands from the party's left for a referendum (Young 1998: 275), this process was less a response to the pressure of public opinion than a device to maintain Labour Party unity. As he told the German chancellor Schmidt: 'We can't let the unity of the party be destroyed over the question of the Common Market' (Geddes 2013: 64; Schmidt 1990: 96).

The main renegotiation issues were the UK's contribution to the EEC budget and access to the UK market for butter from New Zealand, for which Wilson allegedly had a 'special soft spot' (Young 1998: 280). But, unlike Cameron initially 40 years later, Wilson did not insist on any changes being made to the EEC treaties (Schmidt 1990: 96). Keen to keep the UK in the EEC, the other member states, led by Schmidt and the French president Giscard d'Estaing, made some concessions that Wilson could accept and that for Germany were 'certainly not cheap' (Schmidt 1990: 97). Elsewhere in the EU, Schmidt in fact was the most engaged campaigner in favour to keeping the UK as a member (Mourlon-Druol 2015: 8). His speech to the Labour Party conference in November 1974, in which he implored the UK to stay, was received with a standing ovation by the predominantly 'anti-European' delegates (Schmidt 1990: 95–96; Young 1998: 282). His subsequent meeting with Wilson allegedly had a 'galvanizing effect' on the British leader, hardening his commitment to campaign in favour of continued British membership (Young 1998: 97).

Staged in June 1975, the first UK referendum on EEC membership produced a two-thirds majority in favour of staying in. On the 'remain' side, there was the overwhelming majority of the Conservative Party, whose conference had initially voted eight to one in favour of accession in 1971. The British business community supported membership almost uniformly, as did the major national newspapers. The labour movement, in contrast, was deeply divided. In April 1975, a special Labour Party conference actually rejected the new membership terms by almost two to one. Two-thirds of the members of the Cabinet wanted to stay in, but less than a half of Labour MPs. Among the 46 trade unions represented at the Labour conference, only seven supported membership. The Labour left was overwhelmingly hostile to membership; the Labour right strongly in favour.

The 'remain' camp was able to throw far greater financial resources into its campaign than the 'leave camp', which had to make do with a budget of about a tenth of that of its opponents (Geddes 2013: 64–65). In addition, the 'leave' camp was disadvantaged by the fact that its leading protagonists, especially Tony Benn from the left wing of the Labour Party and Enoch Powell originally from the right wing of the Conservatives, did not enjoy comparable levels of public credibility to those of the leading campaigners for continued UK membership. Although in the two years prior to the referendum, the British public had been evenly split between EU supporters and opponents, opinion shifted strongly in favour of continued membership in the six months preceding the referendum (European Commission 1975). The principal argument made by the 'remain' camp was that continued membership would be good for employment and economic growth. The recent relative economic performance of the UK and the EU, it argued, spoke in favour of staying in. The original six members, the camp's campaign leaflet stated, 'have done well – much better than we have – over the past 15 years' (as quoted in Miller 2015: 22). This was not an argument that could plausibly be made in favour of remaining in the EU in 2016.

The unity of the Labour Party that Wilson had been so keen to preserve did not long survive the party's defeat at the 1979 elections. As, in opposition, the party decided that it would withdraw the UK from the EU once re-elected to office, a large component of its 'pro-European' faction broke away to form the new Social Democratic Party. However, even the governments of the initially much more monolithically 'pro-European' Conservative Party that held office for the following 18 years proved to be a troublesome partner for the other member states. An ongoing conflict over the British budgetary contribution, which the new prime minister Margaret Thatcher wanted to reduce further than was foreseen in the renegotiated terms of British membership, soured the UK's relations with the rest of the EU until it was finally resolved at the EU summit in Fontainebleau in 1984 (Attali 1993 658–61; Thatcher 1993: 541–545). The Thatcher government did then proceed, however, to play a central role in the negotiation and adoption of the Single European Act, which aimed primarily at abolishing remaining non-tariff barriers to trade between member states and bore a British imprint at least as much as that of any other member state (Moravcsik 1991; Young 1998: 334).

In the second half of the 1980s, the British public warmed to the EU in a way that it had not done previously – or would do again in the future (see Figure 6.1). The UK appeared briefly to have become a 'satisfied member state' (Evans and Menon 2017: 4). No sooner had the Single European Act been adopted, however, than new conflicts began to break out between Thatcher and the rest of the EU and between Thatcher and major figures in her own cabinet. There were three significant contentious issues. The first involved a conflict between market-oriented (or 'neo-liberal') and Social (Democratic and Catholic) conceptions of Europe. Here the main protagonists were Thatcher and the European Commission president and (moderate) French Socialist, Jacques Delors. Delors had won over the British trade unions with a speech on the 'social dimension' of European integration at the 1988 Trade Union Congress (TUC) conference (Delors 1992: 66–70). Although the speech did little more than to repeat the standard Social (and Christian) Democratic position on the issue, it riled Thatcher, as did his earlier forecast, made in a speech to the EP, that within a decade 80 per cent of economic and perhaps social and fiscal legislation in the EU might emanate from Brussels. In a speech at Bruges shortly afterwards, she launched a frontal assault on Delors' agenda, culminating in the affirmation that 'we have not successfully rolled back the frontiers of the state in Britain only to see them re-imposed at a European level, with a European super-state exercising a new dominance from Brussels' (Thatcher 1993: 744–745). For British Conservatives and British business, the EU had changed from being a prospective ally to being an opponent in their mission to reduce trade union power in the UK.

Figure 6.1 *The evolution of British attitudes to EU membership, 1983–2011*

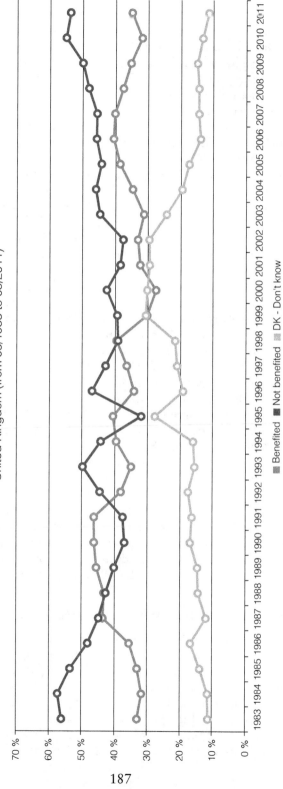

Taking everything into consideration, would you say that (your country) has on balance benefited or not from being a member of the European Union? United Kingdom (from 03/1983 to 05/2011)

Benefited   Not benefited   DK - Don't know

Source: European Commission, various Eurobarometer surveys.

The second issue was that of monetary-political integration, a project which had been conceived by France, in which Germany was to acquiesce, but which Thatcher opposed although she had been persuaded to accept it in the Single European Act as an EU 'goal' (see Chapter 3). This issue pitted Thatcher not only against the other EU member states, but also against key members of her own cabinet. Indeed, in provoking the resignation of one of them, her strong opposition to the introduction of a single European currency precipitated her overthrow as Conservative Party leader and prime minister in autumn 1990.

The third issue was German reunification, the prospect of which, when it emerged with the fall of the Berlin Wall in 1989, ignited Thatcher's 'instinctive anti-Germanism' (her foreign policy adviser Charles Powell, as quoted in Young 1998: 358). Thatcher tried unsuccessfully to stop this process. Whereas France and the other member states reacted to the prospect and reality of German reunification by trying to bind the new and larger Germany more tightly into a politically more closely integrated Europe, Thatcher was inclined to pursue the opposite course: 'In fact, Germany was more rather than less likely to dominate' a more integrated or 'federal' Europe, as, reunited, it was 'simply too big and powerful to be just another player' in such an entity. Rather, she argued, 'only the political and military engagement of the United States in Europe and close relations between the other two strongest sovereign states in Europe – Britain and France – are sufficient to balance German power' (Thatcher 1993: 791).

Isolated in the EU and on EU policy increasingly within her own government, Thatcher survived the achievement of German reunification politically by less than two months. In the short term, the destructive impact of the EU-related conflicts that had arisen during the last years of her prime ministership was felt more in British domestic politics and, specifically, the Conservative Party than in the EU. Her successor, John Major, promptly declared his resolve to put the UK back 'at the very heart of Europe' (Young 1998: 424). In retrospect, however, she played a key role in this period planting the seeds of Euroscepticism that would grow during the next 25 years to the point where this movement not only overwhelmed and destroyed the prime ministerships of her two Conservative successors, Major and Cameron, but also brought the UK to the brink of Brexit (Fontana and Parsons 2015).

An increasingly 'semi-detached' member, 1991–2010

Major's efforts to return the UK to the 'heart of Europe' proved to be conspicuously unsuccessful. Rather, during his premiership, the UK became an increasingly 'semi-detached' member of the EU. Already in the middle of the 1980s, the UK had declined to abolish border controls with other member states. The 'Schengen Area' (see Chapter 5) was launched outside the EU by France, Germany and the Benelux states (see Thatcher 1993: 553–554). At the Maastricht summit in 1991, under intense pressure from Eurosceptic members of his Cabinet and parliamentary party, Major negotiated an opt-out from the single currency for the UK and refused to accept the incorporation of new provisions on workers' rights in the treaty at all, forcing the other members to adopt this as a protocol outside the treaty and excluding the UK. However, he refused to rule out British adoption of the single currency indefinitely or to pledge a popular referendum on the issue (Young 1998: 428). As Chancellor of the Exchequer, he had also persuaded Thatcher in 1990 that the UK should join the Exchange Rate Mechanism (ERM) in the EMS (see Chapter 3). But this step towards a rapprochement with the 'heart of Europe' was to be undone within a few months of his 1992 election victory, when massive speculation against the pound forced the government to withdraw from the ERM. The humiliating circumstances of this decision – in effect, the German Bundesbank, by refusing to support it on foreign exchange markets, ejected the pound from the system – gave additional ammunition to the growing ranks of Conservative Eurosceptics (see also Evans and Menon 2017: 5). The government's popularity plummeted, never to recover before it suffered a landslide defeat in the 1997 elections.

In the intervening period, possessing only a slim parliamentary majority, Major was mercilessly harassed by Eurosceptic cabinet members and MPs, particularly during the parliamentary ratification of the Maastricht Treaty, which came close to failing. Under the Eurosceptics' pressure, Major adopted stances on a series of EU issues – from the size of a blocking minority in the Council after the 1995 enlargement to the choice of Delors' successor as Commission president – that isolated the UK from the other member states (Denman 1997: 272–274; Young 1998: 452–463). His European policy finally descended into farce when, in response to an EU-imposed ban on exports of British beef to other member states during the 'Mad Cow Disease' crisis, the government launched an ineffectual policy of 'non-cooperation' with the EU (Denman 1997: 274–275; Young 1998: 460–462). By the time of Major's 1997 election defeat, the UK was further away from the 'heart of Europe' than at any time since its accession.

Backed by a large parliamentary majority, Major's Labour successor, Tony Blair, came to office as ostensibly the UK's most 'pro-European' prime minister since Edward Heath, the architect of its accession to the EU. In the almost two decades that Labour had been in opposition, Euroscepticism had changed political camps in the UK. As the Conservatives had become increasingly Eurosceptic in office, the experiences of 'Thatcherism' at home and 'Delorism' in Brussels combined with electoral-political considerations had converted Labour into an increasingly and predominantly 'pro-European' party. One of the new government's first acts was to sign up to the Maastricht Social Protocol (see earlier in this section 'An increasingly semi-detached member 1991–2010'). The 13 years that Labour subsequently governed the UK were to witness the accession of 12 new, mainly post-Communist, member states and, partly to 'streamline' the EU's decision-making processes to accommodate this process, the adoption of three new EU treaties (Amsterdam, Nice and Lisbon). With France, through the St Malo Declaration, the UK was the joint instigator of a common

European security and defence policy, designed, after the wars in the former Yugoslavia, to boost the capacity of the EU to undertake collective military intervention autonomous of the USA.

Unlike his two Conservative predecessors, Blair was able to conduct a European policy by and large unencumbered by intra-party opposition to closer European integration. The exception to this rule was the issue of whether the UK should adopt the Euro. Here he was constrained by his inner-party rival, the Chancellor of the Exchequer, Gordon Brown, whose attitude to the Euro was more negative than Blair's, and by the British newspapers, especially the ones owned by Rupert Murdoch, which had grown increasingly hostile to the single currency and European integration more generally. Having pledged in the 1997 campaign (following Major) not to take the UK into the Euro without a popular referendum, Blair was not prepared to use the popularity and authority he enjoyed in the early years of his premiership to champion a cause which he thought – perhaps correctly – was lost in advance (MacShane 2015: 90–96). The UK thus remained outside the Eurozone when the single currency was launched in 1999. Then Blair's support for the US-led invasion of Iraq in 2003 set him at loggerheads with both France and Germany and undermined prospects for the development of an autonomous European military intervention capacity that had been foreshadowed at St Malo. Generally, in the assessment of one of his ministers for Europe, he made 'little effort to enthuse people about Europe or try and reverse the steadily increasing Euroscepticism in political and public life' in the UK (MacShane 2015: 103). Blair himself said that although his 'general posture was pro-European', he was careful 'not to go beyond what was reasonable for British opinion' (quoted in Adonis 2017: 7). As one of his advisers judged: 'On Europe he was a follower not a leader' (Adonis 2017: 7). Blair's successor, Brown, 'did even less to put the case for a positive engagement in Europe' (MacShane 2015: 104). Like most other British prime ministers, Brown had 'no particular cultural connection to or intellectual interest in the political history of post-war Europe. He felt much more affinity with the United States than with Continental Europe' (Wood 2017: 8). Again like most other previous prime ministers, he saw most EU issues 'through the lens of domestic politics' (Wood 2017: 7). It was emblematic of the Labour governments' waning pro-European engagement that, when the Lisbon Treaty was signed in 2007, Brown turned up hours after the official ceremony had taken place. When his government was defeated in the 2010 elections, the UK was not significantly closer to the 'heart of Europe' than it had been when Labour had taken office in 1997, fewer Britons thought belonging to the EU was a 'good thing' than when Labour had taken office in 1997 or 'trusted' the EU than had been the case much earlier during its period in government (see Figures 6.1 and 6.2; Curtice 2017: 21).

The road to the Brexit referendum, 2010–15

The Conservative Party returned to office with Cameron as prime minister in 2010, almost simultaneously with the first peak of the Eurozone Crisis. The party, MPs included, was much more thoroughly Eurosceptic than it had

Figure 6.2 *The evolution of British 'trust' in the EU, 2003–18*

I would like to ask you a question about how much trust you have in certain media and institutions. For each of the following
media and institutions, please tell me if you tend to trust it or tend not to trust it.

The European Union
United Kingdom (from 10/2003 to 03/2018)

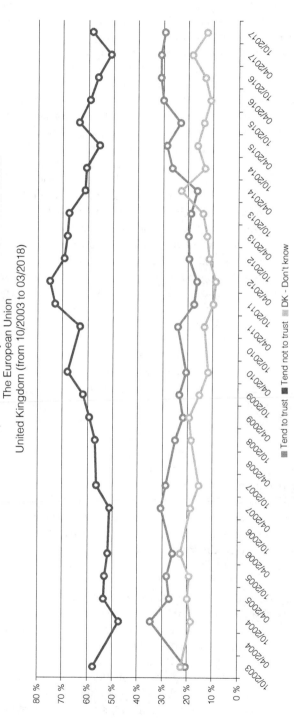

■ Tend to trust ■ Tend not to trust ■ DK - Don't know

Source: European Commission, various Eurobarometer surveys.

been in the 1990s and 'pro-European' voices had been increasingly marginalized (Fontana and Parsons 2015: 99–102). After having become the party's leader in 2005, Cameron had warned the party of the dangers of 'banging on about Europe' while British voters were more concerned about other, domestic issues. However, he had made various concessions to party Eurosceptics while still in opposition. Above all, acting on a pledge he had made when running for the party leadership, he had withdrawn Conservative MEPs from the European parliamentary group of the European People's Party (EPP), of which most other mainstream centre-right parties in the EU, including the German Christian Democrats, were members. In 2007, he also gave a 'cast-iron guarantee' that if elected prime minister he would put the Lisbon Treaty then under negotiation to a popular referendum. Forced to withdraw this pledge once all member states had ratified this treaty in 2009, he replaced it with promises never to take the UK into the Euro and to introduce a 'referendum lock' obliging future governments to stage a referendum on any new European treaty that transferred competences from the member states to the EU (Conservative Party 2010: 113).

Apart from mollifying his Eurosceptic intra-party critics, Cameron had two other motives to adopt a hard-line stance against closer European integration. One was that, in the shadow of the ongoing Eurozone Crisis, public opinion towards the EU in the UK, like in other member states, was growing more negative. The other was that, in the preceding few years, an unequivocally 'anti-European' party, UKIP, had begun to develop traction. Increasingly, electoral-political worries began to complement ideological orientation as galvanizing forces of Conservative opposition to the EU. Although UKIP did not poll well – scarcely any better than in the preceding general elections – in 2010, it had overtaken Labour as the second-biggest party in the 2009 European elections. It looked increasingly capable of mobilizing any discontent among Eurosceptic Conservative supporters with the performance of Cameron's administration on EU issues. Having failed to win a Conservative majority and been forced to form a coalition government with the 'pro-European' Liberal Democrats, Cameron's leeway to accommodate the demands of Eurosceptic Conservatives during his first five-year period in office was, however, limited. His coalition partner did not prevent him from refusing to sign up to the European Fiscal Compact to limit EU government budget deficits in 2011, but Cameron's attempt to veto an accord failed. The other member states – bar one (the Czech Republic) – adopted it nonetheless as an intergovernmental rather than EU treaty, again leaving the UK isolated in its opposition to a major EU project (see Chapter 3).

Squeezed between a 'pro-European' coalition partner and an increasingly strident Eurosceptic parliamentary party and rank-and-file, Cameron reacted with an initiative that at least won him time to try to escape from this entrapment. In his Bloomberg speech in January 2013, he pledged to stage an 'in–out' referendum on the UK's EU membership if the Conservatives won the 2015 elections. Cameron explained his proposal by arguing that the EU that would emerge from the Eurozone Crisis was going to be a 'very different body' to the one that the British had voted to join in 1975. Before staging a referendum, the government would negotiate a 'new settlement' of the UK's membership terms with 'our European partners' (as quoted in *Financial Times* 2013i). Within the government, however, Cameron explained his course of action differently. He had to call a referendum, he explained to the Liberal Democratic leader Clegg: 'It is a party management issue. I am under a lot of pressure on this. I need to recalibrate' (Laws 2016: 241). Warned by Clegg that he was putting the 'international position of the UK for the next few decades' at risk, Cameron responded: 'You may be right. But what else can I do? My backbenchers are unbelievably Euro-sceptic and UKIP are breathing down my neck' (as quoted in Laws 2016: 237). His primary motive seems thus to have been identical to Wilson's in staging the first EU referendum in 1975. Or, as a political analyst expressed it at the time: 'He is held prisoner of fear of a great rupture in his party akin to convulsions about the Corn Laws in the 19th century and imperial trade preferences early in the 20th' (Stephens 2013). Not all his ministers, however, were convinced that the referendum proposal was wise. The Chancellor Exchequer, George Osborne, advised against it, as did a future leading Brexiteer, Michael Gove (Shipman 2016: 10–11). Cameron informed German Chancellor Merkel of his speech in advance. She did not try to dissuade him from his referendum project, but she recommended that he make the case for reforms that would benefit the whole EU rather than just the UK (Shipman 2016: 11–12). In foreign policy circles in Berlin there was widespread incredulity that Cameron would put an issue of such fundamental importance to a popular referendum (interview, Berlin, 2018).

True to the description that they would 'never take "yes" for an answer' (Daniel Finkelstein quoted in D'Ancona 2016), Eurosceptic Conservative MPs pressed Cameron to set out the negotiating stance he would adopt vis-à-vis the other member states in the event of being re-elected and to pledge that if the UK's demands were not met, he would campaign for the UK to leave the EU. Concerned not to reveal his 'bottom line' or fuel an intra-party conflict over his stance, Cameron refused (Parker 2014). At the time of the Bloomberg speech he thought, however, that he would be in a strong bargaining position to obtain concessions on the terms of UK membership from other member states, as there was a widespread belief that, to address the Eurozone Crisis, the EU treaties would need to be changed – something that all members, including the UK, would have to approve (McGowan and Phinnemore 2017: 83; Rogers 2017a and 2017b; Shipman 2016: 12). This analysis was to prove misplaced, as the increasing unpopularity of the EU provoked first by the Eurozone, then the Refugee Crisis persuaded other governments that treaty changes that in some members would have to be ratified by referenda were politically too risky – thus, of course, weakening Cameron's potential bargaining power in any upcoming membership 'renegotiations' (Rogers 2017a, 2017b).

In the short term at least, Cameron's referendum pledge nonetheless secured the acquiescence of his Eurosceptic MPs and restored a semblance of unity to the Conservative Party. But, dangerously for him and his party, it did not slow the UKIP's political momentum. Its leader, Nigel Farage, responded to the pledge with a cricket analogy, observing that the Conservatives were 'coming to play on our pitch' (*Financial Times* 2013j). At the 2014 European elections, with 27 per cent of the vote, the UKIP outpolled the Conservatives and became the biggest UK party. At the 2015 general elections, its share of the vote rose from 3 to 13 per cent. However, its rise did not occur solely at the expense of the Conservatives, who, with a similar share of the vote to 2010 and against most expectations, won a majority of seats and could now govern alone – leaving Cameron little choice but to redeem the pledge he had made two years previously.

The renegotiation of the UK's EU membership terms

By various accounts (and having been on the winning side on referenda on the British voting system and Scottish independence in the previous Parliament), Cameron was very confident that he would win the EU referendum (Clegg 2016a; former EU Council president Herman van Rompuy quoted in Parker and Barker 2016c). He is quoted as having predicted a 'remain' victory of 70 to 30 per cent – which would have exceeded the margin in the 1975 referendum (Parker 2016b). British public opinion appeared to have shifted significantly in favour of remaining in the EU since 2013 (e.g., Pew Research Center 2015a). Moreover, polls suggested that if the government managed to negotiate a deal on new membership terms with other member states and, based on such an agreement, recommended staying in the EU, it would win the referendum comfortably (e.g., Evans and Menon 2017: 47; YouGov 2015).

Much could still depend, however, on the terms of any such deal. Cameron did not have many staunch allies among the other EU heads of government. His decision – before becoming prime minister – to withdraw the Conservative Party from the EPP had greatly antagonized other centre-right leaders, including Merkel. He had found himself completely isolated among the member states in his opposition to the Fiscal Compact in 2011 and in trying to prevent the nomination of Jean-Claude Juncker as president of the European Commission in 2014 and was criticized for not doing enough to build close relationships with other leaders. There was little understanding among other member states for Cameron's demand for a new membership deal, given that the UK already had numerous opt-outs from EU rules and integration projects (Rogers 2017a, 2017b).

Appreciating the UK's military capabilities and, in numerous cases, its liberal political-economic orientation, other member states nonetheless wanted to avert Brexit (Candon 2015). Many of them saw the UK's presence in the EU as contributing to maintain a desirable balance of power: 'The Germans do not want to be left with the French; the French do not want to be left with the Germans; and no one else wants to be left with the French and the Germans' (Anand Menon, quoted in *The Economist* 2015c).

Among their citizens, supporters of continued British membership of the EU outnumbered opponents by six to one, with the largest proportions of supporters in Ireland and the newer member states in Central and Eastern Europe (Murphy 2016). However, although other member states wanted in principle to keep the UK in the EU, this did not guarantee that they would be willing to agree to the new British membership terms that Cameron was going to demand. As they explored the scope for compromise with other governments on the terms Cameron was looking for, his emissaries received a fairly cool reception, especially from governments in Southern and Central Europe (Korski 2016).

To mobilize support for his cause among other members, Cameron relied most heavily on Chancellor Merkel and Germany, appealing to her government to 'help deliver' the changes he was seeking (Kroet 2016). One of his advisers described his strategy from the beginning as having been to 'schmooze the pants off Merkel, get that locked down and then everyone else will fall into line' (Shipman 2016: 11). Not for the first time in the history of the EU, however, the British government overestimated how far Berlin could or would help them (interviews, Berlin, 2018). Above all it failed to recognize to what extent its demands clashed with fundamental German interests in preserving the integrity of the single market and, indirectly, the EU itself.

Germany possessed several compelling motives to try to avoid Brexit. Depending on the terms of any post-Brexit trade agreement between the EU and the UK, German firms' access to the important British market could be impeded (Fuest 2016). The UK was Germany's fifth-biggest trade partner and third-biggest export market, accounting for 6 per cent of its international trade and 7 per cent of its export income (Statistisches Bundesamt 2017). In economic and trade policy, Brexit could also shift the balance of power away from Germany and like-minded, free-trade-oriented states in northern Europe towards the generally more state-interventionist and protectionist southern member states (Fuest 2016; Kornelius 2016a and 2016b; Schwarzer 2015; interview, Berlin, 2018). With its UN Security Council seat, nuclear weapons and military power projection capabilities, the UK also enhanced the EU's weight in international affairs (interview, Berlin, 2018). In as far as Brexit threatened to bolster German dominance in the remainder of the EU, it could also encourage other member states to cooperate to balance German power, reviving the traditional 'nightmare of coalitions' (Grant 2016; Marsh 2016; interview, Berlin, 2018). By no means least, the UK's withdrawal could also strengthen centrifugal political forces in other member states and heighten the risk of political disintegration – a concern also shared by the French government (Kornelius 2016a, 2016b). A senior German minister viewed the prospect of Brexit as a 'disaster' for the UK, but a 'catastrophe' for his country (Parker and Barker 2015). The veteran finance minister Schäuble described it as 'unimaginable', adding that Berlin would do everything in its power to keep the UK in the EU (*Financial Times* 2014i).

At the same time, the German government was constrained in how far it could go to help Cameron and avert Brexit. Knowing that these would give rise to unpredictable and therefore politically unpalatable referenda in other member states, it did not want to make any concessions to Cameron that would require treaty changes (Parker and Barker 2015). It also feared that if the EU were to make too far-reaching concessions to the UK, this would provoke other members to make their own demands for special membership deals – which could provoke the unwinding of the EU in the same way that Brexit itself could (Vasagar 2015). For this reason, but also as a matter of principle, it was especially hostile to any deal that would directly curtail any of the fundamental 'freedoms' in the EU treaties – the free movement not only of goods, services and capital, but also labour and persons. These were regarded in Berlin as belonging to the 'DNA' of European integration and therefore sacrosanct (*Der Spiegel* 2014a; *The Economist* 2014f; interview, Berlin, 2018). Germany wanted to keep the UK in the EU, but, in case of doubt, if it had to choose between having a larger, more loosely integrated EU with the UK (that it feared would unravel) and a smaller, more tightly integrated EU without the UK, it would prefer the latter – in line with its historical stance on the issue.

These constraints may explain why Merkel had said before the 2015 UK elections that she was willing 'to help … a bit' to keep the UK in the EU, but that she could do so only 'on the margins' (as quoted in Laws 2016: 246; *Eurocomment* 2014f: 38). Told that a 'marginal renegotiation' might not suffice for Cameron to win the referendum, her reply was: 'What do they expect me to do about that?' (Laws 2016: 246). She stressed to Cameron that she could not guarantee the UK's place in the EU 'on her own'. He had to stop being so reliant on Germany and go out and make 'some new friends' (Parker and Barker 2016a; Parker et al. 2015).

Having pursued an EU policy of 'not so much Germany first as Germany only' in his first term, Cameron now followed Merkel's advice (Parker and Barker 2016a). In the months before the decisive pre-referendum EU summit in February 2016, he travelled extensively among the member state capitals to press his case and assess the scope for an accord on new UK membership terms that would enable him to win the referendum (Korski 2016). He set out his demands for new UK membership terms in a letter to the European Council president Tusk and other heads of government in November 2015 (Cameron 2015). The main ones related to the safeguarding of the interests of non-Eurozone members, reducing the regulatory burden on business, enhancing the role of national parliaments in EU decision-making, lifting for the UK the treaty obligation to work towards an 'ever closer union', and reducing the flow of immigrants into the UK from other member states (Cameron 2015). However, he did not explicitly demand an immigration cap as such (*Eurocomment* 2016c: 17). Opposition to such a measure among other member states (see later in this section) was huge (Rogers 2017b) and he was concerned to make demands that he considered to be politically 'feasible' for other member states and that therefore had a good chance of being met.

There was a 'presumption' in Brussels and among the member governments that a deal would be reached at the February 2016 summit: 'Cameron
wanted the UK to stay in, his partners wanted the same and the business
which remained to be done was clearly do-able' (*Eurocomment* 2016c: 2).
The negotiations nonetheless proved more difficult and protracted than
anticipated. Although Merkel supported Cameron's demands at the summit,
she did not play a prominent role (*Eurocomment* 2016c: 12–13). In contrast, French president Hollande had strong reservations about Cameron's
demands relating to the rights of non-Eurozone members in the EU, fearing
these could curtail the scope for regulating financial markets and combating
financial instability (*Eurocomment* 2016c: 15–17). In general, though, the
French stance on Brexit was very similar to the German (interview, Berlin,
2018). The Belgian prime minister Charles Michel wanted to be reassured
that if the UK should not be obliged to participate in an 'ever-closer union',
other member states should not be prevented from integrating more closely
(*Eurocomment* 2016c: 21–25). The Visegrad Four, whose members (Poland,
Hungary, the Czech Republic and Slovakia) closely coordinated their positions and tactics, objected to Cameron's demands to curtail the welfare
benefits of citizens of EU member states working abroad (*Eurocomment*
2016c: 17–21). For Tusk and his team, this was the issue on which they
most feared the negotiations could fail (*Eurocomment* 2016c: 17). It was
indeed the topic that provoked the 'most protracted wrangle' at the summit (*Eurocomment* 2016c: 17–21; Rogers 2017b; Shipman 2016: 131–137).
However, none of the Visegrad governments wanted in the end 'to go down
in history' as the country that had 'kicked the British out of the EU' (*Eurocomment* 2016c: 18). A compromise was thus reached on this as well as on
the other contentious issues. The deal made it more difficult for Eurozone
states to adopt rules that would discriminate against non-members (relevant
especially for the City of London). It committed the EU to reduce regulatory
burdens and 'red-tape', authorized the UK not to participate in 'further political integration' and an 'ever-closer union', and gave a threshold of 55 per
cent of national parliaments a 'red card' to block EU legislation. In line with
the specific proposals that Cameron had made in his letter, it also empowered
the UK (and, if they chose, other members), with Commission approval, temporarily to suspend the payment of in-work benefits to migrants from other
EU member states and to index child benefits paid to them to the standard of
living in their home country.

The politically most salient provisions in the deal by far were those related
to *immigration*, which had not actually played a role in Cameron's Bloomberg speech in 2013 (Rogers 2017b). When, with strong UK support, the
post-Communist states in Central and Eastern Europe had acceded to the
EU in 2004, the UK had been one of the few member states not to impose
temporary (maximum seven-year) curbs on their citizens' access to the British labour market. The influx of work-seeking Central and East Europeans
into the UK had subsequently far exceeded official estimates made at the
time (Eyal 2016). By 2015, some one and a half million Central and Eastern

Europeans were living and of these about 1 million were working in the UK. Widespread public unease at this trend had meanwhile been mobilized politically in particular by the UKIP and interwoven with its hostility to European integration into a potent political message (Ford and Goodwin 2014: 185–213). In their 2015 election manifesto (Conservative Party 2015: 29), the Conservative Party felt constrained to reaffirm its ambition to reduce annual net migration into the UK from the hundreds to the 'tens of thousands'.

The February 2016 deal, however, was unlikely to reduce the flow of Central and Eastern European immigrants into the UK. There were no grounds for thinking that access to in-work benefits or child benefits motivated many of these immigrants to move to the UK – for example, only 0.26 per cent of total UK child benefit claims were paid to migrants whose children lived in their home state (Batsaikhan 2016). The UK government could legislate to limit the flow of non-EU immigrants into the UK – who made up 45 per cent of net migration into the UK in 2015 – but not that of EU immigrants. To impose a 'cap' or limits on immigration from other EU member states would be incompatible with the provisions of the EU treaties relating to the free movement of people and non-discrimination between citizens of the member states.

To curb immigration from elsewhere in the EU, the UK government would thus have had to secure the support of the other member states to change the treaties. However, while the other member states accepted to make the provisions of the deal with the UK legally binding, they were not prepared to change the treaty articles on free movement and non-discrimination. According to the UK's Permanent Representative to the EU at the time, there was 'zero preparedness in key capitals, West and East, as well as in the [EU] institutions' to amend the treaties to permit quantitative controls on migration between member states (Rogers 2018). When Cameron floated the idea of a quota or a 'cap' on EU immigration to the UK in 2014, he encountered Merkel's 'furious' opposition (Bernard 2014; Oliver 2016a: 222; *Der Spiegel* 2014a; Parker and Barker 2016a; Shipman 2016: 16). She would not countenance a measure that 'flagrantly breached' EU treaty provisions. Cameron's political aides urged him to continue to push for an immigration cap nonetheless. But advised by the British Permanent Representative and the EU counsellor in the Cabinet Office that neither the German government nor others would bend on this issue, Cameron finally refrained from including the right to cap immigration from elsewhere in the EU in a major speech he made on the issue in late 2014 as well as in his November 2015 letter (Shipman 2016: 16–17, 119–120). He confined himself instead to demanding the power to limit immigrants' access to UK benefits, although he was warned that such measures would not suffice to cut immigration or defuse it as a political issue (Shipman 2016: 21). Cameron and his advisers struggled to convince other governments that there were too many immigrants in the UK (Korski 2016; Roger 2017b). While they accepted the curtailment of EU citizens' entitlement to some benefits when working abroad, the four Visegrad states were viscerally opposed to any curbs or brakes on the free movement of persons as such.

While some of its provisions were arguably significant, the UK's new membership deal was certainly not a 'major new settlement' or 'transformative' (McGowan and Phinnemore 2017: 88). It did little to assuage the Eurosceptics in Cameron's own party, who described the provisions as 'trivial', 'underwhelming to say the least' and not coming 'even close to the fundamental changes promised to the public' (as quoted in Mason and Rankin 2016). Some 140 Conservative MPs – far more than the '40 or 50' with whom Cameron had reckoned – subsequently came out in favour of Brexit (Evans and Menon 2017: 50). The most widely read daily newspaper, *The Sun*, described it as a 'steaming pile of manure … A dismal failure worse than we ever imagined' (*The Sun* 2016). The British public also seemed distinctly unimpressed, one poll finding that only 21 per cent of respondents thought the deal was a good one, while 58 per cent thought the opposite (Parker and Barker 2016b; Shipman 2016: 127). A later opinion survey indicated that more than half of the voters that opted for Brexit in the referendum made their decision after the February 2016 renegotiation (Evans and Menon 2017: 50). In view of such 'bleak' survey findings, Cameron and the remain campaign team concluded that they could not win the referendum on the 'package we had achieved' and therefore abandoned any effort at 'persuading people of its merit' (Korski 2016).

The referendum campaign and outcome

The unfavourable public perception of the renegotiation may not have mattered for the outcome of the referendum if the balance of forces in the campaign had not been much less favourable to the 'remain' camp than it had been in 1975. On the one hand, unlike then, the trade unions, the Labour Party and the (meanwhile much stronger) Scottish National Party were in favour of staying in the EU, although, since the election of a new, radical left-wing leader, Jeremy Corbyn, in September 2015, the Labour leadership was much more lukewarm in its support for membership than it had been under Blair. It turned down an offer from the German Social Democrats to organize a campaign event in the UK in support of continued UK membership, conceivably, however, because it feared that such an intervention would prove counterproductive (interview, Berlin, 2018). On the other, almost all the other actors with the capacity to influence the referendum outcome were significantly less supportive of continued EU membership. Whereas the national newspapers had been unanimously 'pro-European' in 1975, in 2016 the 'quality newspapers' with limited circulation were almost the only ones that came out in favour of remaining. Bar one, all the mass tabloid papers supported withdrawal. The Conservative prime minister Cameron was not used to having campaign against the bulk of the British press (Korski 2016; Shipman 2016: 128). Whereas the business organizations and community had been almost monolithically in favour of continued membership in 1975, in 2016 a sizeable minority favoured Brexit. Among pro-Brexit business actors were numerous hedge funds in the City of London, one out of every three firms belonging to the British Chambers of Commerce and a substantial proportion of small firms – 41 per cent in a survey conducted by the Federation of Small Businesses (Agnew 2015; Gordon 2015; Marshall 2016; Parker and Chassany 2016; Tighe and Bounds 2016). The larger the firm and the stronger its export orientation, the more likely it was to want the UK to remain in the EU, but many large companies were reportedly reluctant to engage in the campaign either because they needed shareholder approval to make donations or because they feared a backlash from Eurosceptic customers (Agnew and Parker 2015). The government told business leaders to 'shut up' while it was renegotiating the UK's membership terms with the other member states, then to 'speak up' for the EU (Gordon et al. 2015; Parker 2016a). The National Farmers' Union, the lobby of the sector most affected by the EU, supported continued membership, but did not play an active part in the campaign (Daneshku 2016).

Most of all, the Conservative Party itself – largely united in favour of membership in 1975 – was split down the middle in its stance on the EU in 2016. A fifth of cabinet members and 43 per cent of Conservative MPs chose to campaign for Brexit, rallying around half of the Conservative electorate in the UK (58 per cent according to the largest last pre-referendum survey; Ashcroft 2016: 6). Cameron was especially damaged by the last-minute decision of the backbench MP and former Mayor of London Boris Johnson to campaign for Brexit, as he was the only leading leave campaigner whose popularity rivalled, if not exceeded, the prime minister's. Also in contrast to 1975, by 2016 a mass party of the national-populist right, UKIP, had emerged. Unsurprisingly, given that withdrawal from the EU was its very raison d'être, almost all its sympathizers were Brexit supporters.

The 'remain' camp relied heavily in the referendum campaign on the so-called 'Project Fear', emphasizing the economic costs that withdrawal from the EU would incur and confident that these would trump popular concerns about immigration (Korski 2016; Shipman 2016: 302–303). In this regard, it was supported by a plethora of economic studies and forecasts – from, among others, the IMF, the Organization for Economic Cooperation and Development (OECD), the Bank of England and the British Treasury – that estimated almost unanimously that Brexit would have more or less serious negative economic consequences for the UK. In the first three weeks of the main phase of the campaign, 'Project Fear' proved effective, with a clear majority of published opinion polls giving the remain camp a lead over its rivals. However, in the last week of May 2016, the credibility of the government's immigration policy and pledges was damaged by the publication of new official statistics showing that net immigration in 2015 had reached 333,000, some 20,000 higher than the year before. This announcement marked a turning point in the campaign (Parker 2016b). In the next three weeks, immigration increasingly superseded the economy and trade as the main campaign issue and polls pointing towards a victory for the 'leave' camp outnumbered the others by two to one.

Cameron and his advisers considered whether the PM should try to persuade Merkel to make a public statement that the EU would enable the

UK to do 'much more … on immigration', but, although he called Merkel, they decided it was too late to launch such an initiative as it would 'look desperate' (Oliver 2016a: 322–323; Shipman 2016: 367–368). Cameron apparently still believed he would win the referendum (Shipman 2016: 368). This may explain why, before the referendum, he did not ask the civil service to prepare any contingency plans for a vote in favour of Brexit. Indeed, opinion surveys conducted after the assassination of the 'pro-European' Labour MP, Jo Cox, a week before the referendum gave the 'remain' camp hope that the trend towards Brexit had been halted, if not turned around. In a strikingly inaccurate prognosis, Cameron's opinion pollsters told him on referendum day that voters had shifted 'decisively in his favour' and he was going to win by a 60 to 40 per cent margin, 'maybe better' (as quoted in Parker 2016b).

The Britons who voted for Brexit in the highest proportions were older, relatively poorly educated and working class – the group(s) which also in most other countries make up the hard-core support of Eurosceptic parties and are frequently labelled globalization or modernization 'losers' or the 'left-behind' (Curtice 2017: 34; Hobolt 2016: 1267–1270; McGowan and Phinnemore 2017: 96; Menon and Fowler 2016: 87). However, this group did not comprise the majority of Brexit voters: only a quarter of these were working class, whereas almost 60 per cent were (to a disproportionate extent, English) middle-class (Dorling 2016). The Leave campaign managed to use the specific issue of immigration to mobilize support for their overall demand to 'take back control' of the UK from the EU. For Brexit supporters overall, it was primarily the in their minds 'closely linked' issues of national sovereignty and immigration that explained their voting choice (see Figure 6.3; Curtice 2017: 28–29; Dennison and Geddes 2018: 1147; Prosser et al. 2016). Paradoxically, the vote for Brexit was lower the higher the proportion of

Figure 6.3 *Immigration and the economy as issues in the UK EU referendum*

Looking ahead to the Referendum on Britain's membership of the European Union on June 23rd, which, if any, issues do you think will be very important to you in helping you decide which way to vote?

	May 2016 (%)	June 2016 (%)	June 2016 (%)
The number of immigrants coming into Britain	28	33	32
The impact on Britain's economy	33	28	31
Britain's ability to make its own laws	15	12	16
The impact on British jobs	9	8	11
The cost ot EU immigration on Britain's welfare system	9	7	11
Britain's ability to trade with countries in the EU	10	6	10
Nothing/none	7	7	7
Don't know	13	11	8

Source: Ipsos MORI opinion survey, published 23 June 2016 (Fieldwork: 21–22 June 2016). Available from: https://ems.ipsos-mori.com/researchspecialisms/socialresearch/eureferendum/interactive.aspx.

immigrants in the locality, but higher the bigger the percentage increase in the number of immigrants between 2001 and 2014 (McGill 2016; *The Economist* 2016e). Outside of Scotland, Northern Ireland and London, the Brexit camp carried the referendum in every British region.

Conclusion

Of the four contemporary crises facing the EU, the Brexit Crisis testifies most powerfully to the impact on European integration of domestic politics, of mass politicization and political polarization around EU issues in the member states. Other than neo-functionalist, transactionalist and liberal intergovernmental theories of European integration imply, the close economic ties that bound the UK to the rest of the EU and the prospect of their disruption failed to dissuade most British voters in the referendum from casting their vote for Brexit. Rather, the (still provisional) outcome of the crisis vindicates postfunctionalist integration theories that emphasize the ultimate primacy of politics over economics.

European integration was always highly politicized in the UK. In the 1950s, there was a constraining consensus against British participation in this process. In more than 50 years since UK accession to the EEC was first proposed in the early 1960s there was never a 'permissive' pro-European consensus. Twice, in 1975 and 2016, British governments prioritized the exigencies of domestic politics over long-term political and strategic orientations by resorting to referenda as a means of arbitrating protracted and intractable conflicts over the UK's EU membership in the governing political parties. In 1975, the UK voted to remain in the EU, but the Labour Party split anyway over Europe six years later, two years after having been voted out of office. Whether the unity of the Conservative Party survives the 2016 referendum remains to be seen. In any case, by potentially fostering stronger support for Scottish independence and complicating relations between Northern Ireland and the Republic, Brexit exacerbated the threat to the unity of the UK. This also belonged to the collateral damage provoked by Cameron's referendum decision, described by a venerable economics commentator as 'the most irresponsible act by a British government in my lifetime' (Wolf 2016).

Referenda arguably represent the highest and most pristine expression of the primacy of domestic politics in international relations. Governments can negotiate with each other to resolve conflictual issues in international politics. Referenda, however, place the arbitration of such conflicts in the hands of a mass public. Governments cannot negotiate in any direct way with the mass publics of other countries. Conflict-mediation over a negotiating table is no longer possible. By their pronouncements, governments can, however, send 'signals' to foreign publics to encourage them to vote this way or that in referenda. In the case of the 2016 Brexit referendum, the principal means by which they could influence the voting behaviour of the British public was through the terms of an accord with the Conservative government over new British membership terms.

In the referendum post-mortem, the question arose as to whether, to keep the UK in the EU, the other member states could or should have made greater concessions to Cameron on immigration and the free movement of persons and whether, with a more confrontational style in the negotiations, the prime minister could have secured a 'better' deal for the UK on this issue (see, e.g., Shipman 2016: 591). But this was almost certainly not the case. Merkel assured Cameron after the referendum that there 'could never have been an emergency brake on migrants' to the UK from other member states (as quoted in Oliver 2016a: 383, 401; Korski 2016; Rogers 2018).

One of Cameron's advisers wrote after the referendum that 'in today's EU, you either rely on Germany, or you have nobody to rely on at all'. As Merkel had been willing to give the UK 'some of what we asked for, but not all of it', other EU leaders had gone 'an extra mile, but not two or three' (Korski 2016). A former British ambassador to Germany wrote after the referendum that Merkel and her government did 'nothing to help' Cameron in the Brexit referendum: 'Neither Chancellor Merkel nor any other German minister put any pressure on the Commission or on the Poles and others to be more accommodating to British concerns', despite the EU having had a 'long history of finding solutions to political problems through special or transitional arrangements or the like' (Lever 2017: 157). While it is an exaggeration to say that Merkel was inactive in the Brexit Crisis, she and her government did indeed keep a lower profile in it than in any of the other contemporaneous EU crises. The decisive intervention from the German chancellor that Cameron and his government was banking on – one in which she would lay down the line for the other member states and the Commission to follow, as they conceived – never came. Nor did she make any comparable effort to influence the British campaign to that made by her predecessor Schmidt in 1975 – whereby it is conceivable, of course, given the strength of Eurosceptic sentiment in the UK, that such an intervention would have been counterproductive.

Why was Merkel less willing to 'lead' on Brexit than on the other crises in which she was less reluctant to deploy Germany's power resources? One possible answer to this question is that Berlin was conflicted on Brexit and acted correspondingly ambivalently. While, on the one hand, wanting to accommodate the UK and keep it in the EU, it was prepared to grant it concessions that would have 'loosened' the existing degree of integration, it was fearful, on the other, that, if these went too far, this would trigger a wider *dis*integration process that ran counter to fundamental German interests. The tough stance that the German government subsequently took in talks over the terms of Brexit confirms that, if forced to choose, Germany preferred a smaller, more tightly integrated EU to a larger, more loosely integrated one that the UK sought.

A second conceivable explanation of Germany's leadership reticence on Brexit – not inconsistent with but rather complementary to the first – is that this simply recognized Germany's incapacity to orchestrate a more accommodating response to British demands, given the breadth and depth of opposition to these among other member states and the (closely related) fact that this would have required treaty changes to which all of them would have had to agree, which some of them would have had to put to a referendum and which would therefore in all likelihood have proved politically unfeasible. Overall there certainly does not seem to have been a German 'master plan' either to avert Brexit or, after the referendum, to manage its consequences (Hockenos 2016). Merkel's reply to the observation that the UK might vote for Brexit if the other member states did not make extensive concessions to it over its membership terms – 'what do they expect me to do about that?' – may summarize well how limited she thought her scope was to influence the outcome of the referendum. Even if they had been willing to change the free movement provisions in the EU treaties to accommodate Cameron, what Merkel and the German government could have done to bring especially the Visegrad states into line on this issue is not obvious. Berlin's efforts around the same time to persuade or coerce them to accept refugees from the war-torn Middle East had proved fruitless. Both crises revealed the limits of German power in the EU.

In the absence of the much more assertive style of German leadership that characterized the other three crises, the primary actor in the Brexit negotiations became, by default, the Council and its president, Tusk (*Eurocomment* 2016a, 2016b, 2016c). As Council president he could not mobilize similar resources to the head of government of a major member state to rally other member states around a common position. Tusk was also constrained in his mediation efforts by the fact that any accord had to be adopted unanimously, thus giving each member a right of veto over the outcome. Of all the EU's crises, the Brexit Crisis, involving the withdrawal of a major member state, was the one that culminated in the most disintegrative outcome. The weaker the (stabilizing) leadership supplied in any given crisis, it seems, the greater is the risk of significant political disintegration as opposed to limited disintegration (Schengen/Refugee Crisis), no disintegration (Ukraine Crisis) or closer integration (Eurozone Crisis).

Merkel described the referendum outcome as a 'turning point for Europe'; the French prime minister Manuel Valls called it 'an explosive shock' that could provoke the 'break-up, pure and simple, of the union' (as quoted in Parker et al. 2016). Before and immediately after the referendum, widespread fears were expressed that the Brexit vote would unleash a significant 'contagion' effect in the EU that could result in other member states following the British lead. In as far as the UK is a uniquely Eurosceptic member state (see Figure 6.2), it is conceivable that, assuming Brexit is ultimately executed, it will remain the only one to leave the EU, as Vollaard has argued (Vollaard 2014: 1155). As it belongs to neither the Schengen Area nor above all the Eurozone, the costs of withdrawal from the EU for the UK are also arguably more manageable than for any other member state – the UK is not Greece, which may have plunged over a financial abyss if it had left or been expelled from the Eurozone in 2015. Prior to the Brexit referendum, however, substantial minorities of citizens in the other major states – from 38 per cent in Germany to 46 per cent in Italy and 48 per cent in France – seemed to want their countries to leave the EU – given the chance (see Figure 6.4). Such findings suggested that Brexit could indeed prove contagious elsewhere.

Figure 6.4 *A 'domino effect' after Brexit?*

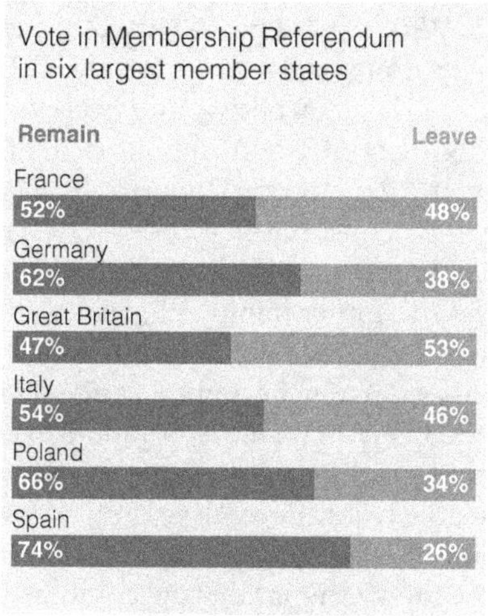

Vote in Membership Referendum
in six largest member states

Remain | Leave

France
52% | 48%

Germany
62% | 38%

Great Britain
47% | 53%

Italy
54% | 46%

Poland
66% | 34%

Spain
74% | 26%

Source: Catherine E. de Vries and Isabell Hoffmann, *Keep Calm and Carry on. What Europeans Think About a Possible Brexit* (June 2016, Bertelsmann Foundation), p. 9, available online here: https://www.bertelsmann-stiftung.de/fileadmin/files/BSt/Publikationen/GrauePublikationen/Survey_EZ_Keep_calm_and_carry_on_2016.pdf.

In fact, however, in the short term at least the Brexit referendum result had not so much the widely feared 'contagion' as an 'inoculation' effect on the rest of the EU. The vote did not dissuade six western Balkans states from maintaining their interest in joining the EU, although the earliest date mooted for the accession of any of them was 2025. Opinion polls in the following months pointed to a resurgence of 'pro-European' sentiment in the existing member states (Oltermann et al. 2016; Salles 2016). In as far as this was a reaction to the British referendum result, it suggests that the image of political and economic uncertainty if not instability that the post-referendum UK projected cooled the Eurosceptic ardour of some of those citizens of other member states who were previously attracted by the idea of their country leaving EU. This kind of sentiment might also have been strengthened by the election of the national-populist Donald Trump as US president in November 2016. Coming on top of the Ukraine Crisis (see Chapter 4) and the Arab Spring and wars in the Middle East, this event conceivably combined with the prospect of Brexit to foster the growing perception that the EU was facing a gathering storm of 'external' threats in the face of which the (future 27) member states had to stick together and thus to strengthen the sense of a common European identity. In this analysis, combined with other changes in the international environment, the UK referendum result had more a centripetal than centrifugal impact on the EU. This trend may also have been favoured by the relative stabilization since 2015 or 2016 of the other – Eurozone, Ukraine and refugee – crises that had fragilized the EU during the preceding years.

It is nevertheless noteworthy that the (provisional) lull in the EU's quadruple crisis did not bring the rise of Eurosceptic parties in the EU to a halt (see Table 7.2, Chapter 7). Where these parties waxed, the danger of the secession of other member states than the UK from the EU could not be entirely excluded. The fortunes of these parties would, however, be only one relevant factor shaping the probability of any further horizontal disintegration of the EU. Politico-institutional variables, particularly the extent to which popular referenda are facilitated by constitutional provisions, laws or political norms and traditions, would also affect the likelihood of other member states following the same path as the UK. Other things being equal, the member states most likely to secede from the EU may be those whose citizens and elites have the strongest collective sense of external economic and security-related invulnerability. In effect, these are likely to be more populous member states, relatively distant from security threats such as those posed by Russia, net contributors to the EU budget, and relatively less dependent on trade with other EU member states. The most propitious conditions for secession from the EU may develop in member states where these structural traits combine with conjunctural variables (such as strongly felt economic and/or other crises) that are favourable to the growth of Euroscepticism. The states thus likely to be most tempted by secession from the EU may not be found among the smaller, financially EU-dependent, more EU-trade-dependent and 'insecure' member states in Central and Eastern Europe, but rather in two of the largest, West European member states in which Euroscepticism has grown strongly since the Eurozone and Refugee Crisis – namely the 'pioneer' member states France and, above all, Italy, whose economic performance, after that of Greece, has been the worst of any member of the Eurozone since the single currency was introduced and which was disproportionately heavily hit by the Refugee Crisis.

An 'Italexit', at least from the Eurozone, became more than a mere hypothetical possibility with the formation of a Eurosceptic coalition government of populist parties in Rome following elections in March 2018. Both new governing parties were, to different degrees, hostile to both the Euro and accommodating refugees in Italy. Once in office, the new government toned down its anti-EU rhetoric and pledged to respect EU fiscal rules. If, however, they should come under strong domestic political pressure to implement the far-reaching fiscal pledges they made in the election campaign, they would have to break these rules, thereby risking a collapse of confidence of international financial markets and a new sovereign debt crisis that, given the size of the Italian economy, the Eurozone's third-biggest, could rapidly jeopardize Italian membership of the Eurozone and the very survival of the Euro. Equally, by explicitly or implicitly encouraging refugees living in Italy to move elsewhere in the EU, they could precipitate the restoration of border controls by other member states and thus the collapse of the Schengen Area. In any case, for the time being, Italy looked as if it would be the next crucible of the quadruple crisis that had broken out in Greece almost a decade earlier.

Chapter 7

Conclusion

Introduction

The process of European political integration has seldom flowed like a tranquil stream. Even before 2009, its history was punctuated with crises, some of which were more and others less severe (see Chapter 1). While some of these may have held up this process temporarily, ultimately, however, none had the effect of reversing it. The competences of the EU were extended into more and more policy domains, more and more states joined it, and the authority of the supranational organs vis-à-vis the member states steadily expanded. The unidirectional nature of the process – perhaps inevitably – spawned a great deal of theoretical reflection on the topic that suggested that European integration was fundamentally irreversible.

Much of this literature emphasized that the integration process was driven by socio-economic trends, notably the growing volume of cross-border trade and exchange, which exerted irresistible pressure on national governments to lower the costs of transactions across borders. However, a cursory glance at world, including European, history tells us that such processes are subject to disruption and ultimately rest on political foundations, whose presence and resilience it may be dangerous to take for granted. Comparing post-World War II European history with that of earlier periods and the evolution of European regionalism with that of other regions points towards two variables that account more than any others for the uniquely high level of political integration meanwhile achieved in Europe: the domination of the party systems in the member states of 'pro-European' political movements from the centre-left to the centre-right (essentially Christian and Social Democracy and Liberalism) and the existence of a 'hegemonic coalition' comprising France and Germany that, while not dominating the everyday politics of the EU, exercised a predominant influence over the overall direction and rhythm of the integration process (Webber 2017).

The analyses contained in previous chapters underline the centrality – prior to the contemporary crisis – of the role of Franco-German cooperation (and conflict) in 'shaping' European integration (Krotz and Schild 2013). The Euro, the Schengen Area with its accompanying measures and the CFSP – all these three major integration projects emerged from the dynamics of the Franco-German relationship, from the bilateral negotiations between Paris and, at this time, Bonn that provided a template for their subsequent 'multilateralization' in the EU. The case of the first British bids to join the EU in the

1960s – which Germany supported, but de Gaulle's France vetoed – exemplified how decisive a Franco-German accord or compromise was for the – in this case, horizontal – expansion of the integration process.

Over time, however, the balance of power in this relationship shifted towards Germany and the capacity of France to provide a major impetus to the integration process was weakened by the increasing political contestation of the EU, illustrated by the defeat of the Constitutional Treaty in a referendum in 2005, and the country's growing economic difficulties, which seemed to be exacerbated by successive governments' unwillingness or incapacity to reform the French welfare state and labour market (Webber and Gehlen 2007). This trend coincided approximately with the post-Communist enlargement of the EU in Central and Eastern Europe, so that at a time when the 'periphery' of the EU was expanding and the EU was becoming increasingly heterogeneous, the 'core', in contrast, was shrinking and the task of mediating conflicts between member states was arguably becoming more challenging. When the GFC and, in its wake, the Eurozone Crisis broke, Germany increasingly became 'indispensable' as the EU's leader. The new 'German Question' now became whether, increasingly alone, it was both willing and able to play the role of a stabilizing hegemonic power, exercising a predominant influence over the rules according to which the crisis was managed, ensuring that the burdens of crisis adjustment were distributed equitably, mobilizing support for crisis policies among the other member states and thereby holding the EU together. The quadruple crisis of the EU thus became a litmus test of Germany's capacity and willingness to provide stabilizing leadership.

The findings

The most influential 'optimistic' (transactionalist, neo-functionalist, and liberal intergovernmentalist) theories of European integration reassure us that the EU 'house' is resistant to all prospective political 'disasters'. Political decision-makers are the prisoners of tight socio-economic, legal and institutional constraints that in the end, as with Syriza in Greece, compel them not to stray too far from the pre-established integration path. If these theories were accurate, one would have expected the EU to survive the quadruple crisis without any manifestations of political disintegration. But this is not the case. In contrast to these approaches, 'pessimistic' (postfunctionalist) theories err in the opposite direction. If these theories were accurate, given especially the highly politicized Eurozone and Schengen crises, one would have expected the 'downward pressure on the scope and level of integration' to become irresistible and a significantly larger part of the EU 'house' to be flattened and destroyed than was the case. In sum, both sets of theories are too blunt to provide a satisfactory explanation of the variable impact of the four crises on political integration. The one set underestimates the autonomy of politics; the other set underestimates the autonomy of political leaders in the face of (domestic) political pressures. Neither allows sufficient scope for political agency, for the statecraft of political leaders. For the one set, political decision-makers are helpless vis-à-vis transnational economic (business) interests; for the other, they have little choice, at least if their goal is to maximize voter support in democratic elections, but to accommodate rising popular support for nationalist or Eurosceptic policies, making the mediation of conflicts between member states in the EU consequently increasingly political unfeasible.

A hegemonic-stability-theoretical explanation of crisis outcomes

In this study I have provided an explanation for this apparent anomaly, the divergent outcomes of the four crises in respect of their impact on political integration, rooted in hegemonic stability theory. The four crises each had (provisionally, at least) different outcomes in this regard. The Eurozone Crisis culminated in a higher level of political integration, with the creation of the ESM to 'bail out' crisis-stricken Eurozone member states, the adoption of more constraining rules relating to member states' fiscal policies, and the launching of an (incomplete) banking union. In the Ukraine Crisis, there was no change in the existing degree of political integration. Unlike in the Eurozone Crisis, there was no need for the creation of new instruments of crisis management. The existing treaties provided for the adoption and implementation of economic sanctions against Russia for its annexation of Crimea and covert military intervention in south-eastern Ukraine. The EU member states adopted and over a period of several years have maintained a common stance on this conflict. The Schengen/Refugee Crisis has resulted, in contrast, limited political disintegration, illustrated by the resurrection and, it seems increasingly, indefinite maintenance of controls on some borders in the Schengen Area, the defiance by some Central and Eastern European member states of EU decisions and ECJ judgments on refugee relocation and member states' pursuit of very divergent policies towards political asylum-seekers and other migrants. Finally, the UK's choice to leave the EU, as determined in the referendum of 23 June 2016, represents a very significant case of political disintegration. The UK will be the first member state to leave the EU after having joined it. While it is only one of meanwhile 28 member states, it was in 2016 the third-biggest member state in terms of population, had the second-biggest economy, and, with France, was the only other member state to possess nuclear weapons, to possess a significant capacity to project military power externally, and to occupy a permanent seat in the United Nations (UN) Security Council. It is no longer a big power, but it is still a medium-sized one. Given the specificity of the UK's relationship with and participation in the EU, Brexit may not have a 'domino effect' precipitating the secession of other member states (Vollaard 2014). By itself, however, it may bring about a tangible reduction in the EU's weight in international economic and security affairs.

Overall therefore the crises ended in increased (*sectoral*) integration in respect of the Eurozone, an unchanged degree of (*sectoral*) integration in foreign and security (trade sanctions) policy in respect of the Ukraine Crisis, limited (*sectoral*) disintegration in respect of the Schengen Area and refugee policy, and significant (*horizontal*) disintegration in the form of the UK's vote for Brexit. In respect of *vertical* (dis)integration there was no uniform trend. In the Eurozone Crisis, the powers of the ECB were clearly strengthened, particularly by the fact that it was empowered to supervise EU banks. In contrast, compared not only with that of the ECB, but also that of the Eurogroup, the role of the European Commission in managing this crisis was relatively marginal and that of the German government, to varying degrees depending on the issue, often central (see Chapter 3). In contrast also to the ECB, the new 'bail-out' agency, the ESM (like the Fiscal Compact too) was created outside the EU treaties as an intergovernmental organ, in which Germany and France each possesses a right of veto. In the management of the Ukraine Crisis, the Commission, which had played the leading role in negotiating the AA with the Ukraine government, was quickly sidelined once the crisis came to a head and the crisis was subsequently managed predominantly in intergovernmental style, by France and Germany, largely outside of the EU institutions (see Chapter 4). This style of crisis management corresponded closely, however, to the norm for the management of foreign policy crises in the EU, reflecting the relatively weak competences of the EU's supranational organs in this domain. In the Schengen/Refugee Crisis, the authority of both the Commission and the ECJ was challenged and weakened. Border controls were reinstated and maintained against the opposition of the Commission, which seemed to resign itself to the fact that it could not persuade or coerce member states to lift them. Several governments in Central and Eastern Europe defied EU decisions and a subsequent ECJ judgment concerning refugee relocation. And, at the height of this crisis in 2015–16, a handful of member states, first and foremost Germany, but also, for example, Austria, wielded the initiative, with the Commission and Council Secretariat consigned at best to supporting roles, depending mainly on which was thought to be more supportive of the German stance on the crisis at any given time (see Chapter 5). It was only in the Brexit Crisis that neither Germany nor any other single or subgroup of member states sprang to the fore as crisis managers, by default leaving the task of negotiating the prospective new 'terms' of British EU membership prior to the 2016 referendum primarily in the hands not of the Commission but of the Council president Tusk and the Council. The quadruple crisis thus witnessed a resurgence of intergovernmentalism, a waning of the Community or Monnet 'method' and an overall, albeit not uniform, trend towards vertical political *dis*integration (Bickerton et al. 2015; Buras 2013; *The Economist* 2017; Fabbrini 2013; Janning 2013, 2015a; Nugent 2017: 9–10).

The Eurozone Crisis

The (dis)integration outcomes of the four crises cannot all be explained in terms of the role played in their management by Germany. However, all four outcomes are nonetheless explicable very largely or to a significant extent in terms of hegemonic stability theory. The outlying and, at first glance, most puzzling case among the four is the Eurozone Crisis. This is the only crisis in which closer political integration was forged – and this although the role played in this crisis by Germany, with its very strong insistence on austerity among bailed-out Eurozone members, was far from that of a *stabilizing* hegemonic power. In this crisis, the constraints of economic and financial interdependence that the 'optimistic' integration theories emphasize indeed exercised a powerful disciplining effect on Eurozone member states at opposite poles of the distributional conflict. Not only were the costs of exiting the Eurozone too high for the radical Leftist Syriza government in Greece in 2015. The – political as much if not more than financial – costs of a collapse of the Eurozone were also seen by the German government as being so high or at least so hard to calculate that it wanted as far as possible to avoid this scenario. It is nonetheless quite conceivable that, under other circumstances, the interest rates that some Southern European Eurozone members had to pay on government bonds and consequently the volumes of financial aid they required would have risen to such heights in the middle of 2012 that, given the intensity of political opposition to such aid, the 'creditor' states led by Germany would have balked at providing it. 'Under other circumstances' means here: If the ECB had not intervened in and defused the crisis with the pledge of its governor, Mario Draghi, to 'do whatever it takes' to prevent the Eurozone from collapsing.

In his study of the Great Depression, Kindleberger (1973) expressed doubt as to whether (in 1973), in the light of the relative economic decline of the USA, there was a strong prospect of a single state or bloc emerging to fill the vacuum that the USA would likely leave and to provide stabilizing hegemonic leadership in the international economic system. He thought it for this reason all the more important that international institutions with 'real authority and sovereignty' be created – but feared that, of all conceivable scenarios, this one was the 'least likely' to materialize (see Chapter 2). Several decades later, however, when confronting the Eurozone Crisis, the EU had, in the ECB, precisely the kind of institution that Kindleberger had had in mind. While it may not possess much democratic legitimacy, given its lack of political accountability, it had all the requisite legal powers and (capacity to create) financial resources to intervene decisively in the crisis – and did. In the other crises, though, there was no supranational actor with comparable powers to intervene and shape the EU's response; so stabilizing hegemonic leadership, if it was to be provided at all, had to come from the member states – concretely, for the reasons discussed above (see Chapter 2) from Germany.

The Ukraine Crisis

The outcomes of the other three crises in respect of (dis)integration in fact varied closely with the strategies followed by the German government (see Table 7.1). In the Ukraine Crisis, supported by the French government, Berlin played the role of the ideal-typical stabilizing hegemonic power. It coordinated closely with other EU member states and kept them well informed

Table 7.1 German leadership and European (dis)integration: an overview

Variable/ crisis	Level of (mass) polarization	EU-level of polarization	Decision making I: process	Decision making II: content	Distribution of burden	Followership?	Political integration outcome	Explanation of outcome
Eurozone (sectoral)	High	High	DE- & ECB-led	Reflected 'creditor state' interests	Unequal (bigger for 'debtor states')	Yes	Closer integration	Strong SI (ECB) & high cost of exit for EZ members
Ukraine (sectoral)	Lower than in other three	Lower than in other three	DE-led	Balanced interests across member states	Fairly equal	Yes	Unchanged	DE = stabilizing HP
Schengen refugees (sectoral)	High	High	DE- (&/v. AT-) led	Collapse of common policies on Schengen/ refugees	Unequal (bigger for Germany and front-line states)	Variable by issue; overall very limited	Limited disintegration	DE tried, but failed, to be stabilizing HP
Brexit (horizontal)	High (at least in UK)	High	No leader (if any, Council)	Reflected 'EU-27' interests	Fell largely on UK	No (UK votes to leave)	(Significant/ partial) disintegration	DE absent as stabilizing HP

Notes: (1) Remarks in asterisks denote explanatory variable not contained in hegemonic stability theory.

(2) DE = Germany

(3) ECB = European Central Bank

(4) HP = Hegemonic Power

(5) AT = Austria

about its contacts and talks with Russia. It was the main architect of the EU's response to Russia's annexation of Crimea and covert military intervention in south-eastern Ukraine, combining support for Ukraine and the threat and implementation of sanctions with the maintenance of a dialogue and negotiations with Russia to try to settle the conflict. At some cost in terms of its trade with Russia, it led the way in the imposition of sanctions and assumed in absolute terms by far the biggest and in relative terms a more than proportionate share of the burden of this policy. With this strategy, whose acceptance in the EU was also facilitated by France's participation in the management of the crisis, Germany succeeded in mobilizing the support or at least acquiescence of the other member states, many of whom initially had been reluctant to impose sanctions on Russia.

The Schengen and Refugee Crisis

German strategy in the Schengen and Refugee Crisis conformed much less to the ideal-type of a stabilizing hegemon. On the one hand, along with the 'front-line' states such as Greece and Italy and a handful of smaller member states, notably Sweden and, at first, Austria and Hungary, Germany assumed a disproportionately heavy burden of the inflow of refugees and migrants. On the other, it managed the crisis – to a certain extent perhaps inevitably, given the speed with which it exploded in summer 2015 – in a largely uni- or mini-lateral style, with little to no consultation or negotiation with other member states before the critical decisions were taken. It played a dominant role in conceiving the accord with Turkey in March 2016, but it is uncertain, even doubtful, whether this accord was decisive for the subsequent sharp fall in the influx of refugees, given that the Austrian government had already orchestrated the closure of the Balkans route. German-led efforts to relocate refugees to ease the pressure on the 'front-line' states and on Germany itself failed on the resistance of numerous member states, especially in Central and Eastern Europe. The latter were not susceptible to threats of a withdrawal or a reduction of EU financial aid that could not easily be implemented and therefore lacked credibility. The opponents of German refugee policy were nowhere near as vulnerable to the threat of material sanctions as the member states that had to be bailed out in the Eurozone Crisis.

The Brexit Crisis

Of all the four crises, the Brexit Crisis – which gave rise to the clearest-cut case of disintegration – is the one in which Berlin adopted the lowest profile. Contrary to the expectations and hopes of the Cameron government in the UK and despite its strong vocal support for continued British membership, it did not play a very active role trying to mobilize support among the other 26 member states for more far-reaching concessions to Cameron than the limited ones contained in the February 2016 agreement between the UK and other EU members. Neither in respect of the process by which this crisis was managed nor in terms of the provisions of the February 2016 accord did the German government provide stabilizing hegemonic leadership. That it did not undertake more vigorous efforts to stave off Brexit may be explained partly at least by its recognition of the limits of its capacity to influence the outcome of the crisis once Cameron had decided to put the UK's continued EU membership to a popular referendum and given the strong resistance not only among other member states to changing the EU treaties, which would have been required to enable the UK to limit immigration from other EU members, but also to this specific British demand among the Central and Eastern European member states. Also important, however, was Berlin's own conviction that to concede the UK's demands on this issue would threaten the integrity of the Single Market and could lead to the unravelling of the EU, the avoidance of which was the overriding priority of German European policy (see Chapter 6). In case of doubt, Germany preferred a smaller, but more tightly integrated EU to a wider, more loosely integrated one.

(Mass) politicization: a necessary but not sufficient condition of disintegration

An alternative, post-functionalist explanation of the variation in (dis)integration outcomes of the four crises might – in principle – revolve around the levels of mass politicization that they provoked. However, with variations by member state according to the degree to which they were affected by the specific crisis (the issue of Brexit, for example, inevitably provoked much greater political debate in the UK than in other member states), three of the four crises appeared to generate comparably high levels of politicization – that is to say, they became highly salient public political issues, how they should be managed was publicly very contested, and they were highly polarizing. In many of the member states most strongly affected by them, the crises produced huge swings of support between political parties, breaking some old ones and making some new ones. If politicization levels were the main variable explaining (dis)integration outcomes, one might have expected not only Brexit, but also greater disintegration in respect of both borderless travel in the Schengen Area and refugee policy than in fact occurred and particularly more monetary disintegration – that is, the partial if not complete collapse in the Eurozone. The Ukraine Crisis, however, did not provoke a comparable level of mass politicization as the other crises. Moreover, to the extent that it did, notably after the shooting-down of flight MH17 in July 2014, this had a uniting effect on public opinion in the member states, making it harder for member states sceptical about sanctions to articulate their opposition to them (interview, Berlin, 2018). The lower level of mass politicization of the Ukraine Crisis thus arguably facilitated the German government's management of this crisis in the style of a stabilizing hegemon. But the principal explanation of the variation in crisis outcomes in respect of political (dis) integration remains the divergent strategies by which the German government managed them and the varying extent to which it played this stabilizing role.

The rising threat of Euroscepticism

By 2018, the EU's quadruple crisis, if one locates its beginning with the announcement of the new, much higher figure for the Greek government deficit in October 2009, was almost a decade old. Overall, the four crises that it comprised had subsided. The Eurozone Crisis had not experienced any major new flare-up since the July 2015 accord over the third Greek bail-out, which was to expire in August 2018, leaving the Greek government, which had fulfilled its terms, to meet its future borrowing requirements on international financial markets. Although small-scale violence persisted on the line of conflict between Ukrainian and separatist forces in south-eastern Ukraine, there had been no major flare-up of this conflict either since the Minsk II accords in February 2015. The influx of refugees had slowed dramatically since the closure of the Balkans route and adoption of the EU–Turkey agreement on this issue in March 2016. While these measures deflected the influx towards the Central Mediterranean route and Italy, the overall number of refugees fleeing to Europe had dropped sharply. As for Brexit, the terms of the UK's post-Brexit relations with the EU-27 remained uncertain, but this issue was being handled by the two sides within the channels foreseen for such negotiations by the European treaties.

But for the (very significant) exception of Brexit, it could therefore be argued that the EU 'house' had managed to traverse and survive the quadruple crisis *largely* intact. Moreover, elections in France and Germany in 2017 had been won by 'pro-European' candidates and parties. Above all the victory in the French presidential elections of Emmanuel Macron and the defeat of the candidate of the extreme right-wing and Eurosceptic *Front National*, Marine Le Pen, banished – for the time being at least – the threat of a potentially existential crisis for the EU. Macron's 'pro-European' zeal exceeded that of any of his predecessors in the Fifth Republic (see, e.g., Macron 2017). At the same time, parliamentary elections in Germany culminated in the continuation in office of the Grand Coalition of CDU/CSU and SPD, Christian and Social Democrats, the most 'pro-European' governmental constellation conceivable in light of the election results. In as far as the stabilization of the EU depended on the existence of fundamentally 'pro-European' governments in Berlin and Paris, it seemed fairly unlikely that any major disintegrative events would occur prior to the next scheduled national elections in 2021 and 2022. The increasingly uncertain, not to say turbulent, international environment that it was facing, characterized by growing Russian aggression, growing American nationalism under President Trump and ongoing war in the Middle East, could have a unifying effect on the EU.

On closer inspection, however, the results of the elections in France and Germany and other member states in 2017 and early 2018 were, in their implications for the EU and European integration, more ambivalent and equivocal. Macron owed his election victory in no small measure to good fortune – to the corruption scandal that destroyed the chances of the mainstream centre-right presidential campaign, François Fillon. Popular adhesion to Macron's personality and programme was shallow. According to one opinion poll, after just over a year in office, the new president enjoyed the 'confidence' of barely a third of French citizens (Ipsos Sofra-Steria opinion poll conducted between 27 June and 2 July 2018, as published in *Le Monde* 2018). Macron had succeeded in introducing a range of reforms to flexibilize elements of the French labour market against trade union opposition, but these measures had not proven popular and if they failed to rejuvenate the French economy, his support could melt away quite quickly (Schild 2017a). Particularly if by 2022 the mainstream left and right should have failed to rebuild themselves as credible political forces, he may face a far tougher challenge from the Eurosceptic radical right or radical left than he faced in 2017. Although Marine Le Pen's presidential bid failed, support for the *Front National* in the 2017 presidential and parliamentary elections was higher than ever before. Its continuing rise compelled the mainstream Right, following the 2017 elections, to choose a leader who aimed to reshape his party in a more national-populist guise to undercut the *Front National*'s appeal. Hence even if a 'mainstream' right-wing candidate should succeed Macron as French president, he may prove to be more Eurosceptic than his predecessors.

In Germany, the 2017 elections resulted in the spectacular breakthrough of the AfD, the first extreme right-wing, Eurosceptic party to win seats in the federal parliament since 1953. Germany was no longer exceptional in not having an extreme right-wing party in Parliament. With 12.6 per cent of the vote, the AfD became, following the return of the Grand Coalition government, the biggest opposition party. Its success would put existing parties, especially those of the centre-right, under greater pressure than hitherto to try to accommodate Eurosceptic strands in German public opinion, in turn making it prospectively more difficult for German governments to make the concessions required to hold the EU together. Support for the Grand Coalition parties had already slumped from 67 per cent in the 2013 elections to 53 per cent in 2017. An opinion survey conducted in July 2018, within a few months of the new government having been formed, found that support for the governing parties had already slumped to 47 per cent and, for the first time, at over 17 per cent, support for the AfD was as high as for the SPD (*Bild-Zeitung* 2018). If the erosion of support for the Grand Coalition should continue in the current parliamentary period, the AfD stood a good chance of being among its primary beneficiaries. Moreover, the continuation of such a trend would also imply that a government based on a parliamentary majority would have to include more parties than hitherto, making it, other things being equal, more difficult to form governments and for these governments, once formed, to provide stabilizing hegemonic leadership in the EU. For such a role, German governments would then no longer possess the domestic-political scope that they possessed, prior to the quadruple crisis, to promote closer European integration or, conceivably, the scope that they required to stave off growing European *disintegration*. All this suggested that the domestic political constellations in France and Germany might prove relatively favourable for European integration during the period up to 2022, but then could change significantly for the worse.

In other words, the years from 2018 to 2022 might represent a brief window of opportunity to build a stronger, more crisis-resilient EU that subsequent, new domestic political constellations would close a window that could actually be shut more quickly if, as was increasingly conceivable, the Grand Coalition government in Berlin should collapse prematurely.

Political trends elsewhere in the EU were more ominous than promising for the future of European integration. The Eurosceptic Freedom Party of Geert Wilders did not make the breakthrough that had been widely anticipated in the 2017 elections in the Netherlands. However, having narrowly failed to win the country's presidential elections in 2016, the Eurosceptic FPÖ increased its share of the vote in Austrian parliamentary elections from 20.5 to 26 per cent and entered into a governing coalition with the conservative ('pro-European') Austrian People's Party (ÖVP). Most strikingly and spectacularly, parliamentary elections in spring 2018 in Italy, historically one of the most 'pro-European' member states, witnessed an unprecedented success for Eurosceptic parties, which together won well over 50 per cent of the popular vote. The subsequent formation of a coalition government comprising these parties, the Five Star Movement and the League, raised the spectre of new crises, whether over refugees or, not least because Italy is far bigger than any state that was rescued between 2010 and 2015 and consequently far harder to bail out, in the Eurozone.

The election results in France, Germany, the Netherlands, Austria and Italy in 2017–18 were, of course, illustrative of a broader trend in the EU and wider Western liberal-democratic world, including the USA. For the most part, the creation of the Eurosceptic parties had preceded the quadruple crisis and their growth, not least in the case of Italy, had often had mainly nationally specific causes. Nonetheless, the EU's quadruple crisis – first the Eurozone Crisis, then, to an even greater extent, the Refugee Crisis – provided these parties with an enormous political boost (see Table 7.2). There might have been a lull in the quadruple crisis post-2016, but the political fallout from the crisis was still unfolding. While it is possible that some of the new Eurosceptic parties will fall apart and disappear again from their respective domestic political landscapes, as appears to have happened with the British UKIP, this seems less likely now than in the past, as their growth arguably reflects the emergence of a durable new open-closed, cosmopolitan-nationalist cultural cleavage in the party systems of the EU's member states (Inglehart and Norris 2016). It is conceivable that, in time, these parties will be integrated into the party systems and 'tamed' as happened with many radical left-wing parties in post-World War II Western Europe. Something like this occurred in Finland with the new Eurosceptic party, the 'True Finns', who entered the government and subsequently collapsed in disarray. The impact of the Eurosceptics' rise, however, is likely to depend primarily on the balance of power that emerges between them and the established parties. Where the Eurosceptic parties begin to gain the political upper hand, the established parties may equally adapt their stance on EU issues to their Eurosceptic counterparts rather than vice versa, as began to occur in France (see earlier in this section).

Table 7.2   *The decline of pro-European and the rise of anti-European parties during the EU's quadruple crisis, 2010–18*

20 largest member states; percentage of vote							
Member	Last pre-2010 elections			Most recent elections			2010/most recent elections
	AEL	PE	AER	AEL	PE	AER	AEL & AER
Austria	1	68	28	1	72	26	−2
Belgium	2	84	8	2	85	4	−4
Czech Rep	13	48	36	8	36	55	+14
Denmark	15	67	14	12	67	21	+4
Finland	9	79	4	7	69	18	+12
France	7	79	10	21	50	27	+31
Germany	12	83	2	9	73	13	+8
Greece	13	80	6	46	41	11	+38
Hungary	–	49	49	–	28	68	+19
Ireland	2	87	–	18	62	–	+16
Italy	5	81	11	1	38	56	+40
Netherlands	17	73	6	9	66	24	+10
Poland	–	64	33	4	45	52	+23
Portugal	18	77	–	20	70	–	+2
Spain	4	85	–	22	65	–	+18
Sweden	6	88	3	6	77	13	+10
UK	–	58	35	1	50	43	+9
Romania	–	74	5	–	92	5	0
Bulgaria	–	82	13	1	78	14	+2
Slovakia	4	79	12	1	61	35	+20

AEL = anti-European (Communist & far) Left.
PE = pro-European (Green, Social Democratic, Liberal, Christian Democratic & non-Eurosceptic Conservative) parties.
AER = anti-European (extreme, nationalist, national-populist and Eurosceptic Conservative) Right.
Parties have been classified primarily according to their group affiliations in the European Parliament: and, where they are divided in their attitudes to the EU, according to the mainstream sentiment in them.
Numbers set in bold indicate the evolution of the vote of anti-European parties of the Left and the Right.
Totals do not all add up to 100, because some minor parties could not be classified.
Percentages are for the presidential elections in France and for Parliamentary elections in the other 19 states.
The table excludes eight EU member states with population below 4.5 million (Estonia, Latvia, Lithuania, Slovenia, Croatia, Cyprus, Luxembourg and Malta).

With Eurosceptic parties on the rise and meanwhile in or on the verge of winning political office in numerous EU member states, domestic political environments in the EU are thus likely overall to change in ways more conducive to political *dis*integration than integration over the next decade. This may not matter too much for the fate of the EU if, during this period, the quadruple crisis can be contained, the EU is no longer in crisis mode, and, in Brussels, 'everyday politics' resumes. However, although there was a lull in the quadruple crisis after 2016, none of the four crises that constitute it had been resolved to the point where one could be certain that they would not flare up again, as the Schengen and Refugee Crisis then did in Germany and the EU in summer 2018 (see the conclusions of Chapters 3, 4 and 5). Moreover, the emergence of new crises could not be excluded – as the German expression goes, *die nächste Krise kommt bestimmt* – a new crisis is bound to come. The next one could concern the fundamental values on which the EU is founded and be unleashed by reforms adopted by the national-conservative and Eurosceptic government in Poland that the European Commission judged would undermine the rule of law. If a new crisis should develop or a pre-existing one should flare up again, the critical question is whether there will be a sufficient supply of stabilizing hegemonic leadership to hold the EU together – and which state or, more likely, coalition of states, if any, is capable of providing and willing to provide it.

Hegemonic leadership in the EU: alternatives to the 'hobbled' German hegemon?

This study has shown that, during the quadruple crisis, Germany alone was at best able to supply no more than spasmodic, intermittent stabilizing hegemonic leadership to the EU. It has proved a 'hobbled hegemon'. Initially, it was indeed the 'reluctant hegemon' (Paterson 2011). However, in the Eurozone Crisis it was less reluctant to lead as such than it was to provide the financial aid required to keep the Eurozone afloat. Then, as the new crises broke out alongside that of the Eurozone, German elites increasingly recognized that German leadership was indispensable to the EU's survival and rallied to the challenge of providing it. Neither Chancellor Merkel nor, less still, Finance Minister Schäuble were very reluctant about imposing extremely tough conditions on the provision of financial aid to Greece and other 'debtor' states in the Eurozone. Germany was nonetheless severely constrained in the extent to which it could supply stabilizing leadership to the EU. The magnitude of its advantage over other EU member states in terms of relative power resources is much smaller than that of other regional big powers vis-à-vis their neighbouring countries. It is indeed 'first among equals' in the contemporary EU, but it is not omnipotent. The way in which political power is dispersed and fragmented in Germany's federal system facilitates its capacity to veto EU-related projects that it opposes, but the same politico-institutional structure renders more difficult the purposeful use of its (potential) power to secure the adoption and implementation of those that it supports. Institutional, domestic-political and ideological-normative constraints prevented it playing the role of a stabilizing hegemon in the Eurozone Crisis. It failed to mobilize very broad support among other member states for its stance in the Refugee Crisis, in which many remained impervious to its appeals for them to accept more refugees, even when they were threatened with the withdrawal or reduction of financial transfers from the EU budget. Also on some issues in the Eurozone Crisis it found itself isolated. Its influence was greatest when other Eurozone members had their backs to the financial wall, German financial aid was indispensable for their rescue, and Germany's stance was backed by a large number of other 'creditor' states, mainly in Northern and Central Europe. Ultimately, it is only in the Ukraine Crisis that Germany played the role of a stabilizing hegemonic power virtually to perfection.

For the reasons discussed above, it is improbable, following the 2017 federal elections, that the German government will be better able and more willing to play the role of a stabilizing regional hegemon than it was during the last decade. If, in prospective future crises, stabilizing hegemonic leadership of the kind required to hold the EU together is to materialize, it will not come from Germany alone, albeit German participation in any such coalition will remain essential. Rather, such leadership will have to be provided by a hegemonic coalition. In theory at least, three such coalitions – and one alternative to a hegemonic coalition – are conceivable.

The one conceivable alternative to a hegemonic coalition would be a kind of *supranational 'Great Leap Forward'* leading to the creation of something much more akin than the contemporary EU to a federal European state. Some elements of such a project were visible in the rhetoric at least of French president Macron (Macron 2017). However, Macron's vision of the EU's future did not initially find a very strong echo in other member states and is also highly contested in France itself. Given how strongly the political wind was blowing against closer European integration in many other member states, it is unlikely that a federal European state in which supranational organs have far more extensive competences and far stronger powers vis-à-vis member states than is currently the case will see the light of day in the foreseeable future. Even those – probably few – governments that could warm to such a vision would be reluctant to entertain such a project where its adoption would require approval in popular referenda. The ECB will thus remain singular among supranational agencies in respect of its powers and authority vis-à-vis EU members. This means that there will be no other supranational EU agencies capable of staving off disintegration in other crises in the way that the ECB managed to achieve this in the Eurozone in 2012.

Among the three conceivable hegemonic coalitions, the politically most feasible one is a *rejuvenated Franco-German coalition* (see, e.g., Krotz and Schild 2018; Schild 2017a). Macron's election as French president in 2017 and the return of the Grand Coalition government in Berlin in 2018 created favourable political conditions for a resurrection of the EU's traditional leadership constellation. In a new such coalition, however, initially at least, the roles would likely be reversed compared with the last two decades in which France largely ceased to be a source of new integration initiatives. Paris would be looking to accelerate the speed of change, whereas, given the changed domestic political constellation in Germany, Berlin would be trying to slow it down, particularly in as far as French initiatives aimed at raising the volume of financial transfers between Eurozone member states. The German government recognized that, to hold the EU together, Macron was the best French president that it was ever likely to have. Worried that he might 'fail', it was prepared to help him and saw plenty of scope for compromises concerning his agenda for reforming the Eurozone (interview, Berlin, 2018). Macron's possible 'failure' – which would be visible in a decline in the level of his domestic political support – indeed represented the principal threat to a rejuvenation of the Franco-German tandem. This in turn would be shaped primarily by the success or failure of his efforts at domestic economic and social reform and to accelerate economic growth and reduce France's relatively high level of unemployment. Germany's capacity to assist Macron in mastering his domestic political challenges was, however, limited.

Even in the enlarged EU with 27 members, as was visible very sporadically during the quadruple crisis (most of all in the Ukraine Crisis), Franco-German cooperation can still be a powerful magnetic force in the EU and a bilateral Franco-German bargain can still often provide a template for a pan-EU agreement. The two states still represent, to a certain extent, 'opposite poles' in the EU towards which distinctive groups of other member states gravitate (former French foreign minister Maurice Couve de Murville, quoted in Webber 1999a: 127). Geographical proximity is the strongest determinant of cooperation patterns between EU member states (ECFR 2017). The northern member states tend to align themselves more closely with Germany and the more southern with France, so that a Franco-German bargain may lay the ground for a compromise that reconciles the interests of northern and southern member states (ECFR 2017). A rejuvenated Franco-German coalition, however, may not be able to mobilize the support of some of the Central and Eastern European member states. The gap between Macron's – and German – visions of the EU and those of notably the Eurosceptic Polish and Hungarian governments is vast. If a rejuvenated Franco-German coalition were to try to forge closer European integration in the near future, this would probably be possible only in the guise of a more differentiated, 'multi-speed' Europe that would decouple at least some of the Central and Eastern European member states more strongly from the rest of the EU than is currently the case. On this issue too, there had been a reversal of roles between France and Germany. Whereas, in the early 1990s, there was significant support in Germany for forging a 'hard-core' Europe, France was opposed, ostensibly fearing that it would not be able to balance German power in a 'hard-core' group from which all other Southern European member states would (at least initially) be excluded (Webber 2012). Now President Macron was an enthusiastic advocate of a multi-speed Europe and Chancellor Merkel, more concerned than him to hold the whole EU together, more reluctant (de Gruyter 2018; Macron 2017).

In principle, the political base of a rejuvenated Franco-German tandem could be widened and a more inclusive hegemonic coalition formed through the expansion of this bilateral cooperation to include Poland and, indirectly, Central and Eastern alongside Northern and Southern Europe. This could be labelled the *Weimar Coalition*, taking its name from the German town where triangular cooperation between France, Germany and Poland was launched in 1991. Given Poland's status as the largest Central and Eastern European EU member and its relatively close relationship with other Central and Eastern European EU members (ECFR 2017), these states would probably regard a trilateral coalition with Polish participation as being more legitimate than bilateral Franco-German leadership. Without a change in the domestic balance of political power in Poland, however, a Weimar Coalition would remain politically unfeasible. Under the national-conservative and Eurosceptic government of the Law and Justice Party in Warsaw since 2015, the Weimar Triangle itself has withered to the point of becoming moribund. No summit of the heads of the three governments has taken place since 2011. It is as likely at future elections that France and Germany will become more Eurosceptic as that Poland will become more 'pro-European'.

The third and final (theoretically) conceivable hegemonic coalition is what might be termed the *Hanseatic Coalition*. This label refers to the association of trading cities that stretched from the Netherlands in the west to the Baltic sea coast in the east from roughly the thirteenth to the fifteenth centuries and had the north German city of Lubeck as its centre. A Hanseatic Coalition would include Germany and the eight other member states whose finance ministers began to meet in early 2018 to discuss alternative proposals to those of France and Germany for reforming the Eurozone and whose cooperation was christened as the 'new Hanseatic League': Ireland, the Netherlands, Sweden, Denmark, Finland and the three Baltic states, Estonia, Latvia and Lithuania (Khan 2018). Some of these states, above all the Netherlands, already cooperate very closely with Germany in the EU (European Council on Foreign Relations 2017; Zunneberg 2017; interview, Berlin, 2018). There is some support in German foreign policy circles for deepening this cooperation (interview, Berlin, 2018). On monetary, fiscal and EU budget policy issues, they are normally closer to Germany than is Germany to France (interview, Berlin, 2018). However, despite comprising a subgroup of economically strong, albeit small, members apart from Germany itself, a Hanseatic Coalition would rest on too narrow a political base to be able to provide hegemonic leadership to the EU. It would not be able to integrate and mobilize the support of Southern and most Central and Eastern European members – unless it was broadened to include France. It is not obvious, however, that Germany could mediate effectively between the other 'Hanseatics', on the one hand, and France, on the other and play a successful long-term broker role between these two sides. If it could not, it is difficult to conceive that it would risk its uniquely close bilateral relationship with the big power France in favour of a closer one with a large group of small member states. To try to lead the EU with a Hanseatic coalition without France would heighten the risk of creating a cleavage and split between Northern and Southern Europe that, historically, close bilateral Franco-German cooperation has served to avert.

As far ahead as one can see, the rejuvenation of the Franco-German tandem thus still offers the best chance of providing stabilizing hegemonic leadership to the EU. The quadruple crisis has shown that, for the most part, this is not a task that Germany can shoulder well alone. Following the 2017 elections, a window of opportunity opened for Berlin and Paris to consolidate and strengthen the EU and make it more resilient in the face of new or the reintensification of already existing crises. It is not certain that they will seize it or that, if they do, they will succeed. Given the rising tide of Euroscepticism across the EU, including in France and Germany, this task will prove more difficult than before. But if this opportunity should be left unexploited, there is a high risk that future crises will result in greater European political disintegration than occurred in the quadruple crisis post-2010.

References

Achen, Christopher H. (2006) 'Evaluating Political Decision-Making Models', in Robert Thomson, Frans N. Stokman, Christopher H. Achen and Thomas König (eds), *The European Union Decides*. Cambridge: Cambridge University Press.

Ademmer, Esther, Barsbai, Toman, Lücke, Matthias and Stöhr, Tobias (2015) *30 Years of Schengen: Internal Blessing, External Curse?* Kiel: Kiel Institute for the World Economy, no. 88, June, 15pp.

Adonis, Andrew (2017) 'Tony Blair and Europe: shattering the Ming vase', lecture delivered at Hertford College, Oxford, 10 November https://www.prospectmagazine.co.uk/politics/tony-blair-and-europe-shattering-the-ming-vase.

Aeschemann, Eric and Riché, Pascal (1996) *La guerre de sept ans*. Paris: Calmann-Levy.

Agnew, Harriet (2015) 'City divided on UK relationship with EU', *Financial Times*, 8 February.

Agnew, Harriet and Parker, George (2015) 'Hedge funds boost campaign to keep Britain in the EU', *Financial Times*, 12 November.

Alexander, Robin (2017) *Die Getriebenen. Merkel und die Flüchtlingspolitik: Report aus dem Innern der Macht*. Munich: Siedler.

Anderson, Perry (2017) *The H-Word: The Peripeteia of Hegemony*. London and New York: Verso.

ARD (*Arbeitsgemeinschaft der öffentlich-rechtlichen Rundfunkanstalten der Bundesrepublik Deutschland* – Consortium of the Public Broadcasters in the Federal Republic of Germany) (2015) 'Wolfgang Schäuble: Macht und Ohnmacht', television documentary broadcast in Germany, 24 August.

Ashcroft, Lord (2016) 'EU Referendum "How Did You Vote?" Poll'.

The Atlantic.com (2015) 'A Controversial Plan to Redistribute Migrants in Europe', 22 September.

Attali, Jacques (1993) *Verbatim*, Vol. 1. Paris: Fayard.

Attali, Jacques (1995a) *Verbatim*, Vol. 2. Paris: Fayard.

Attali, Jacques (1995b) *Verbatim*, Vol. 3. Paris: Fayard.

Aust, Stefan, Bewarder, Manuel, Büscher, Wolfgang, Lutz, Martin, Malzahn, Claus Christian (2015) 'Herbst der Kanzlerin. Geschichte eines Staatsversagens', *Die Welt am Sonntag*, 9 November.

Balkhausen, Dieter (1992) *Gutes Geld & Schlechte Politik*. Düsseldorf: ECON.

Barber, Lionel and Norman, Peter (2001) 'Prodi strikes back', *Financial Times*, 5 December.

Barber, Tony (2015) 'Greece must be saved from political, economic and social collapse', *Financial Times*, 27 June.

Barroso, José Manuel Durão (2011) 'A Europe for all weathers' (speech at meeting with EU Heads of Delegation) (speech/11/838), Brussels, 30 November.

Barthon de Montbas, Alexandre (2010) 'EU or European Differentiated Integration? The Prüm Convention and the Dangers for the EU of Integration Competition'. Fontainebleau: INSEAD, unpublished manuscript.

Bartolini, Stefano (2005) *Restructuring Europe: Centre Formation, System Building, and Political Structuring between the Nation State and the European Union*. Oxford and New York: Oxford University Press.

Bastasin, Carlo (2015) *Saving Europe: How National Politics Nearly Destroyed the Euro*. Washington, DC: Brookings Institution.

Batsaikhan, Uuriituya (2016) 'Child benefits for EU migrants in the UK', *Blogpost Bruegel* Brussels: Bruegel Institute, 18 February.

Bauer, Michael W. and Becker, Stefan (2014) 'The Unexpected Winner of the Crisis: The European Commission's Strengthened Role in Economic Governance', *Journal of European Integration*, 36(3), 213–229.

Baumann, Mechthild (2006) *Der deutsche Fingerabdruck: Die Rolle der deutschen Bundesregierung bei der Europäisierung der Grenzpolitik*. Baden-Baden: Nomos.

Bechev, Dimitar and Buras, Piotr (2014) 'Consequences of Ukraine: Europe's fragile cohesion', commentary, European Council on Foreign Relations, 20 May.

Becker, Peter and Maurer, Andreas (2009) Deutsche Integrationsbremsen, *SWP-Aktuell 41*. Berlin: Stiftung Wissenschaft und Politik.

Becker, Stefan, Bauer, Michael W., Connolly, Sarah and Kassim, Hussein (2016) 'The Commission: Boxed in and Constrained, But Still an Engine of Integration', *West European Politics*, 39(5), 1011–1031.

Bender, Peter (1986) *Neue Ostpolitik: Vom Mauerbau bis zum Moskauer Vertrag*. Munich: Deutscher Taschenbuch Verlag.

Benner, Thorsten (2016) 'Europe's lonely liberal hegemon', *Politico*, 2 March.

Berliner Morgenpost (2017) https://interaktiv.morgenpost.de/analyse-bundestag-swahl-2017/

Bernard, Philippe (2014) 'La surenchère Europhobe de David Cameron', *Le Monde*, 5 November.

Bickerton, Christopher J., Hodson, Dermot and Puetter, Uwe (2015) 'The New Intergovernmentalism: European Integration in the Post-Maastricht Era', *Journal of Common Market Studies* 53:4: 703–722, 1–20.

Bieber, Roland (1995) 'Schlußbetrachtung: Schengen als Modell zukünftiger Integration?', in Alberto Achermann, Roland Bieber, Astrid Epiney and Ruth Wehner (eds), *Schengen und die Folgen: Der Abbau der Grenzkontrollen in Europa*. Bern/Munich/Vienna: Stämpfli/Beck/Manzsche Verlags- und Universitätsbuchhandlung, pp. 179–186.

Bild-Zeitung (2018) 'Groko erreicht nur noch 47 Prozent Zustimmung', 15 July.

Bloomberg (2015) 'Greek polls show Samaras is running out of time', 8 January.

Blustein, Paul (2017) *Laid Low: Inside the Crisis that Overwhelmed Europe and the IMF*. Waterloo: Centre for International Governance Innovation.

Börzel, Tanja (2005) 'Mind the Gap! European Integration between Level and Scope', *Journal of European Public Policy*, 12(2), 217–236.

Börzel, Tanja and Risse, Thomas (2016) 'Three Cheers for Comparative Regionalism', in Tanja A. Börzel and Thomas Risse (eds), *The Oxford Handbook of Comparative Regionalism*. Oxford: Oxford University Press, pp. 621–647.

Bosch, Xavier Vanden (2013) 'Contractual Arrangements: The Overlooked Step Towards a Fiscal Union', in *European Policy Brief*. Brussels: Egmont – Royal Institute for International Relations, December.

Bösche, Monika (2006) 'Trapped Inside the European Fortress? Germany and European Union Asylum and Refugee Policy', in Gunther Hellmann (ed), *Germany's EU Policy on Asylum and Defence: De-Europeanization by Default?* Basingstoke and New York: Palgrave Macmillan, pp. 29–90.

Bozo, Frédéric (2009) *Mitterrand, the End of the Cold War, and German Unification*. New York/Oxford: Berghahn.

Brandt, Willy (1993) *Erinnerungen*. Berlin: Ullstein.

Brattberg, Erik and Pires de Lima, Bernardo (2015) 'Berlin's Unipolar Moment', *Berlin Policy Journal*, July (https://berlinpolicyjournal.com/germanys-unipolar-moment/).

Braun, Stefan (2018) 'Asylstreit: Fehler, Mythen und Lügen in der Flüchtlingskrise', *Süddeutsche Zeitung*, 28 June.

Brinkmann, Bastian (2014) 'Die Rechnung, bitte', www.sueddeutsche.de, 14 March.

Brunnermeier, Markus K., James, Harold and Landau, Jean-Pierre (2016) *The Euro and the Battle of Ideas*. Princeton and Oxford: Princeton University Press.

Buisson, Patrick (2016) *La cause du peuple: L'histoire interdite de la présidence Sarkozy*. Paris: Perrin.

Bulmer, Simon and Paterson, William E. (1987) *The Federal Republic of Germany and the European Community*. London: Allen and Unwin.

Bulmer, Simon and Paterson, William E. (2010) Germany and the European Union: From "Tamed Power" to Normalized Power? *International Affairs*, 86(5), 1051–1073.

Bulmer, Simon and Paterson, William E. (2011) 'A Life More Ordinary? Ten Theses on a Normalization of Germany's Role in the EU', paper presented at the European Studies Association biennial conference, Boston, 3–5 March.

Bulmer, Simon (2011) 'Shop Till You Drop? The German Executive as Venue-Shopper in Justice and Home Affairs', in Petra Bendel, Andreas Ette and Roderick Parkes (eds), *The Europeanization of Control: Venues and Outcomes in EU Justice and Home Affairs Cooperation*. Berlin: Lit Verlag, 41–76.

Bulmer, Simon and Paterson, William E. (2017) 'Germany and the European Union Crises: Asset or Liability?', in Desmond Dinan, Neill Nugent and William E. Paterson (eds), *The European Union in Crisis*. Basingstoke: Palgrave Macmillan, pp. 212–232.

Bundesverfassungsgericht (2011) 'Headnotes to the judgment of the Second Senate of 7 September 2011' (Karlsruhe).

Buras, Piotr (2013) 'The EU's Silent Revolution', *Policy Brief*, Vol. 87. London: European Council on Foreign Relations, September.

Cameron, David (2015) 'A New Settlement for the United Kingdon in a Reformed European Union' (letter to the European Council President Donald Tusk), 10 November.

Candon, George (2015) 'Brexit: The views of Cameron's counterparts', *FTI Consulting*, 3 November.

Carrera, Sergio and den Hertog, Leonhard (2016) 'A European Border and Coast Guard: What's in a Name?' Brussels: Centre for European Policy Studies, Paper in Liberty and Security in Europe No. 88, March.

Chase-Dunn, Christopher., Kawano, Yukio and Brewer, Benjamin D. (2000) 'Trade Globalization since 1795: Waves of Integration in the World-System', *American Sociological Review*, 65 (February), 77–95.

Chastand, Jean-Baptiste and Stolz, Joëlle (2015) 'Le mauvais genie de l'Europe', 24 September.

Checkel, Jeffrey. (2006) 'Social Construction and Integration', in M. Eilstrup-Sangiovanni (ed), *Debates on European Integration: A Reader*. Basingstoke: Palgrave Macmillan, pp. 406–419.

Chollet, Derek (2016) *The Long Game: How Obama Defied Washington and Redefined America's Role in the World*. New York: PublicAffairs.

Christie, Edward Hunter (2016) 'The Design and Impact of Western Economic Sanctions Against Russia', *The RUSI Journal*, 161(3), 52–64.

Clark, Ian (2011) *Hegemony in International Society*. Oxford: Oxford University Press.

Clegg, Nick (2016a) 'Cameron and Osborne are to blame for this sorry pass', *Financial Times*, 25–26 June.

Clegg, Nick (2016b) *Politics: Between the Extremes*. London: The Bodley Head.

Cohen, Benjamin (1998) *The Geography of Money*. Ithaca, NY: Cornell University Press.

Cohen-Tanugi, Laurent (2005) 'The End of Europe?' *Foreign Affairs*, 84(6) (November–December), 55–67.

Connolly, Bernard (1995) *The Rotten Heart of Europe: The Dirty War for Europe's Money*. London: Faber & Faber.

Conservative Party (2010) *Invitation to Join the Government of Britain. The Conservative Manifesto 2010*. London: Conservative Party.

Conservative Party (2015) *Strong Leadership, A Clear Economic Plan, A Brighter, More Secure Future. The Conservative Manifesto 2015*. London: Conservative Party.

Copelovitch, Mark, Frieden, Jeffrey and Walter, Stefanie (2016) 'The Political Economy of the Euro Crisis', *Comparative Political Studies*, 49(7), 811–840.

Council of the EU (2015) 'Council decision (EU) 2015/1601 of 22 September 2015 establishing provisional measures in the area of international protection for the benefit of Italy and Greece', *Official Journal of the European Union* L 248/81 (Brussels).

Council of the EU (2016) 'EU-Turkey statement, 18 March 2016'.

Curtice, John (2017) 'Why Leave Won the UK's EU Referendum', *The JCMS Annual Review of the European Union in 2016*, 19–37.

D'Ancona, Matthew (2016) 'Brexit: How a fringe idea took hold of the Tory party', *The Guardian*, 15 June.

Damro, Chad (2012) 'Market Power Europe', *Journal of European Public Policy*, 19(5), 682–699.

Daneshku, Scheherazade (2016) 'Many British farms not viable without EU support, says NFU', *Financial Times*, 18 April.

Das Parlament (2011a) *DebattenDokumentation*. Peer Steinbrück: 'Europa ist Freizügigkeit, Medien- und Pressefreiheit': 2–3 and Volker Kauder: 'Hier findet ein bedeutender Paradigmenwechsel statt': 1. No. 40–42, 4 October.

Das Parlament (2011b) *DebattenDokumentation*. Angela Merkel: 'Der deutsche Anteil bleibt bei 211 Milliarden Euro', no. 44–45, 31 October: 1–3.

Das Parlament (2012) *DebattenDokumentation*. Angela Merkel: 'Europa scheitert, wenn der Euro scheitert': 1–2 and Peer Steinbrück: 'Das zweite Griechenland-Paket ist auf sehr dunnes Eis gesetzt', no. 10, 5 March: 3–4.

Das Parlament (2013) *DebattenDokumentation*. Wolfgang Schäuble: 'Zur Überwindung der Krise gibt es keine einfache und schnelle Lösung', no. 17, 22 April: 1–2.

Das Parlament (2015a) *DebattenDokumentation*. Thomas Oppermann: 'Wir müssen vom Ich zum Wir kommen', no. 26–27, 22 June, pp. 9–10.

Das Parlament (2015b) *DebattenDokumentation*. Angela Merkel: 'Die Welt schaut auch auf uns': 1 and Sigmar Gabriel: 'Sinn des Referendums ist unklar', 5–7, no. 28–30, 6 July.

Davet, Gérard and Lhomme, Fabrice (2016a) 'Le jour où Poutine a rencontré Poroshenko', *Le Monde*, 26 August.

Davet, Gérard and Lhomme, Fabrice (2016b) *"Un président ne devrait pas dire ça": Les secrets d'un quinquennat*. Paris: Stock.

Davis Cross, Mai'a and Karolewski, Ireneusz (2017) 'What Type of Power Has the EU Exercised in the Ukraine-Russia Crisis? A Framework of Analysis', *Journal of Common Market Studies*, 55(1), 3–19.

Davis, Dane and Gift, Thomas (2014) 'The Positive Effects of the Schengen Agreement on European Trade', *The World Economy* 37:11: 1541–1557.

De Gaulle, Charles (2000) *Mémoires*. Paris: Gallimard.

De Gruyter, Caroline (2018) 'There is Life for the EU After Brexit', (http://www.ecfr.eu/article/commentary_there_is_life_for_the_eu_after_brexit), 28 March.

De Wilde, Pieter, Leupold Anna and Schmidtke, Henning (2016) 'Introduction: The Differentiated Politicisation of European Governance', *West European Politics*, 39(2), 3–22.

Delors, Jacques (1992) *Le nouveau concert européen*. Paris: Odile Jacob.

Delreux, Tom and Keukeleire, Stephan (2017) 'Informal Division of Labour in EU Foreign Policy-Making', *Journal of European Public Policy*, 24(10), 1471–1490.

Dempsey, Judy (2013) 'Is This Ukraine's Turning Point?' Commentary, *Strategic Europe*, 9 December.

Dempsey, Judy (2014) 'Europe's Weakness over Russia', commentary, *Strategic Europe* commentary, 17 July.

Dempsey, Judy (2016) 'Judy Dempsey's *Strategic Europe*: Merkel, Isolated and With No Plan B', *Carnegie Europe*, 21 January.

Denman, Roy (1997) *Missed Chances: Britain and Europe in the Twentieth Century*. London: Cassell.

Dennison, James and Geddes, Andrew (2018) 'Brexit and the Perils of "Europeanised" Migration', *Journal of European Public Policy*, 25(8), 1137–1153.

Der Spiegel (1984) 'Wir müssen wie Wölfe sein', no. 9.

Der Spiegel (1991) 'Eine historische Entscheidung?' 21 October.

Der Spiegel (2013) 'Janukowitsch brüskiert den Westen', 11 December.

Der Spiegel (2014a) 'Rote Linie, roter Kopf', no. 45, 3 November.

Der Spiegel (2014b) 'Steinmeiers Mission in Kiew: Der Marathon-Diplomat', 22 February.

Der Spiegel (2014c) 'Gas, Öl, Autos, Maschinen: So eng sind Deutschland und Russland verflochten', 5 March.

Der Spiegel (2014d) 'Beyond Ukraine: Russia's Imperial Mess', 10 March.

Der Spiegel (2014e) 'Verheugen zur EU-Russlandpolitik: Warum Helmut Schmidt irrt', 19 May.

Der Spiegel (2014f) 'Deutsche befürworten härtere Sanktionen gegen Putin', 27 July.

Der Spiegel (2014g) 'Putin droht mit Einmarsch in Riga und Warschau', 18 September.

Der Spiegel (2015a) 'Luxemburgs Außenminister warnt vor Zerfall der EU', 9 November.

Der Spiegel (2015b) '"Putin will Respekt"' (interview with historian Fiona Hill), 7 February.

Der Spiegel (2016a) 'Putins Aggressionen', 20 February.

Der Spiegel (2016b) 'Ostdeutsche Ministerpräsidenten lehnen neue Russland-Sanktionen ab', 11 October.

Der Spiegel (2016c) '"Wir müssen Deutschland helfen"', 22 January.

Der Spiegel (2017) 'Ukraine wirft Gabriel "Geshaker mit dem Kreml" vor', 6 September.

Deutsch, Karl W. (1957) *Political Community and the North Atlantic Area*. Princeton: Princeton University Press.

Deutsche Gruppe in der Fraktion der Europäischen Volkspartei des Europäischen Parlaments (1984) 'Christdemokraten fordern Beseitigung der Grenzkontrollen', *Nachrichten aus Europa: Pressemitteilung* no. 19, 23 February.

Deutscher Bundestag (1991) *Plenarprotokoll 12/68. Stenographischer Bericht, 68. Sitzung*. Bonn, Friday, 13 December.

Deutscher Bundestag (2015) *Plenarprotokoll 18/120. Stenographischer Bericht, 120. Sitzung.* Berlin, Wednesday, 9 September.

Die Zeit (1984) 'Unterwegs im Mittelalter', 2 March.

Dinan, Desmond (2017) 'Crises in EU History', in Desmond Dinan, Neill Nugent and William E. Paterson (eds), *The European Union in Crisis.* London: Palgrave Macmillan, pp. 16–32.

Dorling, Danny (2016) 'Brexit: The Decision of a Divided Country', *British Medical Journal,* 7 July: 1–2 (https://www.bmj.com/content/354/bmj.i3697)

Drozdiak, William (2017) *Fractured Continent: Europe's Crises and the Fate of the West.* New York: WW Norton.

Duchêne, François (1972) 'Europe's Role in World Peace', in R. Mayne (ed), *Europe Tomorrow.* London: Fontana, pp. 32–47.

Dumas, Roland (2007) *Affaires Étrangères I. 1981–1988.* Paris: Fayard.

Dyson, Kenneth and Featherstone, Kevin (1999) *The Road to Maastricht: Negotiating Economic and Monetary Union.* Oxford: Oxford University Press.

ECFR (European Council on Foreign Relations) (2017) *EU Coalition Explorer.* London: European Council on Foreign Relations, May.

The Economist (2011a) 'How to save the Euro', 17 September.

The Economist (2011b) 'Is this really the end?' 26 November.

The Economist (2013a) 'Charlemagne: Angela all alone', 20 December.

The Economist (2013b) 'Charlemagne: Playing East against West', 23 November.

The Economist (2014a) 'Charlemagne: Keep the door open', 8 February.

The Economist (2014b) 'Charlemagne: Disarmed diplomacy', 8 March.

The Economist (2014c) 'The international reaction: Sixes and sevens', 8 March.

The Economist (2014d) 'Russia and Ukraine: The home front', 15 March.

The Economist (2014e) 'The war in Ukraine: Reversal of fortune', 6 September.

The Economist (2014f) 'Bagehot: Wooing Mrs Merkel', 1 March.

The Economist (2015a) 'Orban the archetype', 19 September: 25.

The Economist (2015b) 'Point taken, Mr Orban', 26 September: 27.

The Economist (2015c) 'Charlemagne: Battling with Britain', 12 December.

The Economist (2016a) 'Europe's migrant crisis: Forming an orderly queue', 6 February, pp. 17–20.

The Economist (2016b) 'Charlemagne: An ill wind', 23 January, p. 22.

The Economist (2016c) 'Putting up barriers', 6 February, p. 18.

The Economist (2016d) 'Charlemagne: The bystander', 10 March, p. 24.

The Economist (2016e) 'The immigration paradox', 16 July.

The Economist (2017) 'Free exchange: Not enough Europe', 18 February: 64.

Eichenberg, Richard C. and Dalton, Russell J. (2007) 'Post-Maastricht Blues: The Transformation of Citizen Support for European Integration', *Acta Politica,* 42, 128–152.

Eilstrup-Sangiovanni, M. (ed) (2006) *Debates on European Integration: A Reader.* Basingstoke: Palgrave Macmillan.

Eisel, Horst (2009) (former high-level civil servant, German Federal Interior Ministry), interview, Bonn-Sankt Augustin, 30 December.

Enderlein, Henrik, Letta, Enrico *et al.* (2016) *Repair and Prepare: Growth and the Euro after Brexit.* Gütersloh, Berlin, Paris: Bertelsmann Stiftung, Jacques Delors Institut-Berlin, Jacques Delors Institute Paris.

Entous, Adam and Norman, Laurence (2014) 'Behind the West's Miscalculations in Ukraine', *Dow Jones,* 3 March.

Epiney, Astrid (1995) 'Das zweite Schengener Abkommen: Entstehung, Konzept und Einbettung in die Europäischen Union', in Alberto Achermann, Roland Bieber, Astrid Epiney and Ruth Wehner (eds), *Schengen und die Folgen: Der Abbau der Grenzkontrollen in Europa*. Bern/Munich/Vienna: Stämpfli/Beck/Manzche Verlags- und Universitätsbuchhandlung, pp. 21–50.

Epstein, Rachel and Rhodes, Martin (2016a) 'International in Life, National in Death? Banking Nationalism on the Road to Banking Union', in James A. Caporaso and Martin Rhodes (eds), *The Political and Economic Dynamics of the Eurozone Crisis*. Oxford: Oxford University Press, pp. 200–232.

Epstein, Rachel A. and Rhodes, Martin (2016b) 'The Political Dynamics Behind Europe's New Banking Union', *West European Politics*, 39(3), 415–437.

Eurobarometer 77 (2012a) *Public Opinion in the European Union. First Results*. Brussels: European Commission Directorate-General for Communication, Spring.

Eurobarometer 78 (2012b) *Public Opinion in the European Union. First Results*. Brussels: European Commission Directorate-General for Communication, Autumn.

Eurobarometer (2015) *Public Opinion in the European Union* (no. 84, autumn).

Eurocomment (2014a) *Preliminary Evaluation, 2014/1: The Extraordinary European Council of 6 March 2014*.

Eurocomment (2014b) *Preliminary Evaluation 2014/2: The European Council of 20–21 March 2014*.

Eurocomment (2014c) *Special Briefing, 2014/2: The Special Meeting of the European Council of 30 August 2014*.

Eurocomment (2014d) *Preliminary Evaluation, 2014/4: June, July and August 2014*.

Eurocomment (2014e) *Preliminary Evaluation 2014/6: December 2014 – A New Beginning?*

Eurocomment (2014f) *October 2014: Climate and Energy, Economic Policy, Ebola and Ukraine, plus an annex on the UK's problems with the EU budget* (Preliminary Evaluation 2014/5).

Eurocomment (2015a) 'The Refugee Crisis' (Preliminary Evaluation 2015/8) 23 September.

Eurocomment (2015b) 'The Refugee Crisis Plus an Annex on EMU and the British Question' (Preliminary Evaluation 2015/9), 15 October.

Eurocomment (2015c) 'The Special European Council Meeting on Migration Policy in Valletta' (Preliminary Evaluation 2015/10), 12 November.

Eurocomment (2015d) 'The EU-Turkey Summit', 29 November.

Eurocomment (2015e) '17–18 December 2015' (Preliminary Evaluation 2015/12).

Eurocomment (2016a) *The British Problem and Migration Policy* (Pre-summit briefing 2016/1).

Eurocomment (2016b) *David Cameron's deal with the EU* (Commentary 2016/2).

Eurocomment (2016c) *February and March 2016: Migration Policy, the British Question and Economic Policy* (European Council Briefing Note 2016/1–3).

European Commission (1975) *Eurobarometer 3*. Brussels: European Commission.

European Commission (2015a) *Eurobarometer 83* spring.

European Commission (2015b) *Eurobarometer 84* autumn.

European Council (2001) 'Laeken Declaration on the Future of the European Union' (Brussels)

European Council (2014a) 'Informal Meeting of Heads of State and Government on Ukraine -6 March 2014. Statement', 6 March.

European Council (2014b) 'Statement by the President of the European Council Herman van Rompuy and the President of the European Commission in the name of the European Union on the agreed additional restrictive measures against Russia', 29 July.

Eurostat (2013) 'Record levels for trade in goods between EU27 and Russia in 2012', 83/2013, 3 June.

Eurostat (2015) 'Asylum in the EU Member States: More than 410 000 first time asylum seekers registered in the third quarter of 2015', *Eurostate Newsrelease* 217/2015 (10 December).

Evans, Geoffrey and Menon, Anand (2017) *Brexit and British Politics*. Cambridge and Medford: Polity Press.

Eyal, Jonathan (2016) 'Immigration blunders that led to Brexit', *The Straits Times* (Singapore), 4 July.

Fabbrini, Sergio (2013) 'Intergovernmentalism and its Limits: Assessing the European Union's Answer to the Euro Crisis', *Comparative Political Studies*, 46(9), 1003–1029.

Faigle, Phillip, Polke-Majewski, Karsten and Venohr, Sascha (2016) 'It Really Wasn't Merkel', *Zeit Online*, 11 October.

Federal Foreign Office (2017) 'Foreign Minister Gabriel on the Independence Day of Ukraine', 24 August.

Ferguson, Niall (2015) 'Fairy tales that conceal the meaning of Minsk', *Financial Times*, 14–15 February.

Financial Times (2009) 'Germany ready to take steps to support eurozone', 19 February.

Financial Times (2011a) 'Europe thinks the unthinkable to solve the debt crisis', 30 September.

Financial Times (2011b) 'Dutch favour tough approach', 11 October.

Financial Times (2011c) 'A weekend to save the euro', 20 October.

Financial Times (2011d) 'Sarkozy softens stance before summit', 26 October.

Financial Times (2011e) 'France and Germany agree new rules', 5 December.

Financial Times (2011f) 'Crisis shows signs of bursting Brussels bubble', 20 December.

Financial Times (2012a) 'Speaking truth to German power' (editorial), 16 January.

Financial Times (2012b) 'Eurozone divisions threaten Greece aid', 14 February.

Financial Times (2012c) 'Berlin split on Greek bailout', 17 February.

Financial Times (2012d) 'ECB "ready to do whatever it takes"', 26 July.

Financial Times (2012e) 'Draghi stance attracts political support', 28–29 July.

Financial Times (2012f) 'A Berlin-Frankfurt alliance for the euro', 30 August.

Financial Times (2012g) 'Businesses call for urgent action on euro', 5 September.

Financial Times (2012h) 'Weidmann isolated as ECB plan approved', 6 September.

Financial Times (2012i) 'Merkel keeps counsel as judges rule', 10 September.

Financial Times (2012j) 'France seeks more time for Greece', 24 September.

Financial Times (2013a) 'Solidarity for solidity drives Berlin debate on "bail-in" rescue', 19 March.

Financial Times (2013b) 'The blunt-speaking reformer who shocked the eurozone', 30–31 March.

Financial Times (2013c) 'German growth figures set to offer election boost to Merkel', 23 August.

Financial Times (2013d) 'Germany and France close on banking union deal', 9 December.

Financial Times (2013e) 'Banking union falls short of EU goal', 20 December.

Financial Times (2013f) 'An exercise in prolonging a bank credit' (W Munchau), 22 December.

Financial Times (2013g) 'Ukraine serves Putin a foreign policy triumph', 21 November.

Financial Times (2013h) 'Thousands take to streets in Kiev after EU deal delayed', 24 November.

Financial Times (2013i) 'Britain and its place within the EU' (excerpts of 'Bloomberg Speech' by Prime Minister David Cameron), 22 January.

Financial Times (2013j) 'Tories split on halting populist upstart', 24 May.

Financial Times (2014a) 'Ex-Barroso aide attacks Brussels on austerity', 8 April.

Financial Times (2014b) 'Russia rattles sabres over fate of Crimea', 21 February.

Financial Times (2014c) 'Obama faces his sternest challenge', 3 March.

Financial Times (2014d) 'Ukraine Crisis tests Berlin's new "culture of engagement"', 5 March.

Financial Times (2014e) 'Scope for sanctions on Russia divides EU', 6 March.

Financial Times (2014f) 'Crimea occupation casts shadow of 1940 over Baltic nations', 12 March.

Financial Times (2014g) 'Europe will feel the bite if it cuts off Moscow', 20 March.

Financial Times (2014h) 'Grieving Dutch reconsider trade relationship with Moscow', 26–27 July.

Financial Times (2014i) 'Germany pledges to keep UK in Europe', 30 June.

Financial Times (2015a) 'Berlin insists it expects Greece to remain in eurozone', 4 January.

Financial Times (2015b) 'Merkel faces growing dilemma over Greece', 5 January.

Financial Times (2015c) 'Sapin open to debt dialogue with Greece', 18 January.

Financial Times (2015d) 'Critics fear ECB quantitative easing will lead to crisis', 22 January.

Financial Times (2015e) 'How Europe's power couple split over QE', 24–25 January.

Financial Times (2015f) 'Alexis Tsipras loses Sigmar Gabriel, his last best hope in Germany', 8 July.

Financial Times (2015g) 'Battle for Ukraine: How the west lost Putin', 2 February.

Financial Times (2015h) 'Battle for Ukraine: How a diplomatic success unravelled', 3 February.

Financial Times (2015i) 'Putin was ready to put nuclear weapons on alert in Crimea crisis', 15 March.

Financial Times (2015j) 'Nemtsov's final report says 220 Russian troops have died in Ukraine', 13 May.

Financial Times (2015k) 'Brussels in fresh push to share out asylum seekers across EU', 20 August.

Financial Times (2015l) 'Merkel and Hollande call for equal spread of refugees across EU', 24 August.

Financial Times (2015m) 'Migrant flows put EU's Schengen under pressure', 1 September.

Financial Times (2015n) 'Europe's eastern states temper stance on refugees', 4 September.

Financial Times (2015o) 'German system creaks under weight of arrivals', 15 September.

Financial Times (2015p) 'German ministers at odds over migrant influx', 20 September.

Financial Times (2015q) 'France will live under terror threat for "several years"', 24 November.

Financial Times (2015r) 'Refugee influx threatens fall of EU, warns Dutch PM', 26 November.

Financial Times (2015s) 'EU stalls over drive to resettle refugees in Turkey', 17 December.

Financial Times (2016a) '"My view was we don't swerve"' (interview with Yanis Varoufakis), 26–27 March.

Financial Times (2016b) 'German blames Mario Draghi for rise of rightwing AfD party', 10 April.

Financial Times (2016c) 'Merkel stance on Russia faces SPD challenge', 23 June.

Financial Times (2016d) 'A last chance to rescue Europe's Schengen pact', 20 January.

Financial Times (2016e) 'Angela Merkel: Lots of foes, fewer friends', 16 February.

Financial Times (2016f) 'EU leaders in disarray over Refugee Crisis', 20–21 February.

Financial Times (2016g) 'EU border controls would cost bloc E470bn, says German think-tank', 22 February.

Financial Times (2016h) 'Turkish rewrite', 8 March.

Financial Times (2016i) 'Donald Tusk moves to patch up migrant deal with Turkey', 15 March.

Financial Times (2016j) 'EU and Turkey harden positions over latest migration plan', 18 March.

Financial Times (2017) 'Economic divide stretches case for EU integration', 13 September.

Financial Times (2018a) 'Dijsselbloem and the lessons of the Eurozone debt crisis', 12 January.

Financial Times (2018b) 'Tsipras warms to role as EU insider and populism critic', 29 June.

Financial Times (2018c) 'The five scenarios for Brexit Britain', 11 July.

Financial Times (2018d) 'German peace deal leaves Merkel's authority dented', 4 July.

Fischer, Joschka (2014) *Scheitert Europa?* Cologne: Kiepenheuer and Witsch.

Fligstein, Neil (2008) *Euro-Clash: The EU, European Identity, and the Future of Europe*. Oxford: Oxford University Press.

Fontana, Cary and Parsons, Craig (2015) '"One Woman's Prejudice": Did Margaret Thatcher Cause Britain's Anti-Europeanism?' *Journal of Common Market Studies*, 53(1) (January), 89–105.

Ford, Robert and Goodwin, Matthew (2014) *Revolt on the Right: Explaining Support for the Radical Right in Britain*. London/New York: Routledge.

Forsberg, Tuomas (2016) 'From *Ostpolitik* to "Frostpolitik"? Merkel, Putin and German Foreign Policy Towards Russia', *International Affairs*, 92(1), 21–42.

Foucher, Michel (2016) 'The Return of the Borders', *European Interview*. Paris: Fondation Robert Schuman, no. 92, 19 July.

Foy, Henry and Buckley, Neil (2015) 'Barbed Rhetoric', *Financial Times*, 27 November.

Frankfurter Allgemeine Zeitung (1984) 'CDU und FDP für Abschaffung der Grenzkontrollen in der EG', 18 April.

Freedman, Laurence (2014) 'Ukraine and the Art of Crisis Management', *Survival*, 56(3), 7–42.

Friedman, George (2014) 'Ukraine: The Perpetual Buffer State', *Real Clear World*, 28 January.

Friedman, Thomas (2014) 'Putin blinked', *New York Times*, 27 May.

Fuest, Clemens (2016) 'How Germany Views Brexit', *Project Syndicate* https://www.project-syndicate.org/brexit-consequences-for-germany-by-clemens-fuest, 19 April.

Gabriel, Sigmar (2012) *Gesprächsprotokoll des Deutschen Bundestags, 17. Wahlperiode, 188. Sitzung, Berlin,* 29 June, 22702–22707.

Galbraith, James K. (2016) *Welcome to the Poisoned Chalice: The Destruction of Greece and the Future of Europe*. New Haven and London: Yale University Press.

Gambarotto, Francesca and Solari, Stefano (2015) 'The Peripheralization of Southern European Capitalism within the EMU', *Review of International Political Economy*, 22(4), 788–812.

Garton Ash, Timothy (2014) 'The next, key step on Ukraine', *latimes.com*, 21 March.

Geddes, Andrew (2013) *Britain and the European Union*. Basingstoke: Palgrave Macmillan.

Gehring, Thomas (1998) 'Die Politik des koordinierten Alleingangs: Schengen und die Abschaffung der Personenkontrollen an den Binnengrenzen der Europäischen Union', *Zeitschrift für Internationale Beziehungen*, 5(1), 43–78.

Genscher, Hans-Dietrich (1995) *Erinnerungen*. Berlin: Siedler.

Germann, Julian (2017) 'Beyond "geo-economics": Advanced unevenness and the anatomy of German austerity', *European Journal of International Relations* 24 (3), 590–613.

Gillingham, John (2003) *European Integration 1950–2003: Superstate or New Market Economy?* Cambridge: Cambridge University Press.

Gilpin, Robert (1981) *War and Change in World Politics*. Cambridge and New York: Cambridge University Press.

Gilpin, Robert (1987) *The Political Economy of International Relations*. Princeton: Princeton University Press.

Gilpin, Robert (2001) *Global Political Economy: Understanding the International Economic Order*. Princeton and London: Princeton University Press.

Giumelli, Francesco (2017) 'The Redistributive Impact of Restrictive Measures on EU Members: Winners and Losers from Imposing Sanctions on Russia', *Journal of Common Market Studies*, 55(5), 1062–1080.

Golub, Jonathan (1999) 'In the Shadow of the Vote: Decision Making in the European Community', *International Organization*, 53(4), 733–764.

Golub, Jonathan (2006) 'Did the Luxembourg Compromise Have Any Consequences?', in J. Palayret, H. Wallace and P. Winand (eds), *Visions, Votes and Vetoes: The Empty Chair Crisis and the Luxembourg Compromise Forty Years On*. Brussels: Peter Lang, pp. 79–99.

Golub, J. (2013) 'Far from dominating EU decision-making, France and Germany are among the least successful member states in negotiating decisions and budgetary contributions', *EUROPP* (http://blogs.lse.ac.uk/europpblog/2013/01/08/countries-which-have-most-success-in-council-negotiations/).

Gordon, Sarah (2015) 'Brexit may suit the hedgies, but others should weigh the risks', *Financial Times*, 5 November.

Gordon, Sarah, Parker, George and Pickard, Jim (2015) 'UK business told to "shut up" over Brexit poll', *Financial Times*, 6 September.

Görtemaker, Manfred (2008) 'The Failure of EDC and European Integration', in Ludger Kühnhardt (ed), *Crises in European Integration: Challenges and Responses, 1945–2005*. New York/Oxford: Berghahn, 33–48.

Gowa, Joanne (1989) 'Rational Hegemons, Excludable Goods, and Small Groups: An Epitaph for Hegemonic Stability Theory?', *World Politics*, 41(3) (April), 307–324.

Grande, Edgar and Kriesi, Hanspeter (2016) 'Conclusions: The Postfunctionalists were (almost) Right', in Swen Hutter, Edgar Grande and Hanspeter Kriesi (eds), *Politicising Europe: Integration and Mass Politics*. Cambridge: Cambridge University Press, pp. 279–300.

Grant, Charles (1994) *Delors: Inside the House that Jacques Built*. London: Nicholas Brealey.

Grant, Charles (2016) 'Brexit would be a challenge for Berlin', *Financial Times*, 15 May.

Gressel, Gustav (2015) 'Russia's military options in Ukraine', commentary, European Council on Foreign Relations, 27 April.

Gressel, Gustav and Wesslau, Fredrik (2017) 'The Great Unravelling: Four Doomsday Scenarios for Europe's Russia Policy', *Policy Brief* (European Council on Foreign Relations), June.

Griffiths, Richard T. (2006) 'A Dismal Decade? European Integration in the 1970s', in Desmond Dinan (ed), *Origins and Evolution of the European Union*, 2nd edn Oxford: Oxford University Press, pp. 169–190.

Gros, Daniel and Alcidi, Cinzia (2014) 'The case of the disappearing Fiscal Compact', *CEPS Commentary* Brussels: Centre for European Policy Studies, 5 November.

The Guardian (2014) 'Ukraine Crisis: Vladimir Putin has lost the plot, says German Chancellor', 3 March.

The Guardian (2015a) 'Refugee Crisis: We must act together, says Merkel ahead of emergency summit', 21 September.

The Guardian (2015b) 'Refugee influx a major opportunity for Germany, leading economist says', 5 November.

The Guardian (2015c) 'Eurozone chiefs strike deal to extend Greek bailout for four months', 20 February.

The Guardian (2016) 'West and Russia on course for war, says ex-Nato deputy commander', 18 May.

The Guardian (2017) 'Alexis Tsipras: "The worst is clearly behind us"', 24 July.

Guigou, Elisabeth (2000) *Une femme au cœur de l'État*. Paris: Fayard.

Guiraudon, Virginie (2011) 'Schengen: Une crise en trompe l'oeil', *Politique Étrangère* no. 4, 773–784.

Haas, Ernst (1958) *The Uniting of Europe: Political, Social and Economical Forces*. Notre Dame: University of Notre Dame Press.

Haas, Ernst (1964) 'Technocracy, Pluralism and the New Europe', in Stephen Graubard (ed), *A New Europe?* Boston: Houghton Mifflin, pp. 62–88.

Haas, Ernst (1976) 'Turbulent Fields and the Theory of Regional Integration', *International Organization*, 30(2), 173–212.

Hacke, Christian (2014) 'Der Westen und die Ukraine-Krise: Plädoyer für Realismus', *Aus Politik und Zeitgeschichte*, 64(47–48), (17 November), 40–47.

Hagemann, Sara and De Clerck-Sachsse, Julia (2007) *Old Rules, New Game: Decision-Making in the Council of Ministers after the 2004 Enlargement*. Brussels: Centre for European Policy Studies, special report March.

Hall, Peter (2014) 'Varieties of Capitalism and the Euro Crisis', *West European Politics*, 37(6), 1223–1243.

Heath, Edward (1998) *The Course of My Life: My Autobiography*. London: Hodder and Stoughton.

Henning, C. Randall (2016) 'The ECB as a Strategic Actor: Central Banking in a Politically Fragmented Monetary Union', in James A. Caporaso and Martin Rhodes (eds), *The Political and Economic Dynamics of the Eurozone Crisis*. Oxford: Oxford University Press, pp. 167–199.

Héritier, Adrienne (1999) *Policy Making and Diversity in Europe: Escape from Deadlock*. Cambridge: Cambridge University Press.

Héritier, Adrienne (2016) 'European Governance in a Changing World: Interests, Institutions and Policy Making' (unpublished manuscript).

Héritier, A. (2017) 'Conclusion: European Governance in a Changing World: Interests, Institutions and Policy Making', *International Journal of Public Administration*, 40(14), 1250–1260.

Hille, Kathrin (2013) 'Russia-Ukraine: Fraternity test', *Financial Times*, 21–22 December.

Hille, Kathrin (2014) 'Russia: Imperialism awakes', *Financial Times*, 15–16 March.

Hirseland, Katrin (2015) 'Aktuelle Zahlen und Entwicklungen', *Aus Politik und Zeitgeschichte* 25/2015 (15 June), 17–25.

Hix, Simon and Høyland, Bjørn (2011) *The Political System of the European Union*, 3rd edn. Basingstoke: Palgrave Macmillan.

Hobolt, Sara B. (2016) 'The Brexit Vote: A Divided Nation, a Divided Continent', *Journal of European Public Policy*, 23(9), 1259–1277.

Hockenos, Paul (2014) 'Can Vladimir Putin Upend Democracy in Europe?' *The Boston Review*, 21 April.

Hockenos, Paul (2015) 'The Stunning Hypocrisy of Mitteleuropa', *Foreign Policy* (commentary), 10 September.

Hockenos, Paul (2016) 'Angela Merkel Doesn't Have a Brexit Plan Either', *Foreign Policy* (http://foreignpolicy.com/2016/06/27/angela-merkel-doesnt-have-a-brexit-plan-either/), 27 June.

Hoffmann, Stanley (1966) 'Obstinate or Obsolete? The Fate of the Nation-State', in Mette Eilstrup-Sangiovanni (ed), *Debates on European Integration: A Reader*. Basingstoke: Palgrave Macmillan.

Hoffmann, Isabell (2016) 'Europe's Reluctant Leader', *Newpolitik*. Berlin: Bertelsmann Foundation, September: 7pp.

Hooghe, Liesbet and Marks, Gary (2008) 'A Postfunctionalist Theory of European Integration: From Permissive Consensus to Constraining Dissensus', *British Journal of Political Science*, 39, 1–23.

Hooghe, Liesbet and Marks, Gary (2014) 'Delegation and Pooling in International Organizations', *Review of International Organizations*, 10(3), 305–328.

House of Lords European Union Committee (2015) *The EU and Russia: Before and Beyond the Crisis in Ukraine*. London: Parliament.

Howarth, David and Quaglia, Lucia (2016) 'The New Intergovernmentalism in Financial Regulation and European Banking Union', in Christopher J. Bickerton, Dermot Hodson and Uwe Puetter (eds), *The New Intergovernmentalism: States and Supranational Actors in the Post-Maastricht Area*. Oxford: Oxford University Press, pp. 146–164.

Howorth, Jolyon (2014) *Security and Defence Policy in the European Union*, 2nd edn. Basingstoke: Palgrave Macmillan.

Howorth, Jolyon (2017) '"Stability on the Borders": The Ukraine Crisis and the EU's Constrained Policy Towards the Eastern Neighbourhood', *Journal of Common Market Studies*, 55(1), 121–136.

Hreblay, Vendelin (1998) *Les accords de Schengen : Origine, Fonctionnement, Avenir* Brussels: Bruylant.

Hsiao, Chen-Hao, Wei, Hao-Chi, Hung, Yi-Hsuan, Shih, Yu and Chang, Ching-Hsuan (2009) 'Prospects for an East Asia Free Trade Area', paper available at: www.ueb.edu.vn/Uploads/file/lethuydzung@gmail.com/2010/09/10/IP_Prospect.

Hubbard, J. (2010) 'Hegemonic Stability Theory: An Empirical Analysis', *ISRJ/th INK Globally*, http://isrj.wordpress.com/2010/05/28/hegemonic-stability-theory/ (accessed 19 July 2012).

Hutter, S., Grande, E. and Kriesi, H. (eds) (2016) *Politicising Europe: Integration and Mass Politics*. Cambridge: Cambridge University Press.

Ifo-Institut (2012) 'The exposure level – Eurozone countries' exposure, highlighting Germany's share, derived from bailouts and other financial support measures for distressed countries', 10 July.

Inglehart, Ronald and Norris, Pippa (2016) 'Trump, Brexit, and the Rise of Populism: Economic Have-Nots and Cultural Backlash', *HKS Faculty Research Working Paper Series*, no. RWP16-026. Cambridge, MA: Kennedy School of Government, August.

Issing, Otmar (2016) 'On the Relation of Monetary and Political Union', *Intereconomics*, 51(1), 16–20.

Janning, Josef (2013) 'State Power within European Integration', *DGAP Journal*, 2 May.

Janning, Josef (2015a) 'More Union for the EU', *Note from Berlin*. Berlin: European Council on Foreign Relations, 17 September.

Janning, Josef (2015b) 'View from Berlin: Pushing for robustness', European Council on Foreign Relations, commentary, 29 September.

Johnston, Alison, Hancké, Bob and Pant, Suman (2014) 'Comparative Institutional Advantage in the European Sovereign Debt Crisis', *Comparative Political Studies*, 47(13), 1771–1800.

Jones, Erik, Kelemen, R. Daniel and Meunier, Sophie (2016) 'Failing Forward? The Eurocrisis and the Incomplete Nature of European Integration', *Comparative Political Studies*, 49(7), 1010–1034.

Kaelble, Hartmut (2013) 'Spirale nach unten oder produktive Krisen? Die Geschichte der Entscheidungskrisen der europäischen Integration', *Integration*, 3, 169–192.

Kalaitzake, Manolis (2017) 'The Political Power of Finance: The Institute of International Finance in the Greek Debt Crisis', *Politics and Society*, 45(3), 389–413.

Kaplan, Robert (2014) 'Crimea: The Revenge of Geography', *Real Clear World*, 13 March.

Katzenstein, Peter J. (1997) 'Introduction: Asian Regionalism in Comparative Perspective', in Peter J. Katzenstein and TakashiShiraishi (eds), *Network Power: Japan and Asia*. Ithaca, NY: Cornell University Press.

Kauffmann, Sylvie (2015) 'Le nouveau rideau de fer', *Le Monde*, 30–31 August.

Kelemen, R. Daniel (2007) 'Built to Last? The Durability of EU Federalism', in Sophie Meunier and Kathleen McNamara (eds), *Making History: The State of the European Union*, Vol. 8. Oxford: Oxford University Press.

Keohane Robert O. (1993) 'Institutional Theory and the Realist Challenge after the Cold War', in David Baldwin (ed), *Neorealism and Neoliberalism: The Contemporary Debate*. New York: Columbia University Press.

Keohane, Robert and Nye, Joseph S. (1993) 'Introduction: The End of the Cold War in Europe', in Robert O. Keohane, Joseph S. Nye and Stanley Hoffmann (eds), *After the Cold War: International Institutions and State Strategies in Europe, 1989–1991*. Cambridge, MA: Harvard University Press.

Kerber, Markus (2014) 'German industry should speak hard truths to Putin', *Financial Times*, 7 May.

Keukeleire, Stephan and MacNaughtan, Jennifer (2008) *The Foreign Policy of the European Union*. Basingstoke: Palgrave Macmillan.

Khan, Mehreen (2018) 'The Franco-German project is no longer enough for the EU', *Financial Times*, 9 March.

Kietz, Daniela (2013) *Politisierung trotz Parteienkonsens: Bundestag, Bundesrat und die Euro-Krise*. Gütersloh: Bertelsmann Stiftung.

Kietz, Daniela and Maurer, Andreas (2007) 'Fragmentierung und Entdemokratisierung der europäischen Justiz- und Innenpolitik? Folgen der Prümer Vertragsavantgarde', in Martin H.W. Möllers and Robert Chr. van Ooyen (eds), *Jahrbuch Öffentliche Sicherheit 2006/2007*. Frankfurt: Verlag für Polizeiwissenschaft/Dr. Clemens Lorei, pp. 439–452.

Kietz, Daniela and Maurer, Andreas (2009) 'Prüm, Brüssel, Washington: Avantgarde-Gemeinschaften und Innere Sicherheitspolitiken der EU', in Martin H.W. Möllers and Robert Chr. van Ooyen (eds), *Europäisierung und Internationalisierung der Polizei. Band 1: Europäisierung*. Second revised edition. Frankfurt : Verlag für Polizeiwissenschaft/Dr. Clemens Lorei, pp. 111–145.

Kindleberger, Charles P. (1973) *The World in Depression, 1929–1939*. Berkeley: University of California Press.

Kindleberger, Charles P. (1981) 'Dominance and Leadership in the International Economy: Exploitation, Public Goods, and Free Rides', *International Studies Quarterly*, 25(2) (June), 242–254.

Kindleberger, Charles P. (1986a) 'International Public Goods without International Government', *American Economic Review*, 76(1) (March), 1–13.

Kindleberger, Charles P. (1986b) 'Hierarchy versus Inertial Cooperation', *International Organization*, 40(4) (Autumn), 841–847.

King, Mervyn (2016) *The End of Alchemy: Money, Banking and the Future of the Global Economy*. London: Little, Brown.

Kipping, Franz (2004) *Rom. 25. März 1957: Die Einigung Europas*. Munich: Deutscher Taschenbuch.

Kohl, Helmut (1993) 'Die aufgestauten Strukturprobleme erfordern eine Generalinventur von Wirtschaft und Gesellschaft', *Handelsblatt*, 31 December.

Kohl, Helmut (1996) *Ich wollte Deutschlands Einheit*. Berlin: Propyläen.

Kohl, Helmut (2007) *Erinnerungen, 1990–1994*. Munich: Droemer.

Kohl, Helmut (2011) '"Wir müssen wieder Zuversicht geben"', *Internationale Politik*, 5 (September–October), 10–17.

Kornelius, Stefan (2016a) 'Merkels Furcht vor dem Brexit' (http://www.sueddeutsche.de/politik/2.220/deutschland-und-grossbritannien-merkels-furcht-vor-dem-brexit), 24 May.

Kornelius, Stefan (2016b) 'Face au "Brexit", Berlin s'inquiète pour l'Europe', *Le Monde*, 26 May.

Korski, Daniel (2016) 'Why we lost the Brexit vote', http://www.politico.eu/article/why-we-lost-the-the-brexit-vote-former-uk-prime-minister, 21 October.

Krampf, Arie (2014) 'From the Maastricht Treaty to Post-crisis EMU: The ECB and Germany as Drivers of Change', *Journal of Contemporary European Studies*, 22(3), 303–317.

Krasner, Stephen D. (1984) 'Approaches to the State: Alternative Conceptions and Historical Dynamics', *Comparative Politics*, 16(2), 223–246.

Krastev, Ivan (2017) *After Europe*. Philadelphia: University of Pennsylvania Press.

Kreppel, Amie (2012) 'The Normalization of the European Union', *Journal of European Public Policy*, 19(5), 635–645.

Kriesi, Hanspeter (2016) 'Mobilization of Protest in the Age of Austerity', in M. Ancelovici, P. Dufour and H. Nez (eds), *Street Politics in the Age of Austerity: From the Indignados to Occupy*. Amsterdam: Amsterdam University Press, pp. 73–96.

Kroet, Cynthia (2016) 'David Cameron asks Germans to help avoid Brexit', *Politico*, 7 January (http://www.politico.eu/article/david-cameron-asks-germans-to-help-avoid-brexit/)

Krotz, Ulrich (2009) 'Momentum and Impediments: Why Europe Won't Emerge as a Full Political Actor on the World Stage Soon', *Journal of Common Market Studies*, 47(3), 555–578.

Krotz, Ulrich and Maher, Richard (2016) 'Europe's Crises and the EU's "Big Three"', *West European Politics*, 39(5), 1053–1072.

Krotz, Ulrich and Schild, Joachim (2013) *Shaping Europe: France, Germany, and Embedded Bilateralism from the Elysée Treaty to Twenty-First Century Politics*. Oxford: Oxford University Press.

Krotz, Ulrich and Schild, Joachim (2018) 'Back to the Future? Franco-German Bilateralism in Europe's Post-Brexit Union', *Journal of European Public Policy*, 25(8), 1174–1193.

Kuhn, Theresa (2011) 'Individual Transnationalism, Globalisation and Euroscepticism: An Empirical Test of Deutsch's Transactionalist Theory', *European Journal of Political Research*, 50(6), 811–837.

Kundnani, Hans (2014) *The Paradox of German Power*. London: Hurst.

Kundnani, Hans (2015) 'Leaving the West Behind', *Foreign Affairs*, 94(1) (January–February), 108–116.

Küsters,HannsJürgenandHofmann,Daniel(1998)*Dokumentezur Deutschlandpolitik: Deutsche Einheit. Sonderedition aus den Akten des Bundeskanzleramtes 1989/90.* Munich: Oldenbourg.

Kuzio, Taras (2015) 'Ukraine says thank you to Vladimir Putin', *Financial Times*, 5 November.

Kuzio,Taras (2017) 'Ukraine between a Constrained EU and Assertive Russia', *Journal of Common Market Studies*, 55(1), 103–120.

Laffan, Brigid and Schlosser, Pierre (2016) 'Public Finances in Europe: Fortifying EU Economic Governance in the Shadow of the Crisis', *West European Politics*, 38(3), 237–249.

Lake, David (1993) 'Leadership, Hegemony, and the International Economy: Naked Emperor or Tattered Monarch with Potential?', *International Studies Quarterly*, 37(4) (December), 459–489.

Lalumière, Catharine (2006) 'Audio interview on the negotiation of the Schengen Accord', *European Navigator – The History of a United Europe on the Internet* (accessible at: http://www.ena.lu), 17 May.

Landler, Mark (2016) *Alter Egos: Hillary Clinton, Barack Obama, and the Twilight Struggle Over American Power.* London: WH Allen.

Lange, Peter (1992) 'Maastricht and the Social Protocol: Why Did They Do It?' Berkeley: University of California Center for German and European Studies, Working Paper I.5.

Lavenex, Sandra (2018) '"Failing Forward" Towards Which Europe? Organized Hypocrisy in the Common European Asylum System', *Journal of Common Market Studies*, 56(5) (July), 1195–1212.

Laws, David (2016) *Coalition: The Inside Story of the Conservative-Liberal Democrat Coalition Government.* London: Biteback.

Le Monde (2012a) 'Plan concerté Etats-BCE pour sauver la zone euro', 28 July.

Le Monde (2012b) 'Pourquoi Paris et Berlin s'opposent', 1 August.

Le Monde (2013a) 'Bagarre entre Berlin et Paris sur la gouvernance de la zone euro', 28 November.

Le Monde (2013b) 'Union bancaire: le difficile partage de souveraineté', 17 December.

Le Monde (2013c) 'Union bancaire: Merkel et Hollande cherchent un accord', 19 December.

Le Monde (2013d) 'Un compromis au forceps sur l'union bancaire', 20 December.

Le Monde (2013e) 'Ukraine: La tentation européenne', 26 September.

Le Monde (2013f) 'Montée de tensions entre la Russie et l'Ukraine', 4 October.

Le Monde (2013g) 'Vladimir Poutine sauve l'Ukraine de la faillite', 19 December.

Le Monde (2014a) 'La menace de sanctions est loin de faire l'unanimité chez les Européens', 5 March.

Le Monde (2014b) 'L'OTAN n'envisage aucune action concrète', 5 March.

Le Monde (2014c) 'L'Allemagne hausse le ton à l'égard de la Russie', 14 March.

Le Monde (2014d) 'Crimée: les Occidentaux sanctionnent en ordre dispersé', 19 March.

Le Monde (2014e) 'Un tir de missile meurtrier et "forcément volontaire"', 19 July.

Le Monde (2014f) 'Face à la Russie, "les sanctions sont la seule arme dont nous disposons"' (interview with the Finnish Prime Minister, Alexander Stubb), 3 October.

Le Monde (2014g) 'Merkel exprime ouvertement son opposition aux visées russes', 17 November.

Le Monde (2014h) 'Hollande au Monde: "Les rebelles syriens méritent notre soutien"', 20 August.

Le Monde (2015a) 'Sans illusion, l'UE durcit ses sanctions contre Moscou', 31 January.

Le Monde (2015b) '"L'Ukraine est devenue un piège pour Poutine"', 7 March.

Le Monde (2015c) '"J'exclus que l'assassinat de Nemtsov ait été possible sans autori-sation"' (interview with Alexeï Navalny), 18 March.

Le Monde (2015d) 'Migrants: L'Europe cherche encore la réponse', 26 August.

Le Monde (2015e) 'Merkel met en garde l'Europe sur les réfugiés', 2 September.

Le Monde (2015f) 'L'UE tente de vaincre les réticences à l'acceuil', 13–14 September.

Le Monde (2015g) 'Des opinions publiques profondément divisées', 16 September.

Le Monde (2015h) 'Nouveau fiasco européen sur les réfugiés', 16 September.

Le Monde (2015i) 'L'UE impose la répartition de 120 000 réfugiés', 24 September.

Le Monde (2015j) 'Le scepticisme croissant des Allemands sur l'acceuil des réfugiés', 28 October.

Le Monde (2015k) 'Migrants : les réticences françaises', 28 October.

Le Monde (2015l) 'Manuel Valls appelle l'Europe à fermer ses portes aux migrants', 26 November.

Le Monde (2015m) 'L'Europe menace d'exclure la Grèce de l'espace Schengen', 2 December.

Le Monde (2015n) 'L'incertitude grecque met le couple franco-allemand à l'épreuve', 2 July.

Le Monde (2016a) 'Deux nouvelles frontières se ferment en Europe', 6 January.

Le Monde (2016b) 'L'Europe renonce peu à peu à Schengen', 20 January.

Le Monde (2016c) 'Face aux réfugiés, Angela Merkel seule en Europe', 24–25 January.

Le Monde (2016d) 'Combien coûterait à la France la fin de Schengen ?', 4 February.

Le Monde (2016e) 'Réfugiés: le face-à-face Berlin-Paris', 16 February.

Le Monde (2016f) 'La fin de Schengen pourrait coûter 1400 milliards d'euros à l'UE', 24 February.

Le Monde (2016g) 'Le couple franco-allemand est en panne sur les réfugiés', 6–7 March.

Le Monde (2016h) 'Réfugiés : l'Europe officialise sa "bunkérisation"', 8 March.

Le Monde (2016i) 'La nuit où Angela Merkel a perdu l'Europe', 17 March.

Le Monde (2016j) 'L'échange de réfugiés esquissé avec Ankara rest contesté', 17 March.

Le Monde (2016k) 'Migrants: pacte sans gloire entre l'UE et Ankara', 20–21 March.

Le Monde (2016l) '«La Bulgarie ne doit pas être l'ennemie de la Russie"'(interview with Roumen Radev), 15 December.

Le Monde (2017a) 'Regain des tensions autour du sauvetage de BMPS', 3 January.

Le Monde (2017b) 'Sarkozy: "Les coups pleuvaient de tous les côtés"', 5 July.

Le Monde (2017c) 'M. Varoufakis : "Macron a déjà échoué face à l'Allemagne"', 14 October.

Le Monde (2017d) 'Sur la ligne de front, la guerre sans fin du Donbass', 4 March.

Le Monde (2017e) 'Le Drian: "Avec la Russie il y a une fenêtre d'opportunité"' (inter-view with the French foreign minister Jean-Yves Le Drian), 30 June.

Le Monde (2018) 'L'optimisme post-élection de Macron s'est dissipé', 10 July.

Legrain, Philippe (2014) *European Spring: Why our Economies and Politics are in a Mess* (published by the author).

Lehmann, Julian (2015) 'Ein Rückblick auf die EU-"Flüchtingskrise" 2015', *Aus Politik und Zeitgeschichte* (65/52/2015), 21 December, pp. 7–11.

Leonard, Sarah (2009) 'The Creation of FRONTEX and the Politics of Institutionalisation in the EU External Borders Policy', *Journal of Contemporary European Research*, 5(3), 371–388.

Leparmentier, Arnaud (2014) 'Avant l'invention des passeports', *Le Monde*, 20 February.

Leparmentier, Arnaud (2015) 'Aidons Merkel', *Le Monde*, 3 September.

Les Echos (2011) 'Les coulisses d'une négociation marathon', 28–29 October.

Lever, Paul (2017) *Berlin Rules: Europe and the German Way*. London and New York: I.B. Tauris.

Libération (2011) 'L'UE ne donne pas cher de la Grèce'.

Libération (2017) 'Yanis Varoufakis : "En Europe, les chiffres prospèrent, les gens désespèrent"', 13 October.

Lieber, Robert (1999) 'Great Britain: Decline and Recovery', in Robert A. Pastor (ed), *A Century's Journey: How the Great Powers Shape the World*. New York: Basic Books, pp. 33–62.

Lindberg, Leon and Scheingold, Stuart (1970) *Europe's Would-Be Polity*. Engelwood Cliffs: Prentice Hall.

Ludlow, N. Piers (2006) *The European Community and the Crises of the 1960s: Negotiating the Gaullist Challenge*. London/New York: Routledge.

Ludlow, Peter (1982) *The Making of the European Monetary System: A Case Study in the Politics of the European Community*. London: Butterworth.

Ludlow, Peter (2010a) 'A View on Brussels. Van Rompuy saves the day: The European Council of 11 February 2010', *Eurocomment Briefing Note* 7:6, February.

Ludlow, Peter (2010b) 'A View on Brussels. In the Last Resort: The European Council and the euro crisis, Spring 2010', *Eurocomment Briefing Note* 7:7/8, June.

Ludlow, Peter (2010c) 'A View on Brussels. The Euro Crisis Once Again: The European Council of 28–29 October 2010', *Eurocomment Briefing Note* 8:3, December.

Ludlow, Peter (2011) 'A Tale of Five Summits: October/November 2011. A preliminary evaluation', 30 November.

Ludlow, Peter (2012a) 'The European Council of 8/9 December 2011', 14 January.

Ludlow, Peter (2012b) 'A turning-point in the euro crisis? The informal European Council of 23 May 2012'.

Ludlow, Peter (2012c) 'Short-term help and long-term conditionality. The European Council of 28–29 June 2012', July.

Ludlow, Peter (2012d) 'Completing EMU: A roadmap not a blueprint. The European Council of 18–19 October 2012'.

Ludlow, Peter (2013a) 'Cyprus: *Chefsache* after all. The making of the settlement on 24–25 March 2013'.

Ludlow, Peter (2013b) 'Economic Policy, EMU and Enlargement. The European Council of 27–28 June 2013'.

Ludlow, Peter (2013c) 'The Digital Economy, EMU, Migration, Cameron's Deregulation Sideshow and Merkel's Mobile Phone. The European Council of 24–25 October 2013'.

Ludlow, Peter (2013d) 'The European Council of 19–20 December 2013. European Defence, Banking Union, Economic Policy Coordination, Migration and Enlargement'.

Luif, Paul (2007) 'The Treaty of Prüm: A Replay of Schengen? Annual policy paper on the interrelation between internal and external security of the future Europe' (Project-No. 513416. EU-Consent. Wider Europe, Deeper Integration? Constructing Europe Network. Network of Excellence. Priority 7 – Citizens and Governance in the Knowledge-based Society. Deliverable No. D38c (Rome: Istituto Affari Internazionali), 19 May.

Lyman, Rick (2015) 'Eastern Bloc's Resistance to Refugees Highlights Europe's Cultural and Political Divisions', *New York Times*, 12 September.

Macron, Emmanuel (2017) 'Initiative for Europe: Sorbonne speech of Emmanuel Macron' (http://international.blogs.ouest-france.fr/archive/2017/09/29/macron-sorbonne-verbatim-europe-18583.html). English version. 26 September.

MacShane, Denis (2015) *Brexit: How Britain Will Leave Europe*. London/New York: I.B. Tauris.

Maillard, Pierre (1995) *De Gaulle et l'Europe: Entre la nation et Maastricht*. Paris: Tallandier.

Majone, Giandomenico (2009) *Europe as the Would-Be World Power: The EU at Fifty*. Cambridge: Cambridge University Press.

Mandra, Allison (2015) 'Measuring Political Muscle in European Union institutions', *Bruegel Blog Post* (http://bruegel.org/2015/04/measuring-political-muscle-in-european-union-institutions/), 12 April.

March, James G. and Olsen, Johan P. (1989) 'The New Institutionalism', *American Political Science Review*, 78(3), 734–749.

Marsh, David (2009) *The Euro: The Politics of the New Global Currency*. New Haven and London: Yale University Press.

Marsh, David (2016) 'Return of a German Nightmare', *OMFIF Commentary*, 7(16), 5, 20 April.

Marsh, David (2017) 'Target-2 and Germany's election dilemmas', 15 February.

Marshall, Paul (2016) 'Hedge funds favour Brexit as refuge from Brussels', *Financial Times*, 29 February.

Mason, Rowena and Rankin, Jennifer (2016) 'EU renegotiation: UK wins partial concession on migrant worker benefits', *The Guardian*, 2 February.

Matthijs, Matthias and Blyth, Mark (2011) 'Why Only Germany Can Fix the Euro: Reading Kindleberger in Berlin', *Foreign Affairs*, 17 November.

Mattli, Walter (1999) *The Logic of Regional Integration: Europe and Beyond*. Cambridge: Cambridge University Press.

Mazzucelli, Colette (1997) *France and Germany at Maastricht: Politics and Negotiations to Create the European Union*. New York and London: Garland.

Mazzucelli, Colette, Guérot, Ulrike and Metz, Almut (2007) 'Cooperative Hegemon, Missing Engine or Improbable Core? Explaining Franco-German Influence in European Treaty Reform', in Derek Beach and Colette Mazzucelli (eds), *Leadership in the Big Bangs of European Integration*. Basingstoke: Palgrave Macmillan, pp. 158–177.

McGill, Andrew (2016) 'Who Voted for Brexit?' *The Atlantic* (www.atlantic.com), 29 June.

McGowan, Lee and Phinnemore, David (2017) 'The UK: Membership in Crisis', in Desmond Dinan, Neill Nugent and William E. Paterson (eds), *The European Union in Crisis*. Basingstoke: Palgrave Macmillan, pp. 77–99.

McKay, David (1999a) *Federalism and European Union: A Political Economy Perspective*. Oxford: Oxford University Press.

McKay, David (1999b) The Political Sustainability of European Monetary Union, *British Journal of Political Science*, 29(3), 463–485.

McKay, David (2004) William Riker on Federalism: Sometimes Wrong but More Right than Anyone Else? *Regional and Federal Studies*, 14(2), 167–186.

McNamara, Kathleen R. (2014) 'The EU after Ukraine: European Foreign Policy in the New Europe', commentary, *Foreign Affairs*, 4 March.

McNamara, Kathleen (2015) 'A Less Perfect Union: Europe after the Greek Debt Crisis', *Foreign Affairs*, 19 July.

Mearsheimer, John J. (1990) 'Back to the Future: Instability in Europe after the Cold War', *International Security*, 15(4), 5–56.

Mearsheimer, John J. (2001) 'The Future of the American Pacifier', *Foreign Affairs*, 80(5), 46–61.

Mearsheimer, John J. (2010) 'Why is Europe Peaceful Today?', *European Political Science*, 9(3), 387–397.

Mearsheimer, John J. (2014) 'Why the Ukraine Crisis is the West's Fault', *Foreign Affairs*, 93(5), 77–89.

Mearsheimer, John J. (2015) 'Don't Arm Ukraine', *New York Times*, 8 February.

Mendras, Marie (2016) 'The West and Russia: From Acute Conflict to Long-Term Crisis Management', commentary, DGAP/Center for Transatlantic Relations, 20 June.

Menon, Anand (2014) 'Defence Policy and the Logic of "High Politics"', in Philipp Genschel and Markus Jachtenfuchs (eds), *Beyond the Regulatory Polity: The European Integration of Core State Powers*. Oxford: Oxford University Press, pp. 66–84.

Menon, Anand and Fowler, Brigid (2016) 'Hard or Soft? The Politics of Brexit', *National Institute Economic Review*, 238 (November), R4–R12.

Mérand, Frédéric (2008) *European Defence Policy: Beyond the Nation State*. Oxford and New York: Oxford University Press.

Merkel, Angela (2014) 'Ein militärisches Vorgehen ist keine Option für uns', *Das Parlament*, minutes of speech to the German Bundestag, 13 March.

Merkel, Angela (2018) 'Deutschland, das sind wir alle' (speech to the German Parliament, 21 March), *Das Parlament: DebattenDokumentation*, no. 13–14, 26 March, 1–5.

Michta, Andrew A. (2017) 'Unchecked migration continues to splinter Europe', *Judy Dempsey's Strategic Europe/Carnegie Europe*, 27 July.

Milesi, Gabriel (1998) *Le roman de l'Euro*. Paris: Hachette.

Miller, Vaughne (2015) 'The 1974–75 UK Renegotiation of EEC Membership and Referendum', *House of Commons Library Briefing Paper No. 7253*, 13 July.

Milner, Helen (1998) 'International Political Economy: Beyond Hegemonic Stability', *Foreign Policy*, No. 110 (Spring, Special Edition), 112–123.

Mitterrand, François (1984) 'Discours de François Mitterrand devant le Parlement européen', *European Navigator – The history of a united Europe on the Internet* (accessible at : *http://www.ena.lu*), 24 May.

Monar, Jörg (2001) 'The Dynamics of Justice and Home Affairs: Laboratories, Driving Factors and Costs', *Journal of Common Market Studies*, 39(4), 747–764.

Monar, Jörg (2006) 'Cooperation in the Justice and Home Affairs Domain: Characteristics, Constraints and Progress', *European Integration*, 28(5), 495–509.

M le magazine du Monde (2015) 'Ils ont signé Schengen', 28 November, pp. 78–82.

Monnet, Jean (1988) *Erinnerungen eines Europäers*. Baden-Baden: Nomos.

Moravcsik, Andrew (1991) 'Negotiating the Single European Act: National Interests and Conventional Statecraft in the European Community', *International Organization*, 45(1), 19–56.

Moravcsik, Andrew (1993) 'Preferences and Power in the European Community: A Liberal Intergovernmentalist Approach', *Journal of Common Market Studies*, 31(4), 473–524.

Moravcsik, Andrew (1998) *The Choice for Europe: Social Purpose and State Power from Messina to Maastricht*. Ithaca, NY: Cornell University Press.

Moravcsik, Andrew (2005) 'The European Constitutional Compromise and the Neofunctionalist Legacy', *Journal of European Public Policy*, 12(2), 349–386.

Moravcsik, Andrew (2008) The European Constitutional Settlement, *The World Economy* (January), 157–182.

Moravcsik, Andrew (2009) Europe Defies the Skeptics: How crisis will make the EU stronger. Available at: www.thedailybeast.com/newsweek/2009/07/31/europe-de-fies-the-skeptics

Moravcsik, Andrew (2010) 'In defense of Europe', *Newsweek* (7 June), 24–27.

Moravcsik, Andrew (2016) 'The Great Brexit Kabuki – A Masterclass in Political Theatre', *Financial Times*, 8 April.

Morelle, Aquilino (2017) *L'abdication*. Paris: Bernard Grasset.

Moret, Erica, Biersteker, Thomas, Giumelli, Francesco, Portela, Clara, Veber, Marusa, Bastiat-Jarosz, Dawid and Bobocea, Cristian (2016) 'The New Deterrent? International Sanctions against Russia over the Ukraine Crisis: Impacts, Costs and Further Action'. Geneva: Programme for the Study of International Governance at the Graduate Institute of International and Development Studies https://repository.graduateinstitute.ch/record/294704/files/The%20New%20Deterrent%20International%20 Sanctions%20Against%20Russia%20Over%20the%20Ukraine%20Crisis%20 -%20Impacts,%20Costs%20and%20Further%20Action.pdf.

Mourlon-Druol, Emmanuel (2015) 'The UK's EU Vote: The 1975 Precedent and Today's Negotiations', *Bruegel Policy Contribution Issue 2015/08*. Brussels: Bruegel.

Munchau, Wolfgang (2011) 'Eurozone really has only days to avoid collapse', 28 November.

Munchau, Wolfgang (2014) 'Once again national interests undermine Europe', *Financial Times*, 9 March.

Münkler, Herfried (2015a) *Die Macht in der Mitte: Die neuen Aufgaben Deutschlands in Europa*. Hamburg: Körber-Stiftung.

Münkler, Herfried (2015b) 'Wir sind der Hegemon', *Frankfurter Allgemeine Zeitung*, 21 August.

Münkler, Herfried (2016) 'Die Mitte und die Flüchtingskrise', *Aus Politik und Zeitgeschichte* 14-15/2016, 4 April, pp. 3–8.

Murphy, Hannah (2016) 'What do Europeans think of Brexit?' *Financial Times*, 25 February.

Natorski, Michal and Pomorska, Karolina (2017) 'Trust and Decision-Making in Times of Crisis: The EU's Response to the Events in Ukraine', *Journal of Common Market Studies*, 55(1), 54–70.

Naurin, Daniel and Lindahl, Rutger (2008) East-North-South: Coalition-Building in the Council before and after Enlargement', in Daniel Naurin and Helen Wallace (eds), *Unveiling the Council of the European Union: Games Governments Play in Brussels*. Basingstoke: Palgrave Macmillan, pp. 64–78.

Naurin, Daniel and Wallace, Helen (2008) 'Introduction: From Rags to Riches', in Daniel Naurin and Helen Wallace (eds), *Unveiling the Council of the European Union: Games Governments Play in Brussels*. Basingstoke: Palgrave Macmillan, pp. 1–20.

Neue Zürcher Zeitung (1984) 'Abbau der Personenkontrollen im EG-Raum', 10 June.

Nevskaya, Anastasia (2016) 'Russia-EU economic relations: Assessing two years of sanctions', *Russia-Direct*, 16 June.

New York Times (2012) 'Huge Step Taken by Europe's Bank to Abate a Crisis', 6 September.

New York Times (2013a) 'Russia Putting a Strong Arm on Neighbors', 22 October.

New York Times (2013b) 'Ukraine's Battle for Europe', 29 November.

New York Times (2014) 'Merkel issues rebuke to Russia, Setting Caution Aside', 17 November.

New York Times (2015a) 'Euro Countries Take Tough Line Toward Greece', 5 January.

New York Times (2015b) 'Optimism for an Agreement on Greek Debt, but Not for Long-Term Stability' (Steven Erlanger and James Kanter), 22 June.

New York Times (2015c) 'Debt Talks May Be Defining Moment for Greece, and for Angela Merkel' (Alison Smale and Andrew Higgins), 24 June.

Niellsen, Katja (2017) *Europa und die Flüchtlinge*, documentary film broadcast by Zweites Deutsches Fernsehen (ZDF), 27 July.

Niemann, Arne (2016) 'Neofunctionalism and EU Internal Security Cooperation', in Raphael Bossong and Mark Rhinard (eds), *Theorizing Internal Security Cooperation in the European Union*. Oxford: Oxford University Press, pp. 129–152.

Niemann, Arne and Speyer, Johanna (2018) 'A Neofunctionalist Perspective on the "European Refugee Crisis": The Case of the European Border and Coast Guard', *Journal of Common Market Studies*, 56(1) (January), 23–43.

Niemeier, Michael and Zerbst, Petra (2007) 'Der Vertrag von Prüm – vertiefte grenzüberschreitende Zusammenarbeit zur Kriminalitätsbekämpfung in der EU', *ERA Forum*, 8, 535–547.

Nitoiu, Cristian and Sus, Monika (2017) 'The European Parliament's Diplomacy – A Tool for Projecting EU Power in Times of Crisis? The Case of the Cox-Kwasniewski Mission', *Journal of Common Market Studies*, 55(1), 71–86.

Nugent, Neill (2017) *The Government and Politics of the European Union*, 8th edn. Basingstoke: Palgrave Macmillan.

Nugent, Neill and Rhinard, Mark (2016) 'Is the European Commission *Really* in Decline ?' *Journal of Common Market Studies*, 54(5), 1199–1215.

OHCHR (Office of the United Nations High Commissioner for Human Rights) (2017) *Report on the Human Rights Situation in Ukraine*, 16 May–15 August 2017.

Oliver, Craig (2016a) *Unleashing Demons: The Inside Story of Brexit* London: Hodder and Stoughton.

Oliver, Tim (2016b) *A European Union without the United Kingdom: The Geopolitics of a British Exit from the EU*. London: LSE Ideas, Strategic Update 16.1, February.

Olsen, Johan P. (2009) 'An Institutional Approach to Institutions of Democratic Government', *European Political Science Review*, 1(1) (March 2009), 3–32.

Oltermann, Philip; Scammell, Rosie and Darroch, Gordon (2016) 'Brexit causes resurgence in pro-EU leanings across continent', *The Guardian*, 15 July.

Orenstein. Mitchell A. and Kelemen, R. Daniel (2017) 'Trojan Horses in EU Foreign Policy', *Journal of Common Market Studies*, 55(1), 87–102.

Ørstrøm Møller, Jørgen (2014a) 'Ukraine: Will Putin strike?' *The National Interest*, 28 February.

Ørstrøm Møller, Jørgen (2014b) 'Will Russia bring down the global system?' *The World Post*, 12 August.

Papaconstantinou, George (2016) *Game Over: The Inside Story of the Greek Crisis* (published by the author).

Parker, George (2014) 'Cameron's uneasy peace on Europe at risk', 1 September.

Parker, George (2016a) 'Cameron urges business to speak up for EU', *Financial Times*, 21 January.

Parker, George (2016b) 'The battle for Britain', *Financial Times*, 19 December.

Parker, George and Barker, Alex (2015) 'Europe: The British question', *Financial Times*, 20 May.

Parker, George and Barker, Alex (2016a) 'How to win friends', *Financial Times*, 23–24 January.

Parker, George and Barker, Alex (2016b) 'Cameron's rocky road to Brussels', *Financial Times*, 20 February.

Parker, George and Barker, Alex (2016c) 'How Brexit spelled the end to Cameron's career', *Financial Times*, 24 June.

Parker, George and Chassany, Anne-Sylvaine (2016) 'European leaders and businesses line up against Brexit', *Financial Times*, 3 March.

Parker, George, Barker, Alex and Wagstyl, Stefan (2015) '"Extremely helpful" Merkel cautions Cameron on EU reform demands', *Financial Times*, 16 December.

Parker, George, MacKenzie, Michael and Hall, Ben (2016) 'Britain breaks with Europe', *Financial Times*, 25–26 June.

Parsons, Craig (2003) *A Certain Idea of Europe*. Ithaca, NY: Cornell University Press.

Parsons, Craig (2006) 'The Triumph of Community Europe', in Desmond Dinan (ed), *Origins and Evolution of the European Union*, 2nd edn Oxford: Oxford University Press, pp. 115–135.

Parsons, Craig and Matthijs, Matthias (2015) 'European Integration Past, Present and Future: Moving Forward Through Crisis', in Matthias Matthijs and Mark Blyth (eds), *The Future of the Euro*. Oxford: Oxford University Press, pp. 210–232.

Paterson, William E. (2008) 'Did France and Germany Lead Europe? A Retrospect', in Jack Hayward (ed), *Leaderless Europe*. Oxford: Oxford University Press, pp. 89–110.

Paterson, William E. (2011) 'The Reluctant Hegemon? Germany Moves Centre Stage in the European Union', *JCMS Annual Review of the European Union in 2010*. Chichester: Wiley-Blackwell, pp. 57–75.

Pedersen, Thomas (1998) *Germany, France and the Integration of Europe: A Realist Interpretation*. London and New York: Pinter.

Peel, Quentin (2011) 'Merkel's mantra brings results without resort to big "bazooka"', 28 October.

Peers, Steve (2017) 'The rise and fall of EU justice and home affairs law', in Maria Fletcher, Ester Herlin-Karnell and Claudio Matera (eds), *The European Union as an Area of Freedom, Security and Justice*. London and New York: Routledge, pp. 11–33.

Pew Research Center (2015a) 'Faith in European Project Reviving' (www.pewglobal.org), 1 June.

Pew Research Centre (2015b) 'NATO Publics Blame Russia for Ukrainian Crisis, but Reluctant to Provide Military Aid', 10 June.

Pew Research Center (2016) 'Europeans Fear Wave of Refugees Will Mean More Terrorism, Fewer Jobs', 11 July.

Peyrefitte, Alain (1994) *C'était de Gaulle*, Vol. 1. Paris: Fayard.

Peyrefitte, Alain (2000) *C'était de Gaulle*, Vol. 3. Paris: Fayard.

Pierson, Paul (1998) 'The Path to European Integration: A Historical Institutionalist Analysis', in Mette Eilstrup-Sangiovanni (ed), *Debates on European Integration: A Reader*. Basingstoke: Palgrave Macmillan.

Pifer, Steven (2017) 'Minsk II's future looks bleak, but what's the alternative?' Order from Chaos blog, Brookings Institution (www.brookings.edu).

Pisani-Ferry, Jean (2017) 'Germany's Dangerous Obsession', *Project Syndicate*, 9 November.

Plickert, Philippe (2017) 'Deutscher Target-Saldo steigt auf mehr als 800 Milliarden Euro', *Frankfurter Allgemeine Zeitung* (7 March).

Policy Department for Citizens' Rights and Constitutional Affairs of the European Parliament (2018) 'The Future of the Schengen Area: Latest Developments and Challenges in the Schengen Governance Framework since 2016'. Brussels: European Union, March.

Politico (2015) 'Greece heads towards euro exit', 29 June (Zeke Turner, Matthew Karnitschnig and Helen Popper).

Politico (2015) 'Why Merkel changed her mind', 15 September.

Politico (2016) 'Final days of the EU's refugee strategy', 20 January.

Pond, Elizabeth (2014a) 'Europe's Long Peace, Shattered', commentary, *Deutsche Gesellschaft für Auswärtige Politik* (DGAP), 13 March.

Pond, Elizabeth (2014b) 'Are Ukrainians Europeans?' Commentary, *Deutsche Gesellschaft für Auswärtige Politik* (DGAP), 23 April.

Portela, Clara (2010) *European Union Sanctions and Foreign Policy: When and Why Do They Work?*. London and New York: Routledge.

Portela, Clara (2015) 'Member States' Resistance to EU Foreign Policy Sanctions', *European Foreign Affairs Review*, 20(1–2), 39–61.

Porter, Eduardo (2017) 'To Punish Putin, Economic Sanctions Are Unlikely to Do The Trick', *New York Times*, 25 July.

Pothier, Fabrice (2017) 'Can Macron reload the Minsk Process?' *Strategic Europe*, 13 July.

Prosser, Chris; Mellon, Jon and Green, Jane (2016) 'What mattered most to you when deciding how to vote in the EU referendum?' (Colchester: British Election Study) (http://www.britishelectionstudy.com/bes-findings/what-mattered-most-to-you-when-de), 11 July.

Putin, Vladimir (2007) 'Speech and the Following Discussion at the Munich Conference on Security Policy' (http://en,kremlin.ru/events/president/transcripts/24034), 10 February.

Quatremer, Jean and Klau, Thomas (1999) *Ces hommes qui ont fait l'euro*. Paris: Plon.

Qvortrup, Matt (2006) 'The Three Referendums on the European Constitutional Treaty in 2005', *Political Quarterly*, 77(1), 89–97.

Rachman, Gideon (2015) 'Putin's survival strategy is lies and violence', *Financial Times*, 3 March.

Reuters (2013) 'Analysis: In Cyprus standoff, Germany refuses to blink', 20 March.

Rinke, Andreas (2014) 'How Putin Lost Berlin', commentary, *Deutsche Gesellschaft für Auswärtige Politik*, 29 September.

Rocholl, Jörg and Stahmer, Axel (2016) 'Where Did the Greek Bailout Money Go?' *EMST White Paper No. WP-16-02* (Berlin: EMST).

Rogalla, Dieter (1983) 'Die Grenzschilder demontieren!' *Sozialdemokratischer Pressedienst*, 38(79), 26 April.

Rogers, Ivan (2017a) Testimony to the UK House of Commons Brexit Committee, *The Guardian*, 22 February.

Rogers, Ivan (2017b) 'The inside story of how David Cameron drove Britain to Brexit', lecture, Hertford College, Oxford, 24 November https://www.prospectmagazine.co.uk/politics/the-inside-story-of-how-david-cameron-drove-britain-to-brexit.

Rogers, Ivan (2018) 'The real post-Brexit options', lecture delivered in the Policy Scotland Brexit series at the University of Glasgow, 23 May https://pastebin.com/print/jMkxVUjs.

Rüdig, Wolfgang and Karyotis, Georgios (2013) 'Beyond the Usual Suspects? New Participants in Anti-austerity Protests in Greece', *Mobilization*, 18(3), 313–330.

Rupnik, Jacques (2015) 'L'autre Europe face à ses contradictions', *Le Monde*, 3 September.

Salles, Alain (2016) 'Le Brexit provoque un regain du sentiment européen', *Le Monde*, 15 July.

Sandholtz, Wayne (1996) 'Money Troubles: Europe's Rough Road to Monetary Union', *Journal of European Public Policy*, 3(1), 84–101.

Sandholtz, Wayne and Stone Sweet, Alec (1999) 'European Integration and Supranational Governance Revisited: Rejoinder to Branch and Øhrgaard', *Journal of European Public Policy*, 6(1), 144–154.

Saurugger, Sabine (2014) *Theoretical Approaches to European Integration*. Basingstoke: Palgrave Macmillan.

Schabert, Tilo (2002) *Wie Weltgeschichte gemacht wird: Frankreich und die deutsche Einheit*. Stuttgart: Klett-Cotta.

Scharpf, Fritz W. (1988) 'The Joint-Decision Trap: Lessons from German Federalism and European Integration', *Public Administration*, 66(3), 239–278.

Scharpf, Fritz W. (2000) 'Institutions in Comparative Policy Research', *Comparative Political Studies*, 33(6/7) (August/September), 762–790.

Scharpf, Fritz W. (2006) 'The Joint Decision Trap Revisited', *Journal of Common Market Studies*, 44(4), 845–864.

Schieder, Siegfried (2011) Germany: Problematizing Europe, or Evidence of an Emergent Euroscepticism?', in Robert Harmsen and Joachim Schild (eds), *Debating Europe: The 2009 European Parliament Elections and Beyond*. Baden-Baden: Nomos.

Schild, Joachim (2010) 'Mission Impossible? The Potential for Franco-German Leadership in the Enlarged EU', *Journal of Common Market Studies*, 48(5), 1367–1390.

Schild, Joachim (2017a) 'Französische Europapolitik unter Emmanuel Macron. Ambitionen, Strategien, Erfolgsbedingungen', *Integration*, 3, 177–192.

Schild, Joachim (2017b) 'Germany and France at Cross Purposes: The Case of Banking Union', *Journal of Economic Policy Reform*, 10, 1–16.

Schimmelfennig, Frank (2016) 'Europe', in Tanja A. Börzel and Thomas Risse (eds), *The Oxford Handbook of Comparative Regionalism*. Oxford: Oxford University Press, pp. 178–201.

Schmidt, Helmut (1990) *Die Deutschen und ihre Nachbarn*. Berlin: Siedler.

Schmidt, Helmut (1993) 'Ein Rückschlag für uns – und Europa', *Die Zeit*, 6 August.

Schmitter, Philippe (1971) 'A Revised Theory of Regional Integration', in Leon Lindberg and Stuart Scheingold (eds), *Regional Integration – Theory and Research*. Cambridge, MA: Harvard University Press.

Schneider, Gerald (2008) 'Neither Goethe nor Bismarck: On the Link between Theory and Empirics in Council Decision-Making Studies', in Daniel Naurin and Helen Wallace (eds), *Unveiling the Council of the European Union: Games Governments Play in Brussels*. Basingstoke: Palgrave Macmillan, pp. 277–289.

Schneider, G., Steunenberg, B. and Widgrén, M. (2006) 'Evidence with Insight: What Models Contribute to EU Research', in Robert Thomson, Frans N.Stokman, Christopher H.Achen and Thomas König (eds), *The European Union Decides*. Cambridge: Cambridge University Press.

Schoeller, Magnus (2017) 'Providing Political Leadership? Three Case Studies on Germany's Ambiguous Role in the Eurozone Crisis', *Journal of European Public Policy*, 24(1), 1–20.

Schoeller, Magnus (2018) 'The Rise and Fall of Merkozy: Franco-German Bilateralism as a Negotiation Strategy in Eurozone Crisis Management', *Journal of Common Market Studies*, 56(5) (July), 1019–1035.

Schönberger, Christoph (2012) 'Hegemon wider Willen: Zur Stellung Deutschlands in der Europäischen Union', *Merkur*, 66(752), 1–8.

Schönberger, Christoph (2013) 'Nochmals: Die deutsche Hegemonie', *Merkur*, no. 764, 25–33.

Schroeder, Paul (2004) 'The Mirage of Empire versus the Promise of Hegemony', in David Wetzel, Robert Jervis and Jack S. Levy (eds), *Systems, Stability, and Statecraft: Essays on the International History of Modern Europe*. Basingstoke and New York: Palgrave Macmillan, pp. 297–305.

Schwall-Düren, Angelika (2006) 'The Way Out of Europe's Constitutional Crisis', *Focus on Germany* (London: Friedrich-Ebert-Stiftung), April.

Schwarz, Hans-Peter (1992) *Erbfreundschaft: Adenauer und Frankreich*. Bonn and Berlin: Bouvier.

Schwarz, Hans-Peter (1994) *Die Zentralmacht Europas: Deutschlands Rückkehr auf der Weltbühne*. Berlin: Siedler.

Schwarz, Hans-Peter (2012) *Helmut Kohl: Eine politische Biografie*. Munich: Deutsche Verlags-Anstalt.

Schwarzer, Daniela (2015) 'It is in Germany's interest to avoid a Brexit', *German Marshall Fund Blog Post* (http://www.gmfus.org/blog/2015/05/18/brexit-views-brussels-berlin-paris-and-warsaw), 18 May.

Seibel, Wolfgang (2017) 'The European Union, Ukraine, and the Unstable East', in Desmond Dinan, Neill Nugent and William E. Paterson (eds), *The European Union in Crisis*. Basingstoke: Palgrave Macmillan, pp. 269–293.

Sellier, André and Sellier, Jean (1995) *Atlas des Peuples d'Europe Centrale*. Paris: La Découverte.

Sénat (2017) *Rapport fait au nom de la commission d'enquête sur les frontières européennes, le contrôle des flux des personnes et des marchandises en Europe et l'avenir de l'espace Schengen*. Paris : French Senate, 29 March.

Servent, Ariadna Ripoll (2018) 'A New Form of Delegation in EU Asylum : Agencies as Proxies of Strong Regulators', *Journal of Common Market Studies*, 56(1) (January), 83–100.

Servent, Ariadna Ripoll and Trauner, Florian (2014) 'Do Supranational EU Institutions Make a Difference ? EU Asylum Law before and after "communitarization"', *Journal of European Public Policy*, 21(8), 1142–1162.

Shipman, Tim (2016) *All Out War: The Full Story of How Brexit Sank Britain's Political Class*. London: Collins.

Siedentop, Larry (2000) *Democracy in Europe*. London: Allen Lane/The Penguin Press.

Sikorski, Radoslaw (2011) 'I fear Germany's power less than her inactivity', *Financial Times*, 28 November.

Simonian, Haig (1985) *The Privileged Partnership: Franco-German Relations in the European Community, 1969–1984*. Oxford: Clarendon Press.

Sjursen, Helene and Rosén, Guri (2017) 'Arguing Sanctions: On the EU's Response to the Crisis in Ukraine', *Journal of Common Market Studies*, 55(1), 20–36.

Snidal, Duncan (1985) 'The Limits of Hegemonic Stability Theory', *International Organization*, 39(4) (Autumn), 579–613.

Spahn, Jens (2016) 'Germany must cut new migrant numbers fast', *Financial Times*, 16 February.

SPD (Sozialdemokratische Partei Deutschlands) (2015) *Mitgliederbrief*, 14 September.

SPD (2017) 'Den Zusammenhalt stärken: Interview mit Sigmar Gabriel', *Aktuelles*, 7 January.

Speck, Ulrich (2014a) 'Has the EU failed Ukraine?' *Strategic Europe*, 21 February.

Speck, Ulrich (2014b) 'Russia's New Challenge to Europe', *Carnegie* Europe, 17 April.

Speck, Ulrich (2014c) 'How Europe Sleepwalked Into a Conflict with Russia', *Carnegie Europe*, 10 July.

Speck, Ulrich (2015) 'German Power and the Ukraine Conflict', *Carnegie Europe*, 26 March.

Speck, Ulrich (2016) 'The West's Response to the Ukraine Conflict: A Transatlantic Success Story', *Transatlantic Academy 2015–16 Paper Series* (4), April.

Spiegel, Peter (2014) 'How the euro was saved', *Financial Times*, 11 May.

Spiegel-Online (2011a) 'Europe shudders at Germany's new-found power', 17 June.

Spiegel-Online (2011b) '80 Prozent der Deutschen würden Griechen kein Geld geben', 21 September.

Spiegel-Online (2011c) 'Berlin und Paris vertagen die Euro-Rettung', 20 October.

Spiegel-Online (2011d) 'So verlief die dramatische Nacht in Brüssel', 27 October.

Spiegel-Online (2011e) 'Die Sprengmeisterin', 27 October.

Spiegel-Online (2012a) 'Finanzministerium zeichnet düsteres Euro-Crash-Szenario', 24 June.

Spiegel-Online (2012b) 'Wirtschaftsbosse warnen vor Euro-Crash', 12 July.

Spiegel-Online (2012c) '"Wir mussten handeln"', 29 October.

Spiegel-Online (2015a) 'Juncker warnt wegen des Euro vor Grenzkontrollen', 25 November.

Spiegel-Online (2015b) 'Unmut in der Union: Merkel droht Griechenland-Aufstand', 2 July.

Spiegel-Online (2018a) 'Germany's Foreign Minister: "We are seeing what happens when the US pulls back"', 8 January.

Spiegel-Online (2018b) 'Deutschland macht 2,9 Milliarden Euro Gewinn mit Griechenland-Hilfe', 21 June.

Spiegel-Online (2018c) 'Geldforderungen der Bundesbank: Sitzt Deutschland wirklich auf einer Billionen-Bombe?', 10 July.

Statista (2017) *Wert der Exporte aus "Deutschland Exporte" nach Ländergruppen im Jahr 2016.* Wiesbaden: Statistisches Bundesamt (https://de.statista.com/themen/563/aussenhandel/).

Statistisches Bundesamt (2017) *Außenhandel: Rangfolge der Handelspartner der Bundesrepublik Deutschland.* Wiesbaden: Statistisches Bundesamt.

Staudinger, Martin and Treichler, Robert (2015) 'Warum Angela Merkel Europa vor einer Katastrophe bewahrt hat', *Profil*, 26 September.

Steinmeier, Frank-Walter (2014) 'Nicht wegschauen', *Vorwärts*, 10 (October).

Steinmeier, Frank-Walter (2016) 'Die SPD weiss: Frieden braucht Dialog', *Vorwärts* (08–09, August–September).

Steinmeier, Frank-Walter (2017) 'Address to the European Parliament in Strasbourg, France' (4 April) (www.bundespraesident.de)

Stephens, Philip (2013) 'No easy relief for Cameron's European headache', *Financial Times*, 18 January.

Stephens, Philip (2014) 'Reset the reset – visa bans will not deter Putin', *Financial Times*, 7 March.

Stephens, Philip (2015) 'Merkel's plan shames Cameron's fear', 4 September.

Stewart, Susan (2016) 'The Future of the Minsk Agreements', *SWP Comments* (14), March.

Stierle, Steffen (2014) 'Is EU's Competitiveness Pact Doomed?' (www.tni.org), 21 February.

Stone Sweet, Alec and Sandholtz, Wayne (1997) 'European Integration and Supranational Governance', *Journal of European Public Policy*, 4(1), 144–154.

Stone Sweet, Alec and Sandholtz, Wayne (eds) (1998) *European Integration and Supranational Governance.* Oxford: Oxford University Press.

Stone Sweet, Alec, Sandholtz, Wayne and Fligstein, Neil (eds) (2001) *The Institutionalization of Europe.* Oxford: Oxford University Press.

Sturm, Roland and Pehle, Heinrich (2005) *Das neue deutsche Regierungssystem: Die Europäisierung von Institutionen, Entscheidungsprozessen und Politikfeldern in der Bundesrepublik Deutschland.* Wiesbaden: VS Verlag für Sozialwissenschaften.

Süddeutsche Zeitung (2012) 'Gabriel lobt Merkel', 3 August.

The Sun (2016) 'The Sun says: Your Brussels deal has done nothing to halt migrants', 3 February.

Tallberg, Jonas (2008) 'Bargaining Power in the European Council', *Journal of Common Market Studies*, 46(3), 685–708.

Taschner, Hans Claudius (1997) *Schengen: Die Übereinkommen zum Abbau der Personenkontrollen an den Binnengrenzen von EU-Staaten.* Baden-Baden: Nomos.

Taylor, Paul (2008) *The End of European Integration: Anti-Europeanism Examined.* London: Routledge.

Teasdale, Anthony (1993) 'The Life and Death of the Luxembourg Compromise', *Journal of Common Market Studies*, 31(4) (December), 567–579.

Thatcher, Margaret (1993) *The Downing Street Years*. London: HarperCollins.

Thelen, Kathleen and Steinmo, Sven (1992) 'Historical Institutionalism in Comparative Perspective', in Sven Steinmo, Kathleen Thelen and Frank Longstreth (eds), *Structuring Politics: Historical Institutionalism in Comparative Analysis*. Cambridge: Cambridge University Press.

Thom, Françoise (2014) 'L'expansion russe se poursuivra si l'Occident ne fait pas preuve de fermeté', *Le Monde*, 5 March.

Thom, Françoise (2015) 'Paris et Berlin accordant une prime à l'aggression de Poutine contre l'Ukraine', *Le Monde*, 18 February.

Thomson, Robert (2008) 'The Relative Power of Member States in the Council: Large and Small, Old and New', in Daniel Naurin and Helen Wallace (eds), *Unveiling the Council of the European Union: Games Governments Play in Brussels*. Basingstoke: Palgrave Macmillan, pp. 238–258.

Tighe, Chris and Bounds, Andrew (2016) 'Pro- and anti-Brexit camps step up efforts to woo business', *Financial Times*, 10 January.

Tokarski, Pawel (2016) 'Die Europäische Zentralbank als politischer Akteur in der Eurokrise', *SWP-Studie* no. 14. Berlin: Stiftung Wissenschaft und Politik.

Transparency International (2017) *Corruption Perceptions Index* (www.transparency.org)

Trauner, Florian (2011) 'Increased Differentiation as an Engine for Integration? Studying Justice and Home Affairs', in Gerda Falkner (ed), *The EU's Decision Traps: Comparing Policies*. Oxford: Oxford University Press, pp. 145–161.

Trauner, Florian (2016) 'Asylum Policy: The EU's "Crises" and the Looming Policy Regime Failure', *Journal of European Integration*, 38(3), 311–325.

Traynor, Ian (2015) 'Three days that saved the euro', *The Guardian*, 22 October.

UNHCR (United Nations High Commission for Refugees) (2015) *Seven Factors Behind Movement of Syrian Refugees to Europe*. Geneva: UNCHR, 25 September.

Varoufakis, Yanis (2016) 'Why we must save the EU', *The Guardian*, 5 April.

Varoufakis, Yanis (2017) *Adults in the Room: My Battle with Europe's Deep Establishment*. London: The Bodley Head.

Vasagar, Jeevan (2015) 'Berlin dismayed over Britain's EU reform push', *Financial Times*, 2 November.

Védrine, Hubert (1996) *Les mondes de François Mitterrand: À l'Élysée 1981–1995* (Paris: Fayard).

Vogel, Hans-Jochen (1984) 'Vogel: Weg mit den Grenzen in Europa!' *Tagesdienst: Informationen der sozialdemokratischen Bundestagsfraktion* (Bonn), 2 March.

Vollaard, Hans (2014) 'Explaining European Disintegration', *Journal of Common Market Studies*, 52(5), 1142–1159.

Walker, Marcus (2013) 'Inside Merkel's Bet on the Euro's Future', *WSJ.com*, 23 April.

Walker, Marchus and Troianovski, Anton (2015) 'Behind Angela Merkel's Open Door for Migrants', *Wall Street Journal*, 9 December.

Wall, Stephen (2008) *A Stranger in Europe*. Oxford: Oxford University Press.

Webb, Michael and Krasner, Stephen D. (1989) 'Hegemonic Stability Theory: An Empirical Assessment', *Review of International Studies* (15), 183–198.

Webber, Douglas (ed) (1999a) *The Franco-German Relationship in the European Union*. London: Routledge.

Webber, Douglas (1999b) 'Agricultural Policy: The Hard Core', in Douglas Webber (ed), *The Franco-German Relationship in the European Union*. London: Routledge, pp. 111–129.

Webber, Douglas (2012) 'The Politics of Differentiated Integration in the European Union: Origins, Decision Making and Outcomes', *Monash University European and EU Centre Working Paper Series*, no. 1. Melbourne: Monash University.

Webber, Douglas (2016) 'Declining Power Europe: The Evolution of the European Union's World Power in the Early 21st Century', *European Review of International Studies*, 3(1) (Spring), 31–52.

Webber, Douglas (2017): 'Can the EU survive?', in Desmond Dinan, Neill Nugent and William E. Paterson (eds), *The European Union in Crisis*. London: Palgrave Macmillan, pp. 336–359.

Webber, Douglas and Gehlen, Claudia (2007) *The Conflict over the French 'First-Job Contract'*. Teaching case. Fontainebleau/Singapore: INSEAD.

Wikipedia (2017a) 'Bundestagswahlen 2017' https://de.wikipedia.org/wiki/Bundestagswahl_2017/Umfragen_und_Prognosen.

Wikipedia (2017b) Euro Plus Pact https://en.wikipedia.org/wiki/Euro_Plus_Pact, accessed 10 April 2017.

Wikipedia (2017c) 'The Russo-Georgian War' https://en.wikipedia.org/wiki/Russo-Georgian_War.

Wilson, Andrew (2014) *Ukraine Crisis: What It Means for the West*. New Haven and London: Yale University Press.

Wilson, Andrew (2016) 'No stability under occupation in Crimea', Commentary, European Council on Foreign Relations, 18 March.

Wolf, Martin (2011) 'A disastrous failure at the summit', *Financial Times*, 14 December.

Wolf, Martin (2012) 'Why the super-Marios need help', *Financial Times*, 18 January.

Wolf, Martin (2014) 'Prise Ukraine from Putin's claws', *Financial Times*, 19 March.

Wolf, Martin (2016) 'The self-inflicted dangers of the EU referendum', *Financial Times*, 26 May.

Wolf, Martin (2018) 'The Italian challenge to the eurozone', *Financial Times*, 20 June.

Wolff, Sarah (2015) 'Integrating Justice and Home Affairs: A Case of New Intergovernmentalism Par Excellence?', in Christopher J. Bickerton, Dermot Hodson and Uwe Puetter (eds), *The New Intergovernmentalism: States and Supranational Actors in the Post-Maastricht Era*. Oxford: Oxford University Press, pp. 129–145.

Wolff, Guntram (2016) *European Parliament Testimony on EDIS*. Brussels: Bruegel.

Wood, Andrew (2014) 'A Russian Requiem', Expert Comment, Chatham House, 8 April.

Wood, Stuart (2017) 'Gordon Brown', lecture at Hertford College, Oxford, 3 November https://www.prospectmagazine.co.uk/politics/read-stewart-woods-lecture-on-what-gordon-brown-got-right-on-europe-and-what-he-didnt.

World Bank (2017) *Quality of Governance Indicators* http://info.worldbank.org/governance/wgi/index.aspx#reports

WTO (World Trade Organization) (2012) *International Trade Statistics 2012*. Geneva: WTO.

Wurzel, Rüdiger and Hayward, Jack (2012) 'Conclusion: European Disunion: Between Solidarity and Sovereignty', in Rüdiger Wurzel and Jack Hayward (eds), *European Disunion: Between Solidarity and Sovereignty*. Basingstoke: Palgrave Macmillan, pp. 314–328.

Yekelchyk, Serhy (2015) *The Conflict in Ukraine: What Everyone Needs to Know*. Oxford and New York: Oxford University Press.

YouGov (2015) 'YouGov Survey Results' (Fieldwork 10–17 September) https://www.yougov.co.uk.

Young, Hugo (1998) *This Blessed Plot: Britain and Europe from Churchill to Blair*. London: Macmillan.

Youngs, Richard (2017) *Europe's Eastern Crisis: The Geopolitics of Asymmetry*. Cambridge: Cambridge University Press.

Zaiotti, Ruben (2011) *Cultures of Border Control: Schengen and the Evolution of European Frontiers*. Chicago and London: University of Chicago Press.

Zeit Online (2011) 'Seehofer lehnt neue Euro-Hilfen ab', 22 September.

Zeit-Online (2013) 'Deutschland spart 40 Milliarden Euro', 18 August.

Zielonka, Jan (2006) *Europe as Empire: The Nature of the Enlarged Union*. Oxford: Oxford University Press.

Zielonka, Jan (2014) *Is the EU Doomed?*. Cambridge: Polity Press.

Zunneberg, Christel (2017) 'Going Dutch: Why Germany needs others besides France' (commentary), European Council on Foreign Relations, 24 October.

Zweig, Stefan (2009) *The World of Yesterday*. London: Pushkin Press.

Index

Please note: page numbers in **bold type** indicate figures or illustrations, those in *italics* indicate tables.

CPSIA information can be obtained
at www.ICGtesting.com
Printed in the USA
LVHW080727010822
724851LV00004B/16

9 781137 529466